The Weird
100

ALSO AVAILABLE IN THE "100" SERIES

THE 100: A RANKING OF THE MOST INFLUENTIAL PERSONS IN HISTORY
THE 100 MOST INFLUENTIAL BOOKS EVER WRITTEN
THE 100 MOST INFLUENTIAL WOMEN OF ALL TIME
THE JEWISH 100
THE BLACK 100
THE GAY 100
THE IRISH 100
THE 100 GREATEST HEROES
THE 100 GREATEST DISASTERS OF ALL TIME
THE 100 GREATEST INVENTIONS OF ALL TIME
THE GOLF 100
THE ITALIAN 100
THE EVIL 100

The Weird
100

Stephen J. Spignesi

CITADEL PRESS
Kensington Publishing Corp.
www.kensingtonbooks.com

CITADEL PRESS BOOKS are published by

Kensington Publishing Corp.
850 Third Avenue
New York, NY 10022

Copyright © 2004 Stephen J. Spignesi

All Kensington titles, imprints, and distributed lines are available at special quantity discounts for bulk purchases for sales promotions, premiums, fund-raising, educational, or institutional use. Special book excerpts or customized printings can also be created to fit specific needs. For details, write or phone the office of the Kensington special sales manager: Kensington Publishing Corp., 850 Third Avenue, New York, NY 10022, attn: Special Sales Department; phone 1-800-221-2647.

CITADEL PRESS and the Citadel logo are Reg. U.S. Pat. & TM Off.

All art courtesy ClipArt.com, except for Chapter 3 (Erich von Däniken), Chapter 18 (Bio-Chart.com), Chapter 25 (Colin Andrews), Chapter 35 (NASA), Chapter 68 (Author's collection), and Chapter 93 (Author's collection).

First printing: May 2004

10 9 8 7 6 5 4 3 2 1

Printed in the United States of America

Library of Congress Control Number: 2003111388

ISBN: 0-8065-2523-1

For one of the all-time greats,

Steve Rapuano

with gratitude and love.

It is an honor to bear your name.

Think where man's glory most begins and ends,
and say my glory was I had such a friend.

       —William Butler Yeats, "The Municipal Gallery
       Revisited," stanza seven

CONTENTS

Introduction: Hubris . . . on a Cosmic Scale   xi

Acknowledgments   xv

A Note about Bold Statements   xvii

Weirdness in 17 Syllables: 100 Weird Haiku   xix

1. Alien Abductions   1
2. The "Alien Autopsy" Film   5
3. The "Ancient Astronaut" Theory   8
4. Angel Hair   12
5. Angels   15
6. Animal Psi   19
7. Area 51   22
8. The Ark of the Covenant   26
9. Are There UFOs in the Bible? Was Jesus an Extraterrestrial?   29
10. The Astral Body, Astral Planes, and Astral Projection   33
11. Astrology   36
12. Atlantis   40
13. Auras and Halos   44
14. Backwards Messages and Reverse Speech   47
15. The Bermuda Triangle   51
16. The Bible Code   55
17. Bigfoot   59
18. Biorhythms   65
19. Bleeding and Weeping Religious Icons   69
20. Cattle Mutilations   73
21. Channeling and Automatic Writing   77
22. Charles Fort and Fortean Phenomena   81
23. Communication with the Dead   85
24. Creationism   89
25. Crop Circles   97
26. Crosses of Light   101

27.	Demons, Possession, and Exorcism	104
28.	Divination and Prophecy	108
29.	Dowsing	114
30.	Dragons	118
31.	The Easter Island Monuments	122
32.	Edgar Cayce	126
33.	Elves, Fairies, and Dwarves	130
34.	ESP	133
35.	The Face on Mars	137
36.	Falls of Animals and Objects	143
37.	Fire Immunity and Firewalking	147
38.	Flat Earth	151
39.	Ghosts, Poltergeists, Haunted Places, and Apparitions	155
40.	Hollow Earth	159
41.	Immanuel Velikovsky and His Theories	164
42.	Incorrupt Corpses	168
43.	Invisibility	172
44.	Ivy League Nude Posture Photos	176
45.	Kirlian Photography	180
46.	Levitation	184
47.	Life After Death	188
48.	The Loch Ness Monster	191
49.	The Lost Colony of Roanoke	195
50.	Lunar Anomalies	198
51.	Marian Apparitions	202
52.	The Men in Black	206
53.	Mermaids	209
54.	Miracles	212
55.	The Mystery of the *Mary Celeste*	216
56.	The Nazca Lines	220
57.	Near-Death Experiences	223
58.	Noah's Ark	228
59.	Nostradamus	232
60.	Numerology	236
61.	The Ouija Board	241
62.	Palmistry	245
63.	The "Paul Is Dead" Mystery	249
64.	Perpetual Motion	260
65.	The Philadelphia Experiment	263

66.	The Planet Vulcan	267
67.	The Powers of Holy Water	271
68.	The Prediction of the Sinking of the *Titanic*	274
69.	Psychokinesis	279
70.	Pyrokinesis	282
71.	Reincarnation and Past-Life Regression	285
72.	Relics of the True Cross	289
73.	Remote Viewing	293
74.	Resurrection	297
75.	Roswell	302
76.	Runes	307
77.	Satanism	310
78.	Savant Syndrome	315
79.	The Shroud of Turin	323
80.	Spells	327
81.	Spontaneous Human Combustion	330
82.	Stigmata	337
83.	Stonehenge	342
84.	Subliminal Messages	346
85.	Suppressed Inventions	351
86.	Synchronicity	355
87.	Tarot	358
88.	Teleportation	362
89.	Theosophy	367
90.	Time Travel	370
91.	Transubstantiation	374
92.	The Tunguska Explosion	378
93.	UFOs (Unidentified Flying Objects)	381
94.	The Ultimate Lincoln/Kennedy Coincidences List	386
95.	Unicorns	392
96.	Vampires	395
97.	Voodoo and Zombies	398
98.	Werewolves	401
99.	Who Is the Antichrist?	404
100.	Witches and Witchcraft	408
	Select Bibliography	413
	Index	417
	About the Author	424

Introduction

Hubris . . . on a Cosmic Scale

The most beautiful thing we can experience is the mysterious. It is the source of all true art and science.
—Albert Einstein

Paranormal: Beyond the range of normal experience or scientific explanation.
— American Heritage Dictionary

This is an introduction, so allow me to introduce you to some of my thoughts:

I am open to the notion of a nonphysical reality, and I believe that the reality in which we live here on earth is not—and quite simply *cannot be*—the *only* reality.

I believe that many of the people who report such things as UFO sightings, or who have had success at dowsing, or who claim to be in contact with the dead are often credible, are not delusional; nor (worse) are they blatant liars.

I believe that because something sounds absurd and impossible, it is not, therefore, de facto, absurd and impossible.

I believe that man as a species does not understand even a hint of the incredible complexities and mysteries of life in our universe.

I believe it is easier to be cynical than open-minded.

I believe that I do not know everything.

The biggest problem with the unrelenting skeptics, those who rule out even the *possibility* that paranormal activity is real, is that their scorn and skepticism leave no room for anything outside their specific worldview. That is hubris on a cosmic scale. Granted, the overwhelming majority of paranormal claims are bogus, but the literature of the supernatural offers countless incidents that are unexplainable, yet powerfully convincing.

Poltergeist activity is a field of paranormal phenomena that is extraordinarily convincing. Multiple witnesses have reported seeing *the same thing*: pictures spinning on a wall; chairs moving across the floor of their own accord; writing appearing out of nowhere. Are all these eyewitnesses to be treated as liars or crazy?

And what about statues that begin to "bleed," and it is later determined conclusively that the fluid they exude is real blood?

Or the people who claim to have been abducted and implanted with something that, when removed, is made of a material that is unidentifiable by scientists and doctors?

In the spring of 2003, a show debuted on the Showtime cable network called *Bullshit!* (Yes, you read that right . . . those wacky cable programmers!)

The show was hosted by the popular magicians Penn & Teller, who became famous for performing astonishing tricks and illusions, and then revealing to the audience how they did them.

The show was a weekly anthology that looked at a range of fringe and paranormal topics, from alien abductions to chiropractics.

The show was defiantly one-sided and the problem with it was its hostility and utter closed-mindedness (not to mention the host's mockery and name-calling). It seemed to be nothing more than an enormous overreaction to the subject matter.

In the first few shows, they attempted to debunk mediums who talk to the dead, people who have been abducted by aliens, magnet therapy, reflexology, and chiropractics. (They later moved on to relationship counselors, sex therapists, and other mainstream enterprises. Guess they ran out of *truly* weird stuff to make fun of.)

The thesis of the show was blatant: *there is no paranormal anything and no matter what anyone claims, it's all bullshit*. This precluded *any* balance whatsoever and, thus, Penn & Teller came across as shrill zealots who accomplished nothing more than to leave the viewer wondering, "Why so angry, boys?"

Chiropractic treatment is paid for by insurance companies. If it is utterly useless (as some of the "experts" appearing on the show claim), then why is it a covered expense?

The benefits of magnet therapy are still inconclusive. Many people claim a great deal of relief from wearing them. Are all these people deluded? Penn & Teller would have you believe so.

Reflexology is based on the science of acupressure and acupuncture points, specifically on the feet. Does it work? For every mocking debunker, there are people who claim results.

One doctor proclaimed that testimonials are all anecdotal, and, thus, completely unreliable. As I say elsewhere in this book, the accounts of infections being cured by the application of a bread poultice were also anecdotal—until science discovered a little something in the mold called penicillin. Also, the accounts of pain being relieved by chewing on the bark of a willow tree were anecdotal—until science discovered something in the bark we now call aspirin.

It is arrogant and foolish to completely rule out all anecdotal evidence as worthless.

Can *all* UFO sightings be false? All of them? Even the ones reported by Air Force pilots?

Penn & Teller would have you believe so.

The Weird 100 is a plea for open-mindedness. It is also my hope that the book gives you something to think about.

I do not think it foolish or naïve to be open to the possibility that science cannot explain everything. If anything, history has proven that repeatedly.

ACKNOWLEDGMENTS

My profound thanks and appreciation to all who assisted me with this book. Some provided research materials; some granted interviews; some offered sage counsel and advice; some supported me in many ways; some were simply kind souls who would never forget to ask, "How's the book coming?" My gratitude to you all knows no bounds.

Carter Spignesi, John White, Lee Mandato, Dolores Fantarella, Mike Lewis, Jim Cole, Bill Savo, Steve and Marge Rapuano, Janet Spignesi Daniw, Ann LaFarge, Bruce Bender, The Zacharius family, ClipArt.com, all my friends and colleagues at Kensington Books, Colin Andrews, Synthia Andrews, Quinn Ramsby, Dr. Michael Luchini, Larry E. Arnold, Jack Kewaunee Lapseritis, Erich von Däniken, Dr. Oleg Atkov, Charlie Fried, Laura Lattrell, Mary Toler, George Beahm, Whitley Streiber, my friends at the East Haven Post Office, Michael Cader, Michael Macrone and all the fine folks at Publishers Marketplace, my friends at the CVS on Main Street in East Haven, my friends at The Office Alternative, Associated Press, Stanley Wiater, Jay Halpern, Ruth Royster, Dave Hinchberger, Minuteman Press, the SKEMERs, Raeleen D'Agostino Mautner, Joe Amarante and Jim Shelton, the *New Haven Register*, the *New York Times*, the *Hartford Courant*, *USA Today*, the *Wall Street Journal*. And Folger's Coffee. And everyone else who had something weird happen to them and took the time to tell me about it.

A Note about Bold Statements

At the beginning of each chapter, we provide the following information:

- Definition
- What the Believers Say
- What the Skeptics Say
- Quality of Supporting Evidence
- Likelihood Phenomena Are Paranormal

These bullet points will provide you with a quick, accessible "executive summary" of the topic, complete with a point/counterpoint assessment of the arguments and counter-arguments regarding the true nature of the subject.

This section will also help you make up your own mind. You will find that you will quickly agree either with what the believers say, or what the skeptics say. You will then be able to fully appreciate and enjoy the remainder of the chapter.

- **Definition:** This is what you would expect: a simple definition of the phenomenon or event. Sometimes we use a strict dictionary definition; sometimes, we provide a more conversational one.

- **What the Believers Say:** This succinctly sums up what the hardcore faithful believe about the phenomenon.

- **What the Skeptics Say:** This briefly explains the main counter-argument.

- **Quality of Existing Evidence:** This rates the quantity and quality of the evidence with one of six quality ratings: *Negligible, Poor, Fair, Good, Very Good,* and *Excellent*. "Is there *something* to study and investigate and, if so, how extensive is the evidence?" is the question this rating seeks to answer. In some cases, there will also be an "Inconclusive" rating; in those cases when evidence exists, but its validity is purely in the eye of the beholder (as in Creationism [Chapter 24], the Lost Colony of Roanoke [Chapter 49], and the Tunguska Explosion [Chapter 92]).

■ **LIKELIHOOD PHENOMENA ARE PARANORMAL:** This gives the phenomenon one of seven ratings: *Nil* (which is less than negligible), *Negligible, Poor, Fair, Good, Very Good,* and *Excellent*.

This category is somewhat subjective, and we did consider anecdotal evidence when deciding on a rating. In some cases, we also interpreted this rating in terms of its "effectiveness," for lack of a better term.

For instance, Tarot readings often provide the "sitter" with insightful personal information which is then used to effect change in his or her life. Paranormal or not, there is no question that the symbology of a Tarot card often results in the person making a change or a decision which, in effect, validates the reading, creating a self-fulfilling prophecy. Thus, as a powerful psychoanalytic tool that may or may not tap into realms of the unconscious or beyond, Tarot readings could be considered a valid paranormal practice.

Also, this rating does not factor in faith. Resurrection is rated as having poor supporting evidence, with the likelihood of the phenomenon being paranormal deemed "Inconclusive." This is a purely scientific evaluation. Resurrection from the dead (and I do not mean being restarting the heart during a cardiac event) is currently a physical impossibility; thus, the open rating.

The Christian faithful, however, believe that Christ rose from the dead. Nothing written in any book will change that. In this volume, we are mostly evaluating phenomena based on provable evidence, however, which accounts for our skeptical rating.

WEIRDNESS IN 17 SYLLABLES:

100 Weird Haiku

Each chapter in *The Weird 100* is introduced by a Haiku concerning the topic of the chapter.

A Haiku is a Japanese poetic form consisting of three lines of five syllables, seven syllables, and five syllables, respectively. Haiku's purpose is to communicate an image, a meaning, or a question in tight, evocative lines and words.

All of the Haiku in *The Weird 100* were written by me exclusively for this volume and ninety-nine of them are published here for the first time. ("Haiku: Titanic" was first published in my book, *The Complete Titanic.*)

It is my hope that reading the Haiku before diving into the chapter will put you in the right mood for the material covered. I hope you enjoy them.

—SjS

The Weird
100

Alien Abductions

HAIKU:

ALIEN ABDUCTIONS

Grey ones come at night
Beings of fear and foul light
Prey you will return

The first thing one must do is overcome fear because alien abductions begin with some sort of paralysis being induced in the person. And if fear itself is present, that might very well deepen the sense of paralysis or inability to act. People have said, "I was paralyzed by fear." It is necessary to assert one's God-given right to be free from that sort of treatment. I don't care if the aliens are from inner or outer space, they do not have the right to treat human beings that way, so a stance of righteous anger and denouncement, telling them to get out of your space, and out of your life, and never come back, is a very useful way to deal with them.

—John White[1]

DEFINITION: Aliens are extraterrestrial beings or creatures from outer or inner space; an alien abduction is the kidnapping of a human being by an alien.

WHAT THE BELIEVERS SAY: Extraterrestrial beings are real, they are regular visitors to our reality and consciousness, and sometimes they abduct earthlings and subject them to invasive physical examinations and reproductive research. Some people say the world governments are in cahoots with the aliens and, in exchange for advanced technologies, have granted aliens permission to abduct human beings for research purposes. The increase in UFO activity in the past several decades is directly related to the tacit permission granted by the government for aliens to continue to visit Earth and abduct humans for their needs.

WHAT THE SKEPTICS SAY: There are no aliens; no one has ever been abducted by aliens, and people who say they were abducted are delusional. All seemingly credible accounts of alien abductions are either dreams or hallucinations, because, we'll say it again, *there are no aliens*. According to Robert Carroll, writing in his *Skeptic's Dictionary*, "The support for these beliefs about aliens and UFOs consists mostly of speculation, fantasy, fraud, and unjustified inferences from questionable evidence and testimony."[2]

QUALITY OF EXISTING EVIDENCE: Inconclusive.[3]

LIKELIHOOD PHENOMENA ARE PARANORMAL: Inconclusive.

The elements of an alien abduction experience are varied, but a majority of victims report some or all of the following:

- The presence of a UFO
- Being taken from a bedroom or a vehicle
- A sense of paralysis
- Feeling or actually seeing oneself float out of the room
- Seeing alien beings
- Lying on a table inside a spacecraft
- Being probed by touch and/or devices
- Having samples of bodily fluids taken
- Having something implanted into the body
- Finding scars and scoop marks on the body after being returned
- The unexplained cessation of a pregnancy, without evidence of a miscarriage
- A period of missing time

- Being given a warning, often about the dangers of nuclear proliferation, or the dire state of the Earth's environment
- The development of new psychic abilities, like ESP and precognition
- Post-traumatic stress disorder

Are people who claim to have been abducted by aliens nothing but publicity seekers? Do they tell their wild stories to get attention? Is everything that they allege happened to them simply made up?

Some skeptics assert that two of the most credible abduction accounts—those of Betty and Barney Hill, and Travis Walton—are both hoaxes. They also assert that the Hills imagined their experience after seeing a TV program prior to their abduction, and that Walton concocted his story because he was late on a lumber contract.

The facts belie this perception, however.

Most people who report abduction experiences are quiet, reserved people who shun media attention and do not want the spotlight. They are often embarrassed by their story, and many try to distance themselves from the whole UFO/abductee subculture. If they were making up their story for attention and possible gain, wouldn't you think they would welcome any and all attention and *encourage* interest in their story?

Dr. John Mack, a professor of psychiatry at Harvard Medical School and the winner of a Pulitzer Prize, believes that many of the stories of alien abductions are true.

His 1994 best-seller, *Abduction*, detailed thirteen in-depth case studies of people Dr. Mack was convinced had been abducted by aliens. These patients showed no sign of mental illness and were from a cross-section of economic, educational, and geographic categories.

A Pulitzer Prize-winning Harvard professor went on the record as believing in aliens and alien abductions?

Yes, and the stories told in his book are compelling, specific, and, above all, convincing.

Dr. Mack sees the alien abduction phenomena as having to do with the "evolution of consciousness"[4] and admits to not fully understanding the alien beings' purpose or methods. He believes the aliens are manifestations of an intelligence beyond our reality and our worldview. And, yes, he believes that the communications from these beings and the experiences of the abductees are, in fact, "real," leaving somewhat open the ultimate, carved-in-stone meaning of that word.

As would be expected, Mack was lambasted by the skeptics when his book was released.

The skeptical viewpoint on alien abductions is, to many, narrow and limited. They interpret any and all of the components of the abduction experience as manifestations of the subconscious, i.e., "it's all in their minds." What used to be angels, fairies, unicorns, dragons, elves, leprechauns, and other fanciful creatures that appeared out of nowhere and interacted with human beings are now Grays, Nordics, and other types of alien beings. Elves weren't real, they tell us, and neither are aliens from another planet.

So, what can we conclude about the alien abduction phenomena? Does it really happen?

Although the ranking for "paranormal likelihood" is "Inconclusive," it seems that something outside the ken of earthly reality is, indeed, going on. There are far too many similarities in abductees' stories, along with a parallel lack of an ulterior self-interest motive.

Can all these people be delusional?

Theoretically, the answer is yes.

But would a reasonable person rule out every single account of abduction as untrue?

That seems unlikely.

[1] *Conscious Living*, July/August 1997, p. 9.

[2] www.skepdic.com, "Alien Abductions."

[3] Verifiable physical evidence (photos, videos, implants, multiple eyewitnesses, etc.) is weak; anecdotal evidence, which is consistent and from many credible sources, is extensive and believable.

[4] *Abduction*, p. 422.

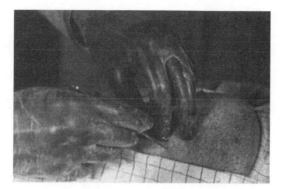

2

The "Alien Autopsy" Film

HAIKU:

ALIEN AUTOPSY

Splayed and silent thing
Staring out of open eyes
Bloody blades proceed

If what you are about to see is real, it's the most startling film footage in history. Although we remain skeptical, some experts believe this is authentic footage of an alien lifeform. Real or not, I must warn you: this appears to be an actual autopsy. Some of the footage you will see in the next hour is very gruesome. Stay with us as we put the question to you: Alien autopsy: fact or fiction?

—Jonathan Frakes[1]

DEFINITION: The "alien autopsy" film is a grainy, black-and-white film allegedly shot by the United States military in 1947 showing an autopsy being performed on one of the three aliens recovered from the July 1947 UFO crash in Roswell (see Chapter 75).

WHAT THE BELIEVERS SAY: The footage shows the autopsy of an extraterrestrial being.

WHAT THE SKEPTICS SAY: The "alien autopsy" film is a blatant hoax; albeit a very well-produced hoax.

QUALITY OF EXISTING EVIDENCE: Very good.[2]

LIKELIHOOD PHENOMENON IS PARANORMAL: Nil (which is even less than Negligible).

When performing an autopsy, real pathologists hold their scissors with their thumb and middle fingers. They use their index finger to steady the blades as needed. Real pathologists would be expected to know this; actors would not.

In the "alien autopsy" film, the gowned and masked "pathologists" hold their scissors with their thumb and index finger, precisely the way an "ordinary person" would hold the instrument.

The alien autopsy footage was supposedly filmed in 1947 by one cameraman with a handheld camera that did not have through-the-lens focusing, which was the standard for cameras of the time. This would undoubtedly explain the occasional out-of-focus shots, but it also mandates a certain fluidity to the shots. If the camera stops filming during a particular sequence, when it starts up again, the scene seen should begin *later on* in the action. There is a scene in the film in which the camera focuses on one of the doctors lifting the edge of a piece of black tissue that covers the alien's left eye. The tip of the tweezers is seen gripping the edge when suddenly the scene changes to a close-up of the eye (the cut in the scene is obvious), and shows the doctor lifting and peeling up the membrane. The problem is that the close-up begins at the *precise moment* that the wide shot concluded. How could the cameraman suddenly zoom in on the scene without the action having progressed? He couldn't, *unless the actors stopped their movements while the camera was moved and refocused—* and then they continued from the same spot.

These are only two of the problems with the alien autopsy film (where is the body block by the way?[3]) that made viewers suspicious and that ultimately confirmed the film as an elaborate hoax.

The alien autopsy film first surfaced in the mid-1990s when music producer Ray Santilli announced that he had purchased it from the cameraman who had shot the footage. It was allegedly in the remaining canisters of film from an extensive military filming of the autopsy that the U.S. government had never retrieved from the cameraman.

Santilli participated in several videos, books, and documentaries about the film. The controversy as to its authenticity only spurred interest in the footage (as well as sales of the books and videos, and high ratings for the TV shows).

Santilli's alien autopsy film is a staged autopsy of a fake alien. Special effects experts have duplicated the film almost identically, and, while comprehensively researched (the old-style equipment and phone), the film is a hoax.

Interestingly, the widespread acknowledgment of the film's bogus nature did not dampen interest in the Roswell incident itself. In fact, some serious Roswell enthusiasts believe that the film was part of a massive disinformation campaign sponsored by the United States government. This is beyond ironic: many who insist that an alien craft did, indeed, crash at Roswell in 1947 and that alien bodies were recovered, believe that the government probably *did* perform an autopsy that was very close to what was seen in the hoaxed film. The labyrinthine nature of this conspiracy theory, however, then concludes that the government staged and released a fake autopsy that was so obviously faked as to make the notion of a real autopsy (which, of course, actually happened, right?) so farfetched that it would throw the researchers off the scent of the truth.

The film, when combined with the official military statement on the "Roswell incident" released in 1997—which stated that nothing happened—comprised the government's attempt to put the Roswell issue to rest once and for all.

Memo to the U.S. government: If all this is true, it didn't work.

Does the alien autopsy film show what an actual autopsy of an actual alien might look like? Yes, if you accept that the alien dummy in the film is what at least one species of extraterrestrials looks like; and yes, if you accept that the autopsy took place in 1947, and was performed by pathologists who did not really know what they were doing.

That is a lot to accept, and yet today there are still those who vouchsafe acceptance of the film as real.

It was, and still is, a real moneymaker, but that's about it.

---

[1] Fox documentary, *Alien Autopsy: Fact or Fiction?*

[2] The quality of existing evidence is rated very good because the footage of the alien autopsy exists and is available in many forms, both on video and in still images, and is easily accessible on the Internet and elsewhere. Thus, there is ample opportunity for interested parties to examine the footage.

[3] Many of the forensic pathologists who viewed the alien autopsy film commented on the absence of a supporting block. The head of the corpse is *never* placed directly onto the table.

3

The "Ancient Astronaut" Theory

HAIKU:

ANCIENT ASTRONAUTS

Ancient visitors
Seeding the human gene pool
Teachers from beyond?

*I think, thousands of years ago, some extraterrestrials
created, by deliberate mutation, our intelligence. This does
not contradict Darwin's theory of evolution. But it's just one
step forward. If you would accept this as a theory, that we
have some extraterrestrial genes in us, then these genes one
day, they will grow and open.*

—Erich von Däniken[1]

DEFINITION: The ancient astronaut theory posits that extraterrestrials visited earth some time between ten thousand and forty thousand years ago. They bred with humans, taught prehistoric humans primitive forms of art and science, built monuments, and invented devices that are still extant today. The chief proponent of the ancient astronauts theory is Erich von Däniken, whose 1969 book *Chariots of the Gods* became an international best-seller.

WHAT THE BELIEVERS SAY: Extraterrestrials visited earth in the distant past, and the evidence of their presence can be found in seemingly unexplainable artifacts like a two-thousand-year-old battery, as well as ancient monuments and archaeological sites such as Easter Island (Chapter 31), Stonehenge (Chapter 83), and the Nazca lines (Chapter 56). All creation myths speak of gods coming to earth in chariots of fire. These ancient writers were describing the landings of extraterrestrials.

WHAT THE SKEPTICS SAY: There is no evidence that aliens visited the Earth and bred with humans. Our DNA shows that all of mankind descended from hominids (*homo sapiens*) living in Africa approximately 120,000 years ago. If today's humans are a hybrid of man and ET, then where's the alien DNA from ten thousand years ago?

QUALITY OF EXISTING EVIDENCE: Poor to Good.[2]

LIKELIHOOD PHENOMENON IS PARANORMAL: Inconclusive.[3]

Does the human race have an inferiority complex?

Do we, as a species, consider ourselves so inferior and incompetent that rather than give ourselves credit for scientific and artistic advancements, we leap at the notion that aliens are responsible for everything from our sacred monuments to our batteries?

This is not a silly question. Erich von Däniken, who put forth precisely such a theory in his 1969 book *Chariots of the Gods?* (and others), had an enormously successful international best-seller with the book, and people all over the world embraced this theory with enthusiasm and, some might say, relief.

Was the book a smash hit simply out of curiosity? Possibly. But why was von Däniken's theory so appealing to so many people? And, an even more important question, how valid is his hypothesis?

The entire ancient astronaut theory hinges on one basic premise: we have been visited.

If that assumption is rejected, then it is impossible to accept the conclusions that follow from that thesis.

What is the evidence put forth to support the idea that aliens visited earth, bred with humans, and taught ancient man technologies he was, at the time, allegedly incapable of achieving on his own?

The Baghdad Battery is a clay vase. Inside this vessel is a copper cylinder held in place by asphalt. Inside the copper cylinder is an iron rod that has an oxodized iron tip. Wilhelm König, the German scientist who found the vase in 1936 while working in a museum in Iraq, said of the object, "After all the parts had been brought together and then examined in their separate parts, it became evident that it could only have been an electrical element. It was only necessary to add an acid or an alkaline liquid to complete the element."[4]

Pouring anything alkaline into the vase, like vinegar or grape juice, causes an electrical charge. The Baghdad Battery was dated to approximately 250 B.C. Two hundred and fifty years before the birth of Christ, someone built a functioning battery. And yet, our textbooks tell us electricity was discovered by the Italian Luigi Galvani sometime around 1790. It is now believed that the Baghdad Battery, and other artifacts that worked similarly, were used to electroplate statuary and jewelry. We still do not know how the ancients acquired the knowledge required to build such devices.

Equally perplexing is a device known as the Antikythera Mechanism, which was built around 80 B.C.

The Antikythera Mechanism was a primitive computer that is believed to have been used to calculate the positions of the Sun, Moon, and planets. It is a wooden box holding many wheel gears and differential gears. Dials are set into the top of the box.

The system of meshing gears in this over two-thousand-year-old device was not invented until the 1500s, when it was used in clocks.

Once again, we do not know how the ancients acquired the knowledge required to build such a device.

Artifacts such as these two (and there are many more equally astonishing discoveries) seem to support selected elements of the ancient astronaut theory, i.e., that advanced beings taught our ancestors about astronomy and electricity.

Then there are the examples of extraterrestrial visitation that do not hold up, most notably the Nazca lines and the Easter Island monuments, both of which seemed to have been explained by solid scientific and archaeological research.

The "ancient astronaut" theory is mocked by serious scientists these days.

The explanations for seemingly unexplainable artifacts exist; it's simply that we have not discerned them yet, but the answers definitely do not include the notion of alien visitation.

Nonetheless, von Däniken stands by his findings, his theories, and his work, and continues to explore mankind's distant and perplexing past.

If the day ever comes where archaeologists come upon a true alien artifact, all the science and history books will have to be rewritten. Von Däniken already has a headstart on that work.

[1] *Florida Today*, August 6, 1997.

[2] Some of the evidence offered by proponents of the ancient astronaut theory is highly questionable or blatantly erroneous; some (like the Baghdad Battery described in this chapter) is quite compelling.

[3] Until we know precisely how cultures and people who did not have the knowledge base to create advanced technological devices dated from their time period made such things, we cannot make a conclusive determination as to the accuracy or errancy of the ancient astronaut theory.

[4] Simon Welfare and John Fairly, *Arthur C. Clarke's Mysterious World*, p. 62.

4

Angel Hair

HAIKU:

ANGEL HAIR

Falling from the sky
Filaments of filagree
Gossamer callers

The substance is described as "cobwebs"—but it fell in flake-formation, or in "flakes or rags about one inch broad and five or six inches long." Also, these flakes were of a relatively heavy substance—"they fell with some velocity." The quantity was great—the shortest side of the triangular space is eight miles long.

—Charles Fort[1]

DEFINITION: Angel hair is a silky, sticky substance that falls from the sky in thin strands that sometimes look like spider webs. It is very unstable and degrades in oxygen.

WHAT THE BELIEVERS SAY: Angel hair is some kind of manifestation from another dimension, or a supernatural realm, or it is a substance that falls from UFOs. Some psychics claim to sense the presence of spirits during and following an angel hair manifestation.

WHAT THE SKEPTICS SAY: Angel hair is made of silicon, magnesium, calcium, and boron and is some kind of atmospheric anomaly, the source of which we still do not yet understand.

QUALITY OF EXISTING EVIDENCE: Good.

LIKELIHOOD PHENOMENON IS PARANORMAL: Fair to Good.

You can touch it, but you can't hold it without it sublimating[2] into nothing. You can see it, but sometimes it doesn't show up in photographs taken of it. It looks like spider webs, but there are never any spiders around when it appears. It often appears after UFO sightings, yet many people who have never seen a UFO report finding it in their yard. Some manifestations occur in the presence of many witnesses; some are reported by only a single person. Charles Darwin reported seeing it fall on his ship, the *Beagle*, in 1832.

It is called "angel hair" and it has been manifesting on earth for centuries, perhaps eons. One of the earliest known reports is from the early eighteenth century (September 21, 1741); recent sightings are commonplace, although often not reported. Some people experience it all the time; others have never even heard of it. Sometimes it falls on an entire town; sometimes it appears in people's houses. It can fall in such quantity as to cover cars and entire fields, or it can appear as a single gossamer strand.

In October 1955, a retired Navy man reported seeing ten silvery balls darting about the sky in North Carolina, followed by a fall of angel hair that covered a field and the telephone lines.

On September 21, 1997 (*another* September 21st sighting), people in Santa Cruz, California reported seeing strands of angel hair falling from the sky. One witness described them as "three-foot strands . . . of a translucent fibrous substance."[3]

On Sunday, August 9, 2001 in Quirindi, South Wales, Australia, multiple witnesses saw approximately twenty silver balls flitting through the sky, followed by a fall of angel hair.

There are many other reports of this weird substance falling from the sky, and what almost all of them have in common is that they are made by credible people, often with corroborating accounts from other witnesses.

So what is this stuff? And where does it come from?

Some people have managed to preserve a sample of angel hair before it dissolved into nothing. Some have paid labs to test it and it was often shown to be made of silicon, magnesium, calcium, and boron—but the source of the substance has consistently been reported as "Inconclusive." The elements of angel hair are common to earth, but the actual substance itself is an anomaly that has yet to be conclusively identified and its origin determined.

Could it be cobwebs from migrating spiders? Spiders don't fly, yet skeptics claim that spiders are carried aloft by winds, and then discharge the webs while in the air. There are reports of angel hair covering entire backyards, and draping like tinsel over great lengths of electrical lines. It would seem that it would take a great many spiders (perhaps millions) floating through the air in a group to create such an outpouring of webs. I, for one, have never seen giant clouds of floating spiders. There may be some who have, but such reports have yet to show up in the literature.

Could angel hair be some kind of material created inside tornadoes or plasma vortices, carried a distance, and then dropped?

Maybe, but there are many, many accounts of angel hair occurring in perfectly calm weather, with no reports of turbulent weather for miles.

Can angel hair be a discharge from UFOs? The connection between UFO sightings and subsequent falling angel hair is strong. And yet, no one has reported ever seeing a UFO actually dropping the stuff, nor has anyone ever photographed such an event.

It is said that the veil between other dimensions and other realms is thin, and that sometimes holes appear, allowing some to see and experience things alien to our world. Ghosts, UFOs, manifestations of the Virgin Mary, sightings of transdimensional creatures like Bigfoot and the Loch Ness monster, and channeled information have all been alleged to come from dimensions parallel, or perhaps above or below our own.

Could angel hair be from such a realm?

Can we be seeing something that is undoubtedly alien to us, but which might be as commonplace "somewhere else" as rain is to us in our world?

Or is it nothing but cobwebs from flying spiders?

---

[1]*The Book of the Damned*, p. 60.

[2]In chemistry, a substance is said to sublimate when it transforms from a solid to a gaseous state (or vice versa) without first becoming a liquid.

[3]*San Francisco Chronicle*, September 22, 1997.

5

Angels

HAIKU:

ANGELS

Celestial friends
Visitors from godly realms
Beings of the light

Likewise, I say unto you, there is joy in the presence of the angels of God over one sinner that repenteth.[1]

DEFINITION: Angels are immortal, spiritual beings attendant to God; they are divine guardians.

WHAT THE BELIEVERS SAY: Angels are divinely created messengers and servants of God who can have a direct and specific influence on human affairs. They are regular visitors to our Earthly realm. Many people have seen them and experienced their blessings.

WHAT THE SKEPTICS SAY: Angels are imaginary creatures that people dream up to explain seemingly inexplicable turns of events as instances of divine intervention. The belief in "guardian angels" is nothing but a projection of man's innate need to feel protected.

QUALITY OF EXISTING EVIDENCE: Good.

LIKELIHOOD PHENOMENA ARE PARANORMAL: High.

Those who believe in angels say they are all around us, and that they often appear at moments of crisis and danger to help their terrestrial charges. I recently heard a story about a woman who ended up stranded on a deserted highway in the middle of a blizzard. Her car stalled and when she turned the key, the engine wouldn't start. There were no other cars on the road, the snow was coming down heavily, and she did not have a cell phone. Just as she was reaching the point of panic, a man suddenly appeared at her window, banged on the glass and shouted, "If you hold your foot down on the gas for five seconds it will start." The woman did as instructed and the car did, indeed, start. She looked for the man who had helped her, but he was nowhere to be found and there was no car stopped anywhere else on the highway. To this day, the woman believes the man was an angel, sent to help her.

Stories of angels permeate the world's cultures, even when it comes to something as scientifically rational as space travel. The January 5, 1986 issue of *Parade* magazine reported that Russian cosmonaut Oleg Atkov saw angels outside the window of *Salyut* 7 in 1985 on his 155th day in orbit. There was also a widely reproduced quote about this incident: "What we saw were seven giant figures in the form of humans, but with wings and mistlike halos, as in the classic depiction of angels. Their faces were round with cherubic smiles."

This angel story flew (sorry) around the world and there wasn't much critical debunking regarding its validity. When I began researching this chapter, I came upon this story in several highly regarded reference books, and it was always presented as a true story.

In December 2002, I contacted Dr. Atkov, now a clinical cardiologist in Moscow and asked him if the story was true.

His response? "Dear Mr. Spignesi, This 'celestial story' is completely false. Dr. O. Atkov."

Did anyone else ever bother to ask Dr. Atkov if the story was true? It seems as if no one did, and I believe that part of the reason was the global fascination with angels. Whether or not it was true didn't much matter: the story of cosmonauts seeing angels in space was too fantastic not to publish. Likewise the current story making the rounds that the Hubbell telescope has taken photos of angelic beings of light; that NASA has the photos, and that there is an airtight lid of secrecy that prevents their release. The Vatican knows about these images, but the official position from everyone is "no comment."

Is the Hubbell story true? Who knows? But many people believe it. In fact, a recent study revealed that the overwhelming majority of Americans believe in the existence of angels.

The possibility of the existence of angels is comforting to many people. The *Catholic Encyclopedia* tells us that angels are spiritual beings intermediate between God and men. They are immortal, and they are often spoken of as messengers. Their job is to communicate the will of God to man, and to offer assistance to us mortals (as in the above highway story). Catholicism also tells us that each person is assigned a personal guardian angel at birth.

Other interesting facts about angels include . . .

- The Koran was supposedly dictated to the Prophet Mohammed by none other than the Angel Gabriel.
- Satan is a fallen angel who challenged the authority of God.
- An angel appeared to Mary to tell her that she was to be the mother of Christ.
- There are several books on the market containing first-hand accounts of people who have seen angels. In a recent book review in *Fate* magazine, the reviewer wrote, "If you, like this reviewer, have ever seen angels, all the research in the world is unnecessary to convince one that they do exist."[2]

According to tradition, there are nine types of angels, and they are organized into three "choirs" as follows:[3]

THE HIERARCHY OF ANGELS

FIRST CHOIR

1. **Seraphim:** They have six wings and are apparently the only holy beings allowed to stand in the presence of God. Seraphim are the "highest ranking" angels.
2. **Cherubim:** They have large wings, a human head, and an animal body.
3. **Thrones:** The Bible is vague on what Thrones look like, but they are mentioned in Colossians 1:16 ("For by him were all things created, in the heavens and on the earth, things visible and things

invisible, whether thrones or dominions or principalities or powers; all things have been created through him, and to him."), and it is assumed that they serve Seraphim and Cherubim in some capacity.

SECOND CHOIR

4. **Dominions:** The chief angels of the Second Hierarchy. They are also mentioned in Colossians.
5. **Virtues:** Angels that report to Dominions.
6. **Powers:** Angels that report to Virtues and which are also mentioned in Colossians.

THIRD CHOIR

7. **Principalities:** An angel with power over Archangels and Angels.
8. **Archangels:** A chief angel, in charge of Angels. Gabriel, Raphael, and Michael are Archangels.
9. **Angels:** Supernatural beings garbed in white robes. They have one set of wings and are superior to humans in powers and intelligence. They are usually assigned the day-to-day work of watching over and helping humans.

So are angels real? We rate the quality of existing evidence as good because the countless stories of human interaction with angelic beings are very convincing. Credible people tell of incredible things and many of them are quite believable. Are they *all* delusional or mistaken? *All of them?*

Faith plays a role, but a reasonable assessment of the many accounts of angels compels us to rate the likelihood of their existence and their paranormal nature as high.

[1]Luke 15:10.

[2]*Fate*, March 2003, p. 43.

[3]This ranking originally appeared in my book, *The Odd Index* (Plume, 1994), as a list titled "9 Types of Angels." Used by permission.

6

Animal Psi

HAIKU:

ANIMAL PSI

Speaking without words,
A mind to mind connection:
Let us know the beasts.

Animals are such agreeable friends—they ask no questions,
they pass no criticisms.

—George Eliot[1]

DEFINITION: Animal psi is the alleged extrasensory, interspecies communication between humans and animals; it also refers to the ability of animals to sense future events, and to the mental connection and communication between animals.

WHAT THE BELIEVERS SAY: Animals can read our minds; animals can sense danger and predict death; animals can travel thousands of miles homed in by psi powers alone.

WHAT THE SKEPTICS SAY: Animals cannot read humans' minds; all their apparent "understanding" actions comes simply from ingrained behaviors imprinted on their psyche by simple reward and punishment interactions between them and their masters; all other instances of seemingly accurate predictions by animals or communication between species are due to chance and chance alone.

QUALITY OF EXISTING EVIDENCE: Excellent.

LIKELIHOOD PHENOMENON IS PARANORMAL: Very high.

Can animals read our minds? Can we talk to our pets simply by thinking? Can animals know when someone is going to die? Can animals travel thousands of miles across lands they have never known to locate their masters?

The answer to all these questions seems to be an unqualified "yes."

There are countless stories of animals who exhibited behaviors impossible without some type of extrasensory ability. And many of these stories have arisen from scientific experiments, with controls and validation techniques.

Item: A mother dog and her pup were both conditioned to cower in fear to a raised newspaper. They were never actually struck with the paper but they were indoctrinated to fear the threatening gesture. As part of an experiment, the mother was placed in a sealed, copper-lined room.[2] Her pup was placed in a similarly secured room, out of earshot of her mother, and some distance away. The experimenter raised a rolled-up newspaper to the mother . . . and the pup cowered in fear.

Item: A woman and her pet boxer were each placed in copper-lined rooms, out of sight and earshot of each other. The dog's heart was monitored by electrocardiogram. A male unknown to the woman then suddenly entered the room where she sat, shouted at her, and threatened her with violence. The woman's pet's heart began to race wildly at the precise moment that her master was in danger. The dog was alone in the room at the time and could not hear or see anything that was going on in the other room.

Item: A man was riding a horse through a forest when the horse stopped and refused to move, no matter how much the rider prodded him. A full minute went by and then suddenly a bolt of lightning erupted from the sky and struck the ground in front of the horse and rider—precisely where they would have been if they had continued on their way instead of stopping.

Item: In August 1923, Bobbie the collie got separated from his owners as they were traveling through Indiana. Bobbie and his family lived in Oregon. In February 1924, Bobbie leaped up onto the bed where his master was sleeping in their home in Oregon and happily licked his face. He was gaunt, and his paws were so worn, the bones were showing through the pads, but Bobbie had survived. The Oregon Humane Society eventually retraced his route, discovering that he had traveled a total of three thousand miles to get home. He had crossed the Rockies, swum the Missouri River, and even shared mulligan stew with a bunch of hobos. Bobbie caught and ate rabbits, and he managed to avoid dying, getting killed, or getting caught by dogcatchers. Also, throughout his entire journey, he did *not* travel the route of his owners, but instead, traversed lands he had never seen, and of which he had no prior knowledge. Bobbie was ultimately given a gold dog collar and the keys to several cities when news of his incredible journey was made public.

Logically, and with a righteous dollop of skepticism, how can these stories be explained without acknowledging the existence of extrasensory perception in these animals?

The answer? They *cannot* be explained without acknowledging the existence of extrasensory perception in these animals.

Pet owners have long known of their animals' ability to read their minds. I myself have experienced such a connection with my pets over the years.

The process is *not* like talking on an interspecies phone; it is simply knowing how your pet will react, or, conversely, your pet knowing what you are planning next. Can any of this be explained by habit and training? Yes, some can. But some cannot.

I once had a cat who would never lick me on the forehead when he was being affectionate. He liked to lick me on the neck. There were exceptions to this rule, however, and it was when I had a migraine. Whenever I was suffering from a terrible headache, he would jump up on the arm of my chair and lick only my forehead, much the way mother animals lick the wounds of their offspring. Did he know I had a headache? I wholeheartedly believe so.

I believe that animal psi is real and that it should be studied. There is a real problem, however, if humans become adept at communicating with animals. We may ultimately be able to more fully understand them and—let's be honest—do we really want to know what animals (and I'm not talking about family pets now) are thinking and feeling, considering the way we treat them?

---

[1] *Mr. Gilfil's Love Story*, Ch. 7.
[2] The copper blocked sound and other vibrations from entering the room.

7

Area 51

HAIKU:

AREA 51

A place with no name
As big as Connecticut
Desert mysteries

Stealth has changed irrevocably the way in which war in the air is being and will be fought. Groom Lake, Nevada, is the epicentre of classified Air Force research into stealth and other exotic aerospace technologies. Thirty years from now, we may still not know the half of what is currently being tested in and around Groom Lake.

—Nick Cook[1]

DEFINITION: Area 51, named for a grid designation on an old map of Nevada, is allegedly a top secret military installation northwest of Las Vegas, located in the heart of the Nevada Test Site, and incorporating part of the enormous Nellis Air Force Range. We say "allegedly" because the U.S. government will not acknowledge that it exists.

WHAT THE BELIEVERS SAY: Area 51 is where the military keeps the alien spacecraft. It is also where top secret, joint alien-military reverse engineering projects take place. What goes on in Area 51 is not only proof that aliens and UFOs are real, but also that the U.S. government has known about them for years and now works regularly with aliens.

WHAT THE SKEPTICS SAY: Area 51 is an "above top secret" military test installation where the U.S. government designs, builds, and tests advanced aircraft, weaponry, and communications systems. Period.

QUALITY OF EXISTING EVIDENCE: Poor.[2]

LIKELIHOOD PHENOMENON IS PARANORMAL: Low.[3]

Item: On September 29, 1995, President Clinton signed Executive Order 95-15, which exempted Area 51 (which, remember, does not exist) from all federal, state, interstate, and local laws.

Item: On October 12, 1996, President Clinton exempted Area 51 from all federal, state, interstate, and local environmental regulations.

Item: On January 31, 2001, President Bush renewed Area 51's exemptions from all federal, state, interstate, and local laws.

What is going on in Area 51 that would justify the President of the United States voiding the area's obligations to obey *all* laws and environmental regulations?

What is going on in Area 51 that could warrant the suppression of evidence—by executive order—of past or future government crimes?

What is going on in Area 51 that the test facility does not appear on any Federal budget allotments, does not appear on Federal Aviation Administration or United States Geological Survey maps?

What is going on in Area 51 that the base does not even have an official name?[4]

Are retrieved alien spacecraft hidden in the many hangars and underground bunkers at Area 51?

Is the United States government working with aliens on joint operations involving space travel and advanced otherworldly weapons?

Do the Area 51 personnel spend their days reverse-engineering alien technology, which has already supposedly given mankind the transistor, superconductors, microwave technology, satellite communications, even Velcro, and the Superball?

Are all these questions utterly ridiculous, since there is no empirical evidence to merit even asking them?

The history of Area 51 begins in the mid-1950s when the CIA needed a place to test the top secret U2 bomber project. Military research, design, and production continued at the site throughout the ensuing decades but, during those years, the area became associated with UFOs, captured extraterrestrial craft, and ultra-secret alien research and programs.

How did this come about? Why is Area 51 believed to be home to UFOs and more?

In the late 1980s, a man named Robert Lazar began appearing on television and in documentaries claiming that he participated in the reverse-engineering of alien technology at the Groom Lake (Area 51) military facility. He had evidence that he did, indeed, at one time work for the Air Force, but all of his claims about UFOs and the work he did at the facility remain, to this day, unsubstantiated.

Lazar's public pronouncements prompted the Area 51 tourist wave. People began visiting the site (or as close as they could get to it without being arrested) and the rumors and stories about the area grew exponentially.

Some conspiracy buffs claim that many of the stories about Area 51 were deliberately disseminated by the government as part of a major disinformation campaign.

It *is* known that there is highly advanced aviation and weaponry research going on at Area 51, an area which is almost the size of Connecticut and which is patrolled by guards who, signs tell visitors, are authorized to use deadly force to prevent encroachment onto the grounds.

Can we arrive at any conclusions about what goes on in what some pilots call "Dreamland?" Yes, we can: Based on the empirical evidence, the anecdotal accounts, and common sense, it seems extremely unlikely that any of the Area 51 "ET" rumors are true.

What is highly likely is that there is very advanced research going on at Area 51, none of which the government wants made public and which easily explains the tighter-than-tight security spanning a large portion of southern Nevada.

We have recently learned, however, through a series of lawsuits against the U.S. government and a segment on *60 Minutes*, that toxic materials are routinely destroyed at Area 51 in giant "burn pits." Some of the workers who participated in burning chemicals and materials developed cancers and skin diseases they attribute to the chemicals that were released in the smoke they were exposed to.

The resolution of these suits will be interesting to watch, since, as noted, anything that goes on at Area 51 is above and beyond all laws.

In the end, such immunity may be the biggest "Area 51" scandal of all.

[1] *Jane's Defence Weekly.*

[2] What kind of concrete evidence can be garnered about a place that the government doesn't even acknowledge exists?

[3] This ranking comes with the caveat that a final conclusion cannot be reached based on unsubstantiated theories and wild allegations alone. If the doors to one of the Area 51 hangars are one day thrown open to *60 Minutes's* cameras and Mike Wallace walks in and shows us aliens and extraterrestrial crafts, then we reserve the right to upgrade this ranking to "Very high."

[4] *The New York Times Sunday Magazine*, June 24, 1994.

8

Ark of the Covenant with the Mercy Seat.

The Ark of the Covenant

HAIKU:

ARK OF THE COVENANT

Sacred chest of truth
Stone tablets reside within?
Washed by Jesus' blood

God's temple that is in heaven was opened, and the ark of the Lord's covenant was seen in his temple. There followed lightnings, sounds, thunders, an earthquake, and great hail.[1]

DEFINITION: In the Old Testament, the Ark of the Covenant was purported to be the chest containing the Ten Commandments which were written on stone tablets and presented to Moses by God. The Ark was carried by the Hebrews during their desert wanderings.

WHAT THE BELIEVERS SAY: The Ark of the Covenant was real; the Ten Commandments were placed inside it; and it may or may not have the blood of Christ on its mercy seat.

WHAT THE SKEPTICS SAY: The Ark of the Covenant is a Biblical legend; the odds of its actual existence are slim.

QUALITY OF EXISTING EVIDENCE: Inconclusive.[2]

LIKELIHOOD PHENOMENON IS PARANORMAL: Inconclusive.[3]

The first mention of the Ark of the Covenant in the Bible occurs in the book of Exodus, when God himself gives Moses the specific dimensions and instructions for constructing the Ark:

They shall make an ark of acacia wood. Its length shall be two and a half cubits, its breadth a cubit and a half, and a cubit and a half its height.

You shall overlay it with pure gold. Inside and outside shall you overlay it, and shall make a gold molding around it.

You shall cast four rings of gold for it, and put them in its four feet. Two rings shall be on the one side of it, and two rings on the other side of it.

You shall make poles of acacia wood, and overlay them with gold.

You shall put the poles into the rings on the sides of the ark to carry the ark.

The poles shall be in the rings of the ark. They shall not be taken from it.

You shall put the testimony which I shall give you into the ark.[4]

A box of wood, covered in gold, carried by poles inserted through rings.

God then continued his instructions, detailing the mercy seat and the two angels that would guard the Ark:

You shall make a mercy seat of pure gold. Two and a half cubits shall be its length, and a cubit and a half its breadth.

You shall make two cherubim of hammered gold. You shall make them at the two ends of the mercy seat.

Make one cherub at the one end, and one cherub at the other end. You shall make the cherubim on its two ends of one piece with the mercy seat.

The cherubim shall spread out their wings upward, covering the mercy seat with their wings, with their faces toward one another. The faces of the cherubim shall be toward the mercy seat.

You shall put the mercy seat on top of the ark, and in the ark you shall put the testimony that I will give you.

There I will meet with you, and I will tell you from above the mercy seat, from between the two cherubim which are on the ark of the testimony, all that I command you for the children of Israel.[5]

People who believe in the Bible state that these passages confirm the construction and, thus, the existence of the Ark of the Covenant. Many historians stipulate that the Ark probably did exist, but that it was likely destroyed when the Babylonians attacked Jerusalem in 587 B.C. and destroyed the Temple.

What about the claims of some that the Ark was a "spiritual capacitor" that channeled the power of God and could be used by the faithful to vanquish their enemies? This was the premise of the Steven Spielberg 1981 blockbuster movie, *Raiders of the Lost Ark*. There is no way to confirm such a theory, though, since the current location of the Ark, if it did, in fact, exist, is unknown.

According to the Bible, however, the Ark is no longer on Earth. It is in Heaven (see the epigraph) and if this were true, it would make the archaeological attempts to locate it exercises in futility.

The theological importance of the Ark that holds the stone tablets given to Moses by God is incalculable, though, and thus, the search goes on.

In more ways than one.

[1]Revelations 11:19.

[2]The only actual "evidence" (to use the term loosely) for the existence of the Ark of the Covenant comes from the Old Testament (with specious validation later in the New Testament, in Revelation). There is no physical evidence that it ever existed, although the late archaeologist Ron Wyatt claimed to have located the Ark in a cave in Jerusalem, but he never provided any verification of his claims. (Many archaeologists believe the Wyatt discovery was a hoax; supporters of Wyatt believe totally in his assertions and are confident that day is coming when someone else will locate the Ark in the area where Wyatt said it was buried.) Whether or not a person believes in the existence of the Ark depends on their depth of faith in the historical and archaeological accuracy of the Bible.

[3]We do not know if the Ark of the Covenant did exist, and/or if it *still* exists; thus, there is no way of knowing whether or not it was/is a paranormal artifact (*Raiders of the Lost Ark* notwithstanding).

[4]Exodus 25: 10–16.

[5]Exodus 25: 17–22.

9

Are There UFOs in the Bible?
Was Jesus an Extraterrestrial?

HAIKU:

ARE THERE UFOS IN THE BIBLE?

High pillars of smoke
Heralding their arrival
Ancient men bow down

Do not neglect to show hospitality to aliens, for thereby some have entertained angels unawares.

—Hebrews 13:2

DEFINITION: There exist biblical passages that some believe describe non-human beings and non-earthly craft coming out of the sky; also, there exist accounts of actions of Jesus that some believe could be those of an alien visitor.

WHAT THE BELIEVERS SAY: Biblical passages in both the Old and New Testaments tell stories, (albeit in metaphorical language) of aliens and alien spacecraft visiting Earth. Also, many accounts of Jesus' doings could easily be interpreted as describing the actions of an extraterrestrial.

WHAT THE SKEPTICS SAY: The religiously minded skeptics say that such speculation is blasphemous and that the Biblical accounts of heavenly manifestations are realistic accounts of divine apparitions. The agnostics and atheists say that everything in the Bible is pure fantasy, all of which was generated from the minds of the writers. The stories do not prove either extraterrestrial or divine interaction with humanity.

QUALITY OF EXISTING EVIDENCE: Good.[1]

LIKELIHOOD PHENOMENA ARE AUTHENTIC: Inconclusive.[2]

UFOs IN THE BIBLE?

Some UFOlogists believe wholeheartedly that the human race has extraterrestrial progenitors, and that all religious symbology is evidence of ancient man's attempts to understand and chronicle alien visitations and the appearance of extraterrestrial craft on Earth.

If we make the assumption that Biblical language is figurative and imagistic, rather than literal and realistic, then the "UFO/alien" interpretation has some validity.

EXODUS 13:21–22:

> And the Lord went before them by day in a pillar of a cloud, to lead them the way, and by night in a pillar of fire, to give them light; to go by day and night: He took not away the pillar of the cloud by day, nor the pillar of fire by night, from before the people.

Interpretation? A UFO led the way for Moses and the Jews fleeing Egypt. The craft was dark gray during the day and lit up at night.

JUDGES 20:40:

> But when the flame began to arise up out of the city with a pillar of smoke, the Benjamites looked behind them, and, behold, the flame of the city ascended up to heaven.

Interpretation? A spacecraft lifted up from Gibeah, and its smoke and exhaust flames could be seen from a distance.

NEHEMIAH 9:11–12:

> You divided the sea before them, so that they went through the midst of the sea on the dry land; and their pursuers you did cast into the depths, as a stone into the mighty waters.

Moreover in a pillar of cloud you led them by day; and in a pillar of fire by night, to give them light in the way in which they should go.

Interpretation? The UFO leading the Jews out of Egypt parted the Red Sea from above, probably using some type of energy beam that spread the waters and opened a path for the Israelites.

WAS JESUS AN EXTRATERRESTRIAL?[3]

Was Jesus an alien sent to Earth as an undercover scout?

Could it also be possible that this alien did *not* intend that an entire religion be created around his presence?

Here is a look at some of the most compelling "ET" interpretations of the idea that Jesus was an extraterrestrial:

Jesus was the Son of God: Jesus was born of a Virgin.
Jesus was an ET: Jesus was a genetically engineered being who was implanted in an Earth woman to be born on Earth.

Son of God: The angel Gabriel visited Mary to tell her that she would be conceived by the Holy Spirit.
ET: An alien emissary visited Mary to inform her of the implantation.

Son of God: The star of Bethlehem guided the Three Wise Men to the place of Jesus' birth.
ET: An alien ship flew across the sky within plain view of three alien scouts whose assignment it was to monitor the alien/human birth.

Son of God: In *The Gospel According to Matthew*, 3:16–17, Jesus is taken up into heaven by God the Father after he was baptized.
ET: Jesus the ET was teleported out of the water by an anti-gravity ray, beamed down upon him from an alien spacecraft.

Son of God: Jesus walked on water.
ET: Jesus the ET had some kind of anti-gravity device that allowed him to appear to be walking on water.

Son of God: Jesus raised Lazarus from the dead.
ET: Jesus the ET had advanced medical abilities that allowed him to revive Lazarus, who was probably not dead but actually just in a deep coma.

Son of God: In the *Gospel According to John*, Chapter 8, Verse 23, Jesus tells his followers, "You are from beneath; I am from above. Ye are of this world; I am not of this world."
ET: "You are Earthlings; I am an extraterrestrial."

Son of God: Jesus changed water into wine.
ET: Jesus the ET had some kind of device that could transmute at the subatomic level the molecules of water into wine molecules.

Son of God: Jesus miraculously multiplied the loaves and fishes.
ET: Jesus the ET had some kind of technologically advanced food synthesizing device that "read" the original and was then able to duplicate as many completely real duplicates as desired.

Son of God: Jesus spent forty days and forty nights in the desert.
ET: Jesus the ET spent forty days and forty nights on the Mothership reporting on his terrestrial findings and taking a much-needed rest.

Son of God: Jesus rose from the dead.
ET: At the moment when onlookers saw Jesus "commend his spirit" to his heavenly Father, his alien colleagues flying above him in the Mothership put him into suspended animation and then "reactivated" him when he was lying in his tomb.

Son of God: Jesus physically ascended into Heaven.
ET: Jesus the ET was "beamed up" to the Mothership as his followers watched. (This is also how his mother Mary "ascended into Heaven.")

Son of God: Jesus spoke to Paul as Paul traveled the road to Damascus and Paul was instantly converted to Christianity.
ET: Jesus the ET spoke to Paul from a spaceship, so terrifying and awing him that he willingly agreed to do whatever the voice told him to.

[1] The evidence is ranked high because the Biblical passages are specific and accessible.

[2] The likelihood of these passages describing UFOs and of Jesus being an extraterrestrial is ranked inconclusive because, even today, we simply do not know what actually happened during the events and times written about in the Bible.

[3] Some of this "Was Jesus an ET?" material originally appeared in a different form in my 2000 book, *The UFO Book of Lists* (Kensington Publishing).

10

The Astral Body, Astral Planes, and Astral Projection

HAIKU:

THE ASTRAL SELF

Silver cord glimmers
Body and soul of white light
Unseen and silent

I and this mystery here we stand.
Clear and sweet is my soul, and clear and sweet is all that
   is not my soul.
Lack one lacks both, and the unseen is proved by
   the seen,
Till that becomes unseen and receives proof in its turn.[1]

DEFINITION: The **astral body** is one of several etheric bodies humans possess[2] in addition to our physical bodies. The astral body is the body that manifests an aura (see Chapter 13) and it can allegedly travel outside the confines of our physical self.

Astral planes are realms or levels of existence above, below, and/or parallel to earthly corporeal reality.

Astral projection, also known as an **out-of-body experience (OBE),** is the act or process of disconnecting the astral body from the physical body and traveling to other places on Earth and/or other planes of being.

WHAT THE BELIEVERS SAY: Within our physical body is an invisible energy body known as our astral body. Within the astral body resides our life energy, and this body is part and parcel of the totality of our individual self. If the physical body is injured or weakened (from drugs, diet, environmental toxins, etc.), the astral body will likewise be weakened. Similarly, if the astral body is bombarded with negative energies (fatigue, stress, anger, negative criticism, faultfinding, and condemnatory family and friends, etc.) then the physical body will reflect the drain and the person will feel unwell. The astral body is as much a part of the human being as the mind, which, although we know it is "resident" within the brain, we nonetheless cannot physically see. The astral body is likewise resident within the body, but is invisible.

WHAT THE SKEPTICS SAY: There is no evidence proving the existence of even one astral body, let alone several. All this nonsense about silver umbilical cords and walking through walls and floating up to the ceiling is nothing but delusions, dreams, hallucinations, or lies. Man may have a spiritual dimension, but this dimension is most assuredly not manifested as a body of ether that can step out of our physical body and go traveling about. Anyone who believes that they have "astral traveled" was either dreaming or experiencing a wonky brain state.

QUALITY OF EXISTING EVIDENCE: Fair.[3]

LIKELIHOOD PHENOMONA ARE PARANORMAL: Fair to Good.[4]

According to clairvoyants who claim to have actually seen the human astral body, it is luminous, resplendently colorful, and it vibrates.

They say the astral body is real, invisible, and inside our physical bodies, an integral part of our being. An apt comparison (as mentioned above) would be the paradigm of our minds being inside our physical brains, real, invisible, yet an integral part of the being we know as our self.

Our astral body operates on its own and, according to occultists, only a tiny percentage of people are ever aware of its existence. People who have had a near-death experience (see Chapter 57), or who deliberately and diligently work to develop their psychic skills, do ultimately interact with their etheric selves, but the majority of humans live only within the rudiments of their physical body.

Interestingly, the generally accepted definition of the "astral self" sounds like nothing so much as the standard definition of the "soul": "The animating and vital principle in human beings, credited with the faculties of thought, action, and emotion and often conceived as an immaterial entity; the spiritual nature of human beings, regarded as immortal, separable from the body at death, and susceptible to happiness or misery in a future state."[5]

So, is the notion of the "astral body" simply camouflaged religious dogma? Is there any real difference between organized religion's conception of the eternal soul and the occult philosophies' understanding and definition of the astral body?

Both seem to be addressing the same mystery.

I once had a conversation with a clairvoyant who told me that she perceived eternal, universal reality (what some call the Godhead) as an infinitely high skyscraper with a limitless (or at least unknown) number of floors. Our physical reality is only one floor in this skyscraper and it is the floor in which our physical bodies must reside. The other floors are off-limits to our corporeal selves, but they are accessible by our etheric/astral/spiritual selves. She believed that our astral bodies could visit these floors, but that not everyone was able to "climb the stairs," so to speak.

Interestingly, this belief system can fit rather neatly into many of the religio-spiritual constructs of man.

It can all be reduced to the idea that man has a soul and it is eternal and does live on.

Is everything else just window dressing?

[1] Walt Whitman, *Leaves of Grass*, "Song of Myself, 3."

[2] Madame Blavatsky, the founder of Theosophy, claimed humans have seven bodies of varied composition.

[3] Granted, most of the evidence for the existence of the astral body comes from people who claim to have had an out-of-body experience, which cannot be proven, but there are far too many anecdotal accounts of such travel and of auras and other elements of the astral body to dismiss the phenomena as *completely* impossible. Fifteen percent of people who have claimed to have had an OBE have reported information they state they could not have known if their consciousness had remained within their physical body. (George, *Alternate Realities*, p. 206.)

[4] The questionable empirical evidence notwithstanding, it does not seem at all unlikely that human beings possess a spiritual dimension. Many (most?) people would reply "yes" if you asked them if they believed that there was a spiritual element to their identity. As discussed in this chapter, the similarities to the usual perception of the astral self and the soul cannot be discounted.

[5] *American Heritage Dictionary.*

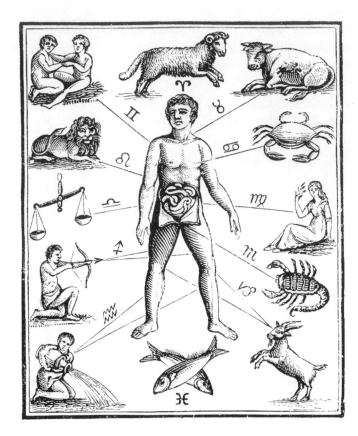

11

Astrology

HAIKU:

ASTROLOGY

As above, below.
Stars impel—or they compel?
Ghosts in the machine

It is the stars,
The stars above us, govern our conditions.[1]

DEFINITION: Astrology is the study and interpretation of the positions of celestial bodies—the Sun, planets, and the Earth's Moon—in the belief that they have a real, direct, and quantifiable influence on earthly events and human affairs.

WHAT THE BELIEVERS SAY: The movements of celestial bodies create enigmatic—yet quite real—"energy fields" and forces that can affect how human beings act and think, much the way a full moon can have a measurable effect on the earth's tides and other activities on earth. This correlation between reality and astrological predictions and interpretations goes well beyond coincidence, or even synchronicity.

WHAT THE SKEPTICS SAY: Astrology is one of the worst examples of pseudoscience, since there is *zero* scientific validity to the belief that Jupiter's orbit (or the orbit of any other planet) can affect humans in any way whatsoever. People who find meaning in astrological readings are simply projecting their own desires and concerns onto a fabricated belief system centering around the movements of planets.

QUALITY OF EXISTING EVIDENCE: Good.

LIKELIHOOD PHENOMON IS PARANORMAL: Fair.[2]

Back in the late eighties, when I was writing my Stephen King encyclopedia, *The Shape Under the Sheet*, I had King's horoscope cast by computer by a firm in New York that promised accuracy and revelatory details. I wasn't sure back then whether or not I actually believed in astrology, but I thought that for the purposes of the book, and considering the fact that King often writes about things beyond the ken of man, a horoscope of the writer would be a fun feature to include. I did include a graphic of King's astrological chart in the book, but ultimately was unable to include the detailed analysis of the natal information for space reasons.

I recall the gist of it, though. It said that King was creative, ambitious, and reserved, and probably would feel most comfortable working in the arts. It specifically mentioned "writer" as a possible career and also spoke of an innate need for privacy and a strong self-effacing personality. Anyone familiar with King's career and public persona would recognize the specificity of those conclusions.

I myself was amazed by the accuracy of this reading—and therein lies the problem with attempting to dismiss astrology or debunk its findings.

Sometimes the personality traits assigned to people with certain astrological signs, and the accuracy of the details of astrological reports, are so compelling, that one cannot help but feel that there simply *must* be something to this astrology thing, since how else could the information be so specific?

The skeptics say that astrological interpretations are too general for them not to strike a chord with almost anyone who reads one.

The question, then, is "are astrological readings accurate *beyond chance?*"

This question seems to have been answered in the affirmative by a French husband and wife research team in the 1950s.

Michel and Françoise Gauquelin studied planetary alignments and birth data and discovered some astonishing facts:[3]

1. A statistically significant number of doctors were born at specific times of the day or night when Mars or Saturn was at its highest point or had just risen.

2. Many soldiers, politicians and actors—outgoing, public types— were overwhelmingly influenced by the planet Jupiter.

3. A great many writers were influenced by the Moon. (This happens to be true for me in particular. My sign is Cancer, which is ruled by the Moon, and I share the sign with Pearl Buck, Ernest Hemingway, and many other writers.)

4. A great many athletes were influenced by the planet Mars. (This came to be known as the "Mars Effect.")

These findings were not welcomed with glee by skeptics and the mainstream scientific community.

In 1978, CSICOP (the Committee for the Scientific Investigation of Claims of the Paranormal) conducted a study with the intention of disproving the Gauquelins' findings. To their horror, their own carefully arrived-at results confirmed the Gauquelins' conclusions. For five years, the group obfuscated their findings by means of the manipulation of some of the statistical findings so as to make the results more in line with what an avowedly skeptical group would desire. The cover-up was obvious, members resigned, and in 1983, CSICOP sheepishly admitted that the Gauquelins' findings were accurate and that their own research had proven it.[4]

Astrology has been around for over two millennia. As far back as five hundred years before Christ, astrologers were casting horoscopes and looking to the heavens, literally, for answers. Catherine de Medici had her own personal astrologer—none other than Nostradamus himself. (See Chapter 59.)

The underlying principle that is fundamental to an understanding (and acceptance) of astrology is the belief that is summed up in the most commonly cited adage about astrology: "As above, so below." Astrology proceeds from the conviction that everything in the universe is designed, everything is interconnected, and nothing occurs by chance. Astrology, therefore, is basically theistic, in that its core functionality is derived from an attempt to understand the design of the universe, and since you cannot have a design without a designer, astrology is, (the Catholic Church's abhorrence of its "apathetic fatalism"[5] notwithstanding), orthodoxly religious in construct.

- Nancy Reagan consulted an astrologer regarding decisions her husband the President should make.
- Millions of people read their horoscope every day in the newspaper.
- Who does not know their astrological sign?

Astrology may never be accepted by mainstream science. But fair-minded seekers would be loath to dismiss it out of hand. Some of the answers mankind is searching for might, in fact, just be in the stars. And the planets, for that matter.

[1] William Shakespeare, *King Lear*, Act IV, Scene 3.
[2] Astrology may or may not be paranormal; there are passionately committed proponents for both sides of the argument.
[3] Bernard Gittelson, *Intangible Evidence*, pp. 344–45.
[4] Ibid., p. 346.
[5] *The Catholic Encyclopedia*, "Astrology," online at www.newadvent.org.

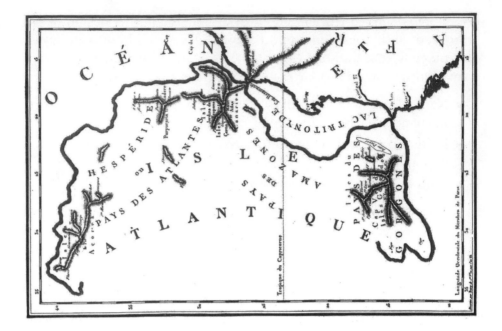

12

Atlantis

HAIKU:

ATLANTIS

Legendary land
West of Gibraltar it reigned
Vanished for all time?

*Way down ... below the ocean ... where I wanna be ...
she may be*

—Donovan[1]

DEFINITION: Atlantis was a legendary island in the Atlantic Ocean west of Gibraltar, said by Plato to have existed circa 9,000 B.C. and to have sunk beneath the sea during an earthquake.[2]

WHAT THE BELIEVERS SAY: Atlantis was real and its inhabitants were superior beings from whom mankind received all of its advanced technical knowledge, as well as its languages and religions.

WHAT THE SKEPTICS SAY: Atlantis is a myth created by Plato as part of a Socratic dialogue to illustrate what would happen when a society degenerated into decadence (Atlantis), as compared to a society that espoused fairness, respect, and dignity (Athens).

QUALITY OF EXISTING EVIDENCE: Poor.

LIKELIHOOD PHENOMENON IS PARANORMAL: Nil.[3]

How popular is the legend of Atlantis? A recent search of the Internet Movie Database (www.imdb.com) turned up over forty movies, four television series, and six "Atlantis"-themed video games. A search for books will turn up hundreds of titles; thousands, if out-of-print titles are included.

What is it about the tale of this ancient land that so engages modern man?

We have the Greek philosopher Plato to thank for the legend of Atlantis. In his fourth century B.C. Socratic dialogues *Timaeus* and *Critias*, Plato posited a scenario in which a perfect society was suddenly subjected to great burdens, including attack by a barbaric enemy accompanied by all the strife and turmoil associated with such aggression. Athens was the idealized society in his dialogues; Atlantis, Athens's hostile assailant. Prior to Plato's writings, there is *no mention anywhere* in surviving literature of such an ancient island and civilization.

In addition to being one of the most profoundly gifted thinkers of all time, Plato was also a great storyteller:

> Now in this island of Atlantis there was a great and wonderful empire which had rule over the whole island and several others, and over parts of the continent, and, furthermore, the men of Atlantis had subjected the parts of Libya within the columns of Heracles as far as Egypt, and of Europe as far as Tyrrhenia. This vast power, gathered into one, endeavoured to subdue at a blow our country and yours and the whole of the region within the straits; and then, Solon, your country shone forth, in the excellence of her virtue and strength, among all mankind.[4]

But the story Plato told was not based in reality. *It was an allegory.*

Plato was trying to impart a moral lesson to his students by telling the story of Athens and Atlantis.

He made it up—probably using an ancient Egyptian myth as his source.

No less a source than Aristotle, Plato's pupil, confirmed that Plato's tale was a fable written to make a point.

Yet, the legend of Atlantis lives on.

Incredibly detailed, fully developed mythologies have been concocted to shoehorn the myth of Atlantis into the tapestry of human history. Reviewing the many interpretations of the Atlantis legend literally rewrites history as we know it.

Supposedly, Atlantis is connected to, or the source of, the Great Pyramids, Noah's Flood, the invention of paper, all of man's laws, arts, and religions, the sciences of mathematics, astronomy, agriculture, metallurgy, ballistics, architecture, and engineering, as well as the occult arts, such as divination and magic.

According to those who believe that Atlantis actually existed as a real island that was destroyed by cataclysmic earthquakes, all of civilization owes its . . . well, owes its *everything* to ancient Atlantis. The fact that the time line of the development of civilization does not coincide with the Atlantean chronology does not seem to matter much to the Atlantisologists.

Is there any hint whatsoever of historical veracity to the story or Atlantis?

Atlantis apologists have long looked to *corroborated* history for validation of the Atlantis story. "It could be here; it could be there," is repeated like a mantra every time a new theory as to Atlantis's likely location is "floated." Yet, the science of geophysics may be the ultimate "invalidator" of the story of Atlantis.

The science of plate tectonics, the movement of the earth's crust over long periods of time, has confirmed that the continents of today were likely one huge land mass that split apart over eons due to volcanism, earthquakes, and other forces. In fact, looking at a map of the world today, it does not take an expert to see how neatly the northeast coast of South America would fit like a piece of a puzzle into the midwest coast of Africa. Or how Indonesia and Australia could have easily been the lower part of southern mainland China.

When continental drift is theoretically reversed and all of today's land masses are put back in their original place, recreating our planet's original solitary continent, there is no room leftover for a piece of property the size of Atlantis.

Yet all of this irrefutable evidence changes nothing in the minds of the believers.

Atlantis was, and continues to be, real to them and their staunch belief is that everyone will know they were right when its ruins are finally discovered, precisely the way archaeologists eventually located the ruins of Troy.

And so, the Atlantis books and movies keep coming, and the Atlantis story continues to be told.

[1] "Atlantis"

[2] In contrast to Plato's account, psychic Edgar Cayce [see chapter 32] claimed that Atlantis was near the Bermuda island of Bimini, and that the Atlanteans possessed super-powerful "fire crystals." He attributed Atlantis's sinking to an accident in which the fire crystals went out of control. Cayce said that the crystals continue to send out powerful waves of energy to this day, and that all the plane disappearances and ship sinkings in the Bermuda Triangle are due to their effects. Another theory regarding Atlantis's destruction lays blame on a six-mile-wide asteroid that laid waste to the island and created the Atlantic Ridge.

[3] This evaluation should be construed to assess the likelihood of Atlantis's reality (nil) as well as the likelihood that if it did, indeed, exist, its inhabitants had supernatural powers (nil).

[4] *Timaeus.*

13

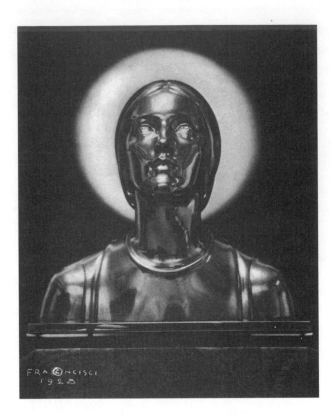

Auras and Halos

HAIKU:

AURAS AND HALOS

Around us glowing
Invisible but to some
Colorful halos

The aura shows everything. And when someone becomes enlightened the master knows it, because the aura reveals everything.

—Osho Rajneesh

Wow, your aura is really fantastic! It's this beautiful purple color! Your aura is purple!

—Beth, from Denver[1]

DEFINITION: An aura is an invisible emanation that surrounds every living thing and changes color based on the health of the person, animal, or plant; a halo is a luminous ring around and above the heads of holy people.

WHAT THE BELIEVERS SAY: An aura is an energy field that visually manifests the state of the energies and health of a person; although only the psychic and highly intuitive can see it, auras are real and are excellent indicators of a person's condition. A halo is an aura around the head of a highly spiritual person. The many depictions of holy figures with halos in paintings prove their existence. We cannot see the scent of flowers, yet we know it is there from our other senses. Seeing auras is simply a matter of developing innate sensory abilities most of us never use.

WHAT THE SKEPTICS SAY: If a person's aura is invisible, how can it be seen? And if it cannot be seen, then how can we believe anyone who says they can "read" it? Anyone who claims to see halos or auras is hallucinating, projecting a fantasy, or simply making it up. People who *truly see* colored rings around people and objects probably have eye problems.

QUALITY OF EXISTING EVIDENCE: Fair to Good.[2]

LIKELIHOOD PHENOMENA ARE PARANORMAL: Poor to Fair.

A friend of mine once went to a therapist who employed alternative modalities of evaluation and treatment, which included the reading of patients' auras. This practitioner examined my friend and told him his aura was badly damaged, and that his overall health was poor.

My friend's reaction was unequivocal: If this was a guess, it was a damn good one. Jeremy (not his real name) had been born with a major birth defect involving his urological and gastrointestinal systems. Since childhood, he had undergone over thirty surgeries, was in constant pain, could not eat normally, and constantly experienced depleted energy levels. Jeremy never felt well, from a combination of many factors, and this therapist was allegedly able to discern all this by studying Jeremy's invisible aura. The therapist was not able to be very specific regarding which organ systems were Jeremy's trouble spots, but he did claim to be able to "see" the result of his problems.

Did the therapist really see anything surrounding my friend? Or did he use his powers of observation and his honed sensitivity to how people felt, and then simply make a good guess? How many times have you yourself "sensed" something was wrong with a loved one or a friend? How many times have you had a hunch that someone was not feeling well? Perhaps the therapist was able to make a snap assessment of Jeremy based on subtle physical clues?

Supposedly, anyone can learn how to see auras. The process usually involves the subject sitting in front of a white wall while the "viewer" stares at the person's third eye. You did not know you had three eyes? Apparently, there is an invisible third eye in every person's forehead between their eyebrows. Psychically advanced people can see it automatically; others have to work at it. After a time spent staring at the third eye, a white aura will appear around the person's body and then the aura will begin to change colors.

Each color means something and, according to the "aura authorities," there are seven layers to the aura; each one represents a particular energy field within the human body. The seven auric layers emanate from a person's chakras, which, according to yoga philosophy, are the seven centers of spiritual energy within the human body.

Is there any validity whatsoever to the belief that the human body emanates a visible field of energy? The ancients believed in auras and surviving writings from ancient Egypt, Greece, Rome, and India speak of emanations from the body that were visible to the priests and psychics.

In the sixteenth century, Paracelsus spoke of a "fiery globe" surrounding certain people.

If auras do not exist, what were all these people seeing?

The existence or non-existence of auras is another of those perplexing mysteries of the transcendental and paranormal world. Is it feasible that *everyone* who has seen auras is mistaken? Science tells us that there is nothing in the human body that could create a color field surrounding the body that would be visible to the human eye. Yet over thousands of years, people have reported seeing what science tells us is impossible.

Like UFOs, the anecdotal evidence for the existence of auras is so overwhelming that it would be unreasonable not to consider the possibility that there might, in fact, be something going on.

---

[1] In Cameron Crowe's 2001 film, *Almost Famous*, Beth says this to William (Crowe's doppelganger). Supposedly, a purple aura signifies intuition, spirituality, and leadership ability.

[2] There is an extraordinary amount of anecdotal evidence for the existence of auras, although the scientific evidence is almost nil.

Backwards Messages
and Reverse Speech

HAIKU:

BACKWARDS MESSAGES AND REVERSE SPEECH

Secret messages
Speaking in the words reversed?
True be this can how?

Number nine, number nine, number nine . . .
—"Revolution 9," *White Album*

DEFINITION: There are two components to backwards speech: Backmasking and reverse speech. **Reverse speech** is a genuine form of communication recently discovered and which, when fully understood, will be a valuable tool in all human endeavors. **Backmasking** is the deliberate insertion of messages into sound recordings that can only be heard when the recording is played backwards. **Reverse speech** consists of the words heard when normal human conversation is reversed; the theory of reverse speech contends that human speech is bi-level and that the human subconscious implants messages in speech that can only be heard in reverse.

WHAT THE BELIEVERS SAY: **Backwards messages** have been planted in records for years in an attempt to control the minds of young people.

WHAT THE SKEPTICS SAY: With few exceptions, almost all alleged **backwards messages** in recordings are simply not there. It is common for words to be heard when sentences are spoken in reverse. All interpretations of these backwards messages are in the eye (sorry, ear) of the listener. **Reverse speech** has no scientific grounding and there is no neurological evidence whatsoever that the human brain inserts backwards messages in common speech.

QUALITY OF EXISTING EVIDENCE: Backmasking: Poor; Reverse speech: Fair.

LIKELIHOOD PHENOMENA ARE PARANORMAL: Backmasking: Nil; Reverse speech: Fair.

BACKMASKING

Backmasking is the deliberate insertion of words and sentences into a sound recording that can only be heard if the recording is played backwards.

Fundamentalists who regularly rail against that "evil rock and roll" point to backwards Satanic messages in rock records as proof that the music is from the Devil himself. While there is evidence that some rock artists do intentionally insert backwards messages into their recordings, the allegations that this practice is rampant are overblown and mostly unfounded.

At the end of the track "Goodbye Blue Sky" on Pink Floyd's *The Wall* album, for instance, Roger Waters can be heard saying in reverse, "You have just discovered the secret message." This is one of the rare cases where the artists spent the time (and money) to embed a backwards message, and they obviously did it for fun. The overwhelming majority of rumored backward messages on rock recordings, however, are simply that: rumors.

But what about "Turn me on, dead man" being heard when the "Number nine" recitation in "Revolution 9" on the Beatles' *White Album* is reversed? That had to be deliberate, right?

No. It is apparently a phonetic coincidence and was not intentionally inserted by John Lennon and Yoko Ono.

Doesn't Queen's "Another One Bites the Dust" reverse to "It's fun to smoke marijuana"?

According to William Poundstone in his book, *Big Secrets*,[1] what is actually heard is "sfun to scout mare wanna."

So, it's fun to "scout" marijuana?

The Queen example, as was the "Number nine" case, is a phonetic reversal: coincidental recognition of words when normal words are played backwards.

Reverse speech, however, is an entirely different matter.

REVERSE SPEECH

What make you of these?

- If you play Neil Armstrong's "That's one small step for [a] man, one giant leap for mankind" backwards, you will hear, "Man will space walk."

- If you play a reporter's live commentary during coverage of the assassination of John F. Kennedy backwards, you will hear, "He's shot bad! Hold it! Try and look up!"

- During an interview, Patsy Ramsey talks about how there are only two people on earth who know who killed her daughter: the killer, and the person in whom he confided. Played backwards, Patsy is heard to say, "I'm that person."

- A segment of a sermon by a televangelist (who shall remain unnamed), reverses to say, "My advice is rancid."

Can these be true?[2]

Yes, according to David Oates, the discoverer of the phenomenon known as "reverse speech."

Reverse speech is what is heard when ordinary speech is played backwards. According to Oates, the subconscious mind consistently "speaks" via words implanted backwards in our normal speech. This is supposedly outside of our conscious control and we are completely unaware of the process.

This is apparently why O.J. did not know that, during a television interview, something he said was reversed as, "I killed them."

Is reverse speech for real? Or is it nothing but the power of suggestion?

I played the Neil Armstrong clip several times and did not hear anything recognizable. When I visited Oates's Web site and read that I was supposed to be hearing "Man will space walk," damn if that wasn't precisely what I heard the next time I played the clip! (Although to be fair, what I really hear is "man were spacwaw . . .")

Oates states that reverse speech occurs in the right hemisphere of the brain, and spoken speech occurs in the left, and there is a certain kind of logical yin/yang vibe in this theory. But science does not back him up and there is no empirical evidence to prove that an unconscious processing of information relevant to whatever the person is speaking goes on in the right side of the brain at the precise moment that the left side of the brain is working to process spoken speech.

Oates also tells us that infants reverse speak *first*, and then their brain learns how to forward speak. This, too, completely goes against everything we know about how infants learn to talk.

According to Robert Carroll in his *Skeptic's Dictionary*, Oates's theories "belie a profound ignorance of fundamental matters in neuroscience and physiology. Furthermore, a good chunk of his theory is untestable metaphysics, psychobabble and gobbledygook."[3]

Conclusions? Some rockers put backmasked messages in their recordings. They do it for fun and not because they are minions of Satan.

Reverse speech is an intriguing idea, and some of the things that we hear when some spoken statements are reversed are astonishing, but there is little, if any, scientific evidence to bolster its discoverer's claims.

[1] William Morrow and Company, 1983.

[2] All of these can be heard as RealPlayer or MP3 files on the www.reversespeech.com Web site.

[3] www.skepdic.com, "Reverse Speech," available online.

The Bermuda Triangle

HAIKU:

BERMUDA TRIANGLE

Three lines in the sea
Bordering a realm of doom?
The sea is silent.

The Coast Guard is not impressed with supernatural explanations of disasters at sea. It has been their experience that the combined forces of nature and unpredictability of mankind outdo even the most far-fetched science fiction many times each year.[1]

DEFINITION: The "Bermuda Triangle" (or "Devil's Triangle") is an imaginary area located off the southeastern Atlantic coast of the United States. The triangular area is noted for a high incidence of unexplained losses of ships, small boats, and aircraft. The apexes of the triangle are generally accepted to be Bermuda, Miami, and San Juan.[2]

WHAT THE BELIEVERS SAY: The Bermuda Triangle is a supernaturally charged area of the Atlantic Ocean in which extraordinarily high numbers of ships and planes have disappeared in the past several decades. We do not know if the terrible fate of these planes and ships and everyone on them is due to some inexplicable natural forces or supernatural or extraterrestrial powers and agents, but something is definitely going on in the Triangle and it is the fortunate vehicle that makes it out of there safe.

WHAT THE SKEPTICS SAY: The tales of the Bermuda Triangle are overblown myths that have been passed on in any number of books and articles as though they were true, along with outright fabrications of things that allegedly went on in the Triangle. There is no concrete evidence that anything anomalous whatsoever is going on in that area of the Atlantic, and the only reason it remains a topic of discussion is to sell books and get TV ratings. The reasons for losses in the area are environmental, failure of equipment, and human error.

QUALITY OF EXISTING EVIDENCE: Fair to Good.

LIKELIHOOD PHENOMENON IS PARANORMAL: Poor to Fair.

The term "Bermuda Triangle" first appeared in print in the February 1964 issue of *Argosy* magazine in an article entitled, "The Deadly Bermuda Triangle" by Vincent Gaddis. Ten years later, Charles Berlitz wrote a book about the Triangle that became an international best-seller.

The legend of the Triangle seems to have begun with the loss of five Navy airplanes in that area of the Atlantic during a terrible storm. Back then, the aviation navigation equipment was (compared to today's) quite primitive, and it was extraordinarily easy for a pilot to quickly "lose his way," especially during a storm. The accepted belief today is that Lt. Charles Taylor's compass failed or malfunctioned, the planes went off course, they ran out of gas, and they all crashed into the Atlantic.

The Navy issued a four-hundred-page report explaining the disaster, but this was not enough to convince Triangle enthusiasts that there was nothing going on in the Atlantic. In fact, the response from Triangle conspiracists augured the kind of response that would quickly be forthcoming when the U.S. government issued their definitive 1994 statement about the Roswell incident, which likewise stated that nothing untoward or extraterrestrial happened in the desert of New Mexico in 1945.

Is it true that the Bermuda Triangle is a maelstrom of bizarre happenings?

None other than Christopher Columbus reported seeing a ball of fire fly into the sea in the Bermuda Triangle at the same time as his compass malfunctioned.

Ships have disappeared in the Bermuda Triangle. So have planes.

But ships and planes have disappeared all over the waters of the world, oftentimes with nary a remnant of their presence, or an urgent radio call begging for help.

Logic demands that we look for the most ordinary of explanations. The area is enormous. It is heavily trafficked. It experiences a wide spectrum of weather. Equipment failures and malfunctions happen.

These are all levelheaded reasons for trouble in the Triangle.

But are there accurate, validated accounts of happenings that weather and equipment failures cannot explain?

There is a history of "lost time" episodes in the Bermuda Triangle.

One story told is of a National Airlines passenger jet that disappeared from Miami air traffic controller's radar for ten minutes.

The plane then reappeared, landed safely, and everyone onboard seemed fine—except that all of their watches and clocks were ten minutes slow. When the pilot was queried about the missing ten minutes, he reported that nothing out of the ordinary happened during that period, except that they flew through a light fog.

Did the plane travel through a time warp and "lose" those ten minutes?

What about extraterrestrials? Are aliens abducting planes and ships from the Bermuda Triangle? If this is so, one wonders why they did not simply pick and choose their prey from harbors and airports.

The United States Navy has weighed in on the Bermuda Triangle. First off, they state that they do not recognize the term "Bermuda Triangle" as a geographic name.

They state the following as the most likely explanations for ship and plane losses in the Triangle:[3]

- The "Devil's Triangle" is one of the two places on earth where a magnetic compass does point towards true north. Normally it points toward magnetic north. The difference between the two is known as compass variation. The amount of variation changes by as much as twenty degrees as one circumnavigates the earth. If this compass variation or error is not compensated for, a navigator could find himself far off course and in deep trouble.[4]

- Another environmental factor is the character of the Gulf Stream. It is extremely swift and turbulent and can quickly erase any evidence of a disaster.

- The unpredictable Caribbean-Atlantic weather pattern also plays its role. Sudden local thunderstorms and water spouts often spell disaster for pilots and mariners.

- The topography of the ocean floor varies from extensive shoals around the islands to some of the deepest marine trenches in the world. With the interaction of the strong currents over the many reefs the topography is in a state of constant flux and development of new navigational hazards is swift.

- Not to be underestimated is the human error factor. A large number of pleasure boats travel the waters between Florida's Gold Coast and the Bahamas. All too often, crossings are attempted with too small a boat, insufficient knowledge of the area's hazards, and a lack of good seamanship.

Disinformation?

A "Bermuda Triangle" conspiracy?

An attempt to hide the dark secrets about the Triangle that people at the highest levels of government are privy to?

Perhaps, but the official explanations make bedrock sense to me. And the number of losses do not seem all that disproportionate for such an enormous expanse of wide, wide ocean.

[1]Department of the Navy/Naval Historical Center, "Bermuda Triangle Fact Sheet."

[2]Ibid.

[3]All excerpts are from the aforementioned Department of the Navy "Bermuda Triangle Fact sheet."

[4]An area called the "Devil's Sea" by Japanese and Filipino seamen, located off the east coast of Japan, also exhibits the same magnetic characteristics. It is also known for its mysterious disappearances.

The Bible Code

HAIKU:

BIBLE CODE

Hidden predictions
A tapestry of letters
Coded works from God?

"Never forget, gentlemen," he said to his astonished hearers, as he held up a copy of the "Authorized Version" of the Bible, "never forget that this is not the Bible," then, after a moment's pause, he continued, "This, gentlemen, is only a translation of the Bible."

—Richard Whately, Archbishop of Dublin[1]

DEFINITION: The Bible Code is a complex, arcane code hidden in the original Hebrew translation of the first five books of the Old Testament (the Torah) that was recently deciphered by mathematicians working with computers, and which predicts future events with uncanny accuracy.

WHAT THE BELIEVERS SAY: God encrypted predictions in code in the Hebrew Old Testament and waited for man to develop the technology to understand it.

WHAT THE SKEPTICS SAY: There is no such thing as an "original" Hebrew Old Testament and any perceived messages hidden in its words are simply random flukes arrived at by statistically analyzing all the letters in the Bible in varying configurations.

QUALITY OF EXISTING EVIDENCE: Very good.

LIKELIHOOD PHENOMENON IS PARANORMAL: Good.

Is there a hidden code in the Bible that has successfully predicted momentous historical events—with specific details, including names, places, and years?

Michael Drosnin, the author of two best-selling books about the Bible Code, is an atheist. He states unequivocally in his books that he does not believe in God. And yet he is the investigative reporter who revealed to the world that there was a secret code hidden in the Torah, and that one of its most astounding predictions was the assassination of Yitzhak Rabin, a year before it actually happened. (Drosnin told Rabin of the prediction, but his letter was ignored.)

According to Drosnin, the Bible Code also predicted the Stock Market Crash, the Great Depression, the Shoemaker-Levy comet hitting Jupiter in 1994, the assassinations of John F. and Robert Kennedy, the Holocaust (including Eichmann's and Hitler's names, and the name of the nerve gas they used in the death camps, Zyklon B), the Moon landing, and Bill Clinton's victory in the 1992 Presidential election (as well as foretelling the Monica Lewinsky affair and Clinton's impeachment).

The Bible Code also predicted the Watergate scandal, Edison's inventions, the Wright Brother's first flight, Newton's work with gravity, William Shakespeare and his plays, and the exact date—January 18, 1991—of the start of the Gulf War.

Following the events of September 11, 2001, Drosnin also found predictions of the attacks on the World Trade Towers and the Pentagon encoded in the Bible, with the words "twin towers," and "airplane" intersecting with, "It caused to fall, knocked down." The Bible Code also named the perpetrator of the attacks. In a section of Genesis which contained the words "the city and the tower" were the words, "the sin, the crime of bin Laden."

The Bible Code also predicts that World War III, which will be a nuclear war, will begin in 2006 in Jerusalem.

Can any of this be true? If it is, then the *Baltimore Sun's* description of the Bible Code as "the biggest news of the millennium—maybe of all human history"—is, if anything, an understatement.

Drosnin is not the one who uncovered the hidden code in the Bible. Israeli mathematician Eliyahu Rips, expanding on work begun by a Czechoslovakian rabbi over fifty years ago, first discovered the code using a mathematical formula called Equidistant Letter Sequences in which all of the spaces and punctuation in the first five books of the Bible are removed, creating one continuous strand of letters—304,805 letters to be precise. From *The Bible Code*:

> The computer searches that strand of letters for names, words, and phrases hidden by the skip code. It starts at the first letter of the Bible, and looks for every possible skip sequence—words spelled out with skips of 1, 2, 3, all the way up to several thousand. It then repeats the search starting from the second letter, and does it over and over again until it reaches the last letter of the Bible.[2]

Researchers hunt for specific words or names, and then, once the key word is found, search for related words in the same place in the Bible.

Rips published a paper called "Equidistant Letter Sequences in the Book of Genesis" in the August 1994 issue of the journal *Statistical Science*. The paper discussed an experiment in which Rips and his colleagues searched in the Torah for the names of thirty-two rabbis and sages. Their lives spanned a period of five thousand years. All thirty-two names were found encoded in the Bible, *along with all of the men's accurate birth and death dates*.

The editors of *Statistical Science* submitted Rips's paper for peer review an unprecedented three times and each time, the math checked out. The findings were irrefutable, and the paper was published.

Rips had not only uncovered a verifiable code hidden in the Bible; he seemed to have mathematically proven the existence of God—or at the very least, the existence of an intelligence beyond that of man.

Drosnin became fascinated with Rips's work, and shortly after meeting him, uncovered the prediction of Rabin's assassination on his own computer.

What do the skeptics have to say about Drosnin's books?

Ironically, Rips himself has distanced himself from Drosnin and stated publicly that he does not support Drosnin's books, or his conclusions.

Others have come forth with all manner of ELS findings specifically intended to debunk and ridicule Drosnin's work. One writer claims to have found predictions of the Roswell UFO crash (see chapter 75) in the book of Genesis; another, using the same mathematical formulas as Drosnin, predictions of the assassinations of Indira Gandhi, Martin Luther King, and Abraham Lincoln—in Tolstoy's *War and Peace*.

Could statistical randomization applied to any massive array of letters produce words that could be interpreted to have meaning—after the fact?

Perhaps, but a careful reading of both *The Bible Code* and its sequel, *Bible Code II: The Countdown*, seem to suggest that there is much more at play here than simple chance.

"Bin Laden," "towers," and "airplane" all appearing in the same section of the Bible, and all encoded with the same ELS pattern is a coincidence?

What are the odds? Whatever they are, I certainly would not want to bet against them.

[1]Said to a meeting of his diocesan clergy, quoted in *These Eighty Years* (1893) by H. Solly, Volume II, Chapter ii, p. 81.

[2]Michael Drosnin, *The Bible Code*, p. 25.

17

Bigfoot

HAIKU:

BIGFOOT

Footprints in the woods
Creatures from another place?
Or men in fake feet?

Science is so full of fear because they know that if they find a glitch in something that they believe in, then they're going to have to rewrite anthropology, or rewrite some other phase of science.

—Jack Kewaunee Lapseritis[1]

DEFINITION: Bigfoot is allegedly a very large, hairy, humanlike creature purported to inhabit the Pacific Northwest and Canada. He is also called Sasquatch. A similar creature known as the Yeti or the

Abominable Snowman is alleged to inhabit the snows of the high Himalayan Mountains.

WHAT THE BELIEVERS SAY: The race of creatures we call Bigfoot or Yeti exist and may be transdimensional. They live beyond our current reality and are able to travel between dimensions.

WHAT THE SKEPTICS SAY: There is no such creature as Bigfoot. All sightings are either delusions or hoaxes.

QUALITY OF EXISTING EVIDENCE: Good.

LIKELIHOOD PHENOMENON IS PARANORMAL: Good.

There are many theories regarding the existence or nonexistence of Bigfoot.

If he is real, is he simply an evolutionary throwback, still surviving from ancient times, much the way the coelacanth lived on, and the way alligators are believed to be very similar now to what they were in prehistoric times?

Or is Bigfoot a species of transdimensional creatures, capable of moving in and out of our reality at will?

Jack Kewaunee Lapseritis, author of *The Psychic Sasquatch and the UFO Connection*, believes the latter and in this interview explains his theories.

When I interviewed Kewaunee (which is what he prefers to be called), three invisible Sasquatch were in attendance during our talk.

Since I did not see them, I had to take Kewaunee's word for their presence because he has been in telepathic contact with Bigfoot for over forty years. He tells us that the Bigfoot people were brought here by alien spaceships and that they taught Homo erectus how to use fire. They use wormholes to travel between dimensions, but can be photographed if caught unawares. They also have great senses of humor and they loved *Harry and the Hendersons*.

In recent years, people have come forward claiming responsibility for Bigfoot hoaxing. One team claimed that they staged the famous Roger Patterson film; a man on his deathbed admitted planting Bigfoot tracks all over the northwest. These claims have not deterred serious Bigfoot researchers and have been received in much the same way as claims for crop circle hoaxing: the believers admit that hoaxing is done, but state with confidence that this does not mean that the phenomenon is false.

Stephen J. Spignesi: What is Bigfoot?
Jack Kewaunee Lapseritis: Bigfoot—also known as Sasquatch—is a paraphysical, interdimensional nature person.

The Sasquatch are members of a "nature people" who have been talking with people telepathically—this is well documented—and who tell them that they were brought here millions of years ago by their friends, the Star People.

Interestingly enough, there are footprints that are in limestone in Paulaxee, Texas, and the gait of these footprints exactly match the gait of a Sasquatch. These footprints are right beside a dinosaur track that is sixty-five million years old.

SJS: What is the connection between Bigfoot and UFOs?
JKL: The connection between Bigfoot and UFOs is that Bigfoot is a *non-technical nature being* and they claim that their planet was disintegrating, and that there were bad extraterrestrials coming to exploit them, including some that would eat them. They then say that other ships came that were friendly and took them all off, and distributed them around different places in the universe, and one of the places they brought them was planet Earth.

They claim that they are the first people here and that there was a two-legged, or bipedal, animal here that they taught about fire. If that be the case, then they would have to be talking about Homo erectus.

They claim that this is their planet, and that they are the keepers, the *spiritual* keepers of Mother Earth and that they have a way of communicating psychically and spiritually with all of nature, including all animals, and all the plants, and that they can control the environment.

They can control weather. I have seen this. I have proof of this. And they are disgusted with us for destroying the planet and the environment, which is precisely what we are doing a little at a time.

And they are disgusted even more by the Bigfoot hunters—not the researchers, but the hunters—who want to shoot them, without even finding out just what the Sasquatch is, which is what I did. If these hunters *did* do as I did, then they would find out that they are systematically hunting a *people*.

SJS: How many Bigfoot are on the planet Earth?
JKL: I'm not sure how many there are on the planet. When I asked the Sasquatch this question, they told me that on the North American continent there was around 660; sometimes a little more or less.

Worldwide, I don't know the number, but they did tell me that there are seven different "races" of their people—just like a Japanese person would be different from an African person who would be different from an Eskimo or Caucasian, and so on. They also told me that the Yeti (the Tibetan "Abominable Snowman") was an example of a less-evolved race of people—not an animal—but a race of people that are more earthy, a race that would kill a yak and eat it, and act in an aggressive manner.

I was also told that there are some Sasquatch, like the race that lives in Africa, that are very small, about four feet tall. There is also a race that's about five feet tall that is mainly found in Sumatra and Borneo.

Dr. Ivan T. Sanderson from Princeton University wrote a book on this subject in 1961, claiming that there are eight different species or subspecies of Sasquatch, but still referring to them as animals.

SJS: How do the Sasquatch communicate with humans?
JKL: The Bigfoot people communicate telepathically.

It happened to me nineteen years ago in September of 1979. I was on Indian land and I received the shock of my life when both a Bigfoot man and a Star Person spoke to me telepathically and simultaneously. At the time, I was assistant director of an Indian Urban Agency; I was working part-time as a hypnotherapist, and I had been lecturing at the Medical College of Wisconsin. I will admit that working in these areas as a social scientist made me totally ill-prepared to accept these communications.

In my book, *The Psychic Sasquatch and Their UFO Connection*, I have documented seventy-six people who have experienced Bigfoot and UFOs, or Bigfoot and ETs at the same time, as well as Bigfoot telepathic experiences and other psi phenomenon.

But I do not believe in a Bigfoot/UFO connection. Let me repeat that. *I do not believe in a Bigfoot/UFO connection.*

And this really has nothing to do with *belief*. What it has to do with is documented research—empirical documentation as I've done for my book, confirming that there are seventy-six other people who have objectified my reality as a social scientist.

For me it's been nineteen years, and they are still coming and going, and my research is still ongoing.

For some of us, the Bigfoot people come and go in our lives, occasionally letting us know they're there. It's a part of being supportive on their part.

I believe that there are many, many people whose lives have been changed by these beings; people who have developed into either very beautiful artists or talented musicians or become skilled in some way. Also many of them, like myself, acquired psychic ability. People often say to me, "If you're a scientist, how can you be a psychic?" I can prove that because it's all documented. I psychically found the most wanted criminal in the state of Oregon back in 1984. I have a letter from the District Attorney, who is now a judge, thanking me and listing all the things that I did for them. That's just one out of dozens of things that I've done by using my abilities to help humanity.

I feel that when both the Bigfoot people and the extraterrestrial beings change people's lives, it's for the better. They help people surge ahead, and to influence other people with their new gift, with their new "belief system."

SJS: Is there any connection between Bigfoot and other creatures of legend such as the Loch Ness Monster, etc.?
JKL: Yes, there is a connection—and what they all have in common is how they all travel through different dimensions of reality, including our dimension here on Earth.

Let's talk about the Loch Ness Monster—and I use the word "monster" very lightly here. [See Chapter 48.] I prefer to call them anomalous animals. They deserve that respect. The "monster" thing connotes that we must shoot or destroy it. Monsters are something that hurt people. So to label them as such is an insult. I prefer to call them anomalous animals.

Sometime in the late sixties in Ireland, people were seeing a Loch Ness-type monster all the time. Ultimately, some people there actually drained a lake where the creature had been seen and then they all stood around with guns ready to blast this thing.

But guess what they found when they drained the lake? Nothing. Why did they find nothing? Because unbeknownst to them, they had been telepathically communicating their hostility towards this creature to the creature itself. And even though this creature can't read, write, or run a computer, it *can* feel. It is clairsentient. It could sense what these hunters wanted to do to it.

And so how did the creature get out of there if they had surrounded the place? It went through a portal—a vortex into another dimension and ended up on the other side somewhere. These portals are all over. There are aquatic portals, and there are extraterrestrial portals in outer space that the spaceships use. This explains why enormous interstellar distances are irrelevant. If the nearest system is fifteen or twenty light years away, extraterrestrials can "dimension-hop" through different portals or different wormholes.

This isn't anything I got out of *Star Trek*. It's only in the last few years that *Star Trek* and other sci-fi shows and movies have started referring to wormholes. This was told to me back in the mid-eighties, though. I never heard the word wormhole used in popular culture until recently.

And there are also *terrestrial* vortices, or portals, that the Sasquatch use, and that other unusual beings—including the reptilians such as the Loch Ness Monster—use.

In South Carolina, a seven-foot reptilian was sighted walking around, leaving tracks, and scaring people for about a week. All of a sudden it disappeared. Yes, it could have come from a spaceship, but there were no spaceships seen in the area, which doesn't mean they weren't there, of course. Generally, if you see a spaceship and you see these other beings, you can safely deduce that two and two equals four and that the creature came from the spaceship. I've seen this over and over again in my research. But when you just see the creature and no one is reporting spaceships or UFOs, the chances are that these creatures are utilizing these invisible portals leading to another dimension.

SJS: Can you see Bigfoot people all the time?
JKL: When they're around, I can. In fact, without you knowing it, they're right here with us now. There's two sitting next to you on the bed and there's one over there in the corner.

[1]Interview with the author.

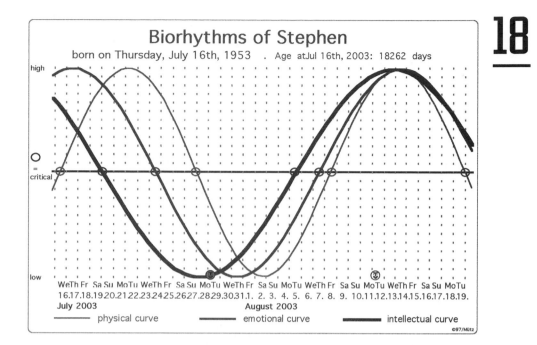

18

Biorhythms

HAIKU:

BIORHYTHMS

Cycles of the cells?
Rhythmic patterns tell the tale?
Ups and downs and ups.

All things have their ends and cycles. And when they have reached their highest point, they are in their lowest ruin, for they cannot last for long in such a state. Such is the end for those who cannot moderate their fortune and prosperity with reason and temperance.

—François Rabelais[1]

DEFINITION: Biorhythms are cyclical biological processes allegedly present in all human beings. The study of biorhythms looks at a person's twenty-three-day physical cycle, twenty-eight-day emotional cycle, and thirty-three-day intellectual cycle. The ups and downs of each cycle, combined with the intersecting of two or more cycles, supposedly provide an accurate picture of a person's fettle on any given day. Each person's biorhythm cycles begin on the day they are born, and they continue in twenty-three-, twenty-eight-, and thirty-three-day cycles until the day the person dies.

WHAT THE BELIEVERS SAY: The existence of biological rhythms is incontestable. Humans are diurnal. Everything in nature functions in rhythmic cycles. The science of biorhythms looks specifically at three biological cycles of human beings. By understanding the highs and lows of these cycles, we can learn more about ourselves, and perhaps predict and prevent problematic times. The techniques for limiting jet lag were formulated by studying biorhythms.

WHAT THE SKEPTICS SAY: Biorhythms are nonsense. These chronobiological cycles have been scientifically tested and there is no empirical evidence that they manifest any accuracy whatsoever regarding the state of an individual on a given day. Also, the number of days in a given cycle (twenty-three, twenty-eight, thirty-three, etc.) is an arbitrary conclusion that has no scientific basis in fact.[2]

QUALITY OF EXISTING EVIDENCE: Fair.[3]

LIKELIHOOD PHENOMENA ARE PARANORMAL: Nil.[4]

The idea of biorhythms does make a lot of sense. Everyone has experienced "good" days and "bad" days. Everyone has had days when they dropped everything they picked up; or they couldn't remember a simple password they've been using every day for a year; or they broke down in tears over an imagined slight that, on any other day, they would have simply ignored.

The pseudoscience of biorhythms attempts to validate and explain these up and down days as individual elements of plottable cycles, and it uses the trappings of hard science, particularly biology, geometry, statistics, and psychology to do so.

On the day we are born, our biorhythm cycles begin, and they continue until we die.[5]

Our physical cycle, for instance, is twenty-eight days long. Half of this cycle, fourteen days, is in the positive zone of our biorhythm chart; the other half is in the negative zone. The day on which the curve goes from positive to negative is considered a "critical" day. The middle of the positive half of the cycle is a peak day; the middle of the negative half is a nadir day. On a graph, this wave looks like a swooping sine curve with a line through the middle of the chart where the top and bottom halves of the arc intersect.

At the beginnning of this chapter is my personal biorhythm chart for the day of my fiftieth birthday. According to my biorhythms, my birthday is a critical physical day (heading upwards); a high intellectual day (heading downward); and a very high emotional day (likewise heading downward). (Note: The original chart is in color. For reference, the top line on July 16, 2003 is the emotional line; the line immediately beneath it is the intellectual line; the line at the axis is the physical line.[6])

Biorhythms were discovered simultaneously around 1900 by German and Austrian physicians working independently in Berlin and Vienna. Dr. Hermann Swoboda, a professor of psychology at the University of Vienna, and Dr. Wilhelm Fleiss, an otolaryngologist[7] at a hospital in Berlin, were both working on analyzing the existence of apparent cycles (in humans) that affected emotional and physical states. Both men arrived at almost the same conclusions without consultation.

Nevertheless (and the jet lag claims notwithstanding), the science of biorhythms has not made the leap into mainstream application. It is still considered pseudoscience and is often lumped into the same category as astrology, reflexology, and numerology, although of this group, I suspect that biorhythms has the likeliest chance at eventual scientific validation.

Something is definitely going on cyclically in human beings. Perhaps biorhythms is not the final reality as to these periodic ebbings, but it does seem to be pointing science in the right direction.

---

[1]*Gargantua* (1995 Pleiade edition), p. 87.

[2]One of the doctors (Swoboda) who discovered biorhythms claimed to have come up with the periods based on careful observation of his patients, but his conclusions cannot be considered scientifically validated. The other discoverer (Fleiss) was simply obsessed with the numbers twenty-three and twenty-eight. Also, additional cycles have been added to the science of biorhythms in recent years: a thirty-eight-day compassion cycle; a forty-three-day aesthetic cycle (whatever that is); and a fifty-three-day spiritual cycle. Also, some hard-core proponents of biorhythms claim that new cycles are also created by the combination of other cycles.

[3]The existing evidence in support of the accuracy of biorhythms is almost solely anecdotal; nonetheless, some of these "anecdotes" are quite persuasive and many people claim great benefits from plotting and studying their personal biorhythms; thus, our "fair" rating.

[4]Remember: This rating evaluates the likelihood phenomena are *paranormal*; i.e., "Beyond the range of normal experience or scientific

explanation" *(American Heritage Dictionary)*. Even if biorhythms are ultimately accepted by all of medical science as quantifiable physical processes, they would fall into the same category as temperature, blood pressure, hormonal levels, the menstrual cycle, pulse, and other rhythmic physical processes. None of these would even remotely be considered "paranormal."

[5] Lately, biorhythmists have been talking about a spiritual cycle. If this refers to the soul, would it be possible for that particular biorhythm cycle to continue past death? Just asking.

[6] Biorhythm chart generated from a shareware program called "Bio-Rhythms" by Martin Muetzenberg and available on the Web site: http://www.bio-chart.com.

[7] A nose and throat specialist.

19

Bleeding and Weeping Religious Icons

HAIKU:

BLEEDING ICONS

Blood rolls down a cheek
Cold hard marble acts like flesh
Statues weep—for whom?

The weeping icon of the Lord's mother, the Blessed Virgin Mary . . . is not a rare occurrence. The phenomenon is rationally unexplainable. It needs no explanation, whether scientific or natural. The believers do not ask the how, but the why.[1]

DEFINITION: Reports appear regularly of the appearance of seemingly real blood, tears, or oil on inanimate religious objects, including statues, paintings, crucifixes, crosses, pictures on plates, and Communion hosts.

WHAT THE BELIEVERS SAY: These manifestations are all real, they are all miraculous, and they are all a sign from God. Many believe that these alleged miracles foretell the imminent appearance of the Antichrist on Earth, and the second coming of Jesus Christ.

WHAT THE SKEPTICS SAY: All such manifestations are either hoaxes, or are easily explained as the melting of resins or some other natural process.

QUALITY OF EXISTING EVIDENCE: Good.

LIKELIHOOD PHENOMENA ARE PARANORMAL: Good.

The elderly Italian widow was alone in the church.

She was dressed all in black and she knelt in a pew, a rosary of black beads entwined in her fingers. As she prayed for her deceased husband, she kept her gaze locked on a ten-foot tall statue of Jesus that stood to the right of the main altar. The widow loved this statue because it showed Jesus' sacred heart, and because the Savior had his hands outstretched, as though he were welcoming everyone into his divine embrace.

As the woman prayed and stared at the face of Jesus, her recitation of Hail Marys slowed as her eyes widened in shock. She suddenly saw tears flowing down Jesus' cheeks. *Red* tears. The statue of Jesus was weeping blood.

The woman gasped, "Mi dios!", made the sign of the cross and quickly fled the church. She ran next door to the rectory and, in rapid-fire Italian, told the pastor what she had seen.

Thus it began for this chosen parish.

This scene has occurred many times and in many places, and what these events all have in common is the mystifying appearance of tears, blood, and oil on inanimate religious icons. Statues weep tears of blood; crucifixes bleed; paintings weep tears of blood and oil; blood suddenly appears on Communion hosts.

Many of the faithful interpret these materializations as signs of divine sadness; messages from God that we have all lost our way. Sometimes these inexplicable events happen in churches; equally as often they occur in people's homes. Skeptics are quick to point out that when a statue or picture appears to weep or bleed in a private residence, the ease with which such an event can be hoaxed must be factored in when considering its possible authenticity.

Are any of these manifestations real? If even a small percentage of them are authentic, they would seem to provide undeniable evidence of the existence of the paranormal and the divine.

Most of the accounts of bleeding and weeping icons seem to come from Italy and the United States, although the phenomena has also been reported in Japan, Korea, Russia, Venezuela, Romania, Syria, Canada, Israel, the Philippines, and many other countries around the world.

The phenomena occurs almost solely in Roman Catholic icons,[2] although sometimes blatantly non-religious images manifest similar behavior. A young man once phoned in to a radio show to report that on the night guitar legend Jimi Hendrix died of a drug overdose, a poster of Hendrix on his bedroom wall began to flow "tears" from Jimi's eyes.[3] Adding to the mystery are accounts of statues that open and close their eyes, move their hands, travel a distance across a floor, and emanate strange, otherworldly noises.[4]

There have been many tests performed on the substances that have reportedly oozed from statues and paintings and on the icons themselves. The tests of the liquids have often revealed that they are indeed human blood or human tears. Sometimes, though, the results show evidence of hoaxing, as when a substance believed to be tears turns out to be fat and water. And even the confirmation that the materials are blood or tears does not rule out the possibility that they are the blood or tears of the person who owns the statue or painting.

Tests on the pictures and statues themselves have been more problematic for true believers. There have been few results that provide conclusive evidence that the icon is, indeed, exuding anything. Sometimes the icon does manifest tears or blood under controlled circumstances but there always seems to be an undertone of suspicion and doubt when the results are released. Apparently no reputable scientist wants to go on the record as having been the one to confirm the existence of a supernatural, divine miracle.

One notable test was performed by paranormal investigator Joe Nickell for a television documentary. He tested a small painting of the Virgin Mary that had reportedly been weeping tears. He wiped the painting clean and dry with cotton, and then placed it on a stand with a camera focused on it for over twenty-four hours. Nothing appeared on the painting during the test.

Some of the devout have been caught squirting red liquid or even real blood onto statues and then claiming it appeared out of nowhere. Sometimes, the explanation for weeping icons is as simple as condensation.

The Catholic Church has long been loath to attribute "miracle" status to weeping and bleeding icons. The Church has validated a handful of Marian apparitions over the centuries, but they have been much more skeptical when it comes to statues of Jesus weeping tears that people collect and give to people on cotton balls.

That said, though, there are some very persuasive anecdotal

accounts of weeping and bleeding statues that could very well be of paranormal origin. Stories of eight or ten statues beginning to bleed simultaneously in front of dozens of witnesses are tough to dismiss out of hand as mass hallucination.

As with all religious "miracles," however, a person's faith (or lack thereof) will commonly rule the day.

[1]"Official Statement on the weeping Icon of the ever Virgin Mary at the St. Nicholas Albanian Orthodox Church in Chicago, IL," December 12, 1986, from *M.C.R.I.*, the newsletter of the Midwest Committee for Rational Inquiry, February 1987, p. 3.

[2]There are also many reports from around the world of Hindu icons of cows drinking milk from a spoon. Witnesses consider these to be similarly divine acts and, on September 21, 1995, government offices in India and the country's stock market reportedly closed down so people could feed statues milk.

[3]Bob Rickard and John Michell, *Unexplained Phenomena*, p. 251–52.

[4]The literature is replete with stories of moving and winking statues, and while most can be discounted as optical illusions, hallucinations, or hoaxes, some reports are just plain strange and baffle even the most jaded of skeptics.

20

Cattle Mutilations

HAIKU:

CATTLE MUTILATION

Eviscerated
Eye sockets staring blindly
Bloody empty shell

What passing-bells for those who die as cattle?

—Wilfrid Owen[1]

DEFINITION: "Cattle mutilations" is the general term used to describe the unobserved death and subsequent mutilation of cattle and other animals.

WHAT THE BELIEVERS SAY: Most cattle mutilations are carried out by aliens from UFOs. The laser-sharp incisions, the lack of blood, and the evidence that the "surgery" is performed inordinately fast all prove that the mutilations are extraterrestrial in origin. Some researchers into cattle mutilations believe that the removal of animal body parts is part of a long-term program of biological and genetic study of terrestrial life forms by visiting alien entities. (Cow blood is very close to human blood.) The few cattle mutilations that are *not* by aliens are by the U.S. government, which has been testing new weapons (including biological) on cattle and other animals for years. Black helicopters[2] have been seen in areas where mutilated cattle corpses were later found.

WHAT THE SKEPTICS SAY: All mutilations can be explained as attacks by other animals, hoaxes, deliberate slaughter by farmers for the insurance money (the mutilations are made to look like animal attacks or vandalism, which is covered by insurance), or secret government study of Transmissible Spongiform Encephalopathies among infected cattle.

QUALITY OF EXISTING EVIDENCE: Good.

LIKELIHOOD PHENOMENA ARE PARANORMAL: Low.

In his final report of his definitive two-year study of the cattle mutilation mystery, "Operation Animal Mutilation," Justice Department investigator and former FBI agent Kenneth Rommel defined a "classic mutilation":[3]

- **The surgically precise removal of certain parts of the animal:** The parts most commonly removed are the sexual organs, one eye, one ear, tongue, and in female animals, the udder.
- **A perfectly cored anus:** It often appears as though a large cookie cutter was used to perform the operation.
- **A lack of blood:** This indicates that the animal has been deliberately drained of its fluid.
- **The unusual rate of decay of the carcass:** The carcass decays either extremely slowly or extremely rapidly. In most cases, the usual "death odors" are absent.
- **The deliberate selection of certain types of livestock:** The New Mexico victims have been described as healthy, native-grown livestock.
- **The absence of human or tire tracks at the scene.**
- **Deliberate avoidance of the carcass by other animals:** Animals who do approach the carcass usually circle at a safe distance. Although flies may avoid the body, dead ones are occasionally found on the carcass.
- **The sighting of strange lights or aircraft within the vicinity of a reported mutilation:** In New Mexico, these aircraft have been variously described as UFOs or helicopters.
- **Unusual reaction of family pets:** On the night a mutilation occurs, the family dog, which usually barks at everything, is exceptionally quiet.

Rommel personally investigated many reported cattle mutilations during the period of his study, as well as digging into the historical archives for reports prior to his study, and he ultimately managed to debunk all of the claims made by those asserting a paranormal explanation. According to Rommel, all of the cattle mutilations are by animal scavengers, including mammals, birds, and insects.

As might be expected, the true believers did not take well to Rommel's report. Some claimed that he was paid off by the U.S. government to cover up and lie about the truth.

And what is the truth? This is summed up in "What the Believers Say"—aliens and secret government ops are responsible.

The cattle mutilation myth is tenacious and long-standing. There are logical, provable explanations for all of the seemingly paranormal occurrences surrounding the mysterious mutilation of cattle.

Here are just some of the explanations for the "classic mutilation" claims:

- **The "surgically precise" removal of organs:** On close examination, what initially looked "surgically precise" often is ragged and torn. Also, some scavengers can chew off an organ or body part quite neatly, leaving behind what looks like an even incision.

- **The absence of human or tire tracks:** This proves nothing, since Rommel showed that animals were the guilty party, not humans in SUVs.

- **A perfectly cored anus:** Blowflies and maggots can, over time, eat away at the rectum of a dead animal so that it eventually looks like it has been cored out.

- **A lack of blood:** This has been shown to be false. The blood of a dead cow pools beneath the body, leaving the internal cavities and organs looking completely dry. Closer examination reveals the blood first pools underneath, and then coagulates.

- **Deliberate avoidance of the carcass by other animals:** Rommel brought his dog with him to several mutilation sites and the pooch was not even slightly averse to walking around the carcass and even smelling it.

- **The lack of a death odor:** Rommel said that all the carcasses he investigated that had allegedly been mutilated reeked with the characteristic smell of decaying cow flesh.

There is no forensic evidence explaining the sightings of strange lights in the vicinity of dead cattle, but those claiming alien perpetrators point to those lights as proof that no matter what is seen in the ground, the truth is in the skies.

It is more likely, however, that the truth is actually on the ground.

[1] *Anthem for Doomed Youth.*

[2] Some supporters of the alien mutilators theory believe that the black helicopters are actually disguised alien spacecraft.

[3] *The Rommel Report*, online at http://www.parascope.com/articles/0597/romindex.htm.

Channeling and Automatic Writing

HAIKU:

CHANNELING AND AUTOMATIC WRITING

Voices from beyond

Voices in a channel's mind

Imaginary?

The glass had slipped thrice, and the sands stood midway through, and still the bird hopped within its wicker. I think the glass had slipped through a score of years, rightfully set at each turning, and the bird had sung through some of these and mourned through others. The hearth's arch yawned sleepily . . ."

—Patience Worth[1]

DEFINITION: **Channeling** (sometimes called *trance channeling*) is a process by which a spirit from beyond allegedly speaks through a living person known as the channeler. **Automatic writing** is the process by which a spirit, while being channeled, writes prose or music that the channeler then transcribes. Sometimes channeling and automatic writing are spoken of as products of a person's subconscious, as more of a psychological tool than a paranormal technique. However, the widely accepted, most popular definition of the term usually refers to spirit channeling.

WHAT THE BELIEVERS SAY: Channelers are gifted psychics who use their consciousness as a "receiver" for spirit entities to communicate wisdom and information. Channelers who do automatic writing or composing are receiving real art from spirits in the beyond. Those who channel great souls like Mozart or Shakespeare should be valued, since the world is being gifted with previously unknown art from these masters.

WHAT THE SKEPTICS SAY: There are no spirits from beyond communicating with anyone. Any and all "wisdom" allegedly channeled from spirits is nothing more than the thoughts of (or, in the case of automatic writers, the prose and music of) the channelers themselves.

QUALITY OF EXISTING EVIDENCE: Inconclusive.[2]

LIKELIHOOD PHENOMENA ARE PARANORMAL: Inconclusive.

Item: Kevin Ryerson is a channeler. One of the spirits he channels is a colleague of Jesus' named John. One of Ryerson's clients is the actress and writer Shirley MacLaine. According to Ryerson, John told him that Shirley MacLaine co-created the universe with God. Apparently, MacLaine believes this to be true.[3]

Item: In 1913, a bored thirty-year-old St. Louis, Missouri housewife named Pearl Curran began to receive communications via a Ouija board from a woman named Patience Worth. Patience told Pearl that she had lived in the mid-1600s on a farm in Dorsetshire, England, and that she had emigrated to America where she was later killed by Indians. It wasn't long before the long-dead British woman began dictating to Pearl Curran. Over a period of twenty-five years, Patience supposedly dictated over 400,000 words of fiction and poetry to Pearl, including five thousand poems, several novels, and a play. Much of this work was published, and Patience Worth, writing through Pearl, became a very successful author. Her historical novels, most notably *Telka* and *The Sorry Tale*, were critically acclaimed at the time, and it was widely accepted that they were, indeed, channeled works, mainly because no one believed Mrs. Curran had the intelligence, education, or talent to produce on her own such a wide range of works in a variety of styles. Today, the work of Worth is nowhere to be found in the mainstream, although out-of-print editions of her books are available, but expensive. Her literary merit is nonexistent, however, and any interest in her today is goaded by the novelty of reading something supposedly written by a dead spirit communicating to the living.

Item: Ludwig van Beethoven wrote nine symphonies, universally considered today to be the epitome of the symphonic form. However, according to British channeler Rosemary Brown, Ludwig actually wrote a total of *eleven* symphonies. The great composer dictated numbers ten and eleven to Mrs. Brown after he died. In addition to Beethoven, Rosemary Brown claimed also to have received original compositions from Brahms, Bach, Rachmaninov, Schubert, Grieg, Debussy, Chopin, and Liszt, as well as many other composers. Over decades of communicating with these musical greats, Mrs. Brown received more than four hundred works, most of which were ultimately determined to be very similar to the style of the attributed composer, and which experts said evinced a level of skill and inspiration well beyond Mrs. Brown's limited abilities.

IMPORTANT . . . OR IMAGINED?

Did Rosemary Brown actually receive new musical compositions from dead composers?

Did Pearl Curran really receive fiction and poetry from Patience Worth?

Or were Brown and Curran simply savants whose subconscious minds were able to summon depths of ability normally inaccessible to them? (See Chapter 78, "Savant Syndrome.")

Whether or not a person believes in channeling and automatic writing hinges on one key question everyone must answer for him or herself: Do you believe that consciousness survives death?

If a person answers "no" to that question, then all talk of channeling and receiving messages and art from dead people is nothing but pure fantasy and delusional thinking. The process itself is called automatism, which is the "suspension of consciousness in order to express subconscious ideas and feelings."[4]

If someone answers "yes" to that question, however, then the door is flung wide, and movies like *The Sixth Sense* and *Ghost* are perceived as fictional renderings of incredible possibilities, rather than entertaining fantasies about utter impossibilities. Higher powers from another realm, and possibly extraterrestrial beings from other planets or dimensions become the "authors" of inspired wisdom and original works of art.

The notion of mankind still being able to receive works of art from the great writers and composers after their deaths is exciting. And some of the music sent to Rosemary Brown by dead composers is apparently in the style of the original. But unless a long-lost manuscript by someone like Beethoven or Bach is unearthed from some dusty archive, the canon of a long-gone composer remains static, all of the channeled works notwithstanding.

And upon reflection, that is probably the wise thing to believe.

[1] Patience Worth, *Hope Trueblood*.

[2] There is simply no way to prove that a channeled musical composition was actually written by Brahms; likewise, there is no way to prove that the advice and guidance allegedly channeled from a wise soul is anything more than the thoughts of the channeler.

[3] www.skepdic.com.

[4] *American Heritage Dictionary*.

Charles Fort
and Fortean Phenomena

HAIKU:

CHARLES FORT

"I do not believe
In everything science says."
—Fortean father

*I am a collector of notes upon subjects that have diversity—
such as deviations from concentricity in the lunar crater
Copernicus, and a sudden appearance of purple Englishmen—
stationary meteor-radiants, and a reported growth of hair on
the bald head of a mummy—and, "Did the girl swallow the
octopus?"*

—Charles Fort[1]

DEFINITION: Charles Fort (1874–1932) was a fulminating skeptic of
scientific dogma, a diligent (some would say obsessive) researcher, a
prolific (some would say tiresome) writer, and a persevering collector
of accounts of odd phenomena he gleaned from newspapers and
other publications.

WHAT THE BELIEVERS SAY: Fort was a rational voice shouting in the wilderness of the "priestcraft" (Fort's word) of science. Fort shone a spotlight on those anomalies of nature and reality that science dismissed out of hand or ignored as irrelevant fantasy. Fort was the father of the study of paranormal phenomena.

WHAT THE SKEPTICS SAY: Fort was just a weirdo crank whose own wife didn't read his books; he was a brilliant curmudgeon who had a profound misunderstanding of the scientific process and he was gullible enough to accept accounts of weird phenomena as truth, without feeling the need for scientific testing of the reported oddity.

QUALITY OF EXISTING EVIDENCE: Very good.

LIKELIHOOD PHENOMENA ARE PARANORMAL: High.[2]

Ghosts. Stigmata. Rains of meat and other effluvia. Levitation. Teleportation. Spontaneous human combustion. Mysterious vanishments. Bleeding icons.

Charles Fort spent almost his entire adult life in libraries chronicling accounts of these oddities, writing in pencil in his own personal shorthand, filling small pieces of paper with dates, places, and details.

Rains of snails.

Real-life firestarters.

Monsters.

Unexplainable lights in the sky.

A Super-Sargasso Sea high in our atmosphere, from which all anomalies manifest—and fall.

At the age of forty-two, Charles Hoy Fort came into an inheritance which allowed him to devote himself full-time to collecting stories of weird happenings on our planet and in our skies and writing about them. He spent countless days reading in the New York Public Library and when he moved to London in the twenties, he did his research in the British Museum Library.

Fort's "mission statement," if it can even be adequately defined, was that science was not to be respected because, he believed, scientists often argue from their own beliefs rather than from provable evidence. He considered scientists to be lackeys of unproven dogma and believed that, since scientific theories are often proven incorrect, nothing that is determined by hard science should be accepted as fact.

Was Fort serious?

It seems he was—for the most part—but he would often mock his own conclusions, as well as those who took it all *so* seriously.

Fort's longtime friend Tiffany Thayer, in his introduction to the 1941 Henry Holt edition of the *Books of Charles Fort*, attempted to explain the sometimes inexplicable Mr. Fort:

> He laughed as he wrote, as he read, as he thought: he roared at his subject, guffawed at the pretensions of his serious practitioners, chortled at their errors, howled at their inconsistencies, chuckled at his readers, snickered at his correspondents, smiled at his own folly for engaging in such a business, grinned at the reviews of his books and became hilarious at my expense when he saw that I was actually organizing the Fortean Society.[3]

Fort's life's work was compiled in four volumes of meticulously reported weirdness:

- *The Book of the Damned* (1919)
- *New Lands* (1923)
- *Lo!* (1931)
- *Wild Talents* (1932, published posthumously)

Fort's books are not easy reads. His "style" is often convoluted, dense, meandering, and almost stream-of-consciousness. Peruse these opening lines from *New Lands*:

Lands in the sky—
> That they are nearby—
> That they do not move.
> I take for a principle that all being is the infinitely serial, and that whatever has been will, with differences of particulars, be again—
> The last quarter of the fifteenth century—land to the west!
> The first quarter of the twentieth century—we shall have revelations.
> There will be data. There will be many. Behind this book, unpublished collectively, or held as constituting its reserve forces, there are other hundreds of data, but independently I take for a principle that all existence is a flux and a re-flux, by which periods of expansion follow periods of contraction; that few men can even think widely when times are narrow times, but that human constrictions cannot repress extensions of thoughts and lives and enterprise and dominion when times are wider times—so then that the pageantry of foreign coasts that was revealed behind blank horizons after the year 1492, cannot be, in the course of development, the only astounding

denial of seeming vacancy—that the spirit, or the animation, and the stimulations and the needs of the fifteenth century are all appearing again, and that requital may appear again—

Yes, Mr. Fort concludes the paragraph with a dash, and then continues on in a similarly abstruse manner, which he sustains for the remaining pages of the book. So, then, Charles Hoy Fort wasn't that great a writer, but this unavoidable fact is irrelevant when his contributions are put in perspective. Today, Fort's name is an adjective; when "Fortean" is used to describe a moment or event of high strangeness, it is immediately understood just what is being discussed.

Granted, Fort went overboard in his rejection (or at the very least, his contempt) for traditional science and the mandates of the scientific method. Yet his enduring legacy is one of calling attention to . . . well, to the many topics discussed in this book, for one thing.

And even if 80 or 90 percent of the anomalous events he wrote about had non-paranormal explanations, the remaining mysteries beckon us even now. And we owe Charles Fort a debt of thanks for calling our attention to them.

[1] *Wild Talents, The Books of Charles Fort*, p. 846.

[2] Since Fort covered a wide-ranging spectrum of allegedly paranormal phenomena, it is almost certain that some of the accounts he collected in his books were beyond scientific explanation. Fort's "casualness" in accepting everything he came upon as paranormal and inexplicable, however, mandates dismissing some of his findings. Yet there is high likelihood that in the tens of thousands of reports he collected, many were probably paranormal, as defined for the purposes of this book.

[3] *New Lands, The Books of Charles Fort*, p. 313.

23

Communication with the Dead

HAIKU:

COMMUNICATION WITH THE DEAD

Message from beyond
Loved ones can send us their thoughts
Is it something else?

Those who are dead are never gone:
They are there in the thickening shadow.
The dead are not under the earth:
They are in the tree that rustles,
They are in the wood that groans,
They are in the water that runs,
They are in the water that sleeps,
They are in the hut, they are in the crowd:
The dead are not dead.[1]

DEFINITION: Communicating psychically with human beings who have died.

WHAT THE BELIEVERS SAY: Human consciousness survives death. Certain people are psychically attuned to the next dimension and can receive information from souls who have "crossed over."

WHAT THE SKEPTICS SAY: Dead is dead. There is no evidence that anyone from the "beyond" has ever told anyone here anything at all.

QUALITY OF EXISTING EVIDENCE: Fair.

LIKELIHOOD PHENOMENON IS PARANORMAL: Fair.

On the hit HBO series *Six Feet Under*, the characters talk to the dead all the time. But unlike the methods practiced by spiritualists (Ouija, seances, automatic writing, etc.) the dead people on the show appear like normal, living human beings, and they converse in regular spoken language with the non-dead.

TV is TV, however, and genuine communication with the dead is a far cry from such powwows. Skeptics would argue with the use of the term "genuine communication"; however, contact with the deceased has been a common element of almost every religion and culture on Earth—from ancient tribal societies' attempt to understand the wisdom of their ancestors, to today's modernized, televised version of the medium's séance.

But is any of it for real?

Using a technique known as "cold reading," self-proclaimed psychics can provide information about someone's deceased loved ones that is uncannily accurate. The trick lies in paying attention to people's responses, reading body language, overhearing things, and speaking in vague generalities that can apply almost to anyone. Once a psychic scores a "hit" with one specific detail ("I'm hearing from an older man named Thomas . . .") they can then embellish the details (without being too specific) until the subject truly believes the psychic has been in touch with their dead father or brother or wife.

The overwhelming majority of those who say they can communicate with the dead are charlatans. The magician David Blaine once demonstrated cold reading on the Howard Stern show (albeit as a technique to pick up chicks) and his performance illustrated how easy it is to say something that many people will instantly agree with. "Sometimes you feel like an outsider." "You put on a happy face many times when you are suffering inside." "You don't feel like you are fully appreciated by your co-workers and your family." "No one truly understands you."

Cold reading is done all the time in private sessions, at psychic fairs, and elsewhere, and many people completely buy into its validity.

But cold reading is not the same as genuine communication with the dead.

Can some people truly communicate with souls existing in the dimension beyond our mortal ken?

John Edward is the latest in a long line of psychics who say they hear from the dead. There are countless articles in print and on the Internet "explaining" (although "debunking" is a better word) how he does what he does, and yet, there are things he has said and done that are not so easily explained away as being part of a parlor trick.

I, and many others, trust Larry King. I believe his show is above-board and legitimate. I believe the calls he receives on the air are not pre-planned. And that is why I am ambivalent about John Edward. During an appearance on *Larry King Live* in June 1998, Edward took a call from a woman whose husband had died. Here is an abridged transcript of the conversation:[2]

Larry King: Hi.
Caller: This is Sherri. I lost my husband about a year and a half ago.
John Edward: He's telling me—this is strange, but did you bury him with cigarettes?
C: Yes.
JE: OK. He's telling me—I know this is going to sound strange—was this the wrong brand?
C: Yeah.
LK: Wait a minute, wait a minute. He was buried with the wrong brand than what he smoked?
C: Yes.
LK: How did you see that?
JE: They just showed me cigarettes and they put a line through it, and like a red circle like "no smoking" and—but I feel like I needed to acknowledge that the cigarettes were there.
LK: So that can't be a wild guess.

The woman sounded stunned that he knew this, but confirmed that it was true.

Was the woman a John Edward plant? Was the whole call staged?

That's where my trust of Larry King comes in. I can not believe Larry King would participate in such a ruse.

So if he didn't, then how did Edward know what he knew? Coincidence? Skeptics say yes; believers say no.

As with many of the other topics covered in this book, one's acceptance or rejection of a phenomenon (especially this one) hinges completely on whether or not that person believes in a human soul, and in life after death.

I believe in both, and so I am willing to lean towards believing that some people can, in fact, communicate with those who have "crossed over." I am not talking about charlatans who have perfected the cold reading. I am talking about spiritually conscious people who attempt and perhaps succeed in communicating with those who have shed this mortal coil.

Is this an error? Perhaps, but I am quite willing to err on the side of open-mindedness.

[1] Traditional African poem, quoted in *Sacred Texts of the World: A Universal Anthology*, Ninian Smaart and Richard D. Hecht, editors.

[2] *Larry King Live*, June 19, 1998.

24

Creationism

HAIKU:

CREATIONISM

Something from nothing?
Glorious nature a fluke?
Or proof of God's will?

And on the seventh day God ended his work which he had made, and he rested on the seventh day from all his work which he had made.[1]

DEFINITION: Creationism is a doctrine stating that the story of the creation of the universe told at the beginning of the Bible in the book of Genesis is *literally* true.

WHAT THE BELIEVERS SAY: In the beginning, God created the Heaven and the Earth. And God said, "Let us make man in our image, after our likeness." And God saw everything that he had made, and, behold, it was very good. All of existence was created by God, in a period of seven days. The Bible is literally true.

WHAT THE SKEPTICS SAY: Genesis is a parable. The Bible is filled with parables and fables, not journalism. The forces of evolution are responsible for life on Earth, and possibly elsewhere in the universe.

QUALITY OF EXISTING EVIDENCE: Inconclusive.

LIKELIHOOD PHENOMENON IS PARANORMAL: Inconclusive.[2]

The arguments between creationists and scientists are wide-ranging, antagonistic, and never-ending. There are, however, some key points that always come up during the debate and, to cover these topics concisely, I have enlisted the assistance of Dr. Tim Berra, author of *Evolution and the Myth of Creationism*.

The following list of sixteen creationism-debunking arguments originally appeared in Dr. Berra's 1990 book. In his lucid, reasoned, and *enlightened* Preface, Dr. Berra said:

> Creationists, for the most part, are fundamentalist Christians whose central premise is a literal interpretation of the Bible and a belief in its inerrancy.
>
> The creationists are determined to force their will on society and the schools, through the courts if possible. Their strategy—ironically enough, considering the moral precepts of Christianity—is founded in deception, misrepresentation, and obfuscation designed to dupe the public into thinking that there is a genuine scientific controversy about the validity of evolution. No such controversy exists, but it is difficult for the lay public to distinguish the scientists, who often disagree on the nuances of evolutionary theory (but not on evolution's existence), from the creationists, who stick together and cloak absurd claims in scientific terminology.

For the record, I do not support creationism, but do believe in intelligent design (which may seem contradictory, but it is not). My position can be summed up by the following comment from Wernher von Braun, Director of NASA's Marshall Space Flight Center from 1960 to 1976.

> To be forced to believe only one conclusion—that everything in the universe happened by chance—would violate the very objectivity of science itself. Certainly there are those who argue that the universe evolved out of a random process, but what random process could produce the brain of a man or the system of the human eye . . . [Some] challenge science to prove the existence of God. But, must we really light a candle to see the sun?

The argument from design makes a lot of sense to me: If you find a pocketwatch on the beach you immediately know two things: 1. It was designed, and 2. There was a designer. Therefore, if you consider the universe and everything in it as being meticulously designed (which the evidence of nature's complexities seems to overwhelmingly suggest), you will conclude that there is a designer. Is that designer God?

SOME CREATIONIST CLAIMS:
DO THEY RAISE ANY LEGITIMATE DOUBTS?

by Dr. Tim M. Berra

1. **The Claim:** *Evolution violates the second law of thermodynamics. Entropy (disorder) is always increasing. Since order does not arise out of chaos, evolution is therefore false.*

   The Truth: These statements conveniently ignore the fact that you *can* get order out of disorder if you add energy. For example, an unassembled bicycle that arrives at your house in a shipping carton is in a state of disorder. You supply the energy of your muscles (which you get from food that came ultimately from sunlight) to assemble the bike. You have gotten order from disorder by supplying energy. The Sun is the source of energy input to the Earth's living systems and allows them to evolve. The engineers in the CRS [Creation Research Society] know this, but they permit this specious reasoning to be published in their pamphlets. Just as the more structured oak tree is derived from the less complex acorn by the addition of energy captured by the growing tree from the Sun, so sunlight, via photosynthesis, provides the energy input that propels evolution. In the sense that the Sun is losing more energy than the Earth is gaining, entropy is increasing. After death, decay sets in, and energy utilization is no longer possible. That is when entropy gets you. What does represent an increase in entropy, as biologists have pointed out, is the diversity of species produced by evolution.

2. **The Claim:** *The small amount of helium in the atmosphere proves that the Earth is young. If the Earth were as old as geologists say, there would be much more helium, because it is a product of uranium decay.*

   The Truth: Helium, used to suspend blimps in air, is a very light gas and simply escapes into space; like hydrogen, it cannot accumulate in Earth's atmosphere to any great extent.

3. **The Claim:** *The rate of decay of the Earth's magnetism leads to the calculation that the Earth was created about ten thousand years ago.*

   The Truth: The Earth's magnetic field does indeed decay, but it does so cyclically, every few thousand years, and it is constantly being renewed by the motion of the liquid core of the Earth. The "fossil magnetism" recorded in ancient rocks clearly demonstrates that polar reversals (shifts in the direction of the Earth's magnetic field) have occurred both repeatedly and irregularly throughout Earth history; the calendar of these reversals was established over two decades ago, and quickly became the linchpin in the emerging theory of plate tectonics and continental drift.

4. **The Claim:** *If evolution were true, there would have to be transitional fossils, but there were none; therefore evolution did not occur.*

   The Truth: There are many transitional fossils, including the ape-human transitional form, *Australopithecus*. *Eusthenopteron* shows marvelous intermediate characteristics between the lobe-finned fishes and the amphibians. The transitional fossils between amphibians and reptiles are so various and so intermediate that it is difficult to define where one group ends and the other begins. *Archaeopteryx* is clearly intermediate between reptiles and birds. In spite of such reptilian affinities as a long bony tail, toothed jaws, and clawed wings, creationists declare that because *Archaeopteryx* had feathers, it was a bird, not a transitional stage between reptiles and birds. Having no explanation of their own, the creationists attempt to deny the transitional fossils out of existence.

5. **The Claim:** *Fossils seem to appear out of nowhere at the base of the Cambrian; therefore, they had to have been created.*

   The Truth: The earliest microfossils date back, in fact, to the Precambrian, about 3.5 billion years ago. A variety of multicellular life appears in the fossil record about 670 million years ago, which is eighty million years before the Cambrian. The Cambrian does seem to explode with fossils, but that is simply because the first shelled organisms, such as the brachiopods and trilobites, date from the Cambrian; their resistant shells fossilize far more readily than their soft-bodied ancestors of the Precambrian. What is more, Precambrian rocks are so old that they have been subjected to a great deal of deformation. We are thus fortunate to have *any* Precambrian fossils of soft-bodied animals. Still more fossils are discovered every year, and each one further weakens the creationist position.

6. **The Claim:** *All fossils were deposited at the time of the Noachian flood.*

   The Truth: There is not a shred of evidence in the geological record to support the claim of a single, worldwide flood. Geological formations such as mountain ranges and the Grand Canyon require millions of years to form, and the fossil record extends over several billion years. The time required for continents to have drifted into their present positions is immense. These things cannot be accounted for by a single flood lasting a few days or years.

7. **The Claim:** *There are places where advanced fossils lie beneath more primitive fossils.*

   The Truth: Earth movements such as faulting and thrusting produce these discontinuities; the older rock has simply been pushed over on top of the younger rocks, as we sometimes see even along highway cuts. These places are easily recognized and explained by geologists. They cannot be explained away by the creationists' belief that all fossils are the result of the Noachian flood. Thus the creationists' attempt to fault evolutionary theory by these means end up demolishing one of their own pet claims.

8. **The Claim:** *The chances of the proper molecules randomly assembling into a living cell are impossibly small.*

   The Truth: Simulation experiments have repeatedly shown that amino acids do not assemble randomly. Their molecular structure causes them to be self-ordering, which enhances the chances of forming long chains of molecules. Simulation experiments also demonstrate that the formation of prebiotic macromolecules is both easy and likely and does not require DNA, which is a later step in the evolution of proteins. The stepwise application of cumulative natural selection acting over long periods of time can make the improbable very likely.

9. **The Claim:** *Dinosaur and human footprints have been found together in Cretaceous limestone at Glen Rose, Texas. Therefore, dinosaurs could not have preceded humans by millions of years.*

   The Truth: This Fred Flintstone version of prehistory is one of the most preposterous and devious claims that the fundamentalists make, and they have made it in both books and films. The "man-tracks" seen by creationists stem from two sources. One is wishful imagination, whereby water-worn scour marks and eroded dinosaur tracks are perceived as human footprints. The other source is deliberate fraud. Creationist hoaxers obscure the foot pads of dinosaur tracks with sand and photograph what remains, the dinosaur's toe impressions. When reversed, the tip of the dinosaur toe or claw becomes the heel of a "human" print. These prints are shown in poor-quality photographs in creationist literature and films. Because the stride length (seven feet) and foot length (three feet) exceed any possible human scale, the fundamentalists call these the giants mentioned in Genesis. In addition to doctored dinosaur tracks, there are other hoaxed prints circulating in this area of Texas. In fact, carved footprints were offered for sale to tourists in curio shops during the Great Depression. These caught the eye of the paleontologist Roland T. Bird, who recognized them as fakes, but they eventually led him to the legitimate dinosaur footprints at Glen Rose. This area has since been extensively studied by paleontologists, and numerous species of reptiles and amphibians have been catalogued. No genuine human tracks exist there, but by leading to genuine new discoveries, the hoax became a boon to science.

10. The Claim: *Biologists have never seen a species evolve.*

The Truth: On a small scale, we certainly have. Using allopolyploidy and artificial selection, scientists have manufactured crop plants and horticultural novelties that are reproductively isolated from the parental stock. In addition, one can see stages of incipient speciation in nature by looking at clinal variations and subspecies, that is, gradual change in the characteristics of a population across its geographical range. Major evolutionary changes, however, usually involve time periods vastly greater than man's written record; we cannot watch such changes, but we can deduce them by inference from living and fossil organisms.

11. The Claim: *Evolution, too, is a religion, and requires faith.*

The Truth: Creationists are beginning to admit that their "science" is not science at all, and that it depends on faith, but, they are quick to add, so does evolution. Not so. Biologists do not have to *believe* that there are transitional fossils; we can examine them in hundreds of museums around the world, and we make new discoveries in the rocks all the time. Scientists do not have to *believe* that the solar system is 4.5 billion years old; we can test the age of Earth, Moon, and meteoritic rocks very accurately. We do not have to *believe* that protocells can be easily created from simple chemicals in the laboratory; we can repeat the experiments, with comparable results. We can also create artificial species of

plants and animals by applying selection, and we can observe natural speciation in action. That is the big difference between science and religion. Science exists *because* of the evidence, whereas
religion exists upon faith—and, in the case of religious funda-
mentalism and creationism, *in spite of* the evidence.

12. **The Claim:** *The numbers of humans today would be much greater
if we have been around as long as evolutionists say we have.*

    The Truth: This notion makes some very naïve assumptions
    about birth and death rates, and the fecundity of early humans,
    and assumes that populations are always growing, when in fact
    most animal populations are at a level somewhat lower than the
    carrying capacity of their environment. Such stable populations
    remain stable for long periods of time, held in check by environ-
    mental constraints. It is only our own species' recently acquired
    ability to modify our environment that has allowed our numbers
    to get dangerously out of control. Ironically, it is our ability to
    master the environment—as the Bible commands us to do—that
    may yet do us in.

13. **The Claim:** *The current rate of shrinkage of the Sun proves that
the Earth could not be as old as geologists say, because the surface
of the Sun would have been near the Earth's orbit just a few million
years ago.*

    The Truth: This simplistic view neglects the fact that stars, such
    as our Sun, have life cycles during which events occur at different
    rates. The characteristics of a newly formed star are quite differ-
    ent from those of stars near death. Astronomers can see these dif-
    ferences today by observing young, middle-aged, and old stars.
    By now, we know a great deal about the Sun, and we know that
    it has not been shrinking at a constant rate.

14. **The Claim:** *A living freshwater mussel was determined by Carbon
14 dating to be over two thousand years old; therefore Carbon 14
dating is worthless.*

    The Truth: When used properly, Carbon 14 is a very accurate time-
    measuring technique. The mussel in this example is an inappro-
    priate case for ^{14}C dating because the animal had acquired much of
    its carbon from the limestone of the surrounding water and sedi-
    ment. These sources are very low in ^{14}C, owing to their age and
    lack of mixing with fresh carbon from the atmosphere. Therefore,
    a newly killed mussel in these circumstances has less ^{14}C than, say,
    a newly cut tree branch. The reduced level of ^{14}C yields an artifi-

cially older date. The ^{14}C technique has no such problems with the tree branch that gets its carbon from the air, or with the campfire sites of ancient peoples. As with arcwelding or Cajun cooking, one must understand the technique to use it properly. This is another example of the self-correcting nature of science.

15. **The Claim:** *The influx of meteoritic dust from space to Earth is about fourteen million tons per year. If the Earth and Moon were 4.5 billion years old, then there should be a layer of dust fifty to one hundred feet thick covering their surfaces.*

   The Truth: This estimate of dust influx is simply out of date. Space probes have found that the level of dust influx from space is about four hundred times less than that. Creationists are aware of the modern measurements, but they continue to use the incorrect figure because it suits their purpose. Such is their honesty and scholarship. Do these people believe that the astronauts would have been allowed to land on the Moon if NASA thought they would sink into one hundred feet of dust?

16. **The Claim:** *Prominent biologists have made statements disputing evolution.*

   The Truth: The out-of-context quote is one of the most insidious weapons in the creationists' arsenal, and reflects the desperation of their position. Biologists do not deny the *fact* of evolution. We do, however, debate its *mechanisms* and *tempo*. The debate reflects the vigorous growth of a major scientific concept; it is what goes on routinely in all healthy, growing branches of scholarship. Creationists dishonestly portray this as a weakness of the theory of evolution.

These sixteen points are just a few of the creationists' arguments. There are others, but they are all of the same character—scientifically inaccurate, willful, or devious.

Reprinted from *Evolution and the Myth of Creationism: A Basic Guide to the Facts in the Evolution Debate* by Tim M. Berra with the permission of the publishers, Stanford University Press, ©1990 by the Board of Trustees of the Leland Stanford Junior University.

[1]Genesis 2:2.

[2]Sorry, but we would not presume to judge within these pages whether or not a divine power created the universe.

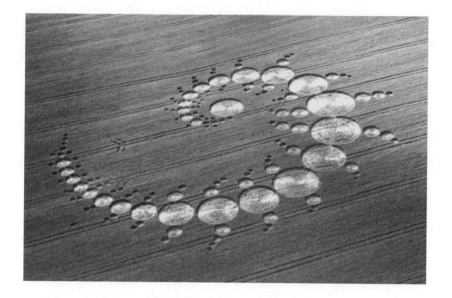

Crop Circles

CROP CIRCLES

Flattened crops beckon
Patterns in the holy grass
Swirling signs of hope

I believe that what is taking place in the fields of our planet is evidence of signs of contact, and that the orbs and other associated phenomena are further proof that this contact is transdimensional and important enough to cross the barriers between these states of being.

—Colin Andrews[1]

DEFINITION: Crop circles are swirled, flattened cereal crops that form geometric patterns, from simple circles to extremely complex designs. They appear annually over the world and often in places inaccessible to casual (human) visitation.

WHAT THE BELIEVERS SAY: Crop formations are a manifestation of troubles with the planet Earth, signs or messages from aliens, communications from the dead, or some unknown energy force that may possess intelligence.

WHAT THE SKEPTICS SAY: Crop formations are either all hoaxes or some kind of weird, *natural* (possibly weather-related) phenomena we still do not understand. None of the formations are paranormal in origin.

QUALITY OF EXISTING EVIDENCE: Excellent.

LIKELIHOOD PHENOMENA ARE PARANORMAL: Very high.

Are they signs? Scars? Alien graffiti? Weird weather? Hoaxes? All of the above?

Crop circles are a mystery in the fields: they are swirled patterns that appear every year, in fields of cereal crops all over the world during the growing season. They have been appearing for centuries and there are numerous historical accounts, by farmers, journalists, and others, going back to the fifteenth century and earlier, of odd circles appearing in crops seemingly overnight and with no sign of a human hand.

So, are they real?

The answer is yes, with an exception: *Some* crop circles are "real," i.e., not made by a human being.

Colin Andrews is the world's authority on crop circles, and the author of three best-selling books. His latest is *Crop Circles: Signs of Contact* (on which I was his co-author). Colin has studied the phenomena since 1983 when he saw five simple circles in a field near Stonehenge in England.

Colin has analyzed the crop circle enigma and has identified the major theories regarding their creation. They are:

- The Gaia Theory
- Magnetism
- Life Force Energies
- Underground Water
- Microwaves
- Plasma Vortexes and Whirlwinds
- ETs and UFO Landing Sites
- Messages from the Dead
- Government Satellites
- Hoaxing

Regarding these ten theories, Colin Andrews believes that 80 percent of the approximately ten thousand formations reported around the world are manmade. He believes the other 20 percent are created by one of the other mechanisms.

In 2000, Colin created a storm of controversy when he stated his 80/20 thesis. He had arrived at this conclusion by analyzing the formation in England for the years 1999 and 2000, determining that 80 percent were counterfeits, and extrapolating that finding for all world manifestations. He has stood by his data, however, and many experts now concede that his findings are probably accurate.

What are the characteristics that determine an authentic formation?

There are several, including:

- There are no tracks into the circle.
- There are no signs of interference with the soil or the plants at points in the circle where hoaxers would have had to stand to create the formation.
- The plants are not damaged. (This is especially important—when a formation is made by hoaxers, the plants are killed.)
- The plants are more vibrant in appearance and the root structure is more extensive than usual.
- The swirl symmetry is even and there are usually two or fewer rotations of the spiral vein of the circle before it strikes the standing wall of the circle's circumference.
- There are magnetic and electrostatic anomalies in the formation, and compass rotation occurs when inside the circle.
- The plants are changed at the cellular level.
- Small quantities of an unknown magnetic material are found in the crop circle's soil and impregnated into the surface plant tissue.
- A magnetic profile as registered on a magnetometer mimics the actual design of the crop circle.
- The profile of the electrostatic field found in a crop circle shows unusual patterning.
- The stalks of the plants show node enlargement that are anomalous to normal growth patterns.

The evidence is clear that there is a genuine phenomenon. But what does the appearance of these patterns every year, all over the world *mean*—to mankind and to the future of the planet?

A bevy of experts, including Colin Andrews, believe that there is an intelligence behind the authentic crop patterns. In this context, "intelligence" does not necessarily mean "entity." The human immune system identifies threats to the body, marshals its defenses, and attacks and destroys the invader. And it does so *intelligently*. Perhaps a similar process is at work in the crop circle phenomena. Most authorities today believe that the crop circle mystery can be explained as a combination of the Gaia Theory and magnetism.

The Gaia Theory posits that the Earth and all its component biological "parts" comprise an enormous living organism and that, like any living entity, it can and does respond to injuries, assaults, and threats. Crop circles may be akin to an autonomic response; a sign that the Earth is communicating through natural energies, especially magnetism, and perhaps some unknown "brother" of magnetism as yet undefined. Many who have studied the placement of authentic crop patterns have noted the alignments of formations with sacred sights and areas of paranormal influence around the world.

What about the theories that crop circles are UFO landing sights, or messages from aliens, or communication from the dead?

There is documented evidence of mysterious balls of light (BOL) appearing above fields, before, during, and after the appearance of a crop circle. The thinking among the experts, however, is that these are not extraterrestrial in nature, but some component of the crop pattern materialization process.

Experiments with posthumous communication via some of the geometric patterns found in crop patterns have provided some tantalizing results, including the repetition of the initials of certain dead paranormal researchers, but there has been nothing conclusive so far.

Crop circles are real, and there is now evidence that paranormal activity occurs even within the hoaxed patterns. Many researchers believe that the hoaxers may also be playing a role in what Colin Andrews describes as a "consciousness experiment." Hoaxers have seen balls of light above their counterfeit patterns, and many cannot explain why they do what they do. Some have spoken of being "called" to make the patterns. Some have experienced their hoaxed patterns being mysteriously and inexplicably added to *without* their participation after they left the fields.

There is clearly a message in the crop circle phenomenon. We are making great strides towards understanding this consciousness communication, but so far we are still having problems with the translation.

[1]Colin Andrews, Stephen Spignesi, *Crop Circles: Signs of Contact.*

26

Crosses of Light

HAIKU:

CROSSES OF LIGHT

Glowing cross appears
Reflection of holy will?
Or a fluke of light?

God appears, and God is Light . . .

—William Blake[1]

DEFINITION: Crosses of light are images of crosses that appear on windows and other objects by known and unknown light sources; some of the crosses allegedly manifest miraculous healing powers. Many of the reported crosses of light are even-armed and centered within a diamond of light. Some appear in church windows; some appear in bathroom windows, on walls, and elsewhere.

WHAT THE BELIEVERS SAY: The crosses of light are a sign from God. They are messages of love and peace and are deliberate communications from Christ.

WHAT THE SKEPTICS SAY: The crosses of light are nothing but an odd confluence of reflected light and ordinary objects that create a cross shape.

QUALITY OF EXISTING EVIDENCE: Very good.[2]

LIKELIHOOD PHENOMENA ARE PARANORMAL: Inconclusive.[3]

I know a woman who recently lost a sister to leukemia. About a week or two after the sister's funeral, a cross of light appeared on the rear wall of the garage opposite the house where the two sisters lived. It was visible from the backyard and anywhere in the house from around three in the afternoon until sunset everyday.

The woman and her husband eventually figured out the source of the cross of light. When a shade in an upstairs bedroom was pulled halfway down, the afternoon sun struck the window and formed a reflected cross using the frame of the window and the edge of the shade. The husband was able to demonstrate that he had located the source by wiggling the shade and making the cross dance, or pulling up the shade and making it disappear.

These people are very religious, and have strong faith. To this day they believe that the cross of light was a sign from God about their deceased loved one, telling them that she was all right. The fact that no one in the two-family house had ever before seen the cross of light convinced them that it was a message from beyond. And the specific optical and geometrical variables that were responsible for the cross's appearance were irrelevant: they were perceived as nothing but tools used to send a divine message.

When a cross of light appears somewhere, in many instances it is not long before the place where it shines becomes a shrine. There are cases in which thousands of people have visited a small suburban house to catch a glimpse of a cross of light in a bathroom window. The yearning for spiritual solace and for a confirmation of the presence of God is palpable in many of these people, and the homeowners or residents are often willing to allow these pilgrims to share in the "miracle" that has occurred in their home.

As in the case of the "Jesus Tortilla" (see Chapter 51, "Marian Apparitions") though, some of these incidents are truly absurd and ripe for mockery by non-believers. One woman who witnessed a cross of light in her bathroom window began allowing people to visit her loo in groups of four to stare at the window. Some prayed; some claimed a sense of the presence of God; some said they were healed of terminal diseases and chronic ailments. Four people crammed into a bathroom, praying to a window, jostling around the toilet and sink is a scene that cries out for ridicule. Yet the pilgrims found nothing at all funny about their visitation.

In addition to bathroom windows, sometimes the crosses appear in churches, above the altar or in the windows of the building. Some-times they appear holographically in the sky; sometimes they only appear during a full moon. Sometimes they appear after being prayed for; sometimes they are reportedly accompanied by the sound of bells, the smell of roses, and the bleeding of statues.

One of the earliest accounts of a cross of light comes from the year 351 A.D. in a May letter from Bishop Cyril[4] to the Emperor Constantine II:

> A great luminous cross appeared in the sky over the holy hill of Golgotha, extending as far as the Mount of Olives, and it was seen most plainly, not by one or two people alone, but by the whole population of [Jerusalem]. Nor was it . . . a cross conjured up by the fancy . . . but for many hours . . . it hung above the earth visible to all . . .[5]

An intriguing process takes place when a cross of light appears. In a community that experiences a cross of light, people report feelings of peace and brotherhood and many witnesses claim an overwhelming sense of well-being, along with a confidence that "everything will be all right."

If the crosses are mere optical illusions, then this "group enlight-enment" is purely a conditioned response to the presence of the divine symbol. But their reactions are *real*, which, in a sense, vali-dates the belief that the crosses of light can, in fact, bring peace and love to the hearts and souls of people.

If you build it, they will come?

Seems so.

---

[1] *Auguries of Innocence.*

[2] The crosses of light undoubtedly exist. They have been photographed all over the world, and they have been witnessed by believers and skeptics alike. The "existing evidence," thus, is very good. The evidence that some of the crosses have been responsible for miraculous healings is somewhat more problematic. There is hard evidence that cures have been reported following an encounter with a cross of light. As with all healings credited to religious phenomena, however (Lourdes, holy water, etc.), the conclusions one arrives at depend solely on the level of faith he or she possesses.

[3] Whether or not the crosses of light are paranormal in origin is impossible to prove; faith, or the lack thereof, provides the answer for each individual who considers the subject.

[4] Cyril of Jerusalem was made a Doctor of the Church in 1882 and later canonized St. Cyril.

[5] Herbert Thurston, *Beauraing and Other Apparitions*, pp. 100–101.

27

Demons, Possession, and Exorcism

HAIKU:

DEMONS

Vile and obscene
Spirits from a darker place
Enemies of man

When he came to the other side, into the country of the Gergesenes, two people possessed with demons met him there, coming forth out of the tombs, exceedingly fierce, so that no man could pass by that way.

Behold, they cried out, saying, "What do we have to do with you, Jesus, Son of God? Have you come here to torment us before the time?"

Now there was a herd of many pigs feeding far away from them.

The demons begged him, saying, "If you cast us out, permit us to go away into the herd of pigs."

He said to them, "Go!" They came out, and went into the herd of pigs: and behold, the whole herd of pigs rushed down the cliff into the sea, and died in the water.

Those who fed them fled, and went away into the city, and told everything, and what happened to those who were possessed with demons.[1]

DEFINITION: **A demon** is an evil supernatural being;[2] **possession** occurs when a human being's identity is taken over by a demon; an **exorcism** is the religious ritual employed to banish a demon from a possessed person.

WHAT THE BELIEVERS SAY: Demons are real, and they are legion. Demons are a supernatural species of purely evil beings that can possess humans and destroy them. Sometimes exorcism works to banish them.

WHAT THE SKEPTICS SAY: There are no such beings as demons. Human beings are certainly capable of "demonic" behavior, but the notion that demons, fallen angels, and evil spirits roam the Earth and possess people is ridiculous. It is nothing but ignorant superstition and an unwillingness to lay blame for evil where it belongs: on the human perpetrators.

QUALITY OF EXISTING EVIDENCE: Fair.

LIKELIHOOD PHENOMENA ARE PARANORMAL: Fair to Good.[3]

Within hours of the collapse of the World Trade Center buildings on September 11, 2001, photos began circulating on the Internet showing an enormous, clearly recognizable demonic face glowering out of the smoke and flames. Many of the religious among us claimed it was Satan (or one of his flunkies) delighting in the mayhem and suffering; the agnostics and non-believers saw it simply as people seeing something in the shapes of the smoke and flames. There were several views of the image, and whether a person believed it was just a trick of light and shadow or an actual demonic manifestation depended solely on his or her belief system. There *was* a face in the fire. That is irrefutable. Its genesis is more problematic.

The Catholic Church states with certainty that the Devil is real, that demons subservient to him are real, and that either Satan or one of his minions can possess human beings and coerce them into saying and doing all manner of evil deeds.

When a person is known to be possessed, sometimes an exorcism is performed.[4] This is an official codified Catholic ritual in which a priest calls on the powers of God to rid the demon from the body of the possessed.

The holiest of the faithful are not immune to demonic possession. In fact, it seems as if they are sometimes specifically targeted by Satan. According to reports, in 1997 a priest in Calcutta, acting on the direct orders of the Archbishop, performed an exorcism on none other than Mother Teresa. Why? Because the saintly nun wholeheartedly believed that she was being attacked by the Devil.

According to a medieval researcher cited in the *Encyclopaedia of Occultism*,[5] there are several telltale signs that a person might be possessed by a demon, including the vomiting of objects, making a pact with the Devil, embracing evil, being excessively violent, making unearthly sounds and noises, and blaspheming God or Jesus.

The medieval researcher also claimed that living alone, being ugly, imagining you are possessed, being chronically sick, and being tired of living also qualified, and therein lies the problem with suspected demonic possession.

Mental illness is often the culprit for "demonic" behaviors, which is why the Catholic Church always refers people who are worried that they or a loved one is possessed by the Devil to a psychiatrist before even discussing the possibility of an exorcism.

When we peruse the stories of human monsters like Hitler, Hussein, Stalin, and Pol Pot (not to mention the Jeffrey Dahmers and Timothy McVeighs of our world), and others of their ilk, it is hard to imagine that these people did what they did of their own *human* accord. It is all too easy to imagine them possessed by some malevolent demon who guided their hand as they went about their abominable lives.

Yet, it is likely that the demons of history were probably all too human.

Does that mean that the evil they committed and fostered could not have been "inspired" by some power beyond our plane of reality? The answer to that question depends on whether or not you believe that true evil exists as an entity, as a power that can "infect" human beings.

Who knows? If someone like Mother Teresa believed she was under attack by a demonic power, who's to say any of us is immune?

[1] Matthew 8:28–33.

[2] There is debate about the number of demons in existence. According to *A Field Guide to Demons, Fairies, Fallen Angels, and Other Subversive Spirits*, a medieval estimate of the number of demons was 7,405,926; an ancient Indian epic called the *Ramayana* cited twenty thousand demons; and the Talmud tells us there is one demon per living person.

[3] The "exorcism" literature repeatedly tells of certain things that have gone on during exorcisms which do seem preternatural, e.g., speaking in tongues, apparent levitation, and precognition. These could all be misinterpretations of what went on, or hoaxes, but on the chance that some of the phenomena are legitimate, we rank the paranormal likelihood as "Fair" to "Good."

[4] Exorcisms are not *pro forma* for suspected possessions. The person must be carefully examined, medical conditions must be ruled out, and the local Bishop must approve and oversee the ritual.

[5] Lewis Spence, University Books, 1960.

28

Divination and Prophecy

HAIKU:

DIVINATION

Glimpsing what will be
Beholding a future time?
Or are we too blind?

Hen and Chickens. To dream of a hen and chickens, is very unfavourable; it portends loss of property, of friends, and reputation—in love it denotes misery and disappointment. After such a dream I would advise the dreamer to change his residence. To dream you hear hens cackling foretells success in love, and an accumulation of riches by means of female relations.

—Mother Shipton[1]

DEFINITION: Divination is the act (some say art) of foretelling future events or revealing occult knowledge by means of augury or an alleged supernatural agency; prophecy is an inspired utterance of a prophet, often viewed as a revelation of divine will. (Also see Chapters 11, "Astrology"; 16, "The Bible Code"; 59, "Nostradamus"; 60, "Numerology"; 62, "Palmistry"; and 87, "Tarot.")

WHAT THE BELIEVERS SAY: Divination is real, and the people who have the power are genuine psychics. There is an enormous amount of concrete evidence proving the accuracy of prophecies since the first days of recorded history.

WHAT THE SKEPTICS SAY: Divination is bunk. There is *no* concrete evidence proving the existence of divinatory abilities. No one can tell the future, especially using any of the methods detailed in this chapter. Rose leaves? Ashes? Burning cinders on the head of an ass? It is all nonsense and a projection of mankind's desperate attempt to control fate.

QUALITY OF EXISTING EVIDENCE: Inconclusive.[2]

LIKELIHOOD PHENOMENA ARE PARANORMAL: High.[3]

The myriad forms of divination are all about one thing: telling the future.

The list below details more than fifty of the ways man has tried to divine.

Many of these are patently ridiculous and clearly originated from superstition and a susceptibility to accept wild interpretations of mundane events.

Yet it must be acknowledged that many of these "mancies" are tools for understanding the subconscious and the unconscious. Often, there is great personal psychological meaning in the way a particular omen is interpreted—again, the "eye of the beholder" often sees more than is actually there, and this can be a path towards understanding.

Can a seer see future events in a crystal ball? Can he or she sit back and observe events unfold like watching a TV show? Is this a supernatural ability? Is time "geographic" instead of linear? Is time a place with different "locations" that certain people can visit at will?

Any and all of the answers to these questions—whether from believers or skeptics—are, in the end, inadequate.

54 FORMS OF DIVINATION[4]

- **Aeromancy:** observation of atmospheric phenomena such as thunder, lightning, clouds, comets, storms, etc.
- **Alectryomancy:** a rooster pecks seeds of grain off letters drawn in a circle and spells out the name of a person.

- **Aleuromancy:** messages written on paper are wrapped in balls of flour and then mixed up nine times and distributed. The person's fate is revealed by the flour ball they receive. (This may have been the ancestral forefather of the Chinese fortune cookie.)
- **Alomancy:** salt is "read" for a prediction.
- **Alphitomancy:** barley is given to people suspected of crimes; whoever gets sick from eating it is guilty.
- **Amniomancy:** the flesh "caul" membrane found on the faces of some newborns is read for information.
- **Anthropomancy:** male and female entrails are studied.
- **Apantomancy:** chance meetings, especially with animals, are interpreted for meaning.
- **Arithmancy:** numbers are interpreted.
- **Armomancy:** a seer examines a person's shoulders for meaning.
- **Axinomancy:** an axe or a hatchet is used as a tool for predicting the future by balancing an agate on the blade, or observing the direction of the handle when the axe is thrown.
- **Belomancy:** arrows are shot into the air and the direction of their shafts when they plunge to the ground is observed.
- **Bibliomancy:** a person suspected of being a wizard or sorcerer is weighed. If he weighs less than the local church's bible, he is innocent.
- **Botanomancy:** questions are carved onto brier branches and then the branches are burned.
- **Capnomancy:** smoke (sometimes from the burning of poppy seeds) is observed.
- **Catoptromancy** (also known as **Enoptromancy**): a mirror predicts a person's fate by the condition of the reflection of their face.
- **Causimomancy:** flammable items are thrown into a fire; if they do not burn, it is a sign of coming good fortune.
- **Ceraunoscopy:** phenomena of the air (clouds? wind?) are observed.
- **Ceroscopy:** melted wax disks are read by a magician.
- **Cleromancy:** black and white beans, bones, and stones are thrown and read; also known as the "**Throwing of Lots.**"
- **Clidomancy:** the name of a person whose fate needs to be decided is written upon a key which is then hung on a Bible. The Bible is then hung on the fingernail of the ring finger of a virgin. The direction in which the swaying book turns determines the fate of the person in question.

- **Coscinomancy:** a sieve, a pair of scissors, and the thumbnails of two people are used in concert to determine innocence or guilt. The sieve is hung by a thread from the shears which are supported on the thumbnails of the two people in question. The direction of the sieve's spin determines the guilty party.

- **Critomancy:** cakes and other food items (mostly baked goods) are read, usually by spreading out the flour of the cake and interpreting it.

- **Crystalomancy:** also known as crystal gazing, this form of divination involves a seer looking into a crystal ball or some similar object to tell the future.

- **Dactylomancy:** a ring is suspended above a table on which are written the letters of the alphabet; the ring's movement over the letters spells out messages; similar to pendulum dowsing.

- **Daphnomancy:** a laurel branch is thrown into a fire and observed.

- **Demonomancy:** demons are consulted for occult knowledge.

- **Eromanty:** the use of air. The Persians devised this method of divination in which they would breathe over a vase filled with water. Bubbles in the water meant that the objects of their desire would come to them.

- **Gastromancy:** seers answer questions by listening to voices emanating from a person's stomach. This is usually a fraudulent form of ventriloquism.

- **Gyromancy:** a small circle is drawn on the ground and the letters of the alphabet are written on its circumference. The person who wants an answer to a question stands inside the circle and is spun around repeatedly until he is too dizzy to stand up. The letters he stumbles over as he falls out of the circle spell out his answer.

- **Hippomancy:** the movement of certain sacred white horses divines the future.

- **Hydromancy:** this refers to various uses of water as a means of divination, including throwing things into water, and suspending things on a string over water.

- **Kephalonomancy:** a piece of carbon is burned on the head of an ass (or sometimes a goat), as the names of suspected criminals are recited. If a crackling sound is heard when a certain person's name is mentioned, he is guilty as charged.

- **Lithomancy:** refers to any number of forms of divination using stones.

- **Margaritomancy:** a pearl is placed beneath an upside down vase and the names of suspected criminals are recited. When a guilty person's name is mentioned, the pearl will fly upwards and shatter the bottom of the vase.
- **Muscle Reading:** a seer reads the unconscious muscle movements of a person who is suspected of knowing some truth that needs to be revealed.
- **Myomancy:** the behavior of rats or mice is observed.
- **Necromancy:** the spirits of the dead are consulted and they reveal the future and answer questions.
- **Onimancy:** divination by observation of a manifestation of the angel Uriel after oil of walnuts mingled with tallow is placed on the fingernails of an "unpolluted" boy or a young virgin.
- **Onomancy:** the spelling of and distribution of vowels and consonants in a person's name is studied for meaning.
- **Onychomancy:** divination by observing the sun's reflection in a person's fingernails.
- **Oomantia:** eggs are observed.
- **Ornithomancy:** the flight and/or song of birds is observed and studied for meaning.
- **Phyliorhodomancy:** rose leaves are read.
- **Psychomancy:** the spirits of the dead are invoked for information and guidance (this is similar to necromancy).
- **Psychometry:** telling the future by holding something possessed by a person.
- **Pyromancy:** telling the future by reading fire.
- **Rhabdomancy:** using a rod or a staff for divination.
- **Rhapsodamancy:** this method of divination involves opening a book of randomly selected poetry and reading the first verse the eye falls upon. There will be occult meaning in the passage.
- **Spodomancy:** divination by reading the ashes and cinders of any number of different sacrificial fires.
- **Stolcheomancy:** a form of Rhapsodamancy in which the works of Homer or Virgil are used.
- **Stolisomancy:** the way a person dresses foretells the future (you can write your own joke for this one).
- **Sycomancy:** the leaves of the fig tree are read for meaning.
- **Xylomancy:** the Slavonic method of telling the future using the position of randomly found small pieces of wood that a person happens to come across during a journey.

[1] *The New Universal Dream-Book,* circa 1686. Shipton was a legendary seventeenth century English prophet who was rumored to be a witch and a child of the Devil.

[2] The interpretation of a reading is in the eye of the beholder and it has been shown that many people will tailor their reaction to a divine revelation so that it "fits" their current situation or answers a question. This is not verifiable data, thus, our "Inconclusive" rating.

[3] There is far too much anecdotal evidence for precognition to dismiss it as a fluke of human behavior. We speak of "women's intuition" and "hunches" and completely accept that they are real; the unavoidable conclusion is that man seems to have nascent psychic abilities that probably utilize the subconscious and the unconscious minds. The day may come when we fully understand these *other* senses.

[4] This is a revised and expanded version of a list that originally appeared in the author's 1994 book, *The Odd Index* (Plume).

29

Dowsing

HAIKU:

DOWSING

The bearded dowser
Places his faith in his stick
Water down below?

Dowsing. It is commonly known as water-divining. It is witchcraft. One cannot say that, because of some unknown chemical, or bio-chemical, affinity, a wand bends in the hand, in the presence of underground water. The wand bends only in the hands of a magician. It is witchcraft. So, though there are scientists who are giving in to its existence, there are others, or hosts of others, who never will give in.

—Charles Fort[1]

DEFINITION: Dowsing is the act of searching for and sometimes locating underground water, minerals, underground mines, or buried objects using a divining rod, which is usually a forked branch or stick made of hazel wood, ash, or rowan, that bends downward when held over a source. A pendulum suspended above the ground or a map is also sometimes used.

WHAT THE BELIEVERS SAY: Successful dowsers are highly sensitive to certain electrical, magnetic, biochemical, or indefinable organic energies surrounding, permeating, and radiating from underground deposits and can read these "fields" for accuracy in locating sites.

WHAT THE SKEPTICS SAY: Dowsing does not work. There is no empirical scientific evidence to prove its efficacy. Any "hits" are due either to chance, or to prior knowledge of an underground lode.

QUALITY OF EXISTING EVIDENCE: Very good.

LIKELIHOOD PHENOMENON IS PARANORMAL: High.

Dowsing has been around for centuries; there are recorded accounts of dowsing being practiced as far back as 3000 B.C. in Brittany, and in ancient Egypt. Dowsing became commonplace in the fourteenth and fifteenth centuries in Europe, where "water witches" were often employed to locate underground wells and to seek out caches of metallic ores for the medieval mining industry. (Although Reginald Scot, writing in *The Discouerie of Witchcraft* [1584], described dowsing rods as "meer toys to mock Apes," proclaiming they "have no commendable [purpose].") The first time dowsing was mentioned in extant literature was 1540.

Dowsing is done with a variety of tools, including a **Y-shaped rod** (the most well-known dowsing tool), an **L-shaped rod** (a piece of wire is bent at a right angle and it pivots in the dowser's hand; often the dowser holds one in each hand), or a **pendulum** (used over ground or a map). Sometimes, experienced dowsers simply walk over an area and try to pick up a sense of underground deposits.

Dowsing is one of those fringe practices that science does not seem to know what to do with. Or rather, because science doesn't fully understand *how* dowsing is done, the usual position is that it *can't* be done. Even though it can, is, and has been done quite effectively for centuries.

A report in Robert Todd Carroll's *The Skeptic's Dictionary* tells of a successful series of dowsing tests performed by a German physicist named Hans-Dieter Betz. Betz's team reported enormously high success rate under controlled circumstances. Yet this did not convince Carroll. He writes:

> The third test was a kind of contest between the dowser and a team of hydrogeologists. The scientific team, about whom we are told nothing significant, studied an area and picked 14 places to drill. The dowser then went over the same area after the scientific team had made their choices and he

picked 7 sites to drill. . . . A site yielding 100 liters per minute was considered good. The hydrogeologists hit three good sources; the dowser hit six. Clearly, the dowser won the contest. *This test does not prove anything about dowsing, however.* [emphasis added][2]

Really?

The hydrogeologists' success rate was 21 percent; the dowser's was 85 percent, and yet this does not prove anything?

If science does not accept the validity of dowsing as a still-unexplainable, yet real skill, then why did the United States military use dowsers to locate unexploded mines during World War I?

Also, why did American troops in Vietnam use dowsing to search for and locate mines, booby traps, and buried mortars?

Also, why do multinational oil, gas, mining, and mineral companies *pay* dowsers to complement their conventional geological analyses?

In *Wild Talents*, Charles Fort tells the story of a U.S. Department of Agriculture scientist, Dr. Charles Albert Browne, who witnessed one of Germany's most famous dowsers locate an underground stream, outline its dimensions, report its depth, and assure that its water was drinkable, all of which were later confirmed through standard scientific tests.[3]

So, is dowsing nothing but an ideomotor physical response, dressed up with centuries of superstition, ritual, local custom, and anecdotal evidence?

Or is it a genuine psychoenergetic ability in which certain people's odd sensitivity to vibrations emitted by underground lodes of water, minerals, and other objects and substances has been used to locate all manner of "buried treasures?"

Scientific testing and empirical data are the benchmarks for truth. Yet, science is often late to the party when it comes to confirming centuries- or millennia-old anecdotal wisdom.

People were applying bread-mold poultices to the sites of infections long before science recognized such mold as a source for the antibiotic penicillin.

People were chewing the bark of poplar and willow trees long before science recognized such bark as a source for the analgesic aspirin.

Again, the fact that we do not fully understand *how* dowsing works does not make its ineffectiveness a de facto reality.

Just ask the Vietnam soldier who did *not* lose his legs by stepping on a mine located by a dowser if dowsing works.

[1] *The Books of Charles Fort*, p. 1046.
[2] Robert Todd Carroll, *The Skeptic's Dictionary*, http://www.skepdic.com, "Dowsing."
[3] *The Books of Charles Fort*, p. 1047.

30

Dragons

HAIKU:

DRAGONS

Winged scaly beast
Breath of fire, lion's claws
Fearsome in the skies

Praise the Lord upon earth: ye dragons, and all deeps;
Fire and hail, snow and vapours: wind and storm, fulfilling
his word.[1]

DEFINITION: A dragon is a legendary monster traditionally represented as a gigantic reptile having a lion's claws, the tail of a serpent, wings, fire breath, and scaly skin. Stories of dragons appear in almost every culture on Earth.

WHAT THE BELIEVERS SAY: Dragons were, and are, real creatures that are rare, reclusive, and deadly. They may be a surviving species from prehistoric times, or they may be creatures from another dimension. Whatever the truth, though, they do exist, and they have been seen countless times on the lands, and in the air and skies, of Earth.

WHAT THE SKEPTICS SAY: Dragons are 100 percent mythical. Any purported sightings of dragons are either mistaken reports of birds, reptiles, or some other natural, *real* animal, or hoaxes. There are no such creatures as dragons, fairy tales and *The Hobbit* notwithstanding.

QUALITY OF EXISTING EVIDENCE: Fair.[2]

LIKELIHOOD PHENOMENON IS PARANORMAL: Fair.

Roman scholar and naturalist Pliny the Elder wrote of a dragon being killed on Vatican Hill in the first century A.D. during the reign of Emperor Claudius. When the dragon was cut open, the body of a small child was found inside.[3]

In 1903, two hunters in Utah saw a gigantic scaled, winged, flying creature with the head of a crocodile and "large, fiercely serrated teeth"[4] fly into a cave with a horse in its mouth. They listened as the beast devoured the "crushed and mangled"[5] equine.

As these two examples illustrate, reports of dragon sightings have spanned the breadth of recorded human history. Dragons were seen eons ago; dragons have been seen this century.

But are what people have seen and reported really dragons, as we have come to understand them—giant, flying, serpent-like creatures who breathe fire and have scales that can break a sword?

Strange Magazine Online and *Fate* editor Mark Chorvinsky has been studying the legend and culture of dragons for decades. In the November 2002 issue of *Fate* magazine, he summed up the "dragon problem":

> The problem of dragon study is complicated by the wide variation in description. There are dragons of the air, sea, and land; of two legs, four legs, and more; winged and wingless; venomous, fire-breathing, and stinging; friendly and fierce. The description of aerial dragons have led ufologists to wonder whether the skyborne entities were in fact UFOs and not animals, and the sightings of aquatic dragons have caused cryptozoologists to suggest that the so-called dragon reports may have been reptilian sea serpents or lake monsters.[6]

The key question regarding the existence or nonexistence of dragons is almost the same question we must ask about UFOs: If dragons are not real, *then what are all these people seeing in the skies?*

We know that fantastic legends arise when seemingly inexplicable events and sightings occur and are witnessed and experienced by humans. The legend of mermaids probably arose from sightings of seals or dugongs. (See Chapter 53.) The legend of the werewolf probably arose from stories of schizophrenics who also suffered from hypertrichosis. (See Chapter 98.) But what naturally occurring animal is bigger than five elephants, can fly, swim, and eat a horse at one sitting?

Therein lies the dragon problem.

Many of the dragon sightings over the centuries are so utterly fantastic, that cryptozoologists and other scientists have a hard time finding a real-world explanation for what people claim to have seen.

Granted, there are reptiles like the komodo dragon, and serpents like the boa constrictor that share similar characteristics with some of the reported physical features and abilities of dragons. But there is no creature that has *all* of the powers and physical attributes of the sighted dragon.

So could these creatures be real, but actually some hardy, atavistic survivor from prehistoric times? Are the dragons that people see today, as well as the dragons people claimed to have seen hundreds of years ago, really flying dinosaurs that somehow resisted extinction? Maybe they are creatures that were in deep, deep caves when that primordial asteroid hit during the Mesozoic Era and, thanks to their truly impressive innate hibernation powers, they managed to stick it out here on earth for, oh, 150 million years or so.

Maybe . . .

Dragons have long had enormous symbolic significance. In the Bible, they represented perfect evil. In the Book of Revelation, the arch-angel Michael and his warriors fought Satan, who took on the guise of a dragon for the battle:

> There was war in the sky. Michael and his angels made war on the dragon. The dragon and his angels made war.
>
> They didn't prevail, neither was a place found for him any more in heaven.
>
> The great dragon was thrown down, the old serpent, he who is called the Devil and Satan, the deceiver of the whole world. He was thrown down to the earth, and his angels were thrown down with him.[7]

In Sumerian folklore, a dragon symbolizes chaos.

In Russian mythology, the dragon is the gatekeeper of the realm beyond the world of the living.

In Chinese tradition, the dragon is a benevolent creature who helped create the universe. Chinese emperors were believed to be descendants of dragons.

And of course there is the symbolic legend of St. George (read: Christianity) who slew a dragon (read: paganism) to save the daughter of a king (read: future generations) and who became the patron saint of England.

Dragon sightings are nowhere near as ubiquitous as UFO sightings, and yet there are reports from around the world of strange flying creatures that many believe to be dragons of legend. (The most recent "dragon" sighting was in October 2002 in southwest Alaska. Was it simply a large raptor? The jury's still out.)

The truth may one day be known. Until then, some of us may choose to keep our eyes on the sky . . . for more reasons than one.

[1] *Prayer Book* (1662), 148:7.

[2] The evidence for dragons is mainly anecdotal. Science does not (yet?) have photos of real dragons, or any physical evidence, such as a corpse, some scales, a wing, a few teeth, etc.

[3] *Historia Naturalis.*

[4] *Dawson Daily News*, September 17, 1903.

[5] Ibid.

[6] Mark Chorvinsky, "Here Be Dragons," *Fate*, November 2002, p. 13.

[7] Revelation 12:7–9.

31

The Easter Island Monuments

HAIKU:

EASTER ISLAND

Ancient giant heads
Standing tall, staring away
On Rapa Nui

The very stones prate of my whereabout . . .[1]

DEFINITION: The Easter Island monuments are mysterious ancient heads known as *moai* that were found on an island of Chile in the southern Pacific Ocean about 2,300 miles west of the mainland. Easter Island, known locally as Rapa Nui, was discovered by Dutch explorers on Easter Day, 1722; and it is known for its ancient remains of unknown origin, including hieroglyphic tablets and colossal heads carved from volcanic rock believed to date from around 1400.

WHAT THE BELIEVERS SAY: There is no way humans could have carved the 887 massive monolithic statues and transported them all over the island[2] using nothing but wood, rope, and natural lubricants. Visiting extraterrestrials had to have been involved and they probably either built the statues themselves or provided some form of anti-gravity transportation technology that simply floated the *moai* to their final locations.

WHAT THE SKEPTICS SAY: The Easter Island statues were carved, transported, and erected by human beings. Although the method of transport is not conclusively known, scientists and archaeologists have theorized several modes of transporting the *moai* that definitely would have worked with enough time and manpower. (See the descriptions of transport methods below.)

QUALITY OF EXISTING EVIDENCE: Very good.[3]

LIKELIHOOD PHENOMENA ARE PARANORMAL: LOW.

Were they simply bored? Is it possible that the natives of Rapa Nui spent years carving the hundreds of stone heads circling the island and then more time transporting many of them into their final location because they had nothing better to do?

What was the purpose of building these monuments?

Some have suggested the heads were built to intimidate rival families and tribes.

There is also the theory that the statues were built to commemorate the visit to the island of extraterrestrials, and that the red "hats" on many of the heads are meant to represent space helmets.

Were the natives visited by aliens who were, of course, perceived to be gods from the heavens?

Recent research and experiments make this scenario unlikely.

Beginning in the mid-1950s, archaeologists and historians have attempted to duplicate the transporting of the *moai* to their final resting places on the perimeter of the island.

The great explorer Thor Heyerdahl (of Kon-Tiki fame, the journey that proved that the natives of Easter Island could have made the journey from Peru) devised a system to move the heads by tying them to a sled made from a tree fork and then pulling the sled with ropes. It took 180 islanders to move a ten-ton *moai*. Heyerdahl calculated it would take fifteen-hundred men to move the heaviest *moai*, which weighed eighty-two tons.

In 1986, Heyerdahl tried another method of moving the statues. The statue was swiveled from side to side and "walked" across the ground. This method, which has originally been tried in Czechoslovakia in 1982, also worked, but it did considerable damage to the base of the statue, damage which is not visible on the surviving *moai*, so the experiment was abandoned.

Another method was tried in Wyoming in the 1980s using two sleds placed on top of log rollers. This method also worked and a team of twenty-five men were able to move a ten-ton concrete replica of a *moai* 150 feet in two minutes.

But What about the Aliens?

In his book *The Space Gods Revealed*, Erich von Däniken listed the main reasons why the Easter Island monuments could not have been a product of terrestrial manpower:

- they were too large to have been carved by men
- the local stone was too hard to carve without advanced technology
- the stones could not have been transported from the quarry to their locations
- there were no trees on the island with which to make the alleged log rollers used to move them
- the "red hats" were space helmets
- there was no way to stand the statues up once they were moved to their locations
- all the stone axes and other carving tools that have been found were not indications that the work had been done by the islanders, but rather that they had abandoned even trying to carve more statues after the aliens left
- the heads found on the ground were left there because the natives could not transport them and erect them after the aliens left

We know now that there were indeed ways for mere mortals to move the stones; that the rock was volcanic lava which was relatively soft and easy to carve, that the red hats probably signified the red hair of the local natives, and that the abandoned statues were, in fact, on their way to their final sites, but for some unknown reason, the islanders could not complete the entire array of standing stones.

The Easter Island monuments are archaeological artifacts from long ago. The eagerness with which many are willing to attribute their construction to extraterrestrials bespeaks the skill, diligence, and commitment of those long-gone ancient builders, men who embodied the human spirit seen today in our highest skyscrapers and longest bridges.

[1]William Shakespeare, *Macbeth*, Act II, Scene 1.

[2]Of the 887 *moai* on Easter Island, 288 are in their final location on the perimeter of the island, 397 remain in the Rano Raraku quarry, and 92 lie outside the quarry "in transit." (Source: Nova Online.)

[3]The 887 statues on Easter Island still exist and provide a wealth of concrete evidence about their composition, weight, height, and age.

32

Edgar Cayce
(1877–1945)

HAIKU:

EDGAR CAYCE

The sleeping prophet
Cayce's trances are his tools
For the Akashic

For mind is the builder and that which we think may become crimes or miracles. For thoughts are things and as their currents run through the environs of an entity's experience these become barriers or stepping stones, dependent upon the manner in which these are laid as it were.

—Edgar Cayce[1]

DEFINITION: Edgar Cayce was America's greatest psychic, and was known as the "sleeping prophet" for his practice of entering a sleep-like trance when making his readings. Cayce could reportedly tap into the Akashic Record, the great field of energy thought to be surrounding the planet, containing the history of all the experience of humanity.

WHAT THE BELIEVERS SAY: Cayce was extraordinarily precognitive, as well as being a gifted psychic healer whose success rate with readings and long-distance diagnoses was repeatedly verified and confirmed by non-partisan observers.

WHAT THE SKEPTICS SAY: There is no evidence that Cayce possessed psychic powers of any kind. His supposed "cures" are very unlikely to have been due to his intercession or precognition and are supported by nothing but anecdotal evidence.

QUALITY OF EXISTING EVIDENCE: Excellent.

LIKELIHOOD PHENOMENON IS PARANORMAL: Very high.

Edgar Cayce's psychic gifts appeared at an early age. When he was six, he told his parents that he could see and talk to deceased relatives and angels. As a young boy, he astonished his teachers by memorizing every word in his spelling book by sleeping with his head on the book rather than reading it. Later, he told of a visit from an angelic being who asked him what he wished to do with his life. Cayce responded that he hoped to help heal the sick, and he was told his aspiration would be fulfilled.

Cayce first discovered that he had a sensitivity for understanding physical ailments when he lost his voice while working as an insurance and book salesman in partnership with his father, Leslie Cayce. Cayce was working as a traveling salesman and was doing well enough to entertain thoughts of marrying. One day, in his twenty-third year, he took a sedative to treat a headache and, soon after, developed a severe case of laryngitis. He could barely speak above a whisper, but at first he was not concerned since he knew that people often lost their voices for brief periods of time. Cayce's voice did not return, however, and, after months of medical treatments and consultations with specialists failed to restore his voice, he had to give up his job and look for something that did not require him to speak.

Eventually, Cayce found a job in his hometown of Hopkinsville, Kentucky as a photographer's assistant. By this time, he had resigned himself to never being able to speak normally again, and he took comfort in his fiancée, Gertrude, his family, and his daily reading of the Bible.

One day, a traveling hypnotist named Hart the Laugh King came to Hopkinsville. Someone in town who knew of Hart's clinical work with hypnosis told him of Cayce's chronic, apparently incurable loss of voice, and Hart offered to try an experiment with Edgar. Edgar agreed and was hypnotized by Hart. To the amazement of all present, Cayce was able to speak normally and clearly while under hypnosis. As soon as he was awakened, however, his voice returned to a faint whisper. This experiment was repeated several times and each time, Cayce's voice would disappear once he was awakened from his hypnotic trance.

March 13, 1901. Hart the Laugh King was long gone, and Edgar Cayce still had no voice.

He had not given up on regaining his ability to speak, however, and he prevailed upon a local man with skill in hypnosis to help him.

Cayce went into a trance and immediately began to speak in a normal voice. He quickly identified his loss of voice as a "psychological condition producing a physical effect."[2] He then "told himself" how to cure it: he needed to increase blood flow to his throat and upper chest. As everyone watched, Cayce's upper body and neck became bright red as he willed blood to flow to the afflicted areas.

Upon awakening, his voice had returned.

This event was the beginning of Edgar Cayce's lifelong practice of providing "readings" for people from all over the world. With no formal education, and no medical training at all, Cayce was able to identify what was wrong with people, and tell them how they could be healed. Often, all he needed was the name and address of the afflicted person. He would lie on a couch, place himself into a fugue state that was a combination of sleep and a trance, and then answer questions put to him. He did not remember what he said when he was "under," and was often amazed at the words he had spoken during a reading. His secretary Gladys Davis transcribed everything he said during his Life Readings, most of which were conducted and guided by his wife Gertrude.

Today, all of Cayce's readings are stored at the Association for Research and Enlightenment in Virginia Beach, Virginia and are available on CD-ROM. It was determined that Cayce answered questions on over ten thousand subjects during his readings. His success rate was extraordinarily high and far exceeded the happenstance vagaries of coincidence.

Cayce's fame spread worldwide, and he was investigated by both skeptics and the police for his "medical advice" and for suspicion of fortune telling. One Catholic writer who visited Virginia Beach with the intention of "exposing" Cayce as a fraud instead ended up writing an acclaimed biography of Cayce.

So, was Edgar Cayce a true psychic? A prophet? A seer? Or was he just incredibly lucky?

The evidence overwhelmingly supports that Cayce was a true clairvoyant. Some fundamentalists rage against his readings as the work of Satan, claiming that he was a promoter of demonology and the occult. This is a curious position to take regarding someone who expressed interest in doing nothing but helping people and who read the Bible cover to cover every year of his life.

To sum up, here is a passage from the article "Edgar Cayce's ESP: Who He Was, What He Said, and How it Came True" by Kevin J. Todeschi. It appears on the A.R.E. Web site, and is evidence that Cayce was the exact *opposite* of a demonically influenced corrupter of mankind:

> Throughout his life, Edgar Cayce claimed no special abilities nor did he ever consider himself to be some kind of twentieth-century prophet. The readings never offered a set of beliefs that had to be embraced, but instead focused on the fact that each person should test in his or her own life the principles presented. Though Cayce himself was a Christian and read the Bible from cover to cover every year of his life, his work was one that stressed the importance of comparative study among belief systems all over the world. The underlying principle of the readings is the oneness of all life, tolerance for all people, and a compassion and understanding for every major religion in the world.[3]

[1] From Edgar Cayce Reading 906–3, quoted in *Pole Shift*, by John White, p. 186.

[2] A.R.E. Web site: www.arebookstore.com.

[3] Ibid.

33

Elves, Fairies, and Dwarves

HAIKU:

ELVES

Magical creatures
Shiny twinkle in their eye
How can they not be?

The splendour falls on castle walls
And snowy summits old in story:
The long light shakes across the lakes,
And the wild cataract leaps in glory.
Blow, bugle, blow, set the wild echoes flying,
Blow, bugle; answer, echoes, dying, dying, dying.
O hark, O hear! How thin and clear,
And thinner, clearer, farther going!
O sweet and far from cliff and scar
The horns of Elfland faintly blowing![1]

DEFINITION: An elf is a supernatural being, smaller than humans, gifted with magical powers, and often associated with the elemental powers of the earth, the sea, and the forest; a **fairy** is a tiny supernatural being in human form, often carefree (but equally as often mischievous) and possessing magical powers; a **dwarf** is a small, sometimes bearded, often cave-dwelling creature gifted with the ability to mine and find gems, and sometimes prone to vindictiveness and mischieviousness.

WHAT THE BELIEVERS SAY: Elves, fairies, dwarves, and other mystical creatures like leprechauns and gnomes are real and have magical powers. They have been our neighbors on Earth since time immemorial and there are countless eyewitness accounts of their appearance and their involvement in human affairs.

WHAT THE SKEPTICS SAY: Elves, fairies, dwarves, and other mystical creatures are all *make-believe*. They exist nowhere except in fairy tales, legend, and fantasy epics like *The Lord of the Rings*. They are completely imaginary and there is no evidence whatsoever that these creatures ever existed anywhere outside of that fanciful realm called *folklore*. People who claim to have seen a fairy or a leprechaun *did not* see a fairy or a leprechaun. They were either dreaming, hallucinating, or they made it up.

QUALITY OF EXISTING EVIDENCE: Poor.

LIKELIHOOD PHENOMENA ARE PARANORMAL: Inconclusive.[2]

The Tooth Fairy brings children money or gifts in exchange for teeth that have fallen out and are placed beneath their pillow. When I was a kid, the going rate was a quarter. I understand that the Tooth Fairy has adjusted her rates and that now a dollar is commonplace for a lost tooth.

Elves help Santa build all the toys he brings to good boys and girls all over the world. These elves are known as Santa's Helpers, and they are diminutive, usually dress in green, and are diligent workers. They must have quite a set-up at the North Pole when you consider the array of toys that children wake up to beneath their Christmas tree.

Our Fairy Godmother watches over us, much like our Guardian Angel. One cannot help but wonder if they work in shifts.

Leprechauns, which are a type of elf, are known for playing mischievous pranks on people and also for knowing where the treasure is hidden. What treasure? you ask. The pot of gold at the end of the rainbow! The next time you see a rainbow, be sure to look around for a leprechaun. If you see him and ask him the location of the treasure, legend has it that he has to tell you. You could retire early.

In J.R.R. Tolkien's *Lord of the Rings* trilogy, the elvish race is immortal; the dwarves are legendary mine dwellers who built enormous and magnificent halls and chambers beneath the mountains. Tolkien's elves look like men; his dwarves are short, stocky, and bearded—even the women.

These are just a few examples of the breadth of mythology concerning elves, fairies, and dwarves.

Are they real?

The legends are such a delightful enrichment of our global culture that one cannot help but feel like a curmudgeon when claiming that elves, fairies, leprechauns and all their mystical, mischievous colleagues are nothing but pure fantasy.

Entire genres of fantasy literature have been created around the legends of elves and their associates. People take elvish names, dress up for fantasy weekends, and learn to speak Elvish.

Mindless diversions, you say?

Perhaps. But can anything that so nourishes man's need for fantasy and whimsy be meaningless and a waste of time?

And therein lies the enduring power of the myths of mythical creatures: Pondering their existence and living within the reality of their worlds expands the mind, stimulates creativity, and gives satisfaction.

The power of fantasy cannot and should not be trivialized or dismissed out of hand as immature and silly.

So, yes, Virginia, there is a Santa Claus.

And Elrond lives in Rivendell, and the Tooth Fairy is the one who left the quarter under your pillow.

Truth, perchance, can come in many sizes and shapes?

[1]Alfred, Lord Tennyson (1809–1892), *Song.*
[2]We choose to err on the side of whimsy for this conclusion.

ESP

HAIKU:

ESP

Beyond the senses
The mysteries of our minds
Latent gifts perhaps?

*[T]here is much about human consciousness that we do
not fully understand and cannot yet explain in terms of
neurobiology . . . a multitude of aspects of the natural world
that were considered miraculous only a few generations ago
are now thoroughly understood in terms of physics and
chemistry . . .*

—Carl Sagan[1]

DEFINITION: ESP, short for extrasensory perception, is communication or perception by means other than the physical senses.[2]

WHAT THE BELIEVERS SAY: Human beings clearly have abilities beyond the physical senses of sight, hearing, touch, taste, and smell. (A recent book was published titled *The Sense of Being Stared At*, a phenomenon which everyone immediately recognizes.) We may not fully understand what these other abilities are, or know how they precisely work, but it is obvious that the full powers of the mind are yet to be completely understood. It is quite possible that there are regions of our brain that serve as the repository of the sensory capabilities some humans are now able to utilize.

WHAT THE SKEPTICS SAY: Human beings have no abilities beyond the physical senses. People can not read other people's minds, predict the future, move things with their thoughts, or receive messages from dead people. There is no hard evidence for psychic powers. Science has failed abysmally in proving the existence of extrasensory perception.

QUALITY OF EXISTING EVIDENCE: Very good.

LIKELIHOOD PHENOMENON IS AUTHENTIC: Very high.

The existence or nonexistence of ESP and all of its ancillary "wild talents" (pyrokinesis, telekinesis, etc.) is not resolved, and yet it is one of the most important questions man must ultimately answer.

What are the powers of the mind? The process of thought is not fully understood; we still do not truly know what "thinking" is, nor do we know precisely how memory works. If ESP is not real, then what is "intuition?" If we have no senses beyond the physical, how can we tell when someone is staring at us? People speak of "feeling" that someone looking at them. Obviously, they are not *physically* feeling this sensation, so how can they "feel" a gaze? Where are the receptors in the brain that can sense someone looking at them? The receptors for the other senses are obvious and understood: the eye for sight, the tongue for taste, the skin for touch, the ears for hearing, the nose for smell. These are concrete physical organs that perform a function that allows us to interact with the physical world. Yet information picked up solely by the mind is often dismissed as nothing but coincidence.

Half of all Americans believe in the existence of ESP. This is a staggering validation that a great many people have experienced something they believe to be real. Anecdotal evidence does not prove anything, of course, and of the millions of people who claim to have had a psychic experience, the overwhelming majority of these events can probably be dismissed out of hand as the result of fraud, trickery, human error, coincidence, wishful thinking, gullibility and many other factors that can convince a person that they have had a paranormal experience.

Yet, as with the millions of reports of UFO sightings, the question must be asked: Can *every single report* of a psychic experience be incorrect?

Every one?

If even one percent of the reports of psychic phenomena are real (and we can postulate the same comparison for UFO sighting) then there is something going on that we do not understand, but which seems to be grounded in reality, albeit on a tiny scale as compared to the claims and reports.

These are the cases a reasonable person cannot ignore, or cavalierly dismiss as false.

The *Catholic Encyclopedia* has addressed the subject of telepathy. Its answer to the question, "Has the fact of telepathy been established?" was the following:

> [T]he literature on the subject is very extensive. After considering the cumulative evidence for the existence of telepathy, there cannot fail to remain in the mind at least a general impression that chance does not account for the number of coincidences, which is far greater than could be expected according to chance-probability. . . . The present impossibility of giving a scientific explanation is *no proof that there is no scientific explanation*. The unexplained is not to be identified with the unexplainable, and the strange and extraordinary nature of a fact is not a justification for attributing it to powers above nature. [emphasis added][3]

J.B. Rhine spent years investigating paranormal phenomena at Duke University in the 1920s and developed the Zener Cards—white cards with symbols on them (square, circle, wavy lines, triangle), still used today to test extrasensory abilities.

Rhine legitimized the study of parapsychology and today there are programs at many universities exploring the untapped psychic capabilities of the human mind.

ESP and other psychic abilities are the oddities of the human experience that will not go away. It seems that the attempts to disprove the existence of other abilities of man are, in the end, self-defeating.

It was once deemed physically impossible for man to run a mile in faster than four minutes. Now, after decades of training, that record is beaten regularly.

What other abilities of men now deemed impossible are simply latent talents needing training and time to evolve to their full capacity?

This is a fair question and it behooves legitimate science to try to answer it.

This book began with my admission that I do not believe that I know everything.

A corollary to that could be my acceptance that I also do not believe that I know everything *the human mind is capable of*.

[1] *The Demon-Haunted World: Science as a Candle in the Dark*, p. 268.

[2] Also see the chapters on divination and prophecy (including numerology, astrology, Ouija board, and palmistry), animal telepathy, channeling and automatic writing, communication with the dead, remote viewing, synchronicity, and telekinesis.

[3] *The Catholic Encyclopedia*, "Telepathy," online at: www.newadvent.org.

35

The Face on Mars[1]

HAIKU:

FACE ON MARS

Staring into space
Martian king, or someone else?
Are your eyes open?

That the Face itself could also have an esoteric or
theosophical meaning is certainly possible, but it will not
redefine our entire gnostic and dharmic heritage; it will
simply translate terrestrial terms into interplanetary or
transgalactic terms, perhaps replacing astral symbology
with actual cosmic geography. But the Face (as artifact)
at very least must redefine the exoteric history and
"anthropology" of our planet.

—Richard Grossinger[2]

DEFINITION: The Face on Mars is literally that: an enormous Sphinx-
like face staring out into space from the Cydonia region of the Mar-

tian landscape. The Face was first seen in a NASA Viking *Orbiter* photo in 1976. It was estimated to measure 1.6 miles from crown to chin, 1.2 miles wide, and approximately 1,500 feet high.

WHAT THE BELIEVERS SAY: The Face is a constructed monument built by a long-dead Martian civilization. The builders of the Face may also be the ones responsible for the Nazca lines in Peru (see Chapter 56), and crop circles (see Chapter 25).

WHAT THE SKEPTICS SAY: The Face is nothing but a trick of shadow and light. It is not a constructed artifact and the new NASA photos prove it once and for all.

QUALITY OF EXISTING EVIDENCE: Mixed. The NASA photos exist; some believe them to be doctored. There is also suspicion that NASA has withheld some of the most compelling images showing the Face.

LIKELIHOOD PHENOMENON IS PARANORMAL: Inconclusive. Is the Face an artifact of long-dead Martians? Or just a geological anomaly? For all the research, computer imaging, calculations, and theorizing, we simply do not know.

The Face on Mars is one of the most fascinating branches of the UFO phenomenon. Books have been written about it; documentaries have been produced about it; and lectures about the Face and the other monuments on Mars always attract huge, passionately interested crowds.

The truth is, we *want* the Face on Mars or be real, i.e., a constructed monument left behind by a long-dead civilization. We want the Face to be more than mere slopes of sand worn into odd shapes by wind erosion and gravity.

Imagine the significance! Imagine knowing with certainty that Mars was once inhabited! Imagine what this would mean to mankind!

Which leads to the question: *Was* Mars once inhabited?

And if there was a civilization on Mars, were its inhabitants related to humankind? Did they build the Face and other monuments as they once allegedly built the Sphinx and the Pyramids at Giza?

Are *we* humans actually Martian colonists, the descendants of a race that had to flee their home planet?

The first pictures of the mesa formation that would become known to the world as the Face on Mars were taken on Sunday, July 25, 1976 by the unmanned spacecraft Viking *Orbiter 1* as it flew eleven hundred miles above the surface of Mars. The photo of the

Face was NASA Frame 35A72 and it was taken during Viking's thirty-fifth orbit around Mars. The Face is located in the northern hemisphere of Mars at approximately 41 degrees north latitude and 9.5 degrees west longitude.

The first person to notice the Face was Viking project scientist Tobias Owen, a member of NASA's imaging team.

Tobias Owen's first words after seeing the Face were, "Oh my God, look at this!"[3]

Viking project scientist Gary Soffen was the NASA official who initially spoke to the media about the Face. He told them, "Isn't it peculiar what tricks of lighting and shadow can do. When we took a picture a few hours later it all went away. It was just a trick, just the way the light fell on it."[4]

Experts now believe that the reason the Face "went away" (in the words of NASA spokesman Gary Soffen) a few hours after the initial photos were taken was not because the Face had been an illusion, but because the Martian night had fallen.

On July 31, 1976, NASA released the first photos of the Face and issued the following press release:

> This picture is one of many taken in the northern latitudes of Mars by the Viking 1 Orbiter in search of a landing site for Viking 2.
>
> The picture shows eroded mesa-like landforms. The huge rock formation in the center, which resembles a human head, is formed by shadows giving the illusion of eyes, nose and mouth. The feature is 1.5 kilometers (one mile) across, with the sun angle at approximately 20 degrees. The speckled appearance of the image is due to bit errors, emphasized by enlargement of the photo. The picture was taken on July 25 from a range of 1873 kilometers (1162 miles). Viking 2 will arrive in Mars orbit next Saturday (August 7) with a landing scheduled for early September.[5]

The Face on Mars has been said by some to resemble the Sphinx from ancient Egypt, leading inevitably to questions about the possible extraterrestrial origin of the Egyptian monuments and the connection between the monuments on Mars and Earth history.

Some believe that there was a horrible cataclysm on Mars that destroyed all civilization on the red planet and that the Face and the other Monuments were constructed as a warning to Earthlings that we may be in line for the same type of catastrophic destruction.

After the Face on Mars was discovered, the Cydonia region of Mars was declared unfit to be used as a landing area for Viking 2.

NASA said it was too hazardous, although the landing region ultimately chosen, Utopia, was deemed by NASA to be as dangerous for Viking 2 to land in as Cydonia, if not even more so.

Several miles southwest of the Face is a set of pyramidal structures that some believe are the abandoned components of an engineered, Martian city.

People who believe the Face on Mars is a sure sign that Mars was once inhabited point to several similarities between Mars and Earth, including:

- Mars's axis is tilted at an angle of 24.935 degrees in relation to the plane of its orbit around the Sun; the Earth's axis is tilted at an angle of 23.5 degrees in relation to the plane of its orbit around the Sun.

- Mars makes a complete rotation around its axis in 24 hours, 39 minutes, 36 seconds; the Earth makes a complete rotation in 23 hours, 56 minutes, 5 seconds.

- Mars and the Earth both manifest a cyclical wobble of their axis known as precession.

- Mars and the Earth both have the same non-spherical shape: Their poles are flattened and their equators bulge.

- Mars has four seasons; Earth has four seasons.

- Mars has icy polar caps; Earth has icy polar caps.

- Mars has deserts; Earth has deserts.

- Mars has dust-storms; Earth has dust-storms.

- Scientists have calculated that Mars's surface temperature was at one point during its existence about the same as that of the Earth's now.

In 1985, computer imaging analysis of photos of the Face by Mark Carlotto identified decorative crossing lines above the eyes that suggest a crown; teeth in the mouth of the object; and a very Egyptian-like striped headdress, similar to the ones worn by Egyptian pharaohs on Earth.

Richard Hoagland, author of *The Monuments of Mars*, asked the following rhetorical question about the possible existence on Mars of engineered Monuments, including the Face: "What better way to call attention to a specific place on Mars as a site for further exploration than by using a humanoid image?"[6]

According to astronomical calculations performed by Dr. Colin Pillinger of the UK Planetary Sciences Research Institute, up to one hundred tons of Martian material—in the form of meteorites and other Martian rocks—land on Earth each year.

Mars is now a dead planet. There is not even a remote possibility that it can now support life. Its average temperature is –23 degrees Celsius and water cannot survive there. On Mars, there is only ice. And yet there is geologic evidence (found in recovered Martian meteorites and on the Martian terrain) of enormous floods as recently as 600,000 years ago. And if there were floods, then Mars would have supported the existence of water, which, by extension, would have supported the existence of life. One recovered Martian meteorite actually contained a droplet of real water.

Other geological analyses of the surface of Mars point to evidence of ancient shorelines, all of which are quite close to the Cydonia region and to the Face on Mars. On Earth, villages and hamlets grew from settlements on the banks of rivers and lakes and by the sea. It does not take much imagination to visualize Martian colonies settling by the planet's long-gone waters, growing and developing, and ultimately constructing monuments and other structures.

Within ten miles of the Face is a five-sided pyramid now known as the D&M Pyramid, named after its discoverers Vincent DiPietro and Gregory Molenaar. Other structures on Mars that many believe to be engineered include monuments christened The Fort, The Cliff, and The City.

During his extensive research on the Face on Mars, Richard Hoagland used computers to come up with an astonishing fact. He discovered that a viewer standing at the center of the configuration of monuments known as The City would have seen the sun rising out of the mouth of the Cydonia Face at dawn on the Martian summer solstice 330,000 years ago.

NASA continues to insist that all of the so-called "Monuments on Mars" are completely natural geologic formations. In response to this assertion, California Institute of Technology professor of geology and planetary science Arden Albee said, "[A]s of yet, there is no natural geological explanation for the Cydonia Structures."[7]

In April 1998, NASA instructed its latest orbiter, Mars Global Surveyor, to make three passes over the Cydonia region. The first pass on April 5 captured the Face with astonishing accuracy—although at first the image appeared to be nothing more than a flat ridged area of the Martian terrain. After computer analysis and enhancement, it became obvious that the photo had been taken through clouds and was underprocessed. Mark Carlotto's computer imaging work with the photos later revealed even more detail of the Face, including nostrils.

Former NASA consultant and acclaimed astronomer Dr. Tom Van Flanders studied the new photos and issued the following statement:

"The humanoid facial features that first drew attention to this area are confirmed by this photo, despite poor lighting and poor viewing angle. Using the ability to change mental perspectives, one can see the object clearly, without imagining details, as an excellent rendition of a sculpted face. In my considered opinion, there is no longer room for reasonable doubt of the artificial origin of the race, and I've never concluded 'no room for reasonable doubt' about anything before in my thirty-five-year scientific career."[8]

Of the debatable quality of the second batch of NASA's Martian Cydonia photos, Richard Hoagland smelled a cover-up and stated the following on April 6, 1998 on the Art Bell radio program: "There is a picture tonight which is, yes, geographically and geometrically of the Face on Mars. Now, it's not anywhere near the kind of picture we should have gotten. It is light years below the level this camera and this technology is capable of giving us, so they're giving us the business, but it is a picture geometrically targeted correctly. So the first part of what I would want has happened. Now we know they can target. Now there's no reason they can't target the important stuff, which is the geometry in the city, the Pyramids, the material that is numerically testable, and that's what we should be demanding, and oh, by the way . . . take the lens cap off the camera. *Tell the media to face the truth!!!*"

Imaging specialists summed up the controversy surrounding the Face on Mars and the endless debate about what, if anything, is going on on the Red Planet: "We're just looking at pretty pictures. We don't know until we get there."[9]

[1] Some of the material in this chapter is based on research conducted for the author's 1998 book, *The UFO Book of Lists* (Kensington Publishing).

[2] From the "Publisher's Foreword" to Richard C. Hoagland's book, *The Monuments of Mars: A City on the Edge of Forever*.

[3] *The Monuments of Mars*, p. 4.

[4] Ibid., p. 5.

[5] NASA press release.

[6] *The Monuments of Mars*.

[7] *The Daily Mail*, May 9, 1998.

[8] *The Daily Mail*, May 9, 1998.

[9] PhoenixNewTimes.com, January 16, 2003.

36

Falls of Animals and Objects

HAIKU:

FALLS

Raining oddities
Falling from the sky like rain
But it is not rain

*On Wednesday before Easter, Anno 1666, a pasture field at
Cranstead near Wrotham in Kent, about Two Acres, which
is far from any part of the Sea or Branch of it, and a place
where there are no Fish Ponds, but a Scarcity of Water, was
all overspread with little fishes, conceived to be rained
down, there having been at that time a great Tempest of
Thunder and Rain; the Fishes were about the length of a
Man's little finger, and judged by all that saw them to be
young Whitings . . .*

—Dr. Robert Conny[1]

DEFINITION: Anomalous falls are sudden, sometimes sustained, downpours of animals, ice, and inanimate objects, seemingly in contradiction to the normal operations of nature.

WHAT THE BELIEVERS SAY: These weird rains are of supernatural origin and should be looked to as a sign of some kind. The "picked up by a whirlwind" theory does not explain how some rains consist of only one type of animal or fish. These odd falls are some type of message, and there is no way for traditional science to explain them.

WHAT THE SKEPTICS SAY: These rains are anything but supernatural, and can be explained scientifically. The most likely explanation is that objects or animals are picked up during freak windstorms and dropped a distance away from where they were taken.

QUALITY OF EXISTING EVIDENCE: Excellent.[2]

LIKELIHOOD PHENOMENA ARE PARANORMAL: Very high.[3]

In Stephen King's 1989 short story "Rainy Season," razor-toothed, carnivorous killer toads rain down on the small town of Willow, Maine every seven years, specifically on June 17th.[4] On that day, hapless, unwitting tourists visit Willow, are warned by the locals not to stay, ignore the warnings, and ultimately are eaten by the killer toads. Once the toads receive their sacrifice, they melt in the morning sun, and the townsfolk of Willow, Maine are thereafter assured of another seven years of peace.

The story is a fun, over-the-top thriller, but its basic premise—a strange rain of toads—is firmly grounded in reality.

Yes, animals and objects rain down from the skies above our planet, and there are countless accounts which, quite simply, cannot be explained rationally.

What has fallen from the sky? The following list was compiled from several sources. Many of these falls have not been satisfactorily explained.

- Algae
- Alligators
- Ants
- Axe heads
- Bags of cookies
- Bent coins
- Black rain
- Black snow
- Blood
- Bricks
- Buckshot
- Canaries
- Cannon balls
- Caterpillars
- Cats and kittens
- Crosses
- Dogs
- Ducks (canvasbacks, redheads, and scaups)
- Eels

- Fish (smelt, bass, shad, whitefish, flounder, catfish, and herring)
- Frogs
- Glass
- Golf balls
- Grain
- Green slime
- Hazelnuts
- Hermit crabs
- Ice (hail-sized to elephant-sized, half-ton chunks)
- Insects
- Jellyfish
- Lemmings
- Lichen
- Limestone
- Lizards
- Mice
- Monkeys
- Moth eggs
- Mussels
- Nails
- Nuts and bolts
- Oyster shells
- Paper money
- Periwinkles
- Pieces of flesh (kidney, liver, and heart)
- Plants
- Rats
- Red rain
- Redbud seeds
- Rocks (pebble- to baseball-sized)
- Salamanders
- Sand
- Scarabs
- Snakes
- Spiders
- Straw
- Sulfur ("rains of fire")
- Toads
- Turtles
- Woodpeckers
- Worms
- Yellow rain
- Zinc

What theories have been floated in an attempt to explain these documented falls?

The Roman scholar and naturalist Pliny believed that living things that fell from the sky were spontaneously generated in rain. (Spontaneous generation was a common belief until the seventeenth century.) We now know enough about cellular theory and parthenogenesis to rule out that explanation.

Anomalous weather phenomena can explain many of these bizarre occurrences. Whirlwinds, waterspouts, tornadoes, windstorms, hurricanes, etc., have been known to pick things up off the ground, carry them a distance away, and then unceremoniously drop them, sometimes on unsuspecting people in the wrong place at the wrong time. Coffins have fallen from the sky, as have all manner of household items, including appliances, clothing, and clocks.

Yet there are accounts of strange falls that cannot be explained by the notion of a tornado picking things up in one place and dropping them someplace else. For instance, in May 1981, frogs from North Africa fell on Greece. Did a tornado or whirlwind of some sort pick up frogs from Egypt, Libya, or Algeria, carry them across the Mediterranean Sea, and deposit them on the Greek mainland? Were a multitude of creatures carried en masse across three hundred miles of open water?

Also, how can the "weird weather" theories explain the selective nature of the things or animals dropped? It is not uncommon to find thousands of the *same type* of fish or frog dropped on a locality.

What about an extraterrestrial explanation?

Charles Fort posited that anomalous falls were from interstellar, extraterrestrial wrecks (although he was not being serious at the time). Are UFOs dropping all manner of detritus and creatures as they leave our atmosphere? Are aliens picking up thousands of frogs, and then unceremoniously dropping them wherever they bloody well please?

What about comets and meteorites?

Perhaps these can explain some of the falls of metallic particles or even ice, but, again, there are simply far too many truly bizarre downpours for such a simple explanation. Some chunks of ice that fell from the sky have later been determined to be waste material from an airplane's toilet. But what about six-foot long rods of ice that plunge down out of the sky, piercing roofs and, in one case, killing a German man who was working on a roof?

There are some weird happenings on this planet of ours, and some of these events are like something—oh, out of a Stephen King story.

[1] From a letter to Dr. Robert Plot, published in 1698 in the British Royal Society's journal, *Philosophical Transactions*.

[2] In this case, we are using "Excellent" to evaluate the quality of physical evidence—the documentation of weird falls is voluminous.

[3] In this case, we are stating that there is a very high likelihood that these phenomena are *real*; i.e., it indisputably happens. The fact that some of these falls cannot be scientifically explained, yet may not have a paranormal genesis, however, leaves the definitive answer regarding these anomalous falls as unknown.

[4] The historical literature is filled with stories of frogs and toads falling from the sky. A rain of toads fell on Toulouse, France in August 1804 and *tens of thousands* of toads fell on Brignoles, France on September 23, 1973. Frogs fell on Kansas City, Missouri on July 12, 1873. Toads fell on London in July 1838, and also in 1921. Also in 1921, frogs rained down on Anton Wagner's farm in Stirling, Connecticut on July 31st. Little almost-white frogs fell on Birmingham, England on June 30, 1892. There was a rain of toads on Chalon-sur-Saône, France in 1922. It is not known if any of these stories provided Stephen King with the inspiration for "Rainy Season."

37

Fire Immunity and Firewalking

HAIKU:

FIREWALKING

Hot glowing embers
Bare feet standing on the grass
Until the first step

*Can a man take fire in his bosom, and his clothes not
  be burned?*
Can one go upon hot coals, and his feet not be burned?

—Proverbs 6:27–8

*Fire has always been and, seemingly, will always remain,
the most terrible of the elements. To the early tribes it must
also have been the most mysterious; for, while earth and air
and water were always in evidence, fire came and went in
a manner which must have been quite unaccountable
to them.*

—Harry Houdini[1]

DEFINITION: Fire immunity and firewalking, while related, are two different things. **Fire immunity** is the (seemingly impossible) ability of certain individuals to not be injured by live fire. They hold it, they put it in their mouth, they place their face and hands in it without harm. **Firewalking** is the practice of deliberately walking barefoot over hot coals—embers smoldering at temperatures up to 1,500 degrees Fahrenheit.

WHAT THE BELIEVERS SAY: Firewalking is a transcendent (as in the sense of "beyond normal perception") spiritual ritual. The preparation for the ceremony, and the actual walking itself, summon paranormal abilities in many (although not all) people. It is a life-changing experience which teaches people to face and vanquish fear in their lives.

WHAT THE SKEPTICS SAY: Firewalking is a learned skill. Although it can be dangerous, it usually is not, and there is nothing supernatural or paranormal about it.

QUALITY OF EXISTING EVIDENCE: Excellent.[2]

LIKELIHOOD PHENOMENA ARE PARANORMAL: LOW.

In Fiji, male firewalkers are forbidden to have sex or eat coconuts for two weeks before walking on hot coals. Also, a Fijian man is forbidden to firewalk if his wife is pregnant.

In Sri Lanka, firewalkers must pray, fast, meditate, chant, take many baths, and abstain from sex before walking on the coals.

In the United States, firewalking has evolved into a corporate bonding ritual, now regularly practiced at seminars and retreats to instill confidence in employees, and bond them together as having literally "walked through the fire" together. All of this will hopefully result in greater productivity and loyalty to the company.[3]

These are all examples of some of the ritualistic preparations attached to the act of walking on hot coals, and they illustrate the commonly held belief that firewalking is a transcendent experience; that it is uplifting, enriching, and empowering; that it allows people to understand how they face fear, and then make the necessary changes in their life to vanquish indecision and doubt.

Is firewalking a transcendent experience? Does it summon paranormal abilities perhaps latent in us all? Does the mind somehow change the very essence of people's feet so that the hot coals will not burn them?

We now know that the answer to these questions is *no*. But that is not the end of the discussion. Experienced firewalkers claim they enter almost a trancelike state during a firewalk. Using a discipline akin to self-hypnosis, they elevate their tolerance to pain, they maintain a placid heart rate and blood pressure, they eliminate transient thoughts and concentrate only on putting one foot in front of the other and reaching the end of the bed of coals or embers. People who have firewalked many times report that the only times they were burned was when they lost their concentration. Consciousness researcher John White describes the state of mind he experienced during his first firewalk:

> My mind was Zenlike: free from thought and mental chatter, focused clearly on the physical aspects of the event, observing without comment, performing without fear. Because of my years in consciousness research, I can say I wasn't in trance or anything like it. No one else reported being in trance, as far as I heard later. Inasmuch as there was an altered state of consciousness in me, it was simply pristine mental clarity, backed by a willingness—a positive mental attitude—to flow with the experience, no matter what.[4]

So do these people summon paranormal powers? After all, they are using mental powers not readily present in most people during their daily lives. Most people experience pain when injured, and experience elevated heart rates and blood pressure when they are stressed or threatened. Firewalkers are able to transcend (there's that word again) these physical responses and walk across glowing embers hot enough to melt a car's aluminum engine block.

So the answer to whether or not firewalking is a paranormal ability lies in one's subjective interpretation of the source of elevated psychic skills.

Are they purely mind over matter? Science says yes, and they have reams of research explaining how yogis who can control their body temperature, breathing, and pulse actually do what they do.

They can explain precisely what happens in the body and, thus, conclude that if one human can do it, all humans can theoretically do it, but, like other learned skills, it takes time and effort.

The more spiritually minded, though, reject the purely empirical evaluation of these abilities and many claim to tap into a higher power in order to do what they do. Prayer and secular affirmations are often the operative engines for entering the state needed for walking over hot coals. They will ardently credit faith that they can accomplish their goals as being the reason they *do* accomplish their goals.

Faith.

But the wood used for firewalking is a poor conductor of heat.

And the feet of the walkers hardly touch the burning embers.

And the bed of coals is very uneven, which means that very little of the surface of the foot actually makes contact with the hot embers.

But . . .

The scientific explanations for the immunity to injury firewalkers manifest when they walk are all true. Yet firewalking has been practiced for centuries all over the world in countless cultures and has almost always been perceived as a religious ritual.

A *religious* ritual. Not a parlor trick designed to entertain and "wow" an audience.

Mind over matter?

Unquestionably.

The mystery, however, lies in the source of the power that allows a walker to control his mind so that the heat doesn't matter.

Once again, as we have seen with many of the phenomena in this volume, the true answer regarding the reality of firewalking comes down to a matter of *faith*.

POSTSCRIPT

True fire immunity is very rare and there is usually some kind of bizarre physiological explanation for those people who can handle fire with seeming impunity. But there are also countless ways of hoaxing fire immunity and many of the anecdotal accounts that have come down through the years are probably untrue.

[1] *The Miracle Mongers and Their Methods.*

[2] The literature is replete with scientific studies proving that what seems like an impossible act (walking on hot coals without getting burned) is understood and explainable, and nothing more than a function of heat conductivity and the rapidity of the firewalker's stride.

[3] Unfortunately, such high-minded goals are not always realized. Some employees with Kentucky Fried Chicken and Burger King received serious burns on their feet while firewalking during a corporate retreat.

[4] *The Meeting of Science and Spirit*, pp. 52–3.

38

Flat Earth

HAIKU:

FLAT EARTH

A flat disk in space
Wanderers beware the edge
Into what you fall?

The facts are simple, the earth is flat. You can't orbit a flat earth. . . . The Space Shuttle is a joke—and a very ludicrous joke. Nobody knows anything about the true shape of the world . . . The known, inhabited world is flat. Just as a guess, I'd say that the dome of heaven is about 4,000 miles away, and the stars are about as far as San Francisco is from Boston. Wherever you find people with a great reservoir of common sense, they don't believe idiotic things such as the earth spinning around the sun. Reasonable, intelligent people have always recognized that the earth is flat.

—Charles K. Johnson[1]

DEFINITION: "Flat Earthers" believe that the planet Earth is a flat disk floating in space, and that it is possible to fall off the edges of the planet.

WHAT THE BELIEVERS SAY: The Earth is flat.

WHAT THE SKEPTICS SAY: Don't be ridiculous. The earth is round.

QUALITY OF EXISTING EVIDENCE: Negligible.

LIKELIHOOD PHENOMENON IS PARANORMAL: Nil.

There are some proponents of the flat earth doctrine who do *not* believe the world is flat. They use their renouncement of proven, accepted science as a "rage against the machine"-type protest against blanket acceptance of what the authority structures of a society put forth as fact. The government, educational institutions, miscellaneous scientific endeavors—all are fair game for these symbolic, "anti-everything" Flat Earthers.

But then there are the *true* Flat Earthers, those folks who still hold to the belief that the earth is a disk, not a globe. The most notable proponent of this belief was the late Charles K. Johnson, the founder of the International Flat Earth Research Society.

From the IFERS' brochure:

Aim: To carefully observe, think freely, rediscover forgotten fact, and oppose theoretical dogmatic assumptions. To help establish the United States . . . of the world on this flat earth. Replace the science religion . . . with SANITY.

The International Flat Earth Society is the oldest continuous Society existing on the world today. It began with the Creation of the Creation. First the water . . . the face of the deep . . . without form or limits . . . just Water. Then the Land sitting in and on the Water, the Water then as now being flat and level, as is the very Nature of Water. There are, of course, mountains and valleys on the Land but since most of the World is Water, we say, "The World is Flat." Historical accounts and spoken history tell us the Land part may have been square, all in one mass at one time, then as now, the magnetic north being the Center. Vast cataclysmic events and shaking no doubt broke the land apart, divided the Land to be our present continents or islands as they exist today. One thing we know for sure about this world . . . the known inhabited world is Flat, Level, a Plain World. The Fact the Earth is Flat is not my opinion, it is a Proved Fact. Also demonstrated Sun and Moon are about

3,000 miles away are both 32 miles across. The Planets are "tiny." Sun and Moon do Move, earth does NOT move, whirl, spin or gyrate. Australians do NOT hang by their feet under the world . . . this is a FACT, not a theory!

As Monty Pythonesque as this tirade reads, Charles Johnson was completely serious when he wrote it, and he was completely serious about his beliefs throughout his tenure as President of the IFERS.

Johnson was at the forefront of Flat Earth philosophy and was the main proponent of the contradictory paradox espoused by serious supporters of the theory: Flat Earthers, rejecting science as a hoax, cite passages in the Bible as irrefutable evidence that the Earth is flat, and yet they then resort to convoluted pseudoscientific arguments to prove their point.[2]

Isaiah 11:12 is often referred to as a key passage supporting the Flat Earthism:

> He will set up an ensign for the nations, and will assemble the outcasts of Israel, and gather together the dispersed of Judah from the four corners of the earth.

How can a globe-shaped planet have four corners? the Flat Earthers ask. And since, to them, literal interpretation of the Bible is, of course, a given, this passage is God's confirmation to Man that the Earth is flat.

Flat Earthers also cite Ezekiel 7:2: "You, son of man, thus says the Lord Yahweh to the land of Israel, An end: the end is come on the four corners of the land"; and Revelation 7:1: "After this, I saw four angels standing at the four corners of the earth, holding the four winds of the earth, so that no wind would blow on the earth, or on the sea, or on any tree." There are many other references in the Bible to the Earth having four corners, and Flat Earthers point to them with satisfaction that they need not defend their position, since God has already done it for them.[3]

But what about science, and satellite photos, and space travel, and the Moon landings, and computer mapping, and the Hubbell telescope?

All lies!

NASA, the United States government, and many governments of other nations around the world are all in on the hoax and people at the highest levels have known the truth for decades: the Earth is not a globe, it does not spin, and space travel has never been successfully accomplished.

On second thought, Monty Python was never so ridiculous.

[1] From "The Flat-out Truth: Earth Orbits? Moon Landings? A Fraud! Says This Prophet" by Robert J. Schadewald, *Science Digest*, July 1980. The article can be found online at http://www.lhup.edu/~dsimanek/fe-scidi.htm.

[2] At http://www.geocities.com/lclane2/hundreda.html, you will find a reprint of the September 1889 pamphlet, "A Hundred Proofs the Earth is Not a Globe" by William Carpenter, which states the most common "scientific" proofs of Flat Earthism.

[3] See http://www.ethicalatheist.com/docs/flat_earth_myth_ch5.html for a detailed time line of Flat Earth beliefs throughout seven thousand years of history.

39

Ghosts, Poltergeists, Haunted Places, and Apparitions

HAIKU:

GHOSTS

Spectral forms appear
Transparent shapes of shades
From the realm of death

What beck'ning ghost, along the moonlight shade
Invites my step, and points to yonder glade?

—Alexander Pope[1]

DEFINITION: A **ghost** or a **poltergeist** is the spirit of a dead person; a **haunted place** is a location frequented by ghosts; an **apparition** is the visual image of a ghost seen by we earth-dwelling mortals.

WHAT THE BELIEVERS SAY: Ghosts are real, and they are everywhere. People have seen them for eons and it is highly unlikely that *every single sighting* was bogus.

WHAT THE SKEPTICS SAY: There are no such things as ghosts.

QUALITY OF EXISTING EVIDENCE: Very good.

LIKELIHOOD PHENOMENA ARE PARANORMAL: High.

THE NIGHT VISITOR

"Forgive us for awakening you, sir, but we come on a matter of great importance."

The old man in bedclothes stared at the two young men who had knocked on his door in the middle of the night.

"Who are you?" he asked, a combination of anger and fear in his voice.

"I am Jacopo Alighieri, son of the poet Dante. This is my friend."

The man's face softened at the mention of the great poet's name.

"Ah, Signore Alighieri. My condolences on the loss of your father. I have always considered it an honor to live in the house in which he spent so many years."

"Thank you, sir," Jacopo replied with respect. "It is because this was my father's house that we visit you this night."

"Come in, come in."

The two men entered the house and Jacopo then told the man of his dream.

"Good sir, my father Dante appeared to me in my dreams this very evening. He was clothed in the purest white and his face shone with a resplendent light. I asked him if he lived, and he replied, 'Yes, but in the true life, not your life.'"

The man remained silent, a look of awe on his face.

"I then asked him if he had completed all of his life's work before he passed into the true life, and he said to me, 'Yes, I finished it.' I then asked him what became of the final thirteen cantos of his *Divine Comedy*, which are missing from the manuscript."

The man nodded. Dante's *Commedia* was known by all.

"My father then took me by the hand, and we traveled to the room in which my father slept in this very house. Yes, good sir, I was here this evening, although not in the form in which you see me now."

The man gasped, but said nothing.

"My father touched one of the walls in the room and said to me, 'What you have sought so much is here.' And then I awakened. I called my friend and, thus, here we are."

The man was silent a moment and then said, "You wish to visit the room."

Jacopo nodded and the man led the way into the master bedroom.

Jacopo walked immediately to the wall his father had touched and found there a hanging mat. He lifted the mat. Behind it was a small compartment. The owner of the house grasped his chest and made the sign of the cross. "Mi dios!" he said softly. He obviously had not known of the existence of the compartment. Jacopo reached in and withdrew a sheaf of papers, which he immediately saw were the missing cantos.

Thanks to the ghost of Dante, the *Divine Comedy* was now complete.[2]

The belief in ghosts has been around for as long as man has possessed bicameral consciousness.

It is likely that the earliest cave dwellers imagined the spirits of their dead kin watching them in the darkness.

People from every culture on Earth have attempted to communicate with the dead; some societies venerate the spirits of their ancestors, pray to them, and ask for their help.

Are ghosts real?

Do the spirits of the dead visit our earthly realm?

Are certain places haunted?

If ghosts are not real, then how can we explain documented poltergeist activity in which chairs fly across the room, pictures spin on the walls, and dishes crash to the floor without being touched?

How can we explain the ghost photographs that remain after we rule out the hoaxes, camera errors, and natural phenomena?

Ghost sightings are akin to UFO sightings. So many people see them, it strains credulity to believe that 100 percent of them are wrong.

What are ghosts and why do they insist on hanging around on Earth?

Theories abound as to the nature and purpose of ghosts. Some ghosts remain and make contact with the living to warn them of danger. Some ghosts linger because they were killed suddenly and their astral selves did not have time to assimilate the transition from life on the earthly plane to life in the realm of the dead. These ghosts need, in essence, to be given permission to let go of their attachment to earth and move on.

Some ghosts are evil, and deliberately try to hurt the living or frighten them out of their wits. Some of these beings manifest themselves through poltergeist activity. They throw the chairs, they spin the pictures, they drip blood from the ceiling, and create other unsettling occurrences, but they do not allow themselves to be seen.

There is a bit of an overlap between the concepts of demonic possession and ghostly infestation. The biggest difference is that ghosts are usually seen in the bodily likeness of their living self. Demons are more elementally evil and usually do not use a body image to appear to humans.

I have never seen a ghost. I have seen a UFO and what I believe to be an authentic crop circle, but never a spectral visitor. Stephen King admitted once that he saw the ghost of an old man in the bedroom of a house he was visiting as he entered to retrieve his and his wife's coats.

Today, there are countless books detailing the location of haunted places all over the world.

None of this means anything to the skeptics. The belief in ghosts is rejected completely as nothing but delusional thinking.

I suppose these people find comfort in believing that they are 100 percent correct—that they know with absolute certainty all that is, and all that isn't.

Knowing everything there is to know, and being able to tell others why they're wrong is quite an achievement, wouldn't you agree?

[1] *Elegy to the Memory of an Unfortunate Lady* (1717) 1.1.
[2] After an account in *Life of Dante* by Giovanni Boccaccio.

40

Hollow Earth[1]

HAIKU:

HOLLOW EARTH

Hollow shell in space
Floating ball of emptiness
Secrets lie within?

It is [my] purpose to present scientific evidence to prove that the Earth, rather than being a solid sphere with a fiery center of molten metal, as generally supposed, is really hollow, with openings at its poles. Also, in its hollow interior exists an advanced civilization which is the creator of flying saucers.

—Dr. Raymond Bernard[2]

DEFINITION: The belief that the planet Earth is a hollow sphere, and that the interior of the earth is honeycombed with chambers, tunnels, and roads, and has its own atmosphere, ecosystem, and vegetation. Some Hollow Earthers also believe that the inside of the planet is populated by beings that may be responsible for all the UFOs sightings on Earth.

WHAT THE BELIEVERS SAY: There is a world inside our world.

WHAT THE SKEPTICS SAY: Nonsense. The Earth is not hollow and only its surface is habitable.

QUALITY OF EXISTING EVIDENCE: Negligible.

LIKELIHOOD PHENOMENON IS PARANORMAL: Nil.

The August 2002 issue of *Discover* magazine featured an article on the possibility of a naturally occurring nuclear power source—a gigantic subterranean cache of solid uranium—at the center of the Earth, four thousand miles beneath our feet.

It is probably a safe bet that Hollow Earthers were not pleased with this article, and quite possibly completely rejected its thesis.

The Earth is, after all, hollow, so how can there be such a solid core in a vacant space?

The Hollow Earth Theory is one of the more fanciful theories of UFOlogy.

Hollow Earth theory states that the Earth is really a hollow sphere and inside this massive globe are rivers, mountains, forests, and most significantly, intelligent civilizations—"super races"—that are the source of many of the UFO sightings seen in the skies above our planet.

As with fringe UFO theories like Bigfoot and others, there are also Hollow Earth "experts." One of the most notable is the above-quoted Dr. Raymond Bernard (the pen name of Walter Siegmeister), author of a most momentously titled book.

Science has proven that the Earth's core is molten and that life can not survive *inside* the planet. And yet, the Hollow Earthers cite a plethora of "evidence" denying these findings. They wholeheartedly believe that the world governments know the truth and that the "scientific findings" about the Earth's molten core are nothing but government disinformation.

Here are two excerpts—the thirteen principles—that spell out the specifics of this bizarre theory. This list is from Dr. Bernard's book and is titled, "What This Book Seeks To Prove."

1. The Earth is hollow and not a solid sphere as commonly supposed, and that its hollow interior communicates with the surface by two polar openings.

2. The observations and discoveries of Rear Admiral Richard E. Byrd of the United States Navy, who was the first to enter into the polar openings, which he did for a total distance of four thousand miles in the Arctic and Antarctic, confirm the correctness of our revolutionary theory of the Earth's structure, as do the observations of other Arctic explorers.

3. According to our geographical theory of the Earth being concave, rather than convex at the Poles, where it opens into its hollow interior, the North and South Poles have never been reached because they do not exist.

4. The exploration of the unknown New World that exists in the interior of the Earth is much more important than the exploration of outer space; and the aerial expeditions of Admiral Byrd show how much exploration may be conducted.

5. The nation whose explorers first reach this New World in the hollow interior of the Earth, which has a land mass greater than that of the Earth's surface, which may be done by retracing Admiral Byrd's flights beyond the hypothetical North and South Poles, into the Arctic and Antarctic polar openings, will become the greatest nation in the world.

6. There is no reason why the hollow interior of the Earth, which has a warmer climate than on the surface, should not be the home of plant, animal and human life; and if so, it is very possible that the mysterious flying saucers come from an advanced civilization in the hollow interior of the Earth.

7. In event of a nuclear world war, the hollow interior of the Earth will permit the continuance of human life after radioactive fallout exterminates all life in the Earth's surface; and will provide an ideal refuge for the evacuation of survivors of the catastrophe, so that the human race may not be completely destroyed, but may continue.

After stating his intentions with the above seven points, Dr. Bernard then proceeds to provide proof of his theories, utilizing scientific fact and theory, ancient writings, and NASA photographs. Dr. Bernard concludes his book by summing up his theory with the following six points:

1. There is really no North or South Pole. Where they are supposed to exist there are really wide openings to the hollow interior of the Earth.

2. Flying saucers come from the hollow interior of the Earth through these polar openings.

3. The hollow interior of the Earth, warmed by its central Sun (the source of Aurora Borealis) has an ideal subtropical climate of about seventy-six degrees in temperature, neither too hot nor too cold.

4. Arctic explorers found the temperature to rise as they traveled far north; they found more open seas; they found animals traveling north in winter, seeking food and warmth, when they should have gone south; they found the compass needle to assume a vertical position instead of a horizontal one and to become extremely eccentric; they saw tropical birds and more animal life the farther north they went; they saw butterflies, mosquitoes and other insects in the extreme north, when they were not found until as far south as Alaska and Canada; they found the snow discolored by colored pollen and black dust, which became worse the farther north they went. The only explanation is that this dust came from active volcanoes in the polar opening.

5. There is a large population inhabiting the inner concave surface of the Earth's crust, composing a civilization far in advance of our own in its scientific achievements, which probably descended from the sunken continents of Lemuria and Atlantis. Flying saucers are only one of their many achievements. It would be to our advantage to contact these Elder Brothers of the human race, learn from them and receive their advice and aid.

6. The existence of a polar opening and land beyond the Poles is probably known to the U.S. Navy in whose employ Admiral Byrd made his two historic flights and which is probably a top international secret.[3]

There are reportedly many entrances to this inner world. They are scattered all over the Earth, and some of the more well-known locations include:

- Secret entrances at the North and South Poles;
- In Zimbabwe at the site of the legendary King Solomon's Mines;
- Mount Epomeo, Italy;
- Mount Shasta in California (reportedly, the Agharthean city of Telos exists beneath this mountain);

- Somewhere in Manaus, Brazil;
- Somewhere in Rama, India (apparently, the legendary subterranean city also called Rama lies beneath this Indian city);
- Somewhere in the Dero Caves (Indonesia?);
- Somewhere in the Giza Pyramid in Egypt;
- Somewhere on the border between Mongolia and China Mongolia (reportedly, the underground city of Shingwa exists somewhere beneath this border);
- The Himalayan Mountains in Tibet (supposedly, the entrance to the underground city of Shonshe is hidden in these mountains and vigilantly guarded by Hindu monks);
- The Iguaçú Falls on the border between Brazil and Argentina;
- The Kentucky Mammoth Cave, in south-central Kentucky in the United States;
- The Mato Grosso plain in Brazil (reportedly, the city of Posid lies beneath Mato Grosso).

The notion of a hollow earth has appeared in countless novels, short stories, and movies, most notably, Jules Verne's *Journey to the Center of the Earth*. Science may have completely disproved the possibility of the existence of such a place, yet, as is often the case with delusional zealotry, the facts are never allowed to get in the way of what a theory's proponents want to believe.

[1] Some of the material in this chapter originally appeared in my 2001 book, *The UFO Book of Lists* (Kensington Publishing).

[2] Dr. Raymond Bernard, *The Hollow Earth: The Greatest Geographical Discovery in History*.

[3] Excerpts drawn from *The Hollow Earth: The Greatest Geographical Discovery in History* (Citadel Press) by Raymond Bernard. ©1969 University Books Inc. Used by permission. All rights reserved.

41

Immanuel Velikovsky and His Theories

HAIKU:

VELIKOVSKY

Worlds in collision
A ridiculous theory?
Tales of Jupiter

The Greeks as well as the Carians and other peoples on the shores of the Aegean Sea told of a time when the sun was driven off its course and disappeared for an entire day. . . . The disturbance in the movement of the sun was followed by a period as long as a day, when the sun did not appear at all. Ovid continues: "If we are to believe the report, one whole day went without the sun. But the burning world gave light."[1]

DEFINITION: Velikovsky proposed that ancient mythological tales were metaphorical accounts of real cosmological events.

WHAT THE BELIEVERS SAY: Velikovsky's work has great validity; it broke new ground, and it was unfairly excoriated by the scientific community.

WHAT THE SKEPTICS SAY: Velikovsky's work has no scientific ground-ing and is nothing but fanciful speculation without any evidence to support it. His followers are uninformed sycophants.

QUALITY OF EXISTING EVIDENCE: Poor.

LIKELIHOOD PHENOMENA ARE AUTHENTIC: Nil.

It sounds like a bad science fiction plot.

Thirty-five hundred years ago, part of Jupiter exploded off the planet and went hurtling through space as a gigantic comet. This comet traveled through our solar system, bumping planets out of their existing orbits and into new rotations, and passing close enough to Earth to envelop us in its gaseous tail. Dust from the Venus comet's tail caused fires and plagues on Earth, and eventually, the gravity of the comet caused the Earth to stop spinning on its axis, and then later restart its rotation. As might be expected from such a devastating cosmological event, the Earth experienced unimaginable tidal waves, earthquakes, volcanic activity, and geological upheavals, including the sinking of Atlantis and the crumbling to dust of enor-mous mountains. Additionally, during its travels, the comet Venus also threw Mars out of its orbit, causing a series of near-collisions between the Earth and Mars. These incredible galactic events also caused the Sun to disappear and nights and days to last many times longer than normal.

Venus the comet then solidified into a planetary body, and trav-eled past the Earth to settle into the orbit where the second planet from the Sun is today.

But all this is not a scenario gleaned from some obscure sci-fi novel or movie. This account of the ordering of our solar system was presented as scientific fact by Immanuel Velikovsky, except that the buttressing proofs of his outlandish theory were anything but scien-tific. Velikovsky used ancient legends, myths, and written traditions to arrive at conclusions that literally shocked the world and created enormous controversy in the scientific community.

Catastrophism is the geological theory which posits that major changes in the Earth's crust are a result of sudden catastrophes— earthquakes, volcanoes, tectonic shifts, etc.—rather than gradual, evo-lutionary changes and processes. This theory was originally proposed in the eighteenth century by the French naturalist Baron Georges Cuvier, but by the nineteenth century, it was largely discarded in favor of the belief that slow, continuing processes were responsible for major geological changes on earth.

Immanuel Velikovsky (1895–1979), a doctor, psychoanalyst, and astronomer born in Russia in 1895, resurrected Catastrophism in 1950 with the publication of his first book, *Worlds in Collision*, but he applied the theory to the cosmos, specifically to the events resulting in the formation of our Solar System as we know it today.

In his best-selling book, Velikovsky stated that the planet Venus did not exist until 1500 B.C., and that it was originally a comet that was ejected from the planet Jupiter.

Velikovsky studied very old writings, including the Old Testament, and myths from China, India, Greece, and Rome, and arrived at scientific conclusions by interpreting events described in these legends and myths as ambitious attempts by the ancients to describe real cosmological events. For instance, Greek mythology tells the story of Athena, the goddess of wisdom and warfare, springing full-blown from the head of Zeus, the ruler of the heavens. Velikovsky came to the dubious conclusion that Athena was the planet Venus, Zeus was the planet Jupiter, and the legend was a metaphorical way for the ancient Greeks to describe the breaking away from Jupiter of the comet that would eventually settle into orbit as Venus.

Robert Todd Carroll, writing in his *The Skeptic's Dictionary*, sums up the problem with the Russian's maverick's theories:

> The essence of Velikovsky's unreasonableness lies in the fact that he does not provide scientific evidence for his most extravagant claims. His claims are based on assuming cosmological facts must conform to mythology. In general, he offers no support for the plausibility of his theory beyond an ingenious argument from comparative mythology. Of course, his scenario is logically possible, in the sense that it is not self-contradictory. To be scientifically plausible, however, Velikovsky's theory must provide some compelling reason for accepting it other than the fact that it helps explain some events described in the Bible or makes Mayan legends fit with Egyptian ones.[2]

The scientific community did not respond well to the publication of *Worlds in Collision*.

The book was originally published by Macmillan, a publishing company that also has a textbook division. Many of Macmillan's textbook authors and editors boycotted the company following the publication of Velikovsky's book, refusing to work on textbooks until the company disavowed Velikovsky. The company buckled and turned Velikovsky's contract over to Doubleday, which did not have a textbook line.

Controversial theories and ideas are commonplace in the scientific arena, and Velikovsky's theories could easily have been quietly dismissed by the leaders in the field but for one unexpected development: the popular success of Velikovsky's books. With *Worlds in Collision* topping the best-seller lists all around the world, Velikovsky could not be so easily dismissed. His theories are still being debated today, yet even the staunchest anti-Velikovskians grudgingly admit that he did get some things right, including the fact that Jupiter emits radiowaves, that moon rocks are magnetic, and that Venus does rotate backwards on its axis.

A close friend of mine met with Velikovsky at Velikovsky's home in 1979, the year the Russian scientist died. My friend's recollection of the then-eighty-four-year-old scholar was of a quiet, almost somber man; an intellectual firebrand who seemed to be taking stock of his life and work; a challenger of conventions who maintained full faith and confidence in his beliefs. Perhaps the decades of pillorying had taken its toll on Velikovsky in this twilight time. "I do not recall him smiling even once during our visit," my friend said.

[1] Immanuel Velikovsky, *Worlds in Collision*, pp. 153, 155.
[2] Robert Todd Carroll, *The Skeptic's Dictionary* (http://www.skepdic.com), np.

42

Incorrupt Corpses

HAIKU:

INCORRUPT CORPSES

Her pristine body
Lying incorrupt in death
Signs of holiness?

The trumpet shall sound, and the dead shall be raised incorruptible.

—1 Corinthians 15:51

DEFINITION: Incorruptibility is the absence of decay in dead human bodies, or parts of bodies, for weeks, months, and even years (sometimes centuries), most remarkably in bodies buried without being embalmed, and in graves in which rapid deterioration would be expected.

WHAT THE BELIEVERS SAY: Incorrupt corpses are signs from God of the holiness of the deceased person, and are also a call to holiness for the faithful.

WHAT THE SKEPTICS SAY: Incorruptibility is a combination of many mundane biological and geological factors, none of which are divine. The temperature, amount of oxygen, and absence or presence of bacteria and fungus all play a role in how long it will take for a body to decay. Plus, it could be possible that the Catholic Church secretly embalmed many "incorruptibles" to foster a widespread acceptance of their divinity.

QUALITY OF EXISTING EVIDENCE: Fair.

LIKELIHOOD PHENOMENA ARE AUTHENTIC: Fair.

Flesh rots.

Once the spark of life is removed from a human body, the rush towards decay is inevitable. Once the warm, gushing, oxygen-carrying blood ceases to flow, and the body's organs are deprived of their sine qua non, then it isn't long before the body is absorbed into the biosphere, this time on the *inanimate* side of the living/dead paradigm.

Such decay can be forestalled, of course, through embalming, refrigeration, and entombment in oxygen-tight vaults. Exhumed bodies buried thousands of years ago have shown remarkably good preservation.

But flesh rots. And eventually, all that is living will die, and all that is dead will become dust. It can take eons or even longer, as evidenced by the recovery of the bodies of intact prehistoric mastodons, preserved only because they were quick frozen in ice shortly after death.

The Catholic Church has long allowed the veneration of the corpses, and even the individual body parts such as hands or hearts, of the holy deceased.

One of the most revered incorruptibles is St. Bernadette Soubirous, the saint to whom the Blessed Virgin Mary reportedly appeared at Lourdes, France in 1858. Bernadette died in 1879 at the age of thirty-five. She was buried as she died, without being embalmed or preserved in any way.

Bernadette's body was exhumed in 1909, thirty years after her death. According to witnesses, there was almost no sign of decay, other than the note that her body was somewhat "emaciated." Her lips had receded slightly so that her teeth were partly visible, and her nose had shrunk a little. Her hands were reportedly perfectly preserved, and her skin was a dull white color. The rosary she held had rusted. Her clothing was damp, but her body exuded no odor of putrefaction. Nuns removed her garments, bathed her body, and dressed her in a clean habit. She was then reburied, along with a document detailing the specifics of the exhumation.

Ten years later, with movement toward Bernadette's canonization progressing at a rapid pace (she was eventually canonized St. Bernadette in 1925), her body was again exhumed. She was found to be as well preserved as she had been ten years prior, except for a slight discoloration of the skin of her face, which was attributed to it being washed during the first exhumation. She was again reburied, in the presence of the Bishop.

In 1925, the year of her canonization, the body of Bernadette was exhumed one final time.

This time, her body would not be reburied, but put on display for all the faithful to see and venerate.

A thin mask of wax was made to cover her face and hands, since her eyes and cheeks had sunk somewhat. There is also rumor that her body was injected with embalming fluid to prevent further decay, although this has not been substantiated and none of the sworn statements taken of the doctors, nuns, and witnesses following the exhumations speak of anything protective being done outside of washing the body.

In addition to washing and preparing the body for viewing, however, the doctors, at the request of the Bishop of Neves, also performed surgery on Bernadette's body. They removed the rear section of her fifth and sixth ribs; pieces of her diaphragm and liver (which was reportedly soft and "almost normal" in consistency); her two kneecaps; and muscle fragments from the right and left sides of her outer thighs. These pieces were all deemed holy relics and were turned over to the Catholic Church.

Bernadette was then placed in an airtight glass case and enshrined in the chapel of the convent of Saint Gildard in Nevers, France.

Her body remains there to this day, over seventy-five years later, still in its perfect, "incorrupt" state.

Is Bernadette's incorruptibility a miraculous sign from God?

The faithful say, "Unquestionably." The skeptics say, "Hardly. Her preserved state is due to fortuitous conditions at the time of initial burial and, among the conspiracy-minded, the possibility that her 'washed only' body may be 'anything but.'"

However, the scientific explanations do not fully satisfy the curious-minded. There are accounts of bodies being buried in the most "decay-favoring" condition—mud, moist underground tombs, etc.—and the bodies of the holy still remaining intact and not the least bit decayed.

Catholic saints are not the only ones who have remained incorrupt after death. There are documented accounts of holy men and women from other religions being in perfect condition after being buried for decades or more.

A sign from God? Or just a fluke of biology we still do not fully understand?

The answer to that question depends—almost entirely—on who you ask.

43

Invisibility

HAIKU:

INVISIBILITY

Private scenes are seen
Private secrets are no more
Unseen visitor.

JAPANESE SCIENTIST INVENTS "INVISIBILITY CLOAK"

A Japanese scientist has developed a coat which appears to make the wearer invisible. The illusion was part of a demonstration of optical camouflage technology at Tokyo University. It is the brainchild of Professor Susumu Tachi who is in the early stage of research he hopes will eventually make camouflaged objects virtually transparent. The photograph was taken through a viewfinder that uses a combination of moving images taken behind the wearer to give a transparent effect. It's hoped the technology will be useful for surgeons frustrated that their own hands and surgical tools can block their view of operations and pilots who wish cockpit floors were transparent for landings.[1]

DEFINITION: The power or ability to make oneself or an object impossible to see.

WHAT THE BELIEVERS SAY: Highly evolved people can manipulate the subatomic nature of their cells, causing them to vibrate at frequencies that do not reflect light. Sight occurs when reflected light enters the eye. If there is no reflected light, the object or person will not be visible. Only very advanced mystics can achieve this level of control. (See the four types of invisibility on the next page.)

WHAT THE SKEPTICS SAY: There are only two types of what could be defined as invisibility: functional invisibility, in which something is rendered invisible to radar and sonar devices; and illusory invisibility (trickery—which is actually not invisibility at all). It is ludicrous to believe that a human being can, through meditation alone, change the subatomic nature of their cells so that light passes through them, instead of reflecting it.

QUALITY OF EXISTING EVIDENCE: For deliberate invisibility and spontaneous involuntary human invisibility, Negligible; for functional and illusory invisibility, Excellent.

LIKELIHOOD PHENOMENON IS PARANORMAL: For deliberate invisibility and spontaneous involuntary human invisibility, Nil to Low; for functional and illusory invisibility, Very high.

THE DAY CAROL VISITED BLOCKBUSTER

Carol locked her car and walked across the parking lot towards the Blockbuster store. She was hoping they had that new documentary about the Salem Witch Trials that had just come out on DVD. She had read a great deal about the film on the Internet and, since it had never been released to theaters, the only way to watch it was to rent it.

She planned on asking at the counter for the documentary, since she always got confused when she tried to find something on her own. All the shelves and aisles and endless array of video boxes made her head spin. It was easier to simply ask for what she was looking for and let one of the clerks get it for her.

A man opened the door to the store and Carol walked in behind him. He ignored her, and didn't even bother to hold the door for her. Carol was quick, though, and she did not get whacked by the closing glass door.

One thing lacking these days is manners, Carol thought as she strode across the front of the store towards the checkout counter.

There were three people in line ahead of her, and they all had videos in their hands. The line moved quickly and then it was Carol's turn.

The clerk was a young girl with a pierced eyebrow, and a name tag that said "Hi, I'm Krystal!" Krystal was also wearing a T-shirt that read, "I Don't Care That I'm Apathetic."

Krystal did not look up when Carol approached the counter. Typical, Carol thought.

"I'm looking for that new documentary about the Salem Witch Trials," Carol began. "Do you have it?"

Nothing.

Krystal did not even look up from the computer terminal on which she was typing in the ID numbers of returned videos.

After a few seconds Carol said, "Excuse me?" with a touch of impatience in her voice.

Krystal continued to completely ignore her.

It was as though Carol wasn't even standing there.

Just as she opened her mouth to begin lambasting this incredibly rude clerk, Krystal looked up, looked right past Carol, and said, "Can I help you?"

Carol turned and saw a man with a baby in his arms walking towards the counter. She stepped out of the way, the man stepped up to the counter and gave his video to Krystal to scan.

Carol was dumbfounded. She was literally so shocked by this treatment that she could not summon the presence of mind to say a single word.

She looked again at Krystal, who was busy taking care of the man and who continued to completely ignore her. Carol walked out of the store.

When Carol got home, she fired off a nasty e-mail to the customer service department of Blockbuster. When Krystal was later questioned about the incident, she had no recollection of Carol and a check of the store's security videotape showed no one at the counter during the time Carol claimed she was ignored.

That day in Blockbuster, Carol had been a victim of spontaneous involuntary human invisibility.

There are four commonly used meanings for the term "invisibility."

One is spontaneous involuntary human invisibility (SIHV), which was Carol's dilemma. This is an unproven paranormal phenomenon which, so far, has nothing but anecdotal claims to support it. Very little information exists about this alleged "condition," and what is out there could be hoaxed.

Another is deliberate invisibility. As defined above, subatomic manipulation of one's cells by gurus and mystics can allegedly render them "immune" to reflected light. This has not been scientifically proven as being possible.

A third is functional invisibility. This is what seems to have been attempted during the Philadelphia Experiment (see Chapter 65). This is when an object like a ship or a submarine is made invisible to enemy radar and other tracking devices. This is commonplace and is regularly used by the military.

A fourth form of invisibility is the illusion of invisibility, a common trick of stage magicians. This usually involves mirrors, misdirection, doubles, and other tricks of the magician's trade.

Is human invisibility, in some distant future, ultimately possible? If the human species someday evolves to the point where the control of such things as reflected light off the body becomes a skill or talent, it would not come without insurmountable problems. The biggest problem, which was conveniently ignored by H.G. Wells in *The Invisible Man*, will be blindness. We see because reflected light strikes our eyes. If our eyes are invisible, they will not be able to receive reflected light. Thus, being invisible will render a person sightless.

Of course, if we are postulating humans evolving to manifest superhero-like powers, than who is to say we could not also evolve an eye that would work while invisible?

I know: these are ridiculous notions. But then again, so was flying before it was actually done.

[1] Ananova News Service, February 5, 2003.

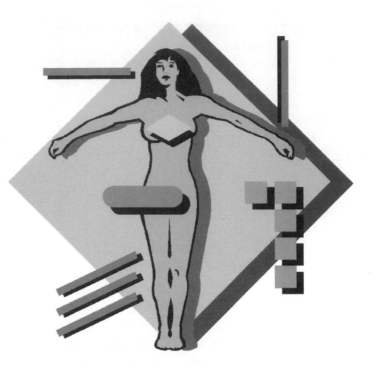

44

Ivy League Nude Posture Photos

HAIKU:

NUDE POSTURE PHOTOS

Take off all your clothes
Smile for the camera
Hearts and minds are numb

*We are ashamed of everything that is real about us;
ashamed of ourselves, of our relatives, of our incomes, of
our accents, of our opinions, of our experience, just as we
are ashamed of our naked skins.*

—George Bernard Shaw[1]

DEFINITION: Ivy League "posture photos" were completely nude photographs taken of all incoming freshmen at Ivy League and Seven Sisters colleges from 1940 through 1960.

WHAT THE BELIEVERS SAY: Nude photos were routinely taken of college freshmen, including then-college students Hillary Rodham Clinton, Diane Sawyer, George Bush, and thousands of others, and these pictures still exist to this day.

WHAT THE SKEPTICS SAY: The nude posture photo practice was stopped in the late 1960s and all the pictures were shredded and burned. They no longer exist, so any prurient interest you may have in seeing Meryl Streep nude in front, back, and side views will go unrequited.

QUALITY OF EXISTING EVIDENCE: Excellent.

LIKELIHOOD PHENOMENA ARE TRUE: Very high.

You are a gifted high school senior and you are excited beyond words to have been accepted to Yale University.

You have always been a little shy, and even though you dated a few boys during high school, you are still a virgin. You never showered after gym class and you always made sure your bedroom door was locked before you got undressed.

A few days after you arrive in New Haven, as you are settling into your dorm room and getting to know your roommate, you are sent a note stating that you must come to the Payne-Whitney Gymnasium the following morning at eleven-thirty. The only reason given for the official summons is "for the taking of academic ID photos."

You show up as ordered, fill out a form, and are told to step behind a large white screen. Behind the screen waiting for you is a nurse who tells you to immediately remove all your clothing, including your underwear. When you question this, you are told it is part of the school's record-keeping procedures and that they will be taking posture photos of you.

You strip and stand there naked and mortified as the nurse tapes three steel rods to your spine. They jut out like the fins of a fish.

She then tells you to follow her and you walk—you cannot believe you are naked—a short ways to a small room. "In there," you are told, and the nurse leaves.

You step inside the room and, to your shock and embarrassment, you find a male photographer standing there waiting for you. You immediately try to cover yourself, but it does no good. The man ushers you by the arm to a lit-up area and tells you to stand perfectly still and face the camera. You obey, because you are a mere freshman and the school is the authority.

The man steps behind the camera, peers through the lensfinder and snaps a picture. The shock of the flash going off sears into your brain the fact that your nude image is now captured on film.

But it's not over.

"Turn around, please."

You do as told and the photographer quickly takes a photograph of your naked behind.

"Turn to your left please, and be sure to stand up straight."

You again comply and a side photo is taken, the steel rods extending out from your back.

Three nude photographs of you, an eighteen-year-old girl, now exist, and they are in the possession of Yale University.

The nurse enters the room and hands you a white paper robe, which you immediately don. You feel only slightly better now that your nakedness is covered.

"Could you please tell me . . ." you begin.

"It's routine," the nurse replies brusquely. "It's for your posture."

You clam up and quickly leave the room, wanting nothing more than to find your clothes and get out of there.

Later you learn that the taking of the nude photographs was, indeed, routine, and that almost everyone on your dorm floor had already had theirs taken.

This story cannot be true, right?

No institute of higher learning, especially an Ivy League school with the legendary reputation of Yale University, would dare to demand that its students pose for naked pictures, right?

No parents would allow their sons and daughters to pose for such photographs, right?

Wrong on all counts.

From 1940 through the late 1960s, thousands of nude photographs were taken of all incoming freshmen at Ivy League schools.

The mind boggles at the cultural, academic, and societal mindsets that would have tolerated such a practice and yet, during those three decades, no one even thought to question the idea.

The practice of taking nude posture photos, which some say began as early as 1880 at Harvard, was stopped at Yale in 1968, although the photos were not destroyed. A Yale employee came upon a cache of the pictures in the late 1970s and the school was so shocked to discover that they still existed and were accessible, they brought in a professional document destruction team to, first, shred them, and then burn the shreds.

But guess what? A great many of these photos still exist and are housed in an archive at the Smithsonian Institution. A reporter looked through them as recently as a few years ago.

It is believed that some of the most famous people in the world had their nude photo taken when they entered one of the Ivy League schools: people like the aforementioned Meryl Streep, Diane Sawyer, and George Bush, along with Dick Cavett, Brandon Tartikoff, Bob Woodward, Wendy Wasserstein, Nora Ephron, and countless others.

So, was the debacle of the nude posture photos simply a group of schools' making idiotic decisions and implementing them until they wised up?

The truth is somewhat darker.

The reality is that the photos were being taken as part of a massive eugenics (the study of hereditary improvement of the human race by controlled selective breeding) study in which the goal was to match intelligence to physique. The study was conceived by Columbia professor W.H. Sheldon and Harvard professor E.A. Hooton, and they wanted to prove that body type predicted all manner of innate capabilities and traits. Their stated purpose was to ultimately weed out "inferior and useless organisms."

Does Hitler's term "Master Race" ring a bell?

Unfortunately, all the photos were not destroyed and who knows what the future may bring? There are many famous people who would certainly prefer that the world not get a glimpse at what they looked like naked when they were eighteen.

Come to think of it, who says you have to be famous to want that?

[1]*Man and Superman*, Act 1.

45

Kirlian Photography

HAIKU:

KIRLIAN PHOTOGRAPHY

Colors sparkling

Halos of radiant hues

Life in a rainbow

Everyone has an aura, but ordinarily your auras are nothing but shadows with no light in them—just dark shadows around you. And those auras reflect your every mood. When you are angry, then your auras become as if blood-filled; they become filled with a red, angry expression. When you are sad, dim, down, then your auras are filled with dark threads, as if you are just near death—everything dead, heavy.

—Osho Rajneesh[1]

DEFINITION: The process of photographing an object by exposing film in a dark room to ultraviolet light that results from electronic and ionic interactions caused by an electric field. The photograph shows a light, glowing band surrounding the outline of the object.[2]

WHAT THE BELIEVERS SAY: Kirlian photography reveals the supernatural, etheric auras—the "life energy" or "life force"—of both living and, paradoxically, inanimate things. Kirlian photographs are glimpses at the bioenergy in our bodies.

WHAT THE SKEPTICS SAY: There is nothing whatsoever supernatural or paranormal about the images produced through Kirlian photography. All the photographs show is a corona discharge, fully understandable and explainable, and due to an electrical charge interacting with the moisture in an object. The "aura" seen is a result of shooting high-frequency, low-voltage electricity though a person or an object and then photographing the subject by placing it directly on film or a photographic plate. Modern photographic techniques now allow Kirlian photographs to be taken with specialized equipment that do not require the subject to be touching the film or photographic plate.

QUALITY OF EXISTING EVIDENCE: Fair.

LIKELIHOOD PHENOMENON IS AUTHENTIC: Fair.

The problem with Kirlian photography is that it is quite possible that both the believers and the skeptics may be right.

The supporters of Kirlian imagery believe that the photos show a person's aura.

The skeptics state that the photos do, indeed, show an aura, but it is a natural discharge that is able to be captured through the Kirlian process.

The problem lies in the *interpretation* of the images; in what the aura that is seen actually means.

Kirlian photography was developed in the 1940s and 50s by the Russian inventor and electrician Seymon Kirlian and his wife, Valentina Kirlian. In a paper published in 1961 in the *Russian Journal of Scientific and Applied Photography*, Kirlian explained the process he had "discovered" and stated that photographs taken using his system showed a glowing aura around the subject.

Paranormal enthusiasts leaped upon this news as scientific proof for the existence of the etheric auras that psychics had been claiming to see around people for eons. The Biblical stories of saints and their haloes are believed by many to be accurate accounts of the auras visible in highly spiritual people.

As Kirlian photography became more widespread, and as Kirlian photos began to show a wide range of colorful halos around people, it wasn't long before interpretations of people's physical, emotional, and spiritual states based on the colors of the auras became commonplace. There are many scales of color meaning, but blue is often interpreted as meaning the person is peaceful and contemplative. Red means desire, and that the person is thinking about sex or is sexually aroused. Green means that the person is intellectually focused, is a teacher, or has recently taught someone how to do something. Yellow means the person is in a good mood and excited about something. Purple signifies a very spiritual person capable of healing others. Browns and blacks mean disease. A shriveled aura means looming death.

Well-known skeptical paranormal researcher Joe Nickell had his aura photographed by Kirlian photography at a psychic fair, and two photographs showed areas of green around him, which he was told meant he was a healer and a teacher. Since Nickell has spent many years "teaching" people through his books and articles, this would seem to be on target.[3] However, a problem arises when we ask the simple question, "How do we know that a green aura signifies teaching?" And the obvious answer is that we don't, and that is where the scientific results of a Kirlian photo clash with the paranormal interpretation of what is seen in the picture.

The human body *does* emit fields of energies. Our nerves emit low-level electrical impulses; our internal organs make sounds as they function; our bodies secrete odors, which are created by biochemical effects. Also, the medical and historical literature is replete with stories of phosphorescent humans—people who physically glowed, often bright enough to be seen with the naked eye.

In the 1937 classic, *Anomalies and Curiosities of Medicine*, the authors tell of a Capuchin monk whose scalp emitted sparks; a man whose penis emitted luminous sparks when he urinated; two patients whose heads were surrounded by a phosphorescent light; a man with glowing perspiration; a woman who had a malignant tumor on her breast that glowed brightly; and a man who found himself surrounded by a phosphorescent halo after an excessive consumption of fats.[4]

Thus, the Kirlian conundrum. It is a scientific fact that Kirlian photographs do capture corona discharges from human, animals, plants, and inanimate objects. And it is a scientific fact that these discharges occur in a range of colors.

The conclusions one reaches about Kirlian imagery depend solely on whether or not an individual believes that these colors signify something and that they communicate information about the person being photographed; or that they are meaningless discharges of ionized electricity that occur within certain color wavelengths that can be captured on film.

[1]Formerly known as the Bagwan Sri Rajneesh.
[2]*American Heritage Dictionary.*
[3]"Aura Photography: A Candid Shot," *Skeptical Inquirer*, May/June 2000.
[4]George M. Gould and Walter L. Pyle, *Anomalies and Curiosities of Medicine*, pp. 422–425.

46

Levitation

HAIKU:

LEVITATION

Floating in the air
Tethered no more to Earth
Sky is her new home

Just as there is the principle of gravitation, in yoga there is the principle of grace, of levitation. Gravitation pulls you downwards, but there is a magnetic force which pulls you upwards. But it depends on your inner state whether you will be influenced from above or below. If your energy is at the lower center you will be influenced from below; if your energy is at the higher center you will be influenced from above.

—Osho Rajneesh

DEFINITION: Levitation is the ability to rise off the ground and float in the air in defiance of gravity.

WHAT THE BELIEVERS SAY: The sacred literature is filled with stories of holy men—truly enlightened spiritual masters—who not only were able to levitate objects in full view of others, but were also known to levitate themselves off the ground in a state of divine bliss. Also, witnesses have seen objects levitate during episodes of poltergeist activity (see Chapter 39). Levitation is not only possible, it might actually be a learned skill.

WHAT THE SKEPTICS SAY: Human beings and solid objects cannot defy gravity at will and levitate themselves off the ground. Any so-called "levitating" is nothing but a magician's illusion.

QUALITY OF EXISTING EVIDENCE: Poor to Fair.

LIKELIHOOD PHENOMENON IS PARANORMAL: Low.

I know how to levitate. I have done it for several people and they have invariably been amazed. I can only rise two or three inches off the ground, but I can unquestionably be seen to float up into the air, with nothing but empty space beneath my feet.

Is Stephen Spignesi, your humble author, gifted with supernatural powers? Can he defy the laws of nature and float his Italian-American carcass off the ground at will?

Hardly.

The truth is that I know how to do a magic trick called the Balducci Levitation. Anyone can learn how to do it with a little practice, and I'll not reveal its secrets here. (Those of you interested in learning it can easily find everything you need to know about it on the Internet.)

There is a difference, however, between intentional trickery and supernatural levitating ability. Is there any concrete evidence that saints and fakirs and ancient builders possessed powers and knowledge unknown to us today?

There are some who believe that the pyramids at Giza were constructed using some type of levitating technology (perhaps using sonics and vibration) that allowed the builders to move the gargantuan blocks of stone into place with ease.

There have been reports of Tibetan monks being able to levitate enormous rocks using drums and other musical instruments. Apparently, if the stories are true, the Tibetan priests have discovered the specific sonic frequencies necessary to nullify gravity and can create these sounds with their instruments.

The Maharishi Mahesh Yogi describes a practice called "yogic flying" in which the acolyte begins by initially bouncing up and down off the ground while seated, actually "levitating" for fractions of a second at a time, and then meditating and refining the skill until the student becomes one with the sky and can actually float through the air in defiance of gravity.

St. Francis of Assisi and St. Teresa of Avila were both said to be able to levitate and the Bible tells of Jesus walking on water,[1] which may have been an act of supernatural levitation. St. Joseph of Cupertino reportedly levitated before witnesses more than seventy times during his life, one time in a church filled with congregants. A Scottish conjurer named Daniel Home (1833–1886) was reportedly able to levitate himself to the ceiling and remain there while conversing with people down below.

But all of these stories are anecdotal and have never been proven to be true. Genuine levitation is impossible.

Or is it?

The Truth about the Indian Rope Trick

A fakir throws a rope up into the sky. The rope immediately stiffens and remains erect, extending up into the clouds. A young boy climbs the rope and disappears when he reaches the top. The fakir himself then climbs the rope, a fierce-looking knife held between his teeth. He, too, disappears; however, his knife can then be heard swishing through the air, and suddenly body parts and limbs begin falling from the sky. The fakir climbs down the rope to the ground, (his knife now covered in blood), gathers up the body parts, and places them in a large wicker basket. He covers the basket, says a few magic words, and the young boy climbs out of the basket, intact and unharmed.

The first news of this amazing feat appeared in a *Chicago Tribune* newspaper article by Fred S. Ellmore published in 1890. The trick was reportedly being performed regularly in India, and shortly thereafter, variations of the stunt began appearing in magicians' acts all over the world.

Thousands of theories were floated (sorry) as to how the trick was actually done, but no one was able to perform it exactly as it had supposedly been performed in India.

The truth?

The truth is that the real Indian Rope Trick *has never been done*.

The original newspaper article describing the trick was a hoax, intentionally published by the newspaper to increase circulation. Apparently, the editors believed the readers would know the piece was a stunt because of the reporter's name. (I'll wait while you go back and look at it again.)

Clever, eh?

Four months after the original article appeared, the paper published a short piece revealing that the Indian Rope Trick did not exist, but by then it was too late: the mystifying, amazing, incredible Indian Rope Trick had entered the lexicon of magic, and there are those to this day who still believe it can be done and that it is still being performed in India.[2]

ANTI-GRAVITY TECHNOLOGY

There is a vibrant subset of scientific endeavor that is studying and experimenting with devices and technologies to legitimately defy gravity.

Many of these technologies use the manipulation and control of magnetism to "float" things in the air. Is this a genuine nullification of gravity or simply another aerodynamic principle utilized to make things appear to be levitating?

The difference between the two is the "mechanism" of making something airborne. Authentic anti-gravity devices would actually *cancel out* gravity, allowing objects of any weight to travel through the air with little or no expenditure of energy. Flying as we know it today, however, requires extraordinary amounts of power to *overcome* gravity, rather than nullify it.

So far, this technology eludes science, although research into anti-gravity is ongoing and, some say, may be further along than widely known. Conspiracy theorists believe that the United States government possesses true anti-gravity craft and that some of the UFO sightings may actually be of top secret government spacecrafts.

---

[1] Matthew 15:25.

[2] The truth about the hoax was uncovered after a five-year investigation by Peter Lamont, a former President of the Edinburgh, Scotland Magic Circle organization. He revealed his findings at the 2001 International Science Festival in Edinburgh.

Life After Death

Life is the art of drawing sufficient conclusions from insufficient premises.[1]

—Samuel Butler

DEFINITION: Life after death is generally defined as the survival of consciousness (perhaps in some form different from human consciousness) after the physical death of the body.

WHAT THE BELIEVERS SAY: We definitely move on after death. Where we go and in what form or state we exist is unknown, but guesses have been made for eons. Our consciousness most assuredly survives the "shedding" of the shell of our physical body. Human life is only one of the lives our consciousness experiences in this universe.

WHAT THE SKEPTICS SAY: When you're dead, you're dead. The only things that survive an individual's death are their legacy, their deeds, and the memories of them in the hearts and minds of their loved ones.

QUALITY OF EXISTING EVIDENCE: Very good.

LIKELIHOOD PHENOMENON IS AUTHENTIC: Very high.

The key question is, of course, does human consciousness survive physical death? This is something that, so far, cannot be conclusively known, and each person has to decide for him or herself whether or not they believe their soul—their essence, their "life force," their *self*—lives on when their body no longer does.

Underlying the question of consciousness surviving physical death is each person's fundamental belief or disbelief in the existence of a soul. If a person holds the belief that they are imbued with a soul, it follows that this "thing" will not show up on a CAT scan or an MRI. It is immaterial, and therefore must be comprised of some type of spiritual energy. Here is where science enters into the mix and may, in fact, prove to some the existence of life after death.

We know from the work of Albert Einstein and others that energy cannot be created or destroyed—it can *only be changed*. This principle is known as the law of conservation of energy.

Therefore, if one believes in a soul and stipulates that it is immaterial, then one is acknowledging and accepting that it is made of some type of energy. Since energy cannot be destroyed, at the time of physical death, the energy that is the soul simply changes to another form. It cannot die. So, does this mean that our consciousness survives? Yes, but with a caveat, which is the essence and foundation of all the religious belief systems on earth: the addition to the equation of the element of *faith*. If a person *believes* the soul lives on, then that person's soul will have the *focus* to move on, and it will cross the threshold to an elevated state of existence. If a person believes that "dead is dead," then his or her soul will not have the impetus to maintain its own transcendental identity, and the energy that is that person's soul will simply dissipate into the eternal ether, not destroyed, but absorbed into the fabric of all reality.

* * *

Recent polls have shown that upwards of 80 percent of Americans believe in life after death, yet only two-thirds of those people believe in the existence of God.

This means that there are people who believe their soul lives on, but who do not believe in a higher power to whom they owe their existence. This bespeaks a pervasive confidence in the continuity of all life.

Belief in life after death has been a common thread running through all of human existence. The Egyptian pyramids are nothing more than elaborate tombs, and we have evidence that many cultures buried food and supplies with their deceased, believing that not only were they going on to another life, but that they would need food and clothing once they arrived there.

Adding to the mystery are phenomena like near-death experiences, ghostly manifestations, channeled messages, Marian apparitions, automatic writings, and other paranormal "events" which suggest the existence of an "other side."

Are all of these oddities, what some would call marvels, explainable as hallucinatory delusions? If people who report near-death experiences simply imagined the entire event, then how could they read what was on the tops of lighting fixtures and report what was being said in the halls outside the room in which they "died?" (See Chapter 57.)

Many who believe in eternal life see it as a necessary component of corporeal life, the "prize" that gives meaning to our existence. If we do not live on, in some form or another, then all of our lives on Earth are essentially meaningless. Could life have evolved from nothing (with or without intelligent design) for no reason whatsoever? Could man have been blessed/cursed with the knowledge of his mortality for no reason whatsoever? Are the constructs of morality and justice nothing more than inevitable responses to the vagaries of human interaction, with all its highs and lows?

Or is life one unimaginable, indefinable matrix of countless realities, all of which are connected, interacting, and eternal?

The spark of life in us all rebels at the notion that all of existence is a random collision of biological and cosmological probablities. We search for meaning, and when we cannot find it, we sometimes create it within ourselves.

Thus, is the idea of life continuing on nothing but a fanciful, optimistic dream in a universe of emptiness and meaninglessness?

As has been the case with many of the phenomena discussed in this book, the answer resides within each person and can only be answered by ourselves.

[1]*Note Books* (1912).

48

The Loch Ness Monster

HAIKU:

LOCH NESS

Scottish loch is deep
See the undulating tail?
Perhaps no one's home?

Descriptions vary: several observers have "seen" an eel-like monster with humps upon its back, a few a creature with small head and long neck attached to an enormous body, and others something that looked like an upturned boat. As a rule, it is said to move swiftly through the water, sometimes to the accompaniment of a "flurry of foam." Guesses at identity have varied, even more than descriptions: from possibilities, such as large eel, grampus, porpoise, whale-shark, seal, otter, to improbabilities such as sunfish, crocodile, "some amphibian," and so to impossibilities, which include Plesiosaurus, "sea camel," and the sea serpent of the Middle Ages. Two professional zoologists have ventured identifications: one suggested an unstable mass of drifting peat, the other a white whale or beluga, but for various reasons neither is likely to be correct.[1]

DEFINITION: The Loch Ness "monster" is reportedly an enormous underwater creature living in a lake in Scotland. Some believe it to be a prehistoric creature (possibly the aforementioned Plesiosaurus?[2]) that surfaces on occasion, and which has also been witnessed on land.

WHAT THE BELIEVERS SAY: Reports of an aquatic creature living in the Loch go back fifteen hundred years. In the past century alone, there have been over four thousand sightings; there have been more than ten thousand sightings all told. The Loch Ness beast is real, anomalous, and reclusive. There is simply no way to reasonably deny that, no matter what the ultimate truth, something weird is living beneath the waters of Loch Ness.

WHAT THE SKEPTICS SAY: There is no such thing as the Loch Ness Monster. The most famous picture of the creature (the so-called 1934 "surgeon's photo") was revealed to have been hoaxed,[3] and all of the other alleged sightings are probably nothing more than fanciful delusions, ordinary animals, or even the visual result of earthquakes, which is the latest theory to explain what people *think* they see. If Nessie is real, and it lives in a specific lake in Scotland, we should have been able to prove its existence by now.

QUALITY OF EXISTING EVIDENCE: Good.

LIKELIHOOD PHENOMENON IS PARANORMAL: Good.

Wouldn't it be wonderful if the Loch Ness Monster were real? Wouldn't it be wonderful if there is a real prehistoric Plesiosaurus living in a loch in Scotland?

Well, perhaps it *is* real.

Technology has made the search for Nessie a global pursuit. There are now Web sites that have Web cams focused on the loch twenty-four seven. People from all over the world sit in front of their computers, staring at the Loch, waiting for Nessie to appear. If a person thinks they see her, they can click a button and take a digital "snapshot" of the lake at that moment.

Thousands of people have reported seeing Nessie, including lawyers, cops, scientists, and even a Nobel Prize winner. These are credible people telling of an incredible thing.

So what precisely is going on beneath the waters of Loch Ness? And what is it that so many people claim to have seen?

In the sixth century A.D., a Catholic priest named Columba (now St. Columba) had a close encounter with the beast of the Loch. According to a biography of the saint, Columba happened to pass by the Loch as some men were burying a friend of theirs who had been killed by a monster in the lake. Columba was angry at such an abominable tragedy and decided to take steps to prevent such an occurrence from happening again. He ordered one of his disciples to swim across the lake. (Why Columba did not volunteer himself as "bait" is not revealed, but his follower obeyed and jumped in the water.) Columba stood on the shore and watched as the man swam across the lake, splashing his way through the cold water. Suddenly, a great aquatic beast, apparently attracted by the man's movements, surfaced and made its way towards the helpless, hapless swimmer. Columba immediately sprang into action. He loudly commanded the beast to leave his disciple alone while, at the same time, he made the sign of the cross over the water. The creature, apparently a God-fearing Christian, responded by abandoning his prey and submerging, desperate to flee the divine power of Columba's invocation.

The first modern-day sighting of the Loch Ness Monster occurred on April 14, 1933. A couple driving by the lake saw something moving about in the water. They parked, got out, and stood and watched the creature for several minutes. They later reported the sighting and an article was published on May 2 in the *Inverness Courier*, in which the beast was dubbed a "monster." Thus, the "Loch Ness Monster" was born.

There have been many attempts to capture on film images of Nessie. Underwater photographs were taken in 1972 which may or may not show a flipper. Some say it's a tree stump. Sonar scans in 1975 picked up the movements of something large at the bottom of the lake, but what the sonar was reading has remained elusive. In fact, all the photographic, radar, audio, and sonar scans of Loch Ness have not resulted in anything conclusive regarding the presence—or absence—of Nessie.

And yet the firsthand reports of Nessie sightings are voluminous, compelling, and believable. And it should also be acknowledged that the legend of Loch Ness has contributed enormously to the tourist revenue at Inverness and surrounding towns, suggesting that perhaps it is not in anyone local's best interests to support debunking efforts.

That said, though, it does seem likely that there is something living in Loch Ness that belies explanation. Lake monsters are reported regularly all over the world and the conclusion a reasonable person must accept is that the species of man may not know everything there is to know about the other myriad species that share this small planet—and its waters.

[1] *Nature*, 132:921, 1933.

[2] If Nessie is a Plesiosaurus, an aquatic dinosaur believed to be extinct for sixty million years, then why are there no Plesiosaurus corpses found floating in the loch? The assumption must be made that if Nessie is real, then there are breeding populations somewhere in Loch Ness and, over the centuries, *some* of them had to have died. The answer lies in one key fact that we know about Plesiosauruses—they routinely swallowed large rocks, which acted as ballast, and which would, therefore, prevent their bodies from floating to the surface after their death.

[3] The famous photo of Nessie taken by gynecologist Robert Wilson on April 19, 1934 (the black and white picture showing the small-headed, long-necked creature swimming through Loch Ness) was revealed in 1994 to have been hoaxed. That said, though, there are still some who believe that the claim of photographic fakery was the *real* hoax, that the picture was real, and that it was ultimately denied to maintain the secrecy about the truth of Nessie's existence (for whatever unknown reasons). Yes, there are even conspiracy theories about the Loch Ness Monster.

49

The Lost Colony of Roanoke

HAIKU:

ROANOKE

Where have they all gone?
"Croatoan" their message
The lost colony

They are all gone into the world of light,
And I alone sit lingering here;
Their very memory is fair and bright,
And my sad thoughts doth clear.
I see them walking in an air of glory . . .

—Henry Vaughn (1622–1695)[1]

DEFINITION: The Lost Colony of Roanoke was a group of English settlers who disappeared from Roanoke Island, North Carolina, without a trace, sometime between 1587 and 1590, leaving behind nothing but the word "CROATOAN" carved into a fence post.

WHAT THE BELIEVERS SAY: The *complete* disappearance of 113[2] or more people, along with *everything* they possessed, suggests the possibility of some kind of supernatural abduction scenario. Perhaps they were all seized by aliens and beamed up to a Mothership?

WHAT THE SKEPTICS SAY: The settlers probably traveled to the nearby settlement of Croatoan (on Hatteras Island) and intermingled with the Chesapeake natives there, resulting, a generation later, in Indians who looked like white people and had grey eyes and light-colored hair.

QUALITY OF EXISTING EVIDENCE: Inconclusive.[3]

LIKELIHOOD PHENOMENON IS AUTHENTIC: Inconclusive.

John White thought it fortunate that he was arriving back at the Roanoke settlement on the day of his granddaughter's third birthday. He had returned to England nine days after Virginia Dare's birth in the New World, and the war with Spain had prevented his return until now. For three years, he had kept his daughter Eleanor and granddaughter Virginia in his thoughts as the British decimated the Spanish Armada, and now he was soon to see them again. "She is probably a spitting image of her mother," he mused as his three ships neared shore. They had fired off a cannon blast to alert the settlers of their return, and they had seen smoke rising from the island, which they believed was from a signal fire.

But John White and his crew were not greeted with a warm welcome from the settlers. Upon landing, they found . . . nothing. All the houses and structures had been "taken downe," and on a palisade fence, White found carved the word "CROATOAN," which he had given them to "signifie the place, where I should find the planters seated, according to a secret token agreed upon betweene them and me at my last departure from them . . . for at my coming away, they were prepared to remove fifty miles into the maine."[4]

More than four hundred years later, the disappearance of the Roanoke settlers remains one of American history's most puzzling riddles.

Are there any theories about the disappearance that are more plausible than others?

Yes, and many historians believe that the notion that the settlers migrated to Croatoan on Hatteras Island makes the most sense. John White had told the settlers to carve the name of their destination on a tree or fence if they decided to pack up and move, and he had also told them to cut a Maltese cross above the name of the place if they were being forced to leave, or if they were being taken away as prisoners. There was no Maltese cross above the word Croatoan, suggesting that their departure was of their own free will.

Were they, thus, assimilated into the bloodline of the Chesapeake Indians?

English explorer John Lawson visited Roanoke Island 119 years after the disappearance of the colony. He spent some time with the Hatteras Indians, who were direct descendants of the original Croatoan tribe. He later wrote that the Indians told him that "several of their ancestors were white people and could talk in a book as we do, the truth of which is confirmed by gray eyes being found infrequently among these Indians and no others."[5]

Could the colonists have been slaughtered by the Croatoan Indians, and one of the colony's last survivors carved the name of their murderers on the palisade? Possibly, but both the Spanish and the English not only carefully investigated the site of the original colony, but also searched far and wide for any sign of the colonists and came up empty-handed. One would think that there would be signs of the bloody massacre of more than one hundred people—even if it was nothing more than blood on the sand.

What about the supernatural theories? Some have posited that the entire colony was abducted by aliens, and that they were beamed up to a spaceship. This would explain the total lack of any evidence whatsoever that there had ever been anyone on Roanoke Island upon John White's arrival.

As with all farfetched, supernatural or paranormal theories, we cannot *disprove* that this is what happened, as implausible as it sounds.

And thus the continuing mystery, and our conclusion here that the fate of the lost colony of Roanoke is, in the end, still inconclusive.

---

[1] "They Are All Gone."

[2] Reports vary as to the number of settlers who disappeared, including 113, 116, 117, 120, and others.

[3] There really is no evidence on which to make a reasoned judgement as to what happened to the Lost Colony. All theories are speculative, although some (especially the traveling to Hatteras Island theory) are more persuasive than others.

[4] Eric Hause, "The Lost Colony: Roanoke Island," www.coastalguide.com/packet/lostcolony01.htm.

[5] John Lawson, *A New Voyage to Carolina.*

50

Lunar Anomalies

HAIKU:

LUNAR ANOMALIES

White light, the night sky
Silent orb of silent rocks
Ancient stone neighbor

Demoniac frenzy, moping melancholy,
And moon-struck madness.

—John Milton[1]

DEFINITION: Lunar weirdness: aliens once inhabited/still inhabit the Moon; there are artificial structures on the moon; the full Moon can affect human behavior; the Moon landing was a hoax; there are lights and UFOs seen on and around the Moon on a regular basis.

WHAT THE BELIEVERS SAY: The Moon is more than just a dead rock. Depending on the interest of the believer, any or all of the reputed lunar anomalies are real. The day will come when we will fully understand the history of our nearest neighbor.

WHAT THE SKEPTICS SAY: The Moon is just a dead rock.

QUALITY OF EXISTING EVIDENCE: Negligible to Fair.

LIKELIHOOD PHENOMENA ARE PARANORMAL: Nil to Fair.

What are lunar anomalies?

Simply put, lunar anomalies are strange goings-on having to do with the Moon, the Earth's natural satellite.

There are several types of anomalies attributed to the Moon. The most prevalent include the following:

- Aliens once inhabited the Moon but are long gone.
- Aliens still inhabit the Moon.
- UFOs are seen and photographed regularly around the Moon.
- Lights are seen and photographed regularly on the Moon.
- There are artificial structures on the Moon, including domes, bridges, pyramids, equipment for mining and traveling across the Moon's surface, as well as areas of vegetation.
- The Moon landing was a hoax.
- There are Nazi bases on the Moon, and the reason the dark side of the Moon is never photographed is because of the giant Swastika banners hanging there.
- The Moon exerts a paranormal influence on human beings.
- The full Moon affects human behavior.
- The Moon is made of green cheese. (Sorry—that one's been conclusively disproved.)

Aliens on the Moon? For centuries, man gazed at the Moon and assumed it was populated. The benign face of the Man in the Moon gazed down upon Earthlings, and although pre-telescope Moon watchers did not know who was on the Moon, they believed that there were beings living there, and that someday we might get a chance to meet them. In recent times, the notion of aliens on the Moon has been relegated to that category of fanciful myths that we bemusedly look upon now and wonder how we could have been so silly.

However, the notion of aliens having once occupied the Moon still holds strong among some who believe that there is evidence there, and that all we need to do is look for it.

This brings us to the belief that there are artificial structures on the moon, and that these edifices are undeniable evidence that the Moon was once inhabited.

I have studied carefully many of the NASA photos that purport-edly show bridges, domes, tracks, pyramids, and all other manner of structures and markings. I have looked at the areas on the photo—pointed to with thoughtfully provided arrows—in many books, and I have tried to see the bridges, and the domes, and the pyramids.

All I could see were things that looked like every other thing on the lunar landscape. Long white lines that were claimed to be bridges looked like every other white line on the surface—which easily could be the edge of a crater, or a line of rocks. Pyramids could easily be giant rocks; domes could easily be rock formations; tracks could easily be ancient lava flows or the skidding trough of a many millennia-ago meteor strike.

Yet, there are many who suspect that NASA found evidence of ancient alien civilizations during our visits to the Moon, and are cov-ering up the truth.

And speaking of the Moon landings, this brings us to those who are certain that we never went to the Moon, and that all the footage we have seen of astronauts gamboling about the lunar surface was filmed on a soundstage. Las Vegas seems to be mentioned quite a bit as being the site of the faked Moon footage. There are books and Web sites devoted to identifying the inconsistencies with lunar photos, and even though some of the questions are intriguing, even the slightest effort in uncovering the truth shows that the conspiracy theories are overblown and unfounded.

In February 2001, the Fox television network broadcast a special called *Conspiracy Theory: Did We Land on the Moon?* During the pro-gram, they showed a photograph of an astronaut descending from the lunar module into its shadow. The astronaut's body was lit up, however, and the narrator asked, "How is it that he is not shrouded in darkness?" Their answer was that there was more than one light source (the Sun was "allegedly" the only light source on the Moon), thus proving the astronauts were not on the Moon, but rather on a soundstage with many lights.

The truth? Surface reflection of light. The astronaut is lit up by sunlight reflecting off the sunlit surface of the Moon.

Americans landed on the Moon in 1969. We went back a number of times, but we have not been back in over twenty years.

Regarding UFOs and lights seen on and around the Moon, some of the supporting photographs are persuasive. Multiple reports vali-date these sightings and it is possible that something is going on that is being withheld from the public. Until more evidence is produced however, a definitive conclusion regarding moonlights and UFOs can not be reached.

Does the Moon exert a paranormal influence on Earthlings? Does the full Moon make people crazy? The evidence supporting these theories is weak and most of the stories of such influence are anecdotal. Yet, I have personally experienced the "full Moon" effect. Years ago, when I managed a family retail jewelry store, we would all notice an increase in the "crazies" during the period of a full Moon. We would see a marked increase in strange customers who acted peculiarly and made bizarre requests. Often, we would remark about the stream of odd customers and then, after checking the calendar, learn that it was a full Moon.

Coincidence? Perhaps. But *every month?*

Anecdotal? Certainly. But I was the one who lived through it, and I can tell you I am not exaggerating. If anything, I am understating the "wackiness factor."

Some women claim to experience heavier than usual menstrual flows during a full Moon. Tides are higher during a full Moon. These are verifiable claims.

Conclusion? It seems that some of the claims of influence by the Moon on us Earthlings stand up to scrutiny. Swastika banners? Doubtful. UFOs? Possible. Remnants of alien civilizations? Possible but unlikely. Physical effects from the moon's pull? Definitely.

Perhaps it is time for us to go back to the Moon?

POSTSCRIPT

Toledo, Ohio police analyzed 122,000 police reports from 1999 through 2001 and discovered that the crime rate rose more than 5 percent on nights when the moon was full.

The police computers analyzed all crimes that occurred between 6:00 P.M. and 6:00 A.M. on the thirty-eight nights from 1999 through 2001 when the moon was full. They then compared this date with crimes during the same time period on all other nights during those years.

The results? Violent crimes were 5.5 percent higher and property crimes were 4.6 percent higher when the moon was full.[2]

[1] *Paradise Lost*, Book IX, lines 485–86.
[2] *The Toledo Blade.*

51

Marian Apparitions

HAIKU:

MARIAN APPARITIONS

Lady clad in blue
Holy mother of Jesus,
Sacred visitor?

*Blessed are the eyes which see the things which ye see: For
I tell you, that many prophets and kings have desired to see
those things which ye see, and have not seen them; and to
hear those things which ye hear, and have not heard them.*[1]

DEFINITION: Marian apparitions are the miraculous, unbidden
appearance or sighting of the Blessed Virgin Mary. Sometimes, Jesus
or saints are also seen.

WHAT THE BELIEVERS SAY: The Blessed Mother and other divinities
appear to certain people to proclaim messages for mankind. Miraculous healings sometimes occur in connection with her appearances.
These events are religious miracles.

WHAT THE SKEPTICS SAY: All Marian and saintly apparitions are hallucinations, mass delusions, or hoaxes; all miraculous healings are
purely biological (albeit often unexplainable) in nature. All inanimate

appearances of images (on windows, etc.) are subjective interpreta-tions by the eyes of the beholders.

QUALITY OF EXISTING EVIDENCE: Fair.

LIKELIHOOD PHENOMENA ARE PARANORMAL: Inconclusive.

"Full church approval" of a sighting or apparition of the Virgin Mary means that the Catholic Church has attested to the supernat-ural authenticity of the manifestation. The Church states that what the percipients saw was divine and real: the Virgin Mary did actually appear to them.

The Church has in the past issued such approval to apparitions in Italy, Mexico, Spain, France, Poland, Slovakia, Ireland, Portugal, Bel-gium, Egypt, Nicaragua, and Japan, and hundreds of apparitions in many other countries (including the United States) are currently under investigation.

After careful investigation of a sighting, its witnesses, and the information relayed during the event, the Church ultimately rules the apparition "not contrary to the Faith," "not worthy of belief," or "worthy of belief."

In addition to the visual presence of the Virgin Mary, oftentimes miraculous healings, unexplainable by medical science, occur at the sight of apparitions. In 1989, an Irish woman named Marion Carroll visited Knock, Ireland, the site of one of the church-approved appari-tions of the Blessed Mother. (In 1879, Mary, St. Joseph, and St. John appeared on the site where a basilica now stands.) Carroll suffered from multiple sclerosis, which had rendered her paralyzed from the waist down and completely incontinent. After she was placed on a stretcher beneath a statue of Mary in the basilica, she claimed she heard a voice telling her to get up. She dismissed it as her imagina-tion, but as she was being carried back to the ambulance that had brought her, she heard the voice again, and this time she asked her nurse if should could try to walk. After seventeen years of paralysis, Carroll walked unaided to the ambulance and, upon her return home, doctors discovered that her muscles showed no sign of the disease that had left her paralyzed. She attributed her healing to the power of the Blessed Mother and later, she reportedly manifested the ability to perform healings herself.

There are an enormous number of apparitions of Jesus and Mary reported regularly all over the world. Are all the witnesses delusional? Are these apparitions genuine gifts from God intended to validate the faith of Catholics and encourage prayerful acts?

Or do people simply "see" what they want to see?

Some of the sightings and manifestations seem tailor-made for mockery by the skeptics. For instance:

- In October 1977 in New Mexico, Maria Rubio fries up a tortilla for her husband Eduardo's breakfast. After it is cooked she sees on the tortilla the unmistakable image of the face of Jesus Christ wearing a crown of thorns. This is immediately accepted as a miraculous manifestation, and the tortilla ends up nicely framed and ultimately venerated by thousands of people who come to see "Tortilla Christ." It is not known what Eduardo ate for breakfast the morning Jesus appeared in his wife's frying pan.

- In Clearwater, Florida in 1997, a two-story-high, multicolored image of the Virgin Mary appears on the windows of a building leased by Ugly Duckling Auto Sales. The image is thirty-five feet high and fifty feet wide, and the parking lot of the building is now a shrine, complete with kneelers, candles, and worshipers.

Granted, neither the tortilla nor the window image has spoken to people, but is it possible that inanimate manifestations of Jesus and Mary are part of the mass delusion that skeptics say occurs when Mary reportedly appears to people and tells them things?

There are certain elements common to many Marian apparitions. The Madonna often appears to children. She often dispenses advice and spiritual guidance, including admonitions to recite the rosary and abstain from fornication. Sometimes, she issues orders, such as telling the people she appears to that a church must be built on the site, or that they must have a spring dug there. Sometimes she makes predictions or reveals information about worldly affairs, the most well-known of these revelations being the three secrets of Fatima. Sometimes healings are reported at sites where the Madonna has appeared.

It must be acknowledged that the majority of Marian sightings around the world are unverifiable and valid only for the individual participants, many of whom are hallucinating or caught up in religious hysteria. That said, however, there are truly astonishing incidents that science cannot explain and for which the explanation of "hallucination" does not suffice.

The Catholic Church is very careful about sanctioning miraculous appearances. Their unwillingness to immediately accept such reports as valid speaks volumes about the widespread proliferation of false accounts.

The most famous Marian apparitions are Fatima and Lourdes.

These sites attract thousands of visitors each year and there are countless anecdotal accounts of miraculous healings and other wonders that occur there. (In addition to faith, however, cynicism also abounds. One well-known remark about the Lourdes shrine is especially snarky: Upon seeing the hundreds of crutches and canes hanging inside the grotto, one skeptic exclaimed, "What? No artificial legs?")

Lourdes water can be purchased today and I know a man who gave his very religious mother a set of rosary beads with a few drops of Lourdes water ("Guaranteed!") embedded in a clear plastic medal. It is one of her prized possessions. Skepticism aside, the faithful believe what they believe and they believe that the Blessed Mother appears on Earth and that her presence can often be a harbinger of miracles or messages.

There is one photograph of a Marian apparition that many consider genuine. It was taken in Zeitoun, Egypt as the Virgin Mary appeared in the sky above a church there.

Many people apparently witnessed the apparition and someone took a photograph.

The picture shows the shape of a woman standing in the air above the roof of the church. Her head is bowed, she has a halo, and she is bathed in white light.

I have never been convinced of the authenticity of this photo. It looks like someone placed a statue on the roof of a church and somehow lit it so its details were obscured in light. Many are confident that I am wrong, however, and perhaps I am.

Does the Virgin Mary appear to people on Earth? I suspect she does, but that the *actual* sightings of the transcendent being that was the mother of Jesus are far fewer than the *reported* sightings.

[1]Luke 10:23.

52

The Men in Black

HAIKU:

THE MEN IN BLACK

Sunglasses at night
Black suits, black ties, no smiles
"I look good in this."

Good things of day begin to droop and drowse,
While night's black agents to their preys do rouse.[1]

DEFINITION: The Men in Black are mysterious men in black suits and sunglasses who may or may not be aliens, and who usually show up unbidden to "interview" people who have had a UFO sighting or an abduction experience.

WHAT THE BELIEVERS SAY: The Men in Black are alien agents whose job it is to monitor and suppress reports of UFOs and alien contact so that other aliens can continue their activities on Earth without

206

interference. It is highly likely that the governments of the world (or at least the U.S. government) are in cahoots with these beings.

WHAT THE SKEPTICS SAY: The Men in Black, if they even exist, are probably nothing more than government agents who drive old cars and who are bad dressers. But the odds are they do *not* exist at all.

QUALITY OF EXISTING EVIDENCE: Poor.

LIKELIHOOD PHENOMENA ARE PARANORMAL: Low.

Who are the Men in Black and are they real?

The 1997 movie *Men in Black* put a different spin on the Men in Black story: They were not aliens. They were human agents whose duty it was to monitor alien activity on Earth and in nearby galactic space. It was a clever "interpretation" of one of the most pervasive elements of UFOlogy.

Reportedly, the Men in Black usually travel in groups of two or three and they appear shortly after someone officially reports a UFO sighting or an abduction experience. (Not all UFO percipients of abductees are visited by the Men in Black, but many are.) In some cases, the Men in Black have shown up at someone's door after they have had a UFO sighting, but before they have had an opportunity to report it to anyone. It was as though they knew everything that had gone on and wanted to stop the person from talking about it.

In 1947, the same year as Kenneth Arnold's Washington state UFO sighting and the Roswell crash (see Chapter 75), Harold Dahl came forward with the first official account of a visit from the Men in Black. Dahl reported that he had witnessed a UFO discharging "metallic" substances (Angel hair, perhaps? See Chapter 4.) into the ocean off the coast of Maury, Washington, and that the following morning he was visited by a stranger clad in a dark suit. This ominous-looking "person" hinted that Dahl and his family would be harmed if he continued to speak about what he had seen. Dahl's story was eventually revealed to be an elaborate hoax, and yet conspiracy theorists embraced the story and charged a cover-up of the truth—which was, of course, that Dahl had been visited by the real Men in Black.

In September 1953, Albert Bender, the founder of the International Flying Saucer Bureau, claimed that he was visited by three men in dark suits after he confided a UFO theory to one of the people with whom he corresponded. This was the true beginning of the Men in Black legend and became known in UFOlogy as the "Bender Mystery."

The Men in Black always wear black suits. Sometimes the suits are impeccably clean and pressed; other times the suits have been reported as being dirty and wrinkled.

Sometimes they have a heavy accent; sometimes they use very formal language; sometimes they attempt to speak in a gangster dialect.

The Men in Black seem amazed by ordinary terrestrial objects like spoons or combs.

Some people who claimed to have been visited by the Men in Black reported being very frightened and said that the Men in Black threatened them with violence if they did not keep their mouth shut.

The Men in Black apparently cannot afford new cars, for they are always said to drive old black Cadillacs (occasionally some other models, like Lincolns or Buicks are mentioned) that were in quite good condition. (If they were government agents, wouldn't they be driving Tauruses or Impalas?) Also, witnesses report that their vehicles seemed to be illuminated from within by an unearthly green light.

Some witnesses claim that the Men in Black wear heavy makeup and have weird facial features. (Wait a minute! I figured it out! Michael Jackson is one of the Men in Black!)

The legend goes on . . .

The Men in Black can disintegrate coins in the palms of their hands. They are impervious to cold and are often seen in below freezing weather wearing nothing but their black suits. And speaking of their suits, many report that they seem to be made of some weird shiny material that is unlike anything any of the witnesses had ever seen.

It is possible that the Men in Black can levitate. There are accounts of them being seen walking across soppy, muddy fields, and appearing at someone's door without a speck of mud or dirt anywhere on them—including their spotless, polished shoes.

Are the Men in Black actors hired by the government and instructed to behave in as odd a manner as possible as part of an ongoing disinformation campaign?

Or are they robots or androids from another planet whose job it is to keep track of UFO activity on Earth?

Or are the Men in Black aliens themselves, perhaps from the planet Sirius, or even from another dimension?

We do not know the answers to these questions.

But there are many people today who believe that the *Men in Black* movies starring Will Smith and Tommy Lee Jones are documentaries.

[1] William Shakespeare, *Macbeth*, Act III, Scene 2.

53

Mermaids

HAIKU:

MERMAIDS

Ocean maidens sing
Beckoning sailors approach
Dreams of the vast seas

She is a beast of the sea, wonderfully shapen as a maid from the navel upward and a fish from the navel downward. With sweetness of song she maketh shipmen to sleep. Then she goeth into the ship and bringeth one out into a dry place. And she maketh him lie with her and if he will not or may not she slayeth him and eateth his flesh.

—Bartholomew Anglicus[1]

DEFINITION: A legendary sea creature having the head and upper body of a woman and the tail of a fish.

WHAT THE BELIEVERS SAY: The mythological stories of mermaids and mermen arose from ancient people's sightings of real beings. Mermaids are real, and people still see them today. They may be an unknown species of fish or aquatic mammal. The movie *Splash* should be viewed as a documentary.

WHAT THE SKEPTICS SAY: Mermaids and mermen are pure fantasy. There is no such thing as a hybrid of man and fish.

QUALITY OF EXISTING EVIDENCE: Poor.[2]

LIKELIHOOD PHENOMENA ARE PARANORMAL: LOW.

At the end of April 1608, Henry Hudson, the seventeenth century English explorer who discovered the Hudson River, left England on a voyage to find a northern route to the East Indies. He was unsuccessful,[3] and after a four-month trip north to the Barents Sea, he and his crew returned to England.

During the voyage, two of Hudson's crewmen, Thomas Hill and Robert Raynor, reportedly saw a mermaid off the coast of Novaya Zemlya, a group of islands off northern Russia. Captain Hudson dutifully recorded the extraordinary sighting in his June 15, 1608 journal entry:

> This evening, one of our company, looking overboard, saw a mermaid, and, calling up some of the company to see her, one more of the crew came up, and by that time she was come close to the ship's side, looking earnestly on the men . . . From the navel upward, her back and breasts were like a woman's . . . her body as big as one of us; her skin very white; and long hair hanging down behind, of color black; in her going down they saw her tail, which was like the tail of a porpoise, and speckled like a mackerel.

Alexander Carmichael's massive 1900 compilation of Scottish and Welsh folktales, *Carmina Gadelica*, contains the story of a mermaid seen by townsfolk on the isle of Benbecula. At first, they tried to capture her, but she was fast and continually eluded their grasp. Finally, as she was attempting to swim out to sea, a young boy did what young boys are wont to do when frustrated. He threw a rock at her and hit her in the back. She submerged, but the blow had been fatal, and her dead body washed up on shore a few days later. Upon examination, the islanders noted that the creature's upper body was the size of a four-year-old, but she had fully developed breasts. Its lower body was like that of a salmon. She had white skin, and long dark hair and, according to eyewitnesses, she looked exactly like what everyone expected a mermaid to look like: half human, half fish.

Her human appearance was so compelling that the sheriff ordered her buried in a shroud and coffin—just like a person.

Was this creature a real mermaid? Or was it a beached whale, a seal or a dugong?

That question begs a second: Is it possible that seafaring islanders would not be able to recognize a beached whale, a seal, or a dugong?

The Benbecula mermaid story is one of the most enigmatic mermaid tales of all time, and it still has not been satisfactorily explained.

The mermaid legend stems from two main sources: Sixth century B.C. Babylonian mythology, and sea creatures that have been mistaken for humans.

Oannes was a Babylonian God that had human form and a fish tail. The first written accounts of mermaids as actual creatures date from the first century in the writings of Pliny the Elder. Pliny claimed that soldiers of Augustus Caesar saw the bodies of dead mermaids strewn along a beach in Gaul.

Adding to these legends and writings were the creatures sailors actually saw; creatures that, glimpsed in fog, or from a distance, could easily have been mistaken for a human with a fish bottom. Seals, dugongs, walruses, whales, and other sea creatures that have humanoid shapes—i.e., head, a torso that slopes towards hips, fins that could be mistaken for arms—have convinced sailors for centuries that they were seeing the legendary merfolk. (Bear in mind also that a great many of the ancient and archival writings concerning mermaids were from a time when there was no such thing as "corrected vision." It is not at all farfetched to imagine a nearsighted sailor glimpsing through fog a dugong lying on a rock and being immediately convinced it was anything but an ordinary sea creature.)

In 1961, Great Britain's Isle of Man Board of Tourism offered a prize to anyone who could come forward with a living mermaid. The prize has yet to be claimed.

[1]Thirteenth century historian. This is one of the few accounts of mermaids being cannibalistic. Although, if they were only half human, then were they half cannibals and half feeders?

[2]The majority of the evidence consists of anecdotal historical accounts. There have been, however, and continue to be dubious sightings of mermaids in modern times.

[3]An extremely long northern water route to Indonesia from England does exist (as it did in the seventeenth century), but it is not a voyage that really makes much sense. In those pre-Panama Canal days, a ship would have had to set out from England, sail west to the North American continent, north to the Baffin Bay, west through the Canadian archipelagos to the Beaufort Sea, south through the Bering Strait, and then southwest in the Pacific Ocean to Indonesia. A difficult, lengthy journey. South around the tip of South America was the shorter, easier, and more economical route.

54

Miracles

HAIKU:

MIRACLES

Impossible act
A miraculous healing
A message from God?

Can we not believe that, at our prayer, God may cause the conditions of natural phenomena so to combine that, through His special agency, we may obtain our heart's desire and yet so that, to the ordinary observer, the event happens in its ordinary place and time. To the devout soul, however, all is different. He recognizes God's favour and is devoutly thankful for the fatherly care. He knows that God has brought the event about in some way. When, therefore, we pray for rain or to avert a calamity, or to prevent the ravages of plague, we beg not so much for miracles or signs of omnipotence: we ask that He who holds the heavens in His hands and who searches the abyss will listen to our petitions and, in His own good way, bring about the answer we need.[1]

DEFINITION: A miracle is an event that appears inexplicable by the laws of nature and so is held to be supernatural in origin or a deliberate act of God.[2]

WHAT THE BELIEVERS SAY: Miracles are real. They are acts of God; they are gifts of divine intervention for the benefit of the faithful. There are healing miracles, apparition miracles, Eucharistic miracles, precognitive miracles, and many other events that bespeak the presence and power of God in earthly affairs.

WHAT THE SKEPTICS SAY: Miracles are impossible. All seemingly "miraculous" occurrences are just a combination of several fortuitous (and possibly unknown) factors, including luck. All of the miracles attributed to Christ in the Bible are fictitious and were made up by the writers of the Gospels.

QUALITY OF EXISTING EVIDENCE: Good.

LIKELIHOOD PHENOMENA ARE PARANORMAL: High.

For several days following the recovery of abducted teen Elizabeth Smart, her father Tom was seen in front of the media stating with passion that her return was a "miracle." The Smart family is devoutly Mormon and her father made the incredible statement that there was no one in the history of the world who had been prayed for more than his daughter Elizabeth.

Was Elizabeth's safe return a true miracle? Did God or one of his saints intervene in the course of human affairs to see that Elizabeth was returned to her family? Or was this happy ending just the result of sharp-eyed civilians, wary cops, and plain old good luck?

The word "miracle" is used almost unthinkingly these days. The woman who walks away from a car accident describes her survival as a miracle. The family of the transplant patient who manages to get the liver he needs credits the availability of the organ to a miracle. Seemingly impossible occurrences like stigmata and bleeding statues are spoken of as miracles.

Ironically, the Catholic Church requires *scientific* proof of a miracle before the saint canonization process can move forward. The Church's archives are filled with accounts of ostensibly "real" miracles. Are these miracles spectacular manifestations of some incredible event? Does a cathedral suddenly levitate off the ground in full view of TV cameras? Are priests seen walking on water?

No. These days, the miracles the Church accepts are almost exclusively medical in nature. The process is similar in most cases. A person—we'll call her Susan—is diagnosed with a terminal disease—

end-stage liver cancer—and her doctors are unanimous in the belief that there is *no* hope for a cure and Susan is, in effect, doomed. The patient's loved ones begin praying to a deceased holy person. Lately, Mother Teresa has been the subject of many such prayers. They pray that Susan be completely cured and restored to health. They beg the intervention of the future saint, they wholeheartedly believe that they will be heard, and they keep detailed records of Susan's medical condition.

One day, Susan's cancer disappears. Her liver checks out as completely normal, and there is absolutely no sign of malignancy.

The doctors are astounded, but they do confirm that she is in complete remission.

Susan and her loved ones credit her recovery to the pending saint, and the details of the healing are submitted to the Church. The Church then does its own medical research to verify the healing. If the doctors and all the other "judges" agree, the miracle is credited to the person under consideration.

Two such miracles must be validated before the Church will decree someone "blessed"; two more before the Church will canonize the person as a saint.

For many, these documented miraculous healings are the most compelling evidence of a paranormal occurrence. Are they irrefutable evidence of a divine presence and intervention? Or simply an event science does not yet understand? These are questions of faith. Regardless of one's religious bent, though, there can be no denying the staggering impact of the restoration to health from the brink of certain death. As to who should get the credit; that, too is a matter of faith.

Are miracles impossible?

Is it possible that the laws of nature can be invalidated (or at the very least, circumvented) by the power of prayer and divine intervention? Could there be some other enigmatic "power" responsible for such events?

In one sense, the existence of a miraculous event *validates* the laws of nature. It is only by knowing and accepting natural laws, can we be conscious of a *violation* of said laws.

In the late twentieth century, the American philosopher William James wrote:

> I confess that at times I have been tempted to believe that the Creator has eternally intended this department of nature to remain *baffling*, to prompt our curiosities and hopes and suspicions all in equal measure, so that, although ghosts and clairvoyances, and rays and messages from spirits, are always

seeming to exist and can never be fully explained away, they also can never be susceptible to full corroboration.

Atheists and agnostics reject even the possibility of miracles because they believe that, first, science is in full possession of all the "rules of reality," and also because acknowledging even the possibility of a miraculous event would, de facto, acknowledge the existence of a paranormal power beyond the realm of scientific fact and the laws of nature, a concession that is in complete defiance of their belief system.

But, as James elucidates, and as we discussed in the Introduction to this book, Man does not know everything. James suspects this bafflement to be intentional on the part of the Creator. Perhaps. My thinking is that we have simply not learned all there is to know yet— and that we probably never will.

This willingness to consider the possibility that there are laws of nature yet to be discovered opens the door to the chance that miracles are simply events we do not yet understand.

It is common for cultures and societies to resort to magical thinking when confronted with something that seems to be beyond their understanding of the laws of nature. Two hundred years ago, a television would have been deemed a magical box in which apparitions appeared out of nowhere. And the remote control would have been seen as a magic wand that could magically make things change in the mysterious box.

Of course, this rationalization puts forth the possibility that so-called "miracles" are not acts of God, but simply yet-to-be understood phenomena. As repellent as this notion might be to the religiously minded, it is, nonetheless, a valid theory and must be considered when trying to comprehend seemingly incomprehensible occurrences.

There are many accounts of miraculous events taking place on Earth.

Ask the person preparing himself to die if his recovery following being prayed for is a fluke, or a true miracle.

---

[1] *The Catholic Encyclopedia*, "Miracle."
[2] *American Heritage Dictionary.*

55

The Mystery of the *Mary Celeste*

HAIKU:

MARY CELESTE

An empty vessel
A floating vacant ghost ship
No clue of their fate

Our vessel is in beautiful trim. I hope we shall have a fine passage; but as I have never been in her before, I can't say how she'll sail.

—Benjamin Briggs[1]

DEFINITION: The mystery of the *Mary Celeste* began with the discovery of the deserted brigantine adrift in the North Atlantic, its captain, his family, and their crew gone. There was no evidence of piracy or foul play, and the ship's six-month store of supplies was intact.

WHAT THE BELIEVERS SAY: Something bizarre happened onboard the *Mary Celeste*. The unexplained disappearance of the people on the ship rivals the disappearance of the Roanoke colony (see Chapter 49) for its enigmatic mystery. Paranormal solutions to the riddle must be considered, including alien abduction, an attack by a monster from the depths, or some kind of time warp anomaly.

WHAT THE SKEPTICS SAY: The captain, his family, and the crew abandoned ship for some unknown reason and were lost at sea. This is the most logical, albeit unsatisfying, explanation of finding the ship yawing in the North Atlantic, its cargo and gear in perfect condition. Why they took to a small lifeboat may never be known, but looking to aliens or monsters as an explanation is ridiculous.

QUALITY OF EXISTING EVIDENCE: Fair.[2]

LIKELIHOOD PHENOMENON IS PARANORMAL: Low or Inconclusive.[3]

The ship ultimately known as the *Mary Celeste* was originally christened the *Amazon*, and there is no way to describe it as anything other than a bad luck boat.

Can a seagoing vessel be lucky or unlucky? Can a ship be cursed?

Sailors and actors share something in common: they are superstitious about their chosen profession and all its rituals and beliefs. A cursory survey of the *Mary Celeste*'s history would quickly convince a sailor that the ship was destined for disaster.

Her history was alarming:

- Two days after taking command of the *Amazon*, her first captain died.
- On her maiden voyage, she collided with a fishing dam and damaged her hull.
- While her hull was being repaired, a fire started onboard, doing further damage.
- After being repaired, she set sail through the Straits of Dover and promptly collided with another ship, sinking it.
- The *Amazon*'s fourth captain ran her aground on Cape Breton Island, doing considerable damage.

After being salvaged (although after the *Amazon*'s series of calamities, one wonders why anyone would want anything further to do with her), she was bought and sold three times, until she was purchased by J.H. Winchester, who rechristened her the *Mary Celeste*. Perhaps he thought a name change would confuse the sea demons who seemed to be particularly set on harming the ship.

The *Mary Celeste* set sail for Genoa, Italy from New York on November 5, 1872. On board were Captain Benjamin Spooner Briggs, his wife Sarah, and their two-year-old daughter Sophie Matilda. Manning the vessel was a crew of seven (although some accounts say there were eight crewmembers). In her brig was a cargo of crude alcohol, and the ship carried enough food and water for a journey of several months.

For twenty days, the *Mary Celeste*'s journey was apparently uneventful. But on November 25, *something* happened, and what that something was, has been the subject of debate (and books and Web sites and articles) for decades.

The night before the *Mary Celeste* set out from New York, Captain Briggs had dinner with his friend, Benjamin Morehouse, the Captain of the *Dei Gratia*, which was berthed next to the *Mary Celeste* in the New York harbor. The next morning, Briggs set sail; ten days later, Captain Morehouse set out for the British colony of Gibraltar on the coast of Spain.

On December 5, Captain Morehouse saw the *Mary Celeste* sailing aimlessly in the North Atlantic, halfway between the Azores and the coast of Portugal. After signaling the ship repeatedly and receiving no response, he decided to have his men board her and investigate.

What did they find?

A mystery that endures to this day.

Most importantly, there was no one on board. Captain Briggs, his family, and his crew were nowhere to be found. Also:

- Two sails had been blown off the ship.
- The box holding the ship's compass (the binnacle) had been broken open and the compass had been smashed.
- There was water belowdecks, but not enough to sink her.
- One of the casks of crude alcohol had been smashed open.
- The crewmembers' lockers were still in place and their contents intact.
- The navigation log and instruments were missing; the Captain's Log remained.
- The food and water stores were intact.
- The last entry in the Captain's Log was dated November 25 and provided the ship's coordinates, which revealed that the ship had traveled approximately seven hundred miles in ten days with no one on board.
- And finally, the lifeboat was missing.

For some reason, Briggs and everyone on board had abandoned ship—*hastily*—on November 25. This was enormously puzzling to Captain Morehouse and his men: The *Mary Celeste* was unquestionably seaworthy. There was no chance of it sinking, so why had everyone fled the safe confines of an able vessel for the perils of a small boat and the open seas?

These are the most commonly cited theories regarding what happened, and the arguments refuting them:

The Captain thought the ship was sinking and abandoned ship. *Why would he think the ship was sinking with so little water belowdecks?*

The crew got into the crude alcohol, got drunk, mutinied, and the captain fled with his family, after which the crew drowned. *Crude alcohol would have made them sick, not drunk, and the* Mary Celeste's *experienced sailors would have known better than to drink it.*

A tornado (waterspout) hit the ship and made the Captain think they were sinking. So he abandoned ship. *Why would they think they could survive a waterspout in a small boat instead of in the* Mary Celeste?

The Captain and his co-owner plotted to abandon the ship to collect the insurance money. *The insurance proceeds would have been less than if they simply sold the ship outright.*

So that leaves alien abduction, right? Or they traveled through a time portal? Or they committed mass suicide?

To this day, no one knows the truth. Much of the speculation about what happened on the *Mary Celeste* arose following the publication of a sensationalistic (and wildly inaccurate) short story about the ship by J. Habakuk Jephson, a pseudonym for Arthur Conan Doyle.

What we do know is that the *Mary Celeste* was abandoned, probably in panic, and everyone on board died at sea.

"Why?" is the question that has still never been answered.

[1] From Captain Brigg's last letter to his mother, written before setting sail on November 5, 1872, *Mysteries of the Unexplained*, p. 122.

[2] The evidence consists mainly of the testimony of the *Dei Gratia* crew, and the *Mary Celeste*'s Captain's Log.

[3] The conclusions regarding the fate of the people on board the *Mary Celeste* can range from prosaic explanations to accounts of incredible occurrences. Since we do not have a definitive answer, the interpretation of the facts that we do have is ultimately, once again, in the eye of the beholder. Those looking for a supernatural explanation can find one; those rejecting such theories can likewise find facts to buttress *their* position.

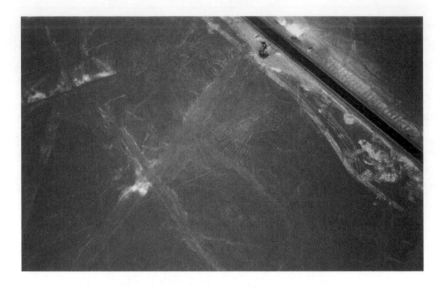

56

The Nazca Lines

HAIKU:

NAZCA LINES

Scripture in the sand
Ancient creatures, lines in sand
No artist signed them

The Spanish conquerors . . . never mentioned these markings in any of their writings; and the present inhabitants of the region, while knowing of them, possess no traditions or legends that might help to explain them. The people sometimes refer to them as "Inca Roads," but their very nature, size, and position indicate that they could never have been used for ordinary purposes of transportation. The possibility that they are the remains of ancient irrigation canals must also be ruled out, for they are often found running over hillocks. And where this is not the case, they have no possible physical connection with the river, which would be the primary requisite for irrigation canals.[1]

DEFINITION: The Nazca lines are enormous, ancient drawings and lines etched into the surface of the Peruvian desert outside of Nazca which depict animals, birds, insects, geometric patterns, and other markings, and which are completely visible only from the air.

WHAT THE BELIEVERS SAY: The Nazca geoglyphs are alien landing strips.

WHAT THE SKEPTICS SAY: The Nazca designs were created by the Nazca people over a period of decades, probably using some kind of grid marking system (ropes, posts, and sketches) by which they could produce on a gigantic scale something plotted out proportionally much smaller.

QUALITY OF EXISTING EVIDENCE: Poor.

LIKELIHOOD PHENOMENA ARE PARANORMAL: Low.

The Nazca lines, like the Great Wall of China, are visible from outer space. However, they are easily overlooked at ground level. Their complete scope cannot be seen anywhere but from the air.

This astonishing aspect of the Nazca ground markings prevented their discovery until the 1930s, and also led to one of the more chimerical theories for their origin. Erich von Däniken, in his 1970 best-seller, *Chariots of the Gods?*, posited that the Nazca lines are extraterrestrial in origin.[2] He suggests that alien spacecraft made the initial lines upon their first landings in the Peruvian desert, and then the Nazca people, working for decades removing the dark upper layer of soil to reveal the lighter level below, created the elaborate designs we see today. It is thought that the Nazca people were either paying tribute to beings they believed to be "gods from the heavens" by making the designs in deliberate imitation of the visitors' "divine" images, or they were attempting to make the ground more amenable to future landings, believing that the designs were integral to the gods' successful return.

There are over three hundred individual images in the Nazca markings, and the complete "canvas" stretches over an area two hundred square miles in size. The images are believed to have been created between 500 B.C. and 500 A.D. and they have remained relatively unchanged since then. The desert of Peru where the Nazca drawings lie is one of the driest places on Earth. It gets twenty minutes of rain a year. (Yes, you read that correctly.) The dryness, combined with the absence of wind (and thus, erosion) allow us to examine these works and know that what they look like now is probably what they looked like when they were first created.

Images in the desert include hands, a baby condor, a dog, a flower, a hummingbird, a lizard, a llama, a monkey, a pelican, a "spaceman," a spider, a spiral, a star, a tree, a triangle, a whale, a wing, and other shapes and creatures.

It is believed that the entirety of the Nazca project was a multi-multi-generational project. The complete layout is so big and so multifaceted, it took decades, and perhaps hundreds of years for what we see today to have been brought into existence.

This reality begs the question, why did they do it?

Maria Reiche, who devoted fifty years of her life to studying the Nazca lines, at first believed that they were astronomical in nature. She discovered that certain lines aligned themselves with the rising and setting Sun during the summer and winter solstices. Her conclusion was that the lines were a way for the Nazca people to keep track of the seasons.

This theory has been discounted of late. Gerald Hawkins, author of *Stonehenge Decoded*, used a computer to discern any correlations between the measurements and locations of the Nazca lines and the seasonal solstices. He found an approximate 20 percent connection between the two sets of variables, which is in the range of chance.

Another theory is that the Nazca lines were iconic figures carved into the land as part of ritualistic worship. The people, it is thought, wanted to do whatever they could to assure bountiful crops, good weather, survival of the tribes, and protection from marauders, and honoring the gods of the earth, sea, and sky seemed like a good place to start. Supporting this theory is the fact that Nazca pottery has been found on which are seen painted images of many of the depictions found in the desert.

Since their discovery, the Nazca lines have been deemed to be roads, irrigation channels, alien landing strips, icons of worship, and Earth art, and yet there are arguments refuting all of these theories.

The truth is that we may know *how* the Nazca lines were created, and *when*, and by *whom*, but we still do not know *why* they were made.

The enigma in the Peruvian desert still manages to hold on to its mystery.

[1]Paul Kosok and Maria Reiche, "The Mysterious Markings of Nazca," *Natural History Magazine*, May 1947, p. 200.

[2]It was actually von Däniken's book that first called worldwide attention to the Nazca lines. Prior to *Chariots*, the markings were known only to a small group of archaeologists and other researchers.

57

Near-Death Experiences[1]

HAIKU:

NEAR-DEATH EXPERIENCES

A floating balloon
Consciousness tethered no more
Gazing down at me

Death can be robbed of its greatest fearfulness
if we practice for it.

—Fulton J. Sheen[2]

DEFINITION: A near-death experience (NDE) is the experience of one's soul or consciousness leaving the body at the point of death. Upon being resuscitated, many NDE percipients report common elements. The person remembers things like rushing through a tunnel towards a light, meeting one's dead relatives and others, sensing the love and joy of God, and being told the deceased was not ready to leave earthly existence.

WHAT THE BELIEVERS SAY: An NDE is evidence of life after death. It is proof that the consciousness survives death. During an NDE, the soul separates from the body and begins the transition to a higher plane of existence. For some reason, the soul returns to the body, but the experiences the person remembers were real and are what all human beings will go through when they die.

WHAT THE SKEPTICS SAY: A near-death experience is an hallucinatory event triggered by changes in the neurochemistry of the dying brain. Science can explain all of the commonalities of an NDE as manifestations of the effects of cardiac arrest and other often-fatal conditions.

QUALITY OF EXISTING EVIDENCE: Excellent.[3]

LIKELIHOOD PHENOMENA ARE PARANORMAL: Very high.[4]

The term "near-death experience" could be considered a misnomer, since the people who experience NDEs are, during their experience, clinically dead, not near death. In fact, some of the most astonishing reports from resuscitated people recount conversations and events that took place while the person was flat-lined on the table. No pulse, no blood pressure, no brain activity . . . and yet the person retained their singular consciousness and was able to talk about what happened to them when they "returned."

The phrase "near-death experience" was first coined by Raymond Moody in 1975, but there are reports of this type of experience in the Bible, and in the writings of the ancient Greeks, Romans, and Egyptians. NDEs have been reported throughout written history; Plato wrote of one experienced by a soldier.

Many scientists and skeptics do not accept that an NDE is a supernatural or paranormal event.

Some scientists and doctors look to *hypoxia* as a cause for an NDE. Hypoxia is a decrease of oxygen to the brain, and, the theory goes, when the brain is oxygen-deprived, hallucinatory sensory experiences occur. Susan Blackmore, writing in the *Skeptical Inquirer*, recounts research showing that "neural noise and retino-cortical mapping" explain the tunnel/light phenomena; the release of endorphins explains the peacefulness, and the aforementioned cerebral anoxia explains the auditory phenomena. Also, it has been proven that the drug ketamine can cause an experience almost identical to an NDE.[5]

More spiritually oriented people such as psychics and clergy choose to believe that a near-death experience is an actual look, an actual *experiencing*, of the next world and the afterlife. They believe that we all experience exactly what all NDE'ers do, except that the majority of us do not come back to life and, thus, the experience remains within the soul of the deceased.

Carl Sagan, in his book, *Broca's Brain*, posits an interesting explanation for the NDE. His theory is that a near-death experience is a re-experiencing of our own birth. This would explain why NDEs are especially common (and similarly remembered and recounted) in three- to nine-year-olds who "die" and are brought back to life. Their latent birth memories are far more recent than those of, say, a seventy-five-year-old.

Sagan put it this way:

> "[E]very human being, without exception, has already shared an experience like that of those travelers who return from the land of death; the sensation of flight; the emergence from darkness into light; an experience in which, at least perceived, bathed in radiance and glory. There is only one common experience that matches this description. It is called birth.[6]

Many people who have had NDEs claim an incredible sense of peace regarding their eventual death, a truly desirable state of mind. Consciousness researcher John White describes this epiphany:

> The aftereffects of the near-death experience are striking. In general, there is a marked shift in values toward the spiritual, and the total effect is akin to a spiritual rebirth. Most often people say they completely lose their fear of death, knowing it to be based on illusion. They also find that they are more alive, more aware, more sensitive to beauty in the natural world and to the feelings of others. They tend to become stronger psychologically and to have a greater sense of self-worth. They also feel strongly a need to be of service to society in some way, as if they now have a purpose for being in the world—a purpose that came clear to them only through the near-death experience. They are more willing and able to express love and concern to others, and they're more tolerant of others. Their religious sense is deepened, not especially by going to church or temple so much as by a constant background feeling of a spiritual dimension underpinning life. They have an inward feeling of closeness to God and to their fellow man. Altogether, they tend to express thanks for having had the near-death experience.[7]

A 1991 Gallup Poll reported that twelve million Americans have had near-death experiences.

Here are the nine most commonly reported elements of the near-death experience.

1. **Being in Another World or Realm:** This is one of the most commonly reported experiences. People feel that they have somehow crossed over into another plane or level of existence.

2. **An Overwhelming Feeling of Peace:** The sense of peace, serenity, and contentment is so palpable to NDE percipients that many have actually chastised the doctor for pulling them away from the afterlife and bringing them back to life.

3. **A Review of the Person's Life:** This is the archetypal experience of having your life flash before your eyes. This experience has also been reported by people who believed they were dying but who remained conscious throughout. People falling off buildings or drowning have all reported a life review.

4. **An Out-of-Body Experience:** Many NDEs begin with the person's astral body floating up and out of their physical body. Many report that they then felt as if they could fly at will.

5. **Accurate Remote Viewing:** People who have NDEs can often relate details about things they could not have seen while clinically dead, including scenes, events, and conversations that take place outside the emergency room or site of their "death." This is one of the most compelling components of the near-death experience and the element that convinces many that an NDE is, indeed, a supernatural experience.

6. **Encountering Other People:** Many people who have NDEs claim to have met and had conversations with deceased relatives and friends on the other side. Some have spoken with Jesus himself.

7. **The Light:** A wondrous and, to some, holy light often bathes and beckons people who have a near-death experience. Most feel that the light is the source of all things or is actually the physical manifestation of God. Chuck Griswold, quoted on Kevin William's NDE site, stated "Life is love is God" after returning from an NDE.[8]

8. **The Tunnel:** This is often spoken of as one of the most common elements of a near-death experience and yet, in fact only 9 percent of people who were interviewed by Raymond Moody reported walking or floating down a tunnel.

9. **Precognition:** Precognition, or being able to predict the future, was the least-reported NDE element. Cynics look to this as proof that there is nothing even remotely supernatural going on here, and thus, the paucity of genuinely provable phenomena. But 6 percent of all of Raymond Moody's NDE'ers reported being able to know at least something of future events after their experience.

[1] Some of the material in this chapter appeared in a different form in the author's 1994 Plume book, *The Odd Index*.

[2] *Peace of Soul*, p. 206.

[3] NDEs are common and the data is available for study.

[4] There are elements of near-death experience that simply cannot be explained away as a result of wonky brain chemistry.

[5] *The Skeptical Inquirer*, 1991, "Near-Death Experiences: In or out of the body?"

[6] *Broca's Brain*, p. x.

[7] *A Practical Guide to Death and Dying*, p. 23.

[8] http://www.near-death.com/skeptic.html.

58

Noah's Ark

HAIKU:

NOAH'S ARK

Built from God's design
Forty days and forty nights
The boundless waters

And it repented the Lord that he had made man on the earth, and it grieved him at his heart. And the Lord said, I will destroy man whom I have created from the face of the earth, both man and beast, and the creeping thing, and the fowls of the air, for it repenteth me that I have made them. But Noah found grace in the eyes of the Lord.

—Genesis[1]

DEFINITION: Noah's Ark is the enormous ship built by Noah on which he carried his family and all the species of the world during the Great Flood described in Genesis.

WHAT THE BELIEVERS SAY: Noah built an Ark on instructions from God, who had decided to destroy all living things on Earth because of man's evil ways. Since Noah and his family lived virtuous lives, God selected them to survive the flood, repopulate the Earth, and restore the saved animal species to the wild.

WHAT THE SKEPTICS SAY: The story of Noah's Ark is nothing but a Biblical myth, which is quite similar to other worldwide flood myths, especially the Babylonian story of Gilgamesh. There may have been a widespread flood at some point in our prehistory, but the Biblical account of Noah and his ark is a fabricated exaggeration for fabling purposes.

QUALITY OF SUPPORTING EVIDENCE: Poor.

LIKELIHOOD PHENOMENON IS AUTHENTIC: Low.

According to Chapters Six through Eight of the book of Genesis, God was so remorseful at having created man that he decided to "destroy all flesh, wherein is the breath of life."

Why was God so upset with his creation?

Because "the wickedness of man was great in the earth" and his thoughts were "only evil continually."[2]

It is not explained in the Bible why God decided also to kill off all of the earth's blameless animals because of man's wickedness. Also left unexplained is why God ordered Noah to make sure he had a pair from each animal species on the Ark for later repopulating of the earth. He's God, for heaven's sake. Why couldn't he have just wiped out evil man and started over, leaving the animals alone? (These are some of the logistical problems with literal interpretation of Bible stories.)

Based on the ages of Adam and his descendants given in Genesis, God grew disgusted with mankind at some point approximately 8,225 years after he created Adam. That year, which is commonly accepted as circa 2345 B.C., Noah was six hundred years old, and God gave him instructions on how to build the Ark, and what to put in it. It took Noah 120 years to build the ark, which is described as 300 cubits long, 50 cubits wide, and 30 cubits high (450 feet x 75 feet x 45 feet). Apparently, God waited patiently for Noah to complete his construction project.

Noah and his family (only eight people all told, including Noah[3]) then assembled all the species of the earth, including mammals, birds, insects, etc. (fish were presumably left on their own in the abundant waters), loaded them onto the ark along with enough food for all, and then God sealed up the great craft. (Experts estimate that the "non-human" contingent of Noah's ark comprised fifty thousand species of animals and more than one million species of insects.) A week later, the rains began.

It rained for forty days and forty nights and, again according to Genesis, "the waters prevailed exceedingly upon the earth, and all the high hills that were under the whole heaven, were covered."[4]

Noah and company were ultimately to spend over a year aboard the Ark. Noah eventually sent out a dove, which returned with an olive leaf, signaling to Noah that the waters had receded and that everyone could "de-Ark."

Genesis then tells us that after they exited the craft, the ship ended up resting "upon the mountains of Ararat."[5]

Is there any literal truth whatsoever to the Biblical account of the Great Flood, Noah's Ark, the destruction of mankind, and the amazingly long lifespans and reproductive capabilities of Noah's family?

According to Robert M. Best's book, *Noah's Ark and the Ziusudra Epic: Sumerian Origins of the Myth*,[6] there actually was an archaeologically confirmed flood in the ancient Near East sometime around 2900 B.C., and that this is the flood on which the Biblical story of Noah and other mythologies is based. This flood was not universal or widespread, however, and only involved the overflowing of a local river. Apparently, a river barge that was carrying cattle and sheep survived the raging waters, and this event was "adapted" into a religious morality tale by several later writers.

What about the specifics of the Ark and its "passengers" and periodic reports that pieces of the Ark, and even the Ark itself, has been found in the mountains of Turkey?

Breathless documentaries notwithstanding (I'm sure you've seen at least one of them—they seem to appear quite regularly, like specials about UFOs, or Barry Manilow specials), there has never been a credible report of anything being recovered that could be part of, or from the Ark. Every now and then, photos of the Ararat site, taken by pilots or from satellites, surface in which something resembling a large, boxy boat appears to be jutting from the earth. None of these have ever turned out to be anything other than a natural formation. One especially memorable sighting of a long, large boat-shaped object turned out to be nothing more than a fossilized mudflow.

Creationists still await the day when the Ark will be found, and the story told in Genesis is proven to be true. Then, the thinking goes, we can extrapolate that if the Noah story is true, then the creation story is now also proven to be a true account of the beginnings of the universe.

As of this writing, they are still waiting.

[1] Genesis 6:6–8.

[2] Genesis 6:5.

[3] Noah, his wife; his three sons Shem, Ham, and Japeth; and his son's three wives (Genesis 7:13).

[4] Genesis 7:19.

[5] Genesis 8:4.

[6] See select bibliography.

59

Nostradamus
(1503–1566)

HAIKU:

NOSTRADAMUS

Hidden messages?

A maze of meaningful lines?

Did he know the truth?

A new law will occupy a new land around Syria, Judea and Palestine.

> —The Nostradamus quatrain (III, 97) which many
> believe predicts the creation of the state of Israel

DEFINITION: Michael de Nostredame was the French physician and astrologer (1503–1566) who wrote *Centuries* (1555), a book of long-range prophecies. (He also wrote the lesser-known *Prognostications*, which made predictions for the year after it was written.)

WHAT THE BELIEVERS SAY: Nostradamus was the world's greatest psychic and he accurately predicted events centuries in the future. His evocative quatrains contain hidden meanings that should be studied and analyzed.

WHAT THE SKEPTICS SAY: Nostradamus's quatrains are abstract, imagistic, and vague, and they can be interpreted to mean almost anything, depending on the predilection of the reader. Nostradamus could not see the future, any more than someone gazing into a crystal ball today can see what will happen fifty years from now.

QUALITY OF EXISTING EVIDENCE: Excellent.[1]

LIKELIHOOD PHENOMENON IS PARANORMAL: Inconclusive.[2]

Around 1540 or so, when Nostradamus was in his late thirties, he was wandering around Italy, trying to keep a low profile. He had embarked on the road after learning that the Church was considering trying him for heresy under the Inquisition for a chance remark he had made may years prior about the lack of artistic beauty of a statue of the Virgin Mary.[3] As he was walking along the road, he happened upon a young monk. Much to the monk's surprise, Nostradamus dropped to his knees before him, bowed, and said breathlessly, "Your Holiness."

The monk, who as a young boy had been a swineherd and was now a novice at the Minorite Convent, was aghast. "Rise, good sir," he likely implored the man bowing to him. "I am not worthy of such veneration." He probably fled quickly, assuming the impassioned man to be not completely of sound mind.

Over forty years later, and twenty years after Nostradamus's death, that young monk and former swineherd, whose name was Felice Peretti, was elected Pope Sixtus V and served as Pontiff from 1585 to 1590.

Legend? Apocryphal? Perhaps. Perhaps not.

Nostradamus was born a Jew and studied Jewish occult literature until he was nine, when his family converted to Roman Catholicism. He became a physician and acquired some acclaim as a healer for his treatment of plague victims in southern France in the early sixteenth century.

Throughout his medical career, Nostradamus was also writing short four-line quatrains or six-line stanzas, which he believed were prognosticatory. He later said that his quatrains, which were collected in *Centuries*, predicted the future, through the years 3797, after which the world might, or might not, end.

Nostradamus wrote almost one thousand quatrains but there are a handful that are always cited when discussing his alleged prophetic abilities.

Did Nostradamus accurately predict the 1666 London Fire, the French Revolution, the terror regime of Adolf Hitler, and the assassination of John F. Kennedy?

The "Hitler" prediction is especially intriguing since, if it were true, it would prove that a sixteenth century seer was able to see the birth, life, and atrocities of what some describe as the most evil person who has ever lived.[4]

Nostradamus scholar Erika Cheetham translated Nostradamus's "Hitler" quatrain (Century II, Quatrain 24) as follows:

> Beasts wild with hunger will cross the rivers, the greater part of the battlefield will be against Hitler. He will drag the leader in a cage of iron, when the child of Germany observes no law.[5]

Can it be that Nostradamus actually mentioned Hitler by name, hundreds of years before he was born?

The original French version of the quatrain reads, *"Plus part du champ encontre Hister sera."* It is now commonly accepted that "Hister" referred to an area of the lower Danube, not a person. Cheetham's translation of "Hister" as "Hitler" is now discredited.

What about the assassination of JFK?

There are several quatrains that speak of "brothers" and "great men" and assassinations. Personally, I do not find much validity in crediting Nostradamus with an accurate prediction of the assassination of JFK.

The problem with the most arcane of Nostradamus's predictions is that they can often be interpreted to mean just about anything.

Sometimes, however, the French seer names names. The twenty-fifth quatrain of Century I translates as follows:

> The lost thing is discovered, hidden for many centuries.
> Pasteur will be celebrated almost as a god-like figure.
> This is when the moon completes her great cycle,
> but by other rumours he shall be dishonoured.[6]

This seems to be uncannily accurate. Louis Pasteur's advancements in germ theory did, indeed, elevate him to the stature of legend. However, there was also great resistance to his ideas in some schools of medical thought and this could easily be the "dishonor" of which Nostradamus writes.

The prophecies of Nostradamus are still being read and interpreted and modern events are oftentimes perceived as a fulfillment of one or more of his prophecies.

Nostradamus has his naysayers and critics, but it is difficult to be skeptical when the French prophet names names.

[1] The writings of Nostradamus survive and are available in many books and also online for anyone to translate and study to their heart's content.

[2] Yet another "eye of the beholder" situation with a paranormal or occult phenomena. If an individual interprets a particular image—"fire in the north," for instance—in a Nostradamus quatrain to mean the bombing of Canada, a forest fire in Wisconsin, or an arson outbreak in Finland, who can say they're wrong, if one of these events actually occurs. And since Nostradamus's quatrains are often interpreted *after* the event, the possibility of assumed "accuracy" is high.

[3] Nostradamus was wise to avoid the emissaries of the Inquisition. If he had been brought in for questioning, he would have been tortured mercilessly with all manner of implements, stretched on the rack, and probably executed for allegedly defiling the name of the Blessed Mother. It would not have mattered much if the charges against him were true or not.

[4] See *The Evil 100* (Kensington Publishing, 2002) by Martin Gilman Wolcott. Wolcott ranks the one hundred most evil people in history and Adolf Hitler is number one on his list.

[5] *The Prophecies of Nostradamus*, p. 82.

[6] *The Prophecies of Nostradamus*, p. 24.

60

$$0123456789$$

Naught One Two Three Four Five Six Seven Eight Nine
Arabic Numerals.

Numerology[1]

HAIKU:

NUMEROLOGY

Do numbers mean more?
Numerical occult truth?
Can we count on it?

*I have often admired the mystical way of Pythagoras,
and the secret magic of numbers.*

—Sir Thomas Brown[2]

DEFINITION: Numerology is a form of divination in which numbers are said to possess prognosticative powers.

WHAT THE BELIEVERS SAY: Numbers have mystical powers.

WHAT THE SKEPTICS SAY: Numbers are merely representational symbols within the construct of mathematics, used to define values. They do not have any paranormal or spiritual significance.

QUALITY OF SUPPORTING EVIDENCE: Fair.

LIKELIHOOD PHENOMENON IS AUTHENTIC: Fair.

Numerology zealots embrace as their hero the Greek philosopher and mathematician Pythagoras and point to the universal notion held by many that particular numbers are "lucky" as evidence of the assumed mystical power of numbers. They assert that our leaning towards (and away, in the case of "unlucky" numbers) a particular number is a subconscious acknowledgment of their sway over our life paths.

Bernard Gittelson, writing in *Intangible Evidence*, defined the subtext of numerology:

> Numbers are the tool of choice for the numerologist. Much as an astrologer uses the position of the planets at the time of your birth as the basis for analysis of character and to forecast your future, numerologists use calculations based on the numerological values of your name and birth date. How can numbers have any predictive value? How can they reveal character? Numbers, say the adepts, have accumulated meanings in the collective unconscious to which we unknowingly respond. Our name, our birth date, is an intrinsic part of our makeup; we are under its influence. We also build personal associations to numbers throughout our lives, which add to the universal associations another layer of significance.
>
> Many adepts claim that numerology is not actually the study of numbers so much as it is the study of the symbols for the numbers and their cultural and psychological significance, both conscious and unconscious, symbolic and literal.[3]

Numerologists differ on assigning carved-in-stone meanings to specific numbers, but generally, the following traits and characteristics apply to the numbers one through nine.

1. Strength of will and individualism
2. Reason and docility
3. Happiness and energy
4. Stability and organization
5. Self-confidence and impatience
6. Art and balance
7. Thought and introspection
8. Leadership and materialism
9. Mental and spiritual wisdom

There are several ways to determine your personal number and thus create your personal numerological reading.

The most important personal number is your *birth force* number. This is arrived at by adding up the digits in the numbers of your birthday.

At the risk of revealing the unvarnished truth about myself, I will now use my own birthday as an example to illustrate the calculation of my own personal *birth force* number.

I was born on July 16, 1953, which is written numerically as 7-16-1953.

Step one is to add up the digits of my date of birth:

$$7+1+6+1+9+5+3 \ = \ 32$$

Step two is to add up the resulting digits:

$$3+2 \ = \ 5$$

Thus, my birth force number is $^{32}\!/\!_5$. The most important reading is generated by the 5, but supposedly you're supposed to also look at the 3 and the 2 to see where the 5 came from.

Therefore, according to my birth force number, self-confidence and impatience are my motivating characteristics, and those specific personality traits are manifested due to an inner happiness, sense of energy (the "3"), and reason and docility (the "2").

Now you know everything there is to know about me, right?

Not quite. Now we move on to my *name* number.

There are several ways to determine your *name* number using the letters in your name, but one popular system (an ancient method that is still used) is one based on the Hebrew alphabet that utilizes the digits one through eight.

The alphabet is laid out according to the following chart:

1	2	3	4	5	6	7	8
A	B	C	D	E	U	O	F
I	K	G	M	H	V	Z	P
Q	R	L	T	N	W		
J		S			X		
Y							

You then spell out your complete name and put the appropriate number beneath the letters . . .

S	T	E	P	H	E	N	J	S	P	I	G	N	E	S	I
3	4	5	8	5	5	5	1	3	8	1	3	5	5	3	1

and then add them up:

$$3+4+5+8+5+5+5 \ + \ 1 \ + \ 3+8+1+3+5+5+3+1 \ = \ 65$$

Reduce the sum down:

$$6+5 \ = \ 11$$

And then again:

$$1+1 = 2$$

My *name* number is 2, which indicates that I have a reserve of reason, but that I can occasionally be too docile and unassertive.

Other important numbers include the *soul* number, which is the numerical total of all the vowels in your name, and the *personality* number, which is the total of all the consonants in your name.

A professional numerologist will take many different calculations to arrive at a series of numbers which he will then interpret for a full-fledged reading.

(Another much-used system utilizes the following chart:

1	2	3	4	5	6	7	8	9
A	B	C	D	E	F	G	H	I
J	K	L	M	N	O	P	Q	R
S	T	U	V	W	X	Y	Z	

You might also try calculating your numbers using this method and see if the results change.)

Other important numbers in the annals of numerology include:

- **11:** This was the number of Christ's faithful disciples and thus stands for revelation and truth.

- **12:** This is a very significant number and some of its associations include the twelve Signs of the Zodiac, the twelve hours in the day and night, the twelve Gods of Olympus, the twelve Tribes of Israel, the twelve apostles, and the twelve days of Christmas. The number twelve thus stands for completeness.

- **13:** Traditionally considered an unlucky number that signifies doom and bad luck, thirteen's bad reputation is said to stem from the fact that Jesus and his twelve apostles totaled thirteen men, and the thirteenth (Judas) was a traitor.

- **22:** This number is said to be important because there are twenty-two letters in the Hebrew alphabet and because there are twenty-two cards in the "major arcana" of the Tarot deck. The number twenty-two also signifies completeness.

- **40:** This number, like the number twelve, has many associations in history and religion, including the forty days and nights of the great Flood, the forty days Moses spent on Mt. Sinai, and the forty days Jesus spent fasting in the desert. Once again, we have a number signifying completeness.

Numerology does have its followers, although it is always included in the basket of pseudosciences (some would call "phony" sciences) that contains astrology, palmistry, and the reading of tea leaves. Regardless of the veracity of its claims, though, if numerology is looked upon as a psychological tool that can possibly reveal truths about oneself, then it must be considered useful. For instance, if during a numerology reading a person is told that his or her number indicates stability and organization and yet he or she knows *the opposite* to be true, the person may then make a conscious effort to change negative traits into positive ones.

Truth be told, it is definitely less expensive than ten years of psychotherapy.

[1]Note: The numerical analysis of the author's name was originally conducted for the author's 1994 Plume book, *The Odd Index*.

[2]*Religio Medici* (1643), Part I, p. 12.

[3]Bernard Gittelson, *Intangible Evidence*, pp. 385–86.

61

The Ouija Board

HAIKU:

OUIJA

Sliding planchette speaks
Dark messages from beyond?
Or naught but a game?

What is it? "Ouija" prophesies, forewarns and advises, as well as prefigures one's destiny. "Ouija's" revelation of what was, what is, and what is to come, rival the Delphic Oracles. The curtain is lifted, revealing the secrets of that debatable land between matter and spirit, and nature's laws have no control over this marvelous instrument. The Unknown Land seems almost within our grasp, and the scientific mind strives to comprehend just where this borderland lies. The "Ouija" is without a doubt the most interesting, remarkable and mysterious production of the twentieth century. Its operations are always interesting and frequently invaluable, answering, as it does, questions concerning the past, present and future with marvelous accuracy. Price: $1.50[1]

DEFINITION: A Ouija board is a trademarked game consisting of a board with letters, numbers, and words on it, and a planchette, which is a small triangular board supported by two casters and a vertical stylus. When a person's fingertips are lightly placed on top of the planchette, it will supposedly move across the board and point to letters that spell out words and messages.

WHAT THE BELIEVERS SAY: The Ouija board is a tool which can be used to communicate with the spirits of the deceased.

WHAT THE SKEPTICS SAY: The Ouija board is only a game. Any movement of the stylus is due solely to the unconscious actions of the players; any messages received are subconsciously "written" by the participants.

QUALITY OF SUPPORTING EVIDENCE: Fair.

LIKELIHOOD PHENOMENON IS AUTHENTIC: Low.

In the chilling film *The Exorcist*, young Regan uses a Ouija board to chat with her friend Captain Howdy. We later learn that Captain Howdy is really Pazuzu, the demon that possesses Regan. She ultimately requires a horrific (and messy) exorcism. (See Chapter 27.)

In the *Witchboard* horror movie series, teenagers use a Ouija board to summon a demon who pretends he is the ghost of a dead young boy. Havoc ensues.

In a fourth season episode of the HBO series, *The Sopranos*, two young children use a Ouija board in an attempt to contact their dead mother, with frightening and unexpected results.

There are countless other pop culture examples of the Ouija board being portrayed as a means to summon demonic spirits; as a portal to the realm of evil.

This, in essence, is nothing but show business.

Believers in the paranormal and the spiritual realm use the Ouija board as a channeling device and are certain that the messages they receive from the spirits channeled by the users of the board are revealed information. The Ouija board is used for channeling and divination (see Chapters 21 and 28), and there are strict guidelines as to using it safely.

Some of these rules include:

- Never use a Ouija board alone and never use it in a place where spirits might be presumed to gather, i.e., graveyards, haunted places, sites of personal tragedy, etc.
- To protect yourself while using the board, visualize white light entering, filling, and then surrounding your body.

- Treat contacted spirits with courtesy and respect.
- Do not let the spirits count the numbers backwards, or recite the alphabet. If they complete either sequence, they will be able to escape from the board.
- If the planchette repeatedly makes a figure eight, it means that an evil spirit is in control of the board.
- The only way to protect yourself if an evil spirit gains control of the board is to immediately begin using the planchette upside down.
- Do not try to destroy a Ouija board by burning it. Reportedly, the board will scream and anyone who hears the scream will have less than thirty-six hours to live.
- Never ask about God.
- Never ask what day or how you are going to die.

There were many precursors to the Ouija board of today. All of these earlier devices used some kind of writing instrument which spirits supposedly "possessed" to communicate with the living.

One of the earliest was the planchette, which was a pencil attached to a heart-shaped pointer that was placed above a sheet of paper. Other early spirit communication instruments were alphabet wheels and boards, and pendulums which swung above letters to form words.

The Ouija board as we know it today was invented in the early 1890's by E.C. Reiche, Elijah Bond, and Charles Kennard. The design was later improved upon by William Fuld who was also responsible for the legend of the origin of the name "Ouija." Fuld revealed to the world that the name came from the French and German words for "yes": *oui* and *ja*. This sounded good, but the truth was that Fuld simply made it up. The other myth surrounding the name was that one of its inventors, Charles Kennard, was told the name of the board *by the board itself*, and that the board also told him that *ouija* was Egyptian for "good luck." This was also untrue.

The truth is that Kennard simply made up the name and *ouija* was how it was known from then on.

The Ouija trademark and game design is now owned by Parker Brothers and is a consistent big seller.

Is there any validity to the belief that a Ouija board can be used to contact the other side?

There are accounts in the literature of people who have used a Ouija board and have been given information that later proved to be correct. However, it is likely that in the vast majority of cases, any messages communicated through a Ouija board are from what is known as the ideomotor effect. Imperceptible muscle movements, triggered by the user's subconscious, move the planchette over the letters. Skeptics assert that there is no validity to the claim that spirits are contacted via the board, and that any seemingly accurate messages are probably due to synchronicity (see Chapter 86).

Nevertheless, Ouija boards will continue to sell, and groups of curious adolescents, drunken teenagers, and the spiritually curious will sit with boards on their laps, place their fingertips on the planchette (not too hard, remember!) and ask the spirits to advise them on romance, money, and the future.

[1]From the 1940 Ralph E. Sylvestre & Company catalog for spiritualists and mediums.

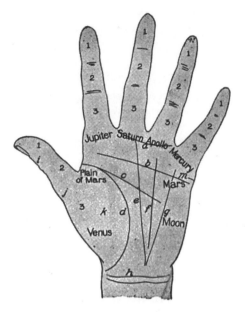

62

Palmistry

PALMISTRY

Open palms beckon
Promises of who you are
The truth in creased lines?

That there is so much information in the hand will be a surprise to many, and when it is seen how logical, rational, and even commonplace, hand reading is, perhaps it will then be taken out of the occult class to which it distinctly does not belong, and placed among the other rational means at the service of mankind, whereby they may be enabled to gain a better knowledge of themselves . . .

—William Benham[1]

DEFINITION: Chiromancy. The practice or art of telling people's character, future, and worries from the lines, marks, and patterns on the palms of the hands.

<small>WHAT THE BELIEVERS SAY:</small> The palm of the hand holds truths and secrets, and can not only reveal details about the individual, but also about their future.

<small>WHAT THE SKEPTICS SAY:</small> There is no scientific evidence whatsoever to support the contention that creases and lines in a person's palm can reveal anything about anything or anybody, especially future events.

<small>QUALITY OF SUPPORTING EVIDENCE:</small> Fair.

<small>LIKELIHOOD PHENOMENON IS AUTHENTIC:</small> Fair.

I once had my palm read at a UFO convention and the first thing the reader said was, "You are the oldest of four children, you have two brothers and a sister, you are married, and you have no children." All true.

When I began to ask questions, she silenced me, continued to tell me what she saw in the lines of my hand, and then I had to cut the reading short to go interview a guy who traveled with a squad of invisible Bigfoots (Bigfeet?).

There are three subsets of palmistry: **Chiromancy**, **Chirognomy**, and **Dermatoglyphics**.

Chiromancy consists of studying and "reading" the lines of the palm and divining information, often quite specific, about the person's life, romances, finances, family, health, and personal relationships.

Chirognomy looks at the innate, genetic shapes of the palm, fingers, and fingernails; along with the texture and consistency of the skin and nails. The personality and traits of a person are said to be revealed in these elements of the hand, and a skilled reader can often provide an in-depth analysis of an individual.

Dermatoglyphics is the study of the skin ridge patterns and creases in the fingertips and the skin of the palm, and it is the closest palmistry comes to real, provable science. Recent studies have shown a specific pattern in the palms of babies born with Down's Syndrome. There is ongoing research into the possibility that Alzheimer's patients may exhibit similarly identifiable palm patterns, and there is also interest in comparable research into the link between palm patterns and diabetes, epilepsy, and certain genetically predisposed cancers.

Following these discoveries, proponents of palmistry ask the (reasonable) question, "If illnesses and diseases can be identified and possibly predicted by studying the palm, is it not possible that there is other information in the hand as well?"

LINES IN THE HAND

Palmists identify many lines in every human being's palm, four of which are considered the major lines. They are the **Life Line**, the **Head Line**, the **Heart Line**, and the **Line of Fate**.

The **Life Line** wraps around the lower left quadrant of the palm (on a left hand), encircling the thumb and its fleshy base. This line indicates the length of a person's life (the longer the line, the longer the life), as well as predicts major life events. One can identify major events by dividing the line into thirds, beginning at the top, with each section signifying a twenty-five-year span. Breaks, splinters, crosses, and other markings at a specific place on the line supposedly pinpoint the period when a major event will occur. My Life Line is well-defined, deep, unbroken, begins with my Head Line, and wraps around the base of my thumb. According to traditional interpretation, this means I will have good health, vitality, long life, and that I am endowed with deep emotion, good judgement, and a sense of caution.

The **Head Line** bisects the middle of the palm. It is the second most important line and can also be divided into thirds. Mine starts beneath my index finger, immediately crosses my Life Line and is long and deep. This apparently means that I think logically, have good self-control, and (again) good judgment.

The **Heart Line** is parallel to the Head Line, directly above it. Mine is long, has a few splinter breaks in it, and is placed in the middle of my palm, halfway between my fingers and wrist. Meaning? Loyalty, trust, sincerity, willingness to sacrifice, emotional upheavals, and a successful love life. (No comment.)

The **Line of Fate** extends down the middle of the palm, beginning beneath the middle finger and stretching almost to the wrist. Mine is pale and thin, meaning that fate does not play that much of a role in the events of my life, which somewhat confirms the other lines' messages of logic, judgment, and caution.

These lines, in a wide array of thicknesses and lengths, are present on almost all hands.

As in all types of divination, the interpretation of palmistry readings is in the eyes and mind of the beholder. One needs to decide for him- or herself if the meaning assigned to particular lines are specific to them, and accurate; or vague, general, and inaccurate.

Interestingly, palm readings *can* serve as a type of psychological self-review. If, for instance, a reading tells a person that she is prone to rash decisions and this person knows that she is, in fact, guilty of such misjudgments, then she could embark on a program of change and self-improvement. In that context, palmistry can be useful and relevant.

But to look to lines in the palm for information about specific incidents in a person's life, such as deaths, financial windfalls or set-backs, and other unknowable events, seems more delusional whimsy than scientific or psychological reality.

[1]William Benham, *The Laws of Scientific Hand Reading.*

63

The "Paul Is Dead" Mystery[1]

HAIKU:

PAUL IS DEAD?

Was the crash for real?
Backwards are the messages
Paul is touring now

However foolish its guise, the McCartney rumor clearly indicates that there is a potential for irrational belief and action—be it constructive or be it destructive to what or whose values—that is alive and well in the modern, industrialized, "enlightened" world.

—Barbara Suzek[2]

DEFINITION: Paul McCartney was killed in a car accident in 1966 and the Beatles decided to keep it a secret . . . but to plant clues in their recordings so that the attentive fan would eventually know the truth.

WHAT THE BELIEVERS SAY: Paul McCartney is dead and the Beatles told the world about the tragic car accident that killed him in a series of hidden clues in and on their records.

WHAT THE SKEPTICS SAY: The "Paul Is Dead" mystery was an elaborate hoax nurtured by the fact that many alleged "clues" on the Beatles records actually *could* be interpreted to mean that Paul had died. Whether these were all astonishing coincidences or deliberately planted is unknown to this day.

QUALITY OF EXISTING EVIDENCE: Excellent. The clues are there.

LIKELIHOOD PHENOMENON IS AUTHENTIC: Nil. Paul is touring this year.

There is no denying that finding and analyzing all the "Paul Is Dead" clues is an enormous amount of fun.

This is probably what prolonged the worldwide frenzy back in September, October, and November of 1969 when the rumor that Paul had died in a car crash first surfaced, thanks to an intentionally satirical review of *Abbey Road* in a college newspaper that claimed to find all kinds of secret messages and clues the surviving Beatles planted to tell the world that Mr. McCartney was no longer with us.

The article that started it all was written by University of Michigan sophomore Fred LaBour. LaBour was inspired to write the review after Detroit's WKNR-FM disk jockey Russ Gibb received a call from a guy named Tom who claimed to have found secret messages on Beatles records revealing that McCartney was dead.

LaBour heard Gibb's conversation with the caller and decided to deliberately expand on the "Paul Is Dead" thesis in his *Abbey Road* review for the University of Michigan's school newspaper, *The Michigan Daily*.

LaBour's article began:

> Paul McCartney was killed in an automobile accident in early November, 1966 after leaving EMI recording studios tired, sad and dejected.
> The Beatles had been preparing their forthcoming album, tentatively entitled *Smile*, when progress bogged down in intragroup hassles and bickering. Paul climbed into his Aston-Martin, sped away into the rainy, chilly night, and was found four hours later pinned under his car in a culvert with the top of his head sheared off. He was deader than a doornail.

LaBour's article discussed the most common "Paul Is Dead" clues, including Paul's "O.P.D." ("Officially Pronounced Dead") jacket patch on the *Sgt. Pepper* album; the "I buried Paul" fadeout on "Strawberry

Fields Forever"; all the appearances of hands above Paul's head in Beatles' photographs; the *Abbey Road* funeral procession; and the backwards message "Turn me on, dead man" in "Revolution Number 9."

The myth immediately took hold and blossomed. It was learned that the surviving Beatles decided that they would *not* reveal this terrible tragedy to their fans but instead, replace Paul with a double, a musical *doppelgänger*.

Paul's "replacement" was a guy by the name of William Campbell, a lucky bloke who just so happened to be the winner of a Paul McCartney Look-Alike Contest. Not only was Campbell the spitting image of the "cute" Beatle, he was also musically and vocally gifted enough to be able to duplicate Paul's writing, playing, and singing abilities. After a period of "training" by John, George, and Ringo, Campbell took Paul's place in The Beatles.

Even though The Beatles did not want to shock the world by revealing the truth about Paul's violent death, they had too much respect for their fans not to let them somehow know of his death. Thus, they began planting "clues" on Beatles albums that would alert the attentive fan to the terrible reality.

The rumors surrounding Paul's alleged death grew into a cottage industry. Special edition magazines and TV and radio programs were devoted to the rumors, and countless newspaper articles fueled the fervor. (I can remember trading clues with fellow Beatlefans when I was in my teens, aghast at the thought that the rumors might actually prove to be true. They weren't, as we now know, and it would be another decade before we actually would have to go through the *real* death of a Beatle.)

This feature compiles some of the more intriguing "hidden" clues. I have concentrated here on primarily visual clues found on record albums and on aural clues heard in The Beatles' songs. I have not focused on song lyrics because they are open to a wide range of interpretation—almost anything can be read into a line from a song. I do, however, examine song lyrics that seem to be a deliberate attempt by The Beatles to address the whole "Paul Is Dead" phenomenon (such as the "walrus was Paul" line in "Glass Onion").

1. **The two *Yesterday and Today* album covers:** *Yesterday and Today* was the first Beatles album released after Paul's rumored death and the two versions of the album's cover are supposed to contain the first of the hidden messages from The Fab Four.

   The first cover, the infamous recalled "butcher" cover, is supposed to contain the most blatant acknowledgment of Paul's death. (The "butcher" cover was originally shot for the "Paperback Writer" single and added to the album as an afterthought.

This cover, which is now an extremely valuable collectible, shows the four Beatles in white butcher coats, covered with decapitated dolls and bloody meat.) The clues here are that the two headless dolls in the picture are resting on Paul's right and left shoulders and a doll's head sits in his lap. (George holds the other severed head.) This is supposed to be The Beatles' way of visually illustrating the bloody results of Paul's car crash. Also, there is a pair of false teeth on Paul's right arm, apparently indicating that his teeth were knocked out during the accident and they could not identify his body from dental records.

The second cover—the "trunk" cover—shows us Paul sitting in a trunk that is standing on its side with its cover open. This trunk is supposed to symbolize a coffin and indicate that Paul is buried somewhere. In the picture, none of The Beatles are smiling and John, George, and Ringo are all standing above the trunk supposedly looking down into Paul's casket.

2. **The *Rubber Soul* album cover:** This cover is supposed to be a photograph taken from inside Paul's grave looking up. The four Beatles are all seen from below in sort of a fisheye view and it is their way of telling fans that Paul is dead. Also, the title *Rubber Soul* is their way of hinting at the bogus nature of the Paul replacement.

3. **The *Revolver* cover:** This cover, designed by Beatlepal and fellow Brian Epstein artist Klaus Voorman, consists of a collage of line drawings and black-and-white photos of the four Beatles. The death clue? Paul's face is the only one shown in profile; all the others are seen full face. Why this means Paul is dead baffles the mind, but cluesters have considered this to be one of the hints.

4. **The "Strawberry Fields Forever"/"Penny Lane" single sleeve:** This sleeve has a framed photo of The Beatles on a stage. Four stage spotlights highlight the boys: one above John's head; one above Ringo's head; and one to the left of George. Paul's spotlight, however, emanates from a mirror directly in front of him, indicating, presumably, that he is on another plane, and that his "inner light" is in a mirror world somewhere. Quite clever, wouldn't you say?

5. **The "Strawberry Fields Forever" video:** Paul is seen in a tree looking down on the other three, symbolically representing once again that he has risen above the survivors to another plane.

6. **The *Sgt. Pepper Lonely Hearts Club Band* album front cover scene:** There are several visual clues on the cover of *Sgt. Pepper*

that indicate that The Beatles are trying to tell the world that Paul is dead. The first and most obvious is that the cover photo depicts a funeral. Whose? Why, Paul's of course!

7. **The flower guitar:** In the foreground is a bass guitar made of flowers that has only three strings. This is Paul's bass and the three strings symbolize the three remaining Beatles. Some people also claim that they can see "Paul?" spelled out in the flowers.

8. **The propped-up Paul:** Paul is the only one facing front and the other three Beatles are all turned towards him as though they were holding him up. If he were dead, he would need to be held up, right? (Shades of *Weekend at Bernie's!*) Outtakes of the *Sgt. Pepper* photo shoot session show Paul in a variety of positions and locations on the set, including sitting down.

9. **Paul's black instrument:** John, George, and Ringo are all holding brass instruments. Paul's is black, symbolizing his death.

10. **The doll and her car:** There is a doll to the left of The Beatles wearing a dress that reads "Welcome the Rolling Stones." On the doll's lap is a toy car that is supposed to be either on fire or filled with blood. This is the Aston-Martin that Paul was driving when he had his fateful accident on November 9, 1966. Also, there appears to be what looks like streaks of blood running down the doll's dress.

11. **The secret message on the bass drum:** If you take a mirror and place it so that you split the words "Lonely" and "Hearts" horizontally, the resultant "words" spell out the secret message "ONE HE DIE." This is a stretch but this message can actually be seen if you're generous about interpreting certain symbols and curves as letters. The actual text that appears if you cover the bottom half of the letters so that the top halves are doubled and reversed is "1ONE1X HE|DIE."

12. **The hand above Paul's head:** There is an open palm above Paul's head. According to the "Paul Is Dead" mythology, this is supposed to be an Eastern gesture that is made over someone about to be buried. No such symbology exists.

13. **The Shiva doll:** A four-armed Indian Shiva doll points his "death" hand (the left rear hand) at Paul.

14. **George's message:** On the back cover of the *Sgt. Pepper* album, George can be seen pointing directly at the lyric "Wednesday morning at five o'clock" in "She's Leaving Home." This was supposed to be the time and day of Paul's fatal accident.

15. **Without Paul?:** Paul's head touches the words "Without You" from George's song, "Within You Without You," indicating that The Beatles—and the world—must, duh, now survive without the esteemed Signore McCartney.

16. **Paul's back?:** On the back cover of the *Sgt. Pepper* album, Paul is the only one with his back to the camera. This means that he is dead. There are conflicting stories explaining why Paul is, indeed, seen only from behind. One explanation was that it wasn't even Paul in the picture. In *The Long and Winding Road: A History of The Beatles on Record*, Neville Stannard wrote:

> Also on the back cover is a small picture of The Beatles, but one Beatles has his back turned. This is because it isn't a Beatles at all, and is, in fact, Mal Evans—Mal deputised for Paul, who was in America to be with Jane Asher on her twenty-first birthday . . . As the sleeve had to go into production by the end of April, before Paul was due to return, Mal donned Paul's Sgt. Pepper gear and stood in for him, but turned his back so that people would not suspect that Paul was absent.

And to further confuse matters, Paul himself has talked about his backwards pose on the cover. Paul claims that he is, in fact, the person seen in the photograph. In 1980, he told *Musician* magazine, "[I]t was just a goof when we were doing the photos. I turned my back and it was just a joke."

Also, in Mark Lewisohn's essential *The Beatles Recording Sessions*, there are several rare, full-color outtakes from the *Sgt. Pepper* photo shoot and Paul is in every one of them.

17. **Paul's "O.P.D." patch:** Inside the album, Paul is seen wearing a patch on his jacket that reads "O P D," initials which supposedly stand for "Officially Pronounced Dead," the British equivalent of the American phrase "Dead On Arrival." This was allegedly a very blatant way for The Beatles to tell us all that Paul was dead. The truth is that the patch actually reads "O. P. P.," which stands for "Ontario Provincial Police." The garment has a fold in it which makes the last "P" look like a "D" to some people. All of The Beatles received these patches as a gift during their 1965 North American tour. (The Fab Four played the Toronto Maple Leaf Stadium on August 17, 1965.)

18. **Paul's Medal of Valor:** In the inside photo, Paul is seen wearing a British Medal of Valor. This was alleged to be the surviving Beatles' way of telling his fans that he died a heroic death. The only

trouble with this clue is that the medal he (and George, for that matter) are wearing is not a British Medal of Valor. What *does* the medal represent? Who knows?

19. **The bloody sleeve:** Some fans have noted that the original inner sleeve of the *Sgt. Pepper* album is colored red at the bottom and gets progressively lighter as the color rises to the top of the sleeve. This is supposed to mean that the album was standing in blood and the red liquid seeped its way up through the paper. This means that Paul is dead.

20. **Selected *Sgt. Pepper* lyrics:** To many "Paul Is Dead" cluesters, *Sgt. Pepper*'s is the album that includes the most candid lyrical admissions that Paul died and was replaced by lookalike William Campbell. The first clue comes in the first song, "Sgt. Pepper's Lonely Heart's Club Band" in which "Paul" sings "So let me introduce to you the one and only Billy Shears." "Billy Shears" is supposed to actually be the words "Billy's here," revealing that Paul has been replaced by William "Billy" Campbell.

   In "She's Leaving Home," is the aforementioned line "Wednesday morning at five o'clock" which is supposed to be the time of Paul's fatal car accident.

   In "Lovely Rita," Paul tells us that he "caught a glimpse of Rita" and was so distracted that he "took her home" and "nearly made it." This leads us to the line telling us that he "didn't notice that the light had changed," from "A Day in the Life." We are also told in "A Day in the Life," that "he blew his mind out in a car."

   In "Good Morning, Good Morning," we once again are told the time of Paul's accident: "People running 'round, it's five o'clock."

   In "Within You Without You" we again are told that life goes on "without you [Paul]."

21. **In the British groove:** I have not heard this one myself, but supposedly on the inner groove of side two of the British *Sgt. Pepper* disk, the words "Never could be any other way" are repeated over and over. This is supposed to be The Beatles' was of telling Paul's fans to accept his death.

22. **Really??!!:** On mono pressings of the album, during the reprise of the title cut, a voice can be heard shouting, "Paul McCartney is dead, everybody! Really, really dead!"

23. **Paul's where?:** On European pressings of *Sgt. Pepper*, after "A Day in the Life," there are two seconds of chatter which apparently can be interpreted as the phrase "Paul's found Heaven."

24. **The *Magical Mystery Tour* album cover phone number:** The word "Beatles" is written in stars on the cover of the *Magical Mystery Tour* album and if you read the word upside down it reveals the phone number 537-1038, or the phone number 231-7438, depending on how you interpret certain "digits." According to the "Paul Is Dead" mythology, if you called this number at a certain time (revealed in the lyrics of "She's Leaving Home") you would be connected with none other than Billy Shears himself (actually Paul's replacement William Campbell), who would then tell you the truth about Paul's death.

25. **The magical Beatles:** On the inside cover of the *Magical Mystery Tour* album, there is a drawing of the four boys dressed as magicians. Paul's hat has black flowers on it which, of course, means that he is dead.

26. **The walrus was Paul?:** On the *Magical Mystery Tour* album cover, Paul is dressed as a black walrus, supposedly a symbol of death in some Scandinavian cultures. This is totally inaccurate and there is no connection between the symbol of the walrus and the concept of death in any of the Scandinavian mythologies.

27. **Paul was?:** On page three of the souvenir booklet that came with the *Magical Mystery Tour* album, Paul is seen sitting behind a desk that has a sign on it that reads "I WAS." Some people see this sign as reading "I YOU WAS." Whatever. This sign means, of course, that Paul is dead.

28. **John buried Paul:** At the conclusion of "Strawberry Fields Forever," John can be heard saying, "I buried Paul." What he is actually saying is "cranberry sauce."

29. **The black flower:** As mentioned in the intro to this chapter, in the "white tails" photograph in the *Magical Mystery Tour* photo booklet, John, George, and Ringo are all wearing red carnations and Paul is wearing a black one. This means that he is dead, even though he just happened to be the Beatles who got the black one after the florist ran out of red flowers. Can you imagine the confusion if one of the other Beatles had worn the black one for that picture? The "Paul Is Dead" legend would have entered a whole new phase and befuddled fans who were certain they had already figured the whole shebang out!

30. **Another hand over Paul's head:** On page twenty-four of the booklet, a man in a bowler hat has his hand held above Paul's head. See number twelve.

31. **"Your Mother Should Know"**: If this *entire song* (sheesh) is played backwards, it supposedly contains such lines as "Why doesn't she know me dead?" and "I shed the light." Tell you what: You play the song backwards and listen for recognizable English and let me know, okay?

32. **"Glass Onion" = casket handles?**: Russ Gibb claimed that the term "glass onion" was British slang for casket handles because that's what the old-style handles looked like. There is no historical documentation that confirms this theory.

33. **"The walrus was Paul"**: When John sang this line in "Glass Onion," fans considered it in light of the *Magical Mystery Tour* photo of a Beatle dressed as a walrus (the supposed symbol of death, remember?) and concluded that John was confirming that Paul was dead. He wasn't, and he wasn't.

34. **The end of "I'm So Tired"**: If you play backwards the mumbling at the conclusion of John's "I'm So Tired" on the *White Album* and listen carefully, you can hear, "Paul is dead, miss him, miss him." In Mark Lewisohn's important chronicle of The Beatles in the studio, *The Beatles: The Recording Session*, he reveals that John actually muttered (in *forward* speech, of course), "Monsieur, monsieur, how about another one?"

35. **George's lament**: At the end of "While My Guitar Gently Weeps," George cries out, "Paul, Paul, Paul." This meant that Paul was dead. What George actually sings/moans is, "oh, oh, oh."

36. **"Number nine, Number nine, Number nine, Number . . ." oh, forget it**: This is a spooky one. When the "Number Nine" mantra from "Revolution Nine" on the *White Album* is played backwards, it *really* does sound like "Turn me on, dead man." John Lennon admitted that all the EMI recording engineers would say the take number onto the tape before beginning a recording and John just happened to like the sound of the guy saying, "Number nine." Andru Reeve, in his definitive "Paul Is Dead" book *Turn Me On, Dead Man*, suggests that the phonetic reversal might have been intentional; that John played "Turn me on, dead man" backwards and decided it sounded enough like "Number nine" to ultimately work. John Lennon himself refutes this theory but, then again, maybe *John's denial* was part of the conspiracy, too! (Only kidding.)

37. **Yet another hand over Paul's head!**: On the *Yellow Submarine* album cover, John is seen holding his hand over Paul's head. See numbers twelve and twenty-nine.

38. **The *Abbey Road* funeral procession:** The *Abbey Road* album cover was the visual confirmation of Paul's death that really pushed a lot of fans over the edge. The photo of The Beatles crossing Abbey Road supposedly contained scads of "how can it not be so!?" clues that drove "Paul Is Dead" theorists nuts.

    First, The Beatles' attire tells the tale. John is dressed in all white. This meant that symbolically he was the priest at Paul's funeral. Ringo is dressed in a tailored black suit. This meant he was the funeral director. George is in denim, meaning he was the gravedigger. And Paul was dressed in a suit, but barefoot, with his eyes closed, and carrying an unlit cigarette in the wrong hand. This meant that he was the corpse. In addition to The Beatles themselves, other clues include the Volkswagen "Beetle" parked on the street. This vehicle has a the license plate "LMW 28IF." The "LMW" was supposed to translate as "Linda McCartney Weeps" and the "28IF" meant that Paul would have been twenty-eight *if* he had lived.

    All of these "clues" have been quite effectively debunked but the fact that fans were able to come up with such detailed interpretations from one photo illustrates the rabid interest the "Paul Is Dead" theory provoked in Beatles watchers.

    The clothes were just what each Beatle happened to decide to wear the day the picture was taken. (During a 1969 radio interview, John said, "We all decided individually what to wear that day for the photograph.") Paul being barefoot is coincidence: He showed up for the shoot in sandals and decided to take them off for one shot. There are five outtakes from this session in which Paul is seen crossing the street wearing the sandals in two of them.

    The VW just happened to be parked there and couldn't be moved. (This car sold for $4,000 at auction in 1986.) The license plate was the car's actual plate.

39. **We've Just Seen a Face?:** On the back of the *Abbey Road* album cover, a girl in a blue dress is seen passing in front of the wall on which "The Beatles" is written. If you look carefully, you can see Paul's face (actually his nose and mouth) in the girl's elbow. To be fair, there *is* something in the photo that can be interpreted as a face, but who the hell would have seen it if no one believed Paul was dead? Also on the back cover are a series of eight dots that form the number "3" when connected with a pen or marker. This was how the surviving Beatles told us that there were only three of them left. In reality, the number could also be seen as a "5" which would add whole new dimension to the rumor, wouldn't it?

40. **One and one and one . . .:** This was blatant. In "Come Together," John sang the line, "One and one and one is three," yet another "three" message about the loss of one Beatle.

41. **Octopus's Garden:** Supposedly, the term "octopus's garden" is a slang British naval term for burial at sea, from either drowning or as an intentional interment. This was Ringo's way of telling us that Paul was dead.

    In a 1996 interview, Ringo talked about writing "Octopus's Garden" and revealed that someone once told him that it was common for octopi to collect shiny things from the ocean floor and neatly arrange them in their nest . . . almost like flowers in a garden. Upon hearing this Ringo thought it was the "happiest" thing he had ever heard and, thus, was inspired to write the song.

[1]Some of the material in this chapter appeared in a different form in the author's 1998 book, *The Beatles Book of Lists* (Kensington Publishing).
[2]*Urban Life and Culture*, 1972.

64

Perpetual Motion

HAIKU:

PERPETUAL MOTION

Ceaselessly moving
Limitless source of power?
Or a futile dream?

*The end of our foundation is the knowledge of causes
and secret motion of things . . .*[1]

DEFINITION: "Perpetual motion" refers to the imagined continuous operation of an isolated mechanical device or other closed system *without* a sustaining energy source and without the addition of energy.

WHAT THE BELIEVERS SAY: A perpetual motion machine is possible; we just don't yet know how to build one. One day we will understand how to defeat the scientific laws of nature that seemingly prevent bona fide perpetual machine devices.

WHAT THE SKEPTICS SAY: Perpetual motion is impossible; it violates the first and second laws of thermodynamics. There is no way a machine can run forever without needing an energy source.

QUALITY OF EXISTING EVIDENCE: Excellent.[2]

LIKELIHOOD PHENOMENON IS PARANORMAL: Nil.[3]

The notion of a machine that, once it is built and started will run forever without needing fuel or power of any sort, has been a seductive, elusive dream of mankind for centuries.

Imagine! An engine that simply runs and runs and runs, never needing gasoline, never wearing out, and never stopping unless someone stops it.

The need for fossil fuels would plummet; drilling would almost completely cease; the environment would rebound and thrive; world economies would soar; poverty would become an anomaly.

This is, in its most literal sense, a "pipe dream."

The first and second laws of thermodynamics, however, tell us that mechanical systems cannot work continuously without external help, i.e., the addition of energy.

This seemingly irrefutable scientific law has not deterred inventors, however, and history is replete with the designs and concepts of all manner of intricate, exotic, and just plain silly machines and devices that their creators claimed would run forever.

The pursuit of true perpetual motion was discouraged somewhat following the mainstream awareness of the first and second laws, but there are still inventors who believe that perpetual motion is possible, even though science tells us the exact opposite.

Many perpetual motion machines use overbalanced wheels, the flow of water, sunlight on mirrors, weights and counterweights, and other systems which seemingly create more energy than they use. Interestingly, many of these machines seem to do precisely what they are designed to do, that is, *create* energy without *requiring* energy. But careful examination of these machines reveal that they are not true perpetual motion machines. No matter how long they will run, or how little energy they will use compared to the energy they produce, they will eventually stop. The wheels or gears will wear out, or the water filters will clog, or the belts will break. And all of these eventualities would require *the addition of energy* to restore motion and the creation of energy, thus invalidating its claim of perpetual motion.

Is a perpetual motion breakthrough possible? Or is the path to a future of limitless energy a chimera, glimpsed intermittently in some of these odd devices, yet, ultimately, scientifically possible?

The first steps on that path may be taken thanks to a revolutionary new concept of energy production called Zero-Point Energy (ZPE). ZPE permeates the universe, and has been identified as a result of the electronic activity of subatomic particles (electrons, photons, neutrons, etc.) in the vacuum of space. Supposedly, this energy is able to be harnessed and, in fact, Nikola Tesla, Henry Moray, and other scientists and engineers in the 1920s built a fully functioning machine that used ZPE, which was then referred to as "Radiant Energy" to create electricity.

The Radiant Energy machine was never brought to market and the stories about why it was suppressed speak of conspiracy theories, death threats, and deliberate destruction of equipment in order to keep the machine from becoming widely known and used. Who would stand to lose if the world was blessed with abundant energy from nothing but the air around us?

The answer to that question may suggest the perpetrators of the movement to keep a free energy machine out of the public domain.

Perpetual motion is scientifically not possible, but almost perpetual motion is not only possible, but has been achieved.

Perhaps it is in our best interest to encourage even seemingly crackpot ideas for perpetual motion machines. So what if an inventor comes up with a machine he says will run forever and, instead, it only runs for, say, a hundred years, before the wheels wear out or the mechanism corrodes? Isn't such an improvement in our current wasteful, fossil-fuel based energy supply chain worth pursuing?

Again, the question must be asked: Who would stand to lose the most from a machine that created energy with no need for fuel?

The track of our future needs lies in the answer to that question.

[1]Francis Bacon, *New Atlantis* (1627).

[2]All purported "perpetual motion" machines are available for careful study and evaluation. Thus, the evidence for evaluation of the attempts to create perpetual motion is excellent.

[3]If perpetual motion is one day achieved, it will be a purely scientific breakthrough, albeit one of epic proportions, with a full and complete understanding and utilization of all the laws of quantum physics. It will almost certainly not be a supernatural occurrence.

65

The Philadelphia Experiment

HAIKU:

THE PHILADELPHIA EXPERIMENT

Elephantine ship
Here one moment, gone the next?
Hiding in plain sight?

Nothing really disappears . . . the sum of matter remains exactly the same . . .

—Francis Bacon[1]

DEFINITION: An alleged experiment in 1943 in which the U.S. Navy rendered the U.S.S. *Eldridge* invisible and then beamed[2] it and its crew from a shipyard in Philadelphia to a shipyard in Norfolk, Virginia.

WHAT THE BELIEVERS SAY: In 1943, the United States Navy did in fact make a destroyer invisible, and transport it from Philadelphia to Virginia, using technology similar to the fictional Transporter's "beaming" capabilities on the TV series, *Star Trek*. The experiment was officially known as Project Rainbow.

WHAT THE SKEPTICS SAY: No Navy ship was ever made invisible, and no ship or crew members were ever "transported" anywhere. The Philadelphia Experiment story is pure myth and has no basis in fact whatsoever. Certain Navy magnetic degaussing experiments to make a ship's magnetic signature "invisible" combined with the written ravings of a delusional "witness" have combined over the years to create one of the most enduring legends of the twentieth century.

QUALITY OF EXISTING EVIDENCE: Poor.[3]

LIKELIHOOD PHENOMENON IS PARANORMAL: Nil.[4]

Scotty is always very careful to verify his coordinates when he beams someone down to a planet or onto another ship. Apparently it is quite possible for the *Enterprise*'s Transporter to beam someone *into* a solid object. The unimaginable horror of suddenly reconstituting inside a wall, or being partially embedded in the bulkhead of another starship must have given the engineers at Starfleet nightmares when designing the Transporter system. One wonders why there wasn't a fail-safe feature preventing such a tragedy? And if it did happen, would it be possible to remove a crewman from the object, or would his molecules be inextricably entwined with the substance of the object?

In 1943, as legend has it, American Navy personnel were subjected to precisely such a horror when they were made invisible and transported from Philadelphia to Virginia. Some of the crewmen were rematerialized inside their ship's bulkhead. Other crew members went insane from being made invisible.

Can any of this be true?

Does the United States Navy, using a sophisticated application of Einstein's "unified field" theory (which is the common allegation) have the capability of making something as large and *solid* as a naval destroyer invisible?

Here are excerpts from the U.S. Navy's official statement about the Philadelphia Experiment:

> Over the years the Navy has received innumerable queries about the so-called Philadelphia Experiment . . .
>
> The genesis of the Philadelphia Experiment myth dates back to 1955 with the publication of *The Case for UFO's*, by the late Morris K. Jessup. Some time after the publication of the book, Jessup received correspondence from a Carlos Miguel Allende [who alleged to have witnessed the experiment].
>
> During the experiment, according to Allende, a ship was rendered invisible and teleported to and from Norfolk, Vir-

ginia, in a few minutes, with some terrible aftereffects for crew members.

Navy personnel in Philadelphia believed that the questions surrounding the so-called Philadelphia Experiment arise from quite routine research which occurred during World War II at the Philadelphia Naval Shipyard. It was believed that the foundation for the apocryphal stories arose from degaussing experiments which have the effect of making a ship undetectable or "invisible" to magnetic mines. ONR has never conducted any investigations on invisibility, either in 1943 or at any other time (ONR was established in 1946). In view of present scientific knowledge, ONR scientists do not believe that such an experiment could be possible except in the realm of science fiction.

Morris Jessup's book about UFOs apparently triggered something in Carlos Allende. In his letters to Jessup, he claimed to have actually witnessed the experiment and, as these claims are sometimes wont to do, they became part of the literature and they were accepted by many people, some of whom held strong beliefs in an ongoing disinformation campaign by the U.S. government and military.

The reality is a bit more prosaic.

Yes, the U.S. Navy was experimenting with "invisibility" in 1943. But they were using the word "invisible" to mean "undetectable by enemy magnetic torpedoes." To accomplish this, they supposedly outfitted certain ships with special propellers which could not be heard by enemy radar. They also wrapped giant electrical cables around ships and sent current through them to "erase" the ships' magnetic signatures.

Someone allegedly overheard an *Eldridge* crew member in a bar talking about being "made invisible." Also, the story goes, the *Eldridge* was docked in Philadelphia one night, then it was gone during the overnight hours, and then it was back in its berth the following morning. This seemed to be impossible, since it was a two-day trip from Philadelphia to Norfolk. Thus, the story took shape and, when Allende's charges surfaced, otherwise explainable events took on the aura of a supernatural occurrence.

Was the ship in Philadelphia one night, Virginia, during the night, and back in Philadelphia the following morning?

No. It is all part of the myth.

According to the Office of Naval Research, the *Eldridge* was *never* docked in Philadelphia.

The aforementioned experiments with degaussing, though, *were* taking place at the Philadelphia shipyard.

Combine *this* truth with the rumors, the conspiracy theories, the unproven allegations and, of course, a movie[5] depicting precisely what the legends tell us and we have a myth that will not die.

Of course, all of this logical analysis and rationalization of reality could be part of a massive disinformation program by the Navy and the U.S. government. (Sorry, I had to say it.)

However, as seductive the notion is of the U.S. having the ability to beam stuff all over the place, it seems that if we did have this technology, we wouldn't still be moving men and material the hard way.

[1] *Cogitationes de Natura Rerum*, p. 5.

[2] Yes, "beaming" means what it does on *Star Trek*—teleporting a solid object from one place to another in a cascade of light.

[3] Other than Allende's wild accusations, there is no concrete physical evidence proving that the Philadelphia Experiment ever took place.

[4] In all likelihood, the Philadelphia Experiment legend is a complete fabrication, based on unsubstantiated witness accounts and the rumored misinterpretation of a crew member's alleged offhand use of the word "invisible."

[5] *The Philadelphia Experiment*, 1984.

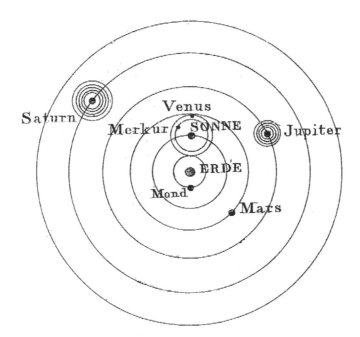

The Planet Vulcan

HAIKU:

VULCAN

Mystery planet
Transiting the Sun's surface
But a chimera

*On the 26th March, about four o'clock, I directed my
telescope to the sun, as I had been in the habit of doing,
when, to my surprise, I observed, at a small distance from
its margin, a black spot well-defined and perfectly round,
and advancing with a very sensible motion upon the disk of
the Sun.*

—Dr. Edmond Modeste Lescarbault[1]

DEFINITION: The planet Vulcan was believed to be a phantom planet
transiting the Sun in orbit between the planet Mercury and the Sun.

WHAT THE BELIEVERS SAY: There is a planet between Mercury and
the Sun.

WHAT THE SKEPTICS SAY: There is no planet between Mercury and the Sun. Einstein proved that the calculations that demonstrated the existence of Vulcan were incorrect. Alleged visual sightings of Vulcan were incorrect, and were probably nothing but asteroids.

QUALITY OF SUPPORTING EVIDENCE: Poor.

LIKELIHOOD PHENOMENON IS AUTHENTIC: Nil.

Anyone who has ever seen even one episode of *Star Trek* knows of the existence of the planet Vulcan, the home planet of *Enterprise* First Officer Mr. Spock. The planet Vulcan is believed to circle the nearby star Epsilon Eridani, and it is approximately 10.5 light years from Earth. (Of course, warp travel makes that trip take about as long as a walk to a store a couple of blocks over.)

The name of Spock's home planet was obviously inspired by the true story of the search for the planet Vulcan, an ultimately futile quest, but one which, nevertheless, became, for a time, the "talk of the town."

The story of the ghost planet began in earnest one afternoon in March 1859 when a country physician with a passion for things astronomical, one Edmond Modeste Lescarbault, saw through his telescope a black object moving slowly across the golden disk of the Sun. He first saw it when it was already transiting the Sun, so he did not know where it first appeared, or how long it had been visible. He took detailed measurements and performed some calculations, continuing to follow the object (interrupted briefly by the needs of a demanding patient), until it moved off the solar disk and out of range of his telescope.

Lescarbault was very excited and believed he had seen the intramercurial planet the French astronomer Le Verrier had predicted existed solely through a complex series of equations and computations. Le Verrier had used a similar set of calculations to mathematically "discover" the planet Neptune, so his assertions about this new planet were taken quite seriously by the scientific community of the time. In order to explain weird anomalies in Jupiter's orbit, Le Verrier had proven the existence of an unknown planet affecting its orbit, and he had been right.

The planet Mercury exhibited similar strange orbital behavior and so Le Verrier concluded that there had to be a planet between Mercury and the Sun, affecting Mercury's orbit. Neither he, nor any of his astronomer colleagues had ever visually confirmed the existence of this planet, yet Le Verrier stood by his calculations and his conclusions.

At first, Dr. Lescarbault did not contact anyone about his sighting, nor did he talk about it. He was hesitant to discuss it until he had seen it again. Thus, he waited nine months before writing to Le Verrier. Finally, in his December 22, 1859 letter, he told the esteemed scientist of his experience, and provided complete technical details.

Le Verrier was secretly thrilled that someone had independently confirmed his calculations, yet he was loath to place much credence in a single letter from a country doctor.

Shortly thereafter, Le Verrier left Paris and personally traveled to Orgéres-en-Beauce to talk to (actually, to mercilessly interrogate) the amateur astronomer. Dr. Lescarbault passed muster and upon his return to Paris, Le Verrier publicly announced the doctor's sighting and declared the existence of a planet between Mercury and the Sun. It was to be called Vulcan. Its orbit was thirty-three days, and his calculations showed that Vulcan would next transit the face of the Sun in March 2, 1877.

Europe and the rest of the world erupted in Vulcan fever. (Vulcanmania?) Articles were written, seminars convened, and Dr. Lescarbault was awarded the Legion of Honor for his discovery.

March 2, 1877. Vulcan did not appear as predicted by Le Verrier. Six months later, on September 23rd, Le Verrier died.

Neither the great astronomer's death nor Vulcan's absence cooled the interest in the new planet, and work continued on both sides of the Atlantic. Scientists labored to prove Vulcan's existence, and both professional and amateur astronomers kept their telescopes pointed at the Sun, hoping for a glimpse of the fugitive intramercurial stellar body.

For thirty-eight years, the belief in Vulcan was strong, although over time, some scientists were beginning to doubt its existence.

In 1915, Albert Einstein completed work on his general and special theories of relativity.

These physical theories of space and time stated that all the laws of physics are valid in all frames of reference, and Einstein concluded that the speed of light is always the same from a uniformly moving source, no matter how fast or slow the source—or its observer—is moving. This scientific breakthrough revealed that time and space actually "warped" within the vicinity of a massive stellar body like the Sun, and thus explained the orbital anomalies of Mercury—*without* requiring the existence of an orbit-effecting planet between Mercury and the Sun.

The search for the planet Vulcan was over.

Le Verrier's legacy of an intramercurial planet was shattered, and yet, great credit is still accorded him for calculating the ecliptic variants of the nonexistent Vulcan. Mercury's orbit *is* affected and the

Sun is the reason. Working pre-Einstein, Le Verrier searched for the most logical and provable answer to the problem—and found it. It would take the genius of Albert Einstein to demonstrate that Le Verrier was explaining a real fluctuation with the wrong cause.

Today, the name "Vulcan" is part of the global culture—but not because of the nineteenth century search for it, however, but because of a TV show.

[1]Quoted in an article by M. L'Abbé Moigno in the January 6, 1860 issue of the journal *Cosmos*.

The Powers of Holy Water

HAIKU:

HOLY WATER

Grace flows from water
Power from blessed waters
Holy stream of life

*We bless these creatures in the Name of Jesus Christ, Thy
only Son; we invoke upon this water and this oil the Name
of Him Who suffered, Who was crucified, Who arose from
the dead, and Who sits at the right of the Uncreated. Grant
unto these creatures the power to heal; may all fevers, every
evil spirit, and all maladies be put to flight by him who either
drinks these beverages or is anointed with them, and may
they be a remedy in the Name of Jesus Christ, Thy only Son.*

—Fourth century blessing[1]

DEFINITION: Water that has either been blessed by a holy person
(priest, shaman, minister, etc.), or that comes from a well, spring, or
river considered "sacred." Such water is believed to possess miraculous healing powers.

WHAT THE BELIEVERS SAY: Holy water is a gift from God, and is a
tool by which He wields His hand to bestow healing miracles upon
the faithful.

WHAT THE SKEPTICS SAY: Holy water is nothing but plain water and it
has no magical, spiritual powers. All supposed cures attributed to
holy water are psychosomatic and probably due to the placebo effect,
and all evidence of such cures is anecdotal.

QUALITY OF EXISTING EVIDENCE: Good.[2]

LIKELIHOOD PHENOMENA ARE PARANORMAL: Fair.

While researching holy water and its alleged powers, I came
across a story that especially interested me, since the events took
place in my hometown of New Haven, Connecticut.

A miraculous holy water healing in my town?

I will leave it to the reader to decide on the validity of this story.

Dr. Richard Selzer of Yale University Medical School is a world-
renowned surgeon who also happens to be a best-selling author. In
his stunning 1974 book, *Mortal Lessons: Notes on the Art of Surgery*,
he tells the story of his patient, Joe Riker of New Haven, Connecticut.

Joe was a short order cook who had a hole in his head.

Literally.

A cancerous tumor had eaten away at Joe's skull, through the
flesh, through the bone, through the membranes, until his actual
brain was fully exposed. Dr. Selzer describes the hole as the size of
Joe's mouth, noting that "you could have dropped a plum into it."[3]

Dr. Selzer saw Joe in his office every Thursday at four o'clock.
The ritual was always the same. Joe would remove his hat, Dr. Selzer
would examine the enormous cavity in his head and then tell Joe that
he could surgically remove the tumor, put in a metal plate, and Joe
would be cured.

Joe's response was also always the same: "No operation."[4]

And Dr. Selzer always came back with the half-joking, "You give
me a headache."[5]

One Thursday, Joe did not show up for his appointment. He also
did not keep his appointment the following week. After a month of no-
shows, an angry Dr. Selzer visited Joe at the diner where he worked,
and Joe agreed to see him that afternoon in the doctor's office.

When Joe removed his fedora later that day, Dr. Selzer was astonished to see that the hole was healing. "Where once there had been a
bitten-out excavation, moist and shaggy," he wrote, "there is now a
fragile bridge of shiny new skin."[6]

When the doctor asked him what happened, Joe replied, "The
wife's sister, she went to France, and brought me a bottle of water
from Lourdes. I've been washing it out with that for a month."[7]

Dr. Selzer concludes his account of Joe's "miraculous cure" wondering to himself, "Could such a man, I think as I sip my coffee, could such a man have felt the brush of wings?"[8]

So, did holy water cure Joe Riker's cancer?

The faithful will answer "Unquestionably"; the skeptics will answer, "Of course not."

In fact, I have read reviews of Selzer's book in which the reviewers dismiss the cure as nothing but a coincidence.

This inevitably leads to the very difficult question, "When is a coincidence more than a coincidence?" According to the skeptics, Joe Riker's cancer would have healed and the hole would have closed up even if he had not washed out the wound with holy water.

The shrine at Lourdes is not the only source in the world of allegedly miraculous water. There are many, many wells and springs in several countries that are reputed to have curative powers. One popular site is the farm village of Tlacote near Mexico City in Mexico. The water there has reportedly been healing pilgrims of everything from AIDS and cancer to diabetes and high cholesterol since a farmer saw a very sick dog drink some of the water and be almost immediately healed.

All holy water that has been tested has been shown to be nothing but plain water. Believers counter the scientific results with, "So what?" God is not going to put some unknown supernatural element into the water to "prove" that it is a divine gift.

All that is needed, they say, is faith.

If you believe you will be healed, you will be. If you are a Doubting Thomas, or Gloria, or Harry, then it probably won't work.

Joe Riker believed the Lourdes water would cure his cancer. After he used it, his cancer was cured.

Are you going to argue with him?

---

[1] This blessing of water and oil was used by the Pontifical of Scrapion of Thumis, a fourth century bishop during Mass (from the *Catholic Encyclopedia*).

[2] Many stories of miraculous cures from holy water are, as noted, mostly anecdotal, but some of these stories are extraordinarily convincing. (There have also been a few medical studies done with surprisingly validating results.) There are accounts of unexplained remissions from cancer, as well as restoration of sight, and cures of diseases like polio and multiple sclerosis. Thus, the "Good" rating of evidence quality, and the "Fair" rating for paranormal likelihood. These stories are voluminous and, even if only a few are a true account of the effects of the water, then there could be the possibility that there is something beyond psychology in the use of these waters.

[3-8] Richard Selzer, from "The Surgeon as Priest" chapter from *Mortal Lessons*.

The Prediction of the Sinking of the *Titanic*

HAIKU:

TITANIC

Vast black glass water
Jet face of ancient iceberg
Still of the new dead

She was the largest craft afloat and the greatest of the works of men.

—The opening line of Morgan Robertson's novella,
The Wreck of the Titan

DEFINITION: The belief that the sinking of the *Titanic* was predicted fourteen years earlier in a novella by a British writer.

WHAT THE BELIEVERS SAY: *The Wreck of the Titan* is prophecy.

WHAT THE SKEPTICS SAY: The facts in the *Wreck of the Titan* that do compare similarly to the *Titanic* are nothing but coincidence.

QUALITY OF SUPPORTING EVIDENCE: Very good.

LIKELIHOOD PHENOMENON IS AUTHENTIC: High.

Did Morgan Robertson predict the sinking of the *Titanic* fourteen years before the great liner's maiden voyage?

In 1898, Robertson, a popular adventure writer of the time, published a novella called *Futility*, which was a thrilling story about the largest passenger steamship ever built striking an iceberg in the north Atlantic and sinking. The ship was called the *Titan* and close to three thousand souls were lost when she foundered.

Fourteen years later, the *Titanic* would strike an iceberg in the north Atlantic and sink within three hours.

Shortly after *Titanic* was lost, Morgan Robertson's publishers re-released *Futility*, but this time it had a new title: *The Wreck of the Titan*.

How close *were* the two ships—and their two stories?

The following table provides a side-by-side look at some of the most amazing parallels. Regardless of the presence—or lack thereof—of precognitive abilities on the part of Morgan Robertson though, there is no denying that the *Wreck of the Titan* is one of the stranger elements of the *Titanic* legend.

	The *Titan*	The *Titanic*
Length:	800 feet	882.5 feet
Number of propellors:	3	3
Watertight compartments:	19	16
Watertight doors:	92	12
Passenger capacity:	3,000	3,000
Passengers on board:	3,000	2,200
Displacement (in tons):	45,000 (1898 edition) 70,000 (1912 edition)	66,000
Gross tonnage:	45,000	46,328
Nickname:	"Unsinkable" (Chapter 1)	"Unsinkable"
Horsepower:	40,000 (1898 edition) 75,000 (1912 edition)	46,000
Lifeboats:	24	20
Speed at time of collision:	25 knots	22.5 knots
Month voyage began:	April	April
Side of ship that struck iceberg:	Starboard	Starboard
Time iceberg was struck:	Near midnight	11:40 P.M.
Itinerary:	New York to England	England to New York

	The *Titan*	The *Titanic*
Location of collision:	North Atlantic, a few hundred miles off U. S. coast	North Atlantic, a few hundred miles off U. S. coast
First warning of danger:	"Ice, ice ahead. Iceberg. Right under the bows"	"Iceberg! Right Ahead!"
Ship's owners:	British company	British company
Ship's owners' headquarters:	Liverpool	Liverpool
Ship's owners' U. S. office location:	New York	New York
Deaths:	2,987	1,507+
Nationality of principal stock owners:	American	American

—————————————————■—————————————————

THE COMPLETE FIRST CHAPTER OF
The Wreck of the Titan

She was the largest craft afloat and the greatest of the works of man. In her construction and maintenance were involved every science, profession, and trade known to civilization. On her bridge were officers, who, besides being the pick of the Royal Navy, had passed rigid examinations in all studies that pertained to the winds, tides, currents, and geography of the sea; they were not only seamen, but scientists. The same professional standard applied to the personnel of the engine-room, and the stewards' department was equal to that of a first-class hotel.

Two brass bands, two orchestras, and a theatrical company entertained the passengers during waking hours; a corps of physicians attended to the temporal, and a corps of chaplains to the spiritual welfare of all on board, while a well-drilled fire-company soothed the fears of nervous ones and added to the general entertainment by daily practice with their apparatus.

From her lofty bridge ran hidden telegraph lines to the bow, stern engine-room, crow's-nest on the foremast, and to all parts of the ship where work was done, each wire terminating in a marked dial with a movable indicator, containing in its cope every order and answer required in handling the massive hulk, either at the dock or at sea—which eliminated, to a great extent, the hoarse, nerve-wracking shouts of officers and sailors.

From the bridge, engine-room, and a dozen places on her deck the ninety-two doors of nineteen watertight compartments could be closed in half a minute by turning a lever. These doors would also close automatically in the presence of water. With nine compartments flooded the ship would still float, and as no known accident of the sea could possibly fill this many, the steamship *Titan* was considered practically unsinkable.

Built of steel throughout, and for passenger traffic only, she carried no combustible cargo to threaten her destruction by fire; and the immunity from the demand for cargo space had enabled her designers to discard the flat, kettle-bottom of cargo boats and give her the sharp dead-rise—or slant from the keel—of a steam yacht, and this improved her behavior in a seaway. She was eight hundred feet long, of seventy thousand tons' displacement, seventy-five thousand horse-power, and on her trial trip had steamed at a rate of twenty-five knots an hour over the bottom, in the face of unconsidered winds, ides, and currents. In short, she was a floating city—containing within her steel walls all that tends to minimize the dangers and discomforts of the Atlantic voyage—all that makes life enjoyable.

Unsinkable—indestructible, she carried as few boats as would satisfy the laws. These, twenty-four in number, were securely covered and lashed down to their chocks on the upper deck, and if launched would hold five hundred people. She carried no useless, cumbersome life-rafts; but—because the law required it—each of the three thousand berths in the passengers', officers', and crews' quarters contained a cork jacket, while about twenty circular life-buoys were strewn along the rails.

In view of her absolute superiority to other craft, a rule of navigation thoroughly believed in by some captains, but not yet openly followed, was announced by the steamship company to apply to the *Titan*: She would steam at full speed in fog, storm, and sunshine, and on the Northern Lane Route, winter and summer, for the following good and substantial reasons: First, that if another craft should strike her, the force of the impact would be distributed over a larger area if the *Titan* had full headway, and the brunt of the damage would be borne by the other. Second, that if the *Titan* was the aggressor she would certainly destroy the other craft, even at half-speed, and perhaps damage her own bows; while at full speed, she would cut her in two with no more damage to herself than a paintbrush could remedy. In either case, as the lesser of two evils, it was best that the smaller hull should suffer. A third reason was that, at full speed, she could be more easily steered out of danger, and a fourth, that in case of an end-on collision with an iceberg— the only thing afloat that she could not conquer—her bows would be crushed in but a few feet farther at full than at half speed, and at the most three compartments would be flooded—which would not matter with six more to spare.

So, it was confidently expected that when her engines had limbered themselves, the steamship *Titan* would land her passengers three thousand miles away with the promptitude and regularity of a railway train. She had beaten all records on her maiden voyage, but, up to the third return trip, had not lowered the time between Sandy Hook and Daunt's Rock to the five-day limit; and it was unofficially rumored among the two thousand passengers who had embarked at New York that an effort would now be made to do so.

———————————■———————————

[1]Some of this material appeared in a different form in the author's 1998 book, *The Complete Titanic* (Citadel).

69

Psychokinesis

HAIKU:

PSYCHOKINESIS

Mentally moving
Solid objects by a thought:
Unattainable?

Eppuor si muove.
"And yet it moves."[1]

DEFINITION: The indisputable physical movement of objects by scientifically inexplicable means, as by the exercise of an occult power, or by using alleged powers of the mind (also known as telekinesis).

WHAT THE BELIEVERS SAY: The ability to move objects using mental powers is real, is proven, and is something anyone can learn to do. Many experiments have proven its existence and the standards most commonly used preclude the possibility of the results being attributable to chance. "In short, recent experiments seem to indicate that the human mind can control delicate machinery by thought alone."[2]

WHAT THE SKEPTICS SAY: Telekinesis, psychokinesis, and all other supposed mental powers are nothing but bunk and stage tricks. The human mind is not capable of moving anything through thought alone.

QUALITY OF EXISTING EVIDENCE: Very good.

LIKELIHOOD PHENOMENON IS PARANORMAL: High.

Psychokinesis is real. It has been proven to exist during controlled experiments, the details of which are available online and in books.

Beginning with J.B. Rhine's experiments in the 1930s, and continuing from the 1950s through today, scientists interested in parapsychology and the untapped powers of the human mind have worked and conducted experiments to prove that psychokinesis exists. Scientists have long wanted to know if, resident within human consciousness, was an ability to physically affect machines and outcomes without actually touching the machine, or the dice, or the balls.

Such thoughts were, for a long time, scientific blasphemy. Scientists studying ESP, remote viewing, and psychokinesis were ridiculed and, worse, ignored by their colleagues. Rational science considered parapsychology a pseudoscience that was not worthy of serious study—or corporate funding. The U.S. government felt otherwise, however, since there was concrete evidence that the Soviet Union was moving full speed ahead with research into psychic abilities with, the CIA assumed, the intent of using such powers as a spying tool and weapon.

Thus, during the Cold War, most of the funding for psychic research came from the government. (See Chapter 73, "Remote Viewing.")

For several decades, scientific protocols were established, experiments were quietly conducted, and subjects were carefully evaluated for abilities that seemed beyond the ken of mortal men. Some experiments involved subjects attempting to affect the direction of the roll of balls. Some tried to change the occurrence of random binary events on a computer through thought alone. Some experiments studied the correlation between such variables as lunar fluctuations, sunspot activity, and geomagnetic variations and their impact on Las Vegas casino pay-offs. Some tried to understand the true nature of the intangible concept of "luck" and whether or not the thoughts and desires of the subject affected "the way the chips fell," so to speak.

Over time, the totality of the results were indisputable: the mind could change outcomes.

Granted, the percentage of "hits" was small, but the successes exceeded random chance and proved the existence of *something* that is, ironically, currently *randomly* present in some people.

So, what is psychokinesis?

Is it a mental faculty that is ultimately controllable by training and self-discipline, like concentration, fortitude, courage, patience, cooperation, compassion, and other psychological facilities?

And if so, why can't everyone do it?

If our minds have within it the power to affect physical reality, then why has it not been obvious and utilized over the past millennia?

Some say it is because it is, yes, a mental power, but it is in the earliest stages of its evolution.

Man's *physical abilities* evolved over time and continue to evolve.

When we started living beneath the trees instead of in them, we began to walk upright.

There has been a steady increase in human brain size over the past four million years, from 450 cc to today's 1350 cc size.

Our earliest ancestor, *Ardipithecus ramidus*, was about 4 feet tall—we are now considerably taller; when we harnessed fire, our molars got smaller; when we moved away from a raw plant diet to a cooked meat diet, our appendix became useless; as we became more dependent on machinery, our skeletons became smaller and weaker.

These physical changes took millions of years. Is it not possible that latent "wild talents" of our gloriously evolved brains may take considerably longer—but we have hints of their presence today?

---

[1] Galileo said this under his breath after he was forced to recant his belief that the Earth moved around the sun.

[2] *Fate*, 1997.

70

Pyrokinesis

HAIKU:

PYROKINESIS

The firestarters
Can use nothing but their thoughts
To bring on a blaze

C'mon baby, light my fire.

—Jim Morrison[1]

DEFINITION: The alleged "psi" ability to ignite fire by the power of the mind.

WHAT THE BELIEVERS SAY: There are people whose psi powers are highly developed and not only can they move things with their minds (telekinesis), they can also create heat and set objects and people on fire with nothing but their thoughts.

WHAT THE SKEPTICS SAY: Pyrokinesis is real only in books and movies. There is no scientific evidence of pyrokinesis and, in fact, it isn't even a word! The notion of being able to ignite objects by thought is not based in anything but fantasy.

QUALITY OF EXISTING EVIDENCE: Negligible.

LIKELIHOOD PHENOMENON IS PARANORMAL: Nil.

For those who believe in the psi abilities of the human mind (telekinesis, ESP, etc.), it does not require much of a leap of faith to also believe in the ability of the human mind to start fires.

Pyrokinesis is the power possessed by "firestarters." Adding to the mix are people who spontaneously burst into flames (see Chapter 81, "Spontaneous Human Combustion"), people who are immune to fire and heat (see Chapter 37, "Fire Immunity and Firewalking"), and so-called "electric people," people who can generate measurable electrical current and sparks. In addition to these anomalous folk, there are those who glow with an aura and emit visible fields of some kind of electrical and/or magnetic energy (see Chapters 13 and 45, "Auras and Halos," and "Kirlian Photography").

But what about firestarters? This potentially deadly psi ability was apparently known to people who studied parapsychology, but it became a *mainstream* "wild talent" with the publication in 1980 of Stephen King's novel *Firestarter*.

From my 2001 book, *The Essential Stephen King:*

> In *Firestarter*, the clandestine government agency The Shop performs ostensibly innocent experiments on college students, telling them that they are testing low-grade hallucinogenics for psychological study. The Shop was actually trying to stimulate paranormal abilities (better psychic powers through chemistry) for covert use and it did not have a contingency plan for what would happen if two of the test subjects married and had a child.
>
> Two of the test subjects—Andy McGee and Vicky Tomlinson—*did* marry and have a child, Charlene Roberta—Charlie—and Charlie was born with pyrokinetic abilities. She was a firestarter.
>
> The Shop inhumanly decides that all of the "Lot Six" (the drug used in the test) experiment subjects must be eliminated and *Firestarter* is the story of the organization's pursuit of Andy and Charlie, and Charlie's ultimate victory over the powers of bureaucratic evil.[2]

In King's book, *drugs* triggered Charlie's pyrokinetic powers.

As clever a narrative device as this unquestionably is, there is no scientific proof that first, mental powers can cause combustion and, second, that drugs of any type can create or stimulate such powers.

Fire, light, and heat happen when flammable substances combine chemically with oxygen. The oxygen is present in the atmosphere, the substances are whatever burns.

The human mind cannot generate or provide any of the elements necessary to create fire.

Yet is it fair to demand normal, empirical behavior of an alleged ability that is supposed to be *para*normal?

Yes, since even the anecdotal evidence for the existence of pyrokinesis is almost nonexistent. When we do not have reams of firsthand accounts of a phenomena (as we do with UFO sightings, ghosts, and near-death experiences), all of which can be examined and evaluated, we must look to the scientific mandates of the alleged ability and make a decision as to whether or not it is even possible. Spontaneous human combustion happens. We have photos and equally vociferous camps of believers and non-believers. Whatever it truly is may be debatable but there is no doubt that it happens and we can study what happens. This is not the case with pyrokinesis.

There is nothing currently known that suggests that the psi power of firestarting is anything but a fictional plot device, as well as a power possessed by many of the characters found in *Dungeons and Dragons* and other role-playing games.

[1]The Doors, "Light My Fire."
[2]Stephen J. Spignesi, *The Essential Stephen King*, "Firestarter," used with permission.

Reincarnation and Past-Life Regression

HAIKU:

REINCARNATION

Are we born again?
Does our soul transcend this life,
Climbing the ladder?

I died a mineral and became a plant.
I died a plant and rose an animal.
I died an animal and I was man.
Why should I fear? When was I less by dying?
Yet once more I shall die as man, to soar
With the blessed angels; but even from angelhood
I must pass on. All except God perishes.
When I have sacrificed my angel soul,
I shall become that which no mind ever conceived.
O, let me not exist! For Non-Existence proclaims,
"To Him we shall return."[1]

DEFINITION: **Reincarnation**, also known as **rebirth**, is a transcendent preternatural act in which an individual's soul is reborn in another body; **Past-life regression** is the accessing and remembering of past lives through hypnosis.

WHAT THE BELIEVERS SAY: We live on, over and over and over, until we get it right. Most of the time we are not aware of our past incarnations, but hypnosis can allow a person to access a past life and recall, sometimes in vivid detail, who a person was and how he or she lived in a prior life. Personality, memory, and intelligence are sometimes able to be transferred from incarnation to incarnation, although usually, such conscious awareness of previous selves is not easily accessible. Nevertheless, our souls climb the ladder of existence to universal God-consciousness (enlightenment) and our reincarnated lives are individual rungs on that ladder. The spiritual cause-and-effect law of karma is the determinant of individual cosmic growth.

WHAT THE SKEPTICS SAY: We each get one life and some of us live it well, and some of us do not. As the old adage tells us, a person born with certain skills can use them to become a knife murderer, a butcher, or a surgeon. Once our life is over, though, it's over, and we do not transfer to another body for a second, or third, of forty-seventh chance. Once again, allow us to repeat the irrefutable: *dead is dead*.

QUALITY OF EXISTING EVIDENCE: Inconclusive.[2]

LIKELIHOOD PHENOMENA ARE PARANORMAL: High.[3]

Jesus believed in reincarnation. There are several passages in the New Testament in which Jesus speaks using language that makes it obvious that the concepts of rebirth and karma were believed in wholeheartedly during his time.

For instance, in the sixteenth chapter of Matthew, these two verses (13–14) tell of Christ's disciples discussing Jesus' possible "past lives":

> When Jesus came into the coasts of Caesarea Philippi, he asked his disciples, saying, "Whom do men say that I, the Son of Man, am?"
>
> And they said, "Some say that thou are John the Baptist, some, Elias, and others, Jeremias, or one of the prophets."

This is clearly an admission by Jesus that people of the time were speaking of him as the reincarnation of someone, and it is also evidence that the disciples were fully cognizant of the concepts of souls being reborn into different bodies.

Apparently this was not good enough for later Christians, however. In 533 A.D., the Fifth Ecumenical Council decided to ban the concept of reincarnation from the liturgy. The official proclamation stated, "If anyone asserts the fabulous pre-existence of souls, and shall assert the monstrous restoration which follows from it: let him be anathema."

Anathema. Excommunication for believing in something espoused by none other than Jesus himself.

Is there any validity to the idea of reincarnation? Spiritual leaders have long believed that birth and death are milestone moments in the life of a soul; moments that are repeated over and over. The individual soul is part of the eternal cosmic matrix, which many believe to be God. As we live each of our lives, our goal must be to better ourselves by doing good, until we achieve oneness with all of eternity—enlightenment—and are assimilated back into the Godhead.

It is said that on the night the Buddha achieved enlightenment, he recalled every one of his previous incarnations—all 900,000 of them. I think it is safe to say that if reincarnation is a reality, the path towards enlightenment is long and slow.

Reincarnation makes sense if you accept two basic principles: first, you believe that human beings possess an invisible eternal soul, and second, you believe that it is in the best interest of all life to *do good*. Karma, reincarnation, and the evolution towards ultimate enlightenment thus follows logically.

There is no agreement amongst believers, however, as to the precise process by which a person reincarnates. There is also no agreement as to the time between incarnations. Some say that there is a period in which the soul and the person's consciousness exist as a disembodied entity floating in the eternal ether. Some say that it's more of an even exchange: a person's soul at the moment of death snaps into another body at the moment of that person's birth.

Does reincarnation contradict spirit communication and ghosts and other experiences in which someone living is in touch with someone on the other side? No, if you believe that souls take time between incarnations. Thus, a person could die, manifest him- or herself to loved ones as a poltergeist or through channeling, and then go suddenly silent when he/she enters another body.

In the grand scheme of things, reincarnation has a neatness and a logic to it that skeptics say is simply a grasping by the fearful at anything that assures them they do not really die.

Ultimately, an individual's answer to that undying question is based on the question that has been asked repeatedly throughout this book: Do you believe you have an eternal soul?

If you say yes, then it's just a matter of designing your own operator's manual.

If you say no, then in your case, as the skeptics say, dead is dead.

[1] Jalal ad-Din ar-Rumi (Rumi the Poet, c. thirteenth century).

[2] Some of the anecdotal evidence for reincarnation is compelling. Some people are quite specific when they are regressed and, while some of what they "recall" could be confabulation, there are instances of accuracy that, at the very least, cast doubt on the "reincarnation is *completely impossible*" school of thought.

[3] If reincarnation is a reality, then it would validate any and all beliefs that this is not the only reality and that there are lives and realities beyond earthly existence. Admittedly, however, that is a big "if."

72

Relics of the True Cross

HAIKU:

THE TRUE CROSS

Tree of agony
Splinters from the distant past?
Or merely wood scraps?

Fulget crucis mysterium;
Qua vita mortem pertulit,
Et vorte vitam protulit.
The mystery of the cross shines bright;
where his life went through with death,
and from death brought forth life.[1]

DEFINITION: Relics of the "true cross" are allegedly pieces of the actual wooden cross on which Jesus Christ was crucified. According to religious legend, these relics have supposedly survived through the ages. Sometimes they can be purchased encased in elaborate monstrance-

like holders. Miraculous powers have been attributed to the pieces
of wood believed to be from Christ's cross.

WHAT THE BELIEVERS SAY: Pieces of the true cross survived the past
two thousand years and exist in collections all over the world. Contrary to popular belief, the sum total weight of all the relics do *not*
equal many crosses; many pieces may be hoaxes, but there is no
question that pieces of the true cross do exist and have miraculous
powers.

WHAT THE SKEPTICS SAY: There is no conceivable way that pieces of a
wooden cross could have survived two thousand years and, even if
pieces from a cross that old *did* survive, there is *no conceivable way*
that the pieces could be confirmed to have been from the cross on
which Christ was crucified.

QUALITY OF EXISTING EVIDENCE: Negligible.[2]

LIKELIHOOD PHENOMENA ARE PARANORMAL: Inconclusive.[3]

The 1948 edition of *The Catholic Almanac*[4] had this to say about
relics of the true cross, and other sacred artifacts:

> There are various relics of the true cross to be found prin-
> cipally in European cities: Brussels, Ghent, Rome, Venice,
> Ragusa, Paris, Limbourg, and Mt. Athos.
> The inscription placed above the cross is preserved in the
> Basilica of the Holy Cross of Jerusalem at Rome.
> The crown of thorns is kept at Paris. One of the nails was
> supposedly thrown into the Adriatic to calm a storm; another
> was made into the famous iron crown at Lombardy; another
> is in the Church of Notre Dame, Paris.
> The sponge is in Rome at the Basilica of St. John Lateran.
> The point of the lance is in Paris, the rest is in Rome. The
> robe is in the Church of Treves.
> The tunic is in the Church of Argenteuil near Paris. A part
> of the winding sheet is in Turin.
> The linen with which Veronica wiped Christ's face is in
> Rome.
> Part of the pillar of the Scourging is in Rome, part in
> Jerusalem.[5]

These are incredible claims. Tellingly, this passage no longer
appears in the latest edition of *The Catholic Almanac*, which speaks to
the problem of relics in general: How are Catholics supposed to know
if they are real? The church has never vouched for a relic as authen-

tic, although it does allow veneration of "honour being paid to those relics which with reasonable probability are believed to be genuine and which are invested with due ecclesiastical sanctions."[6]

According to Catholic tradition, the true cross described by the *Catholic Almanac*, the actual cross on which Jesus was crucified, was discovered in Palestine by Helena, later known as St. Helen, in or around the year 326. The legend of St. Helen tells us that she committed herself to finding the True Cross, and that during her investigation, she learned that it was common Jewish practice to dig a large hole following an official execution and to bury in this hole all the tools and objects of the means of execution. After asking around, she learned that a temple to the Roman God Venus had been constructed above the pit in which the cross of Christ was buried. Apparently, Helen was someone who could get things done. After traveling to Palestine, she ordered the Temple to Venus torn down and, again according to legend, her orders were carried out. She then dug into the pit and uncovered three crosses. She also found the piece of wood on which was carved the inscription that was hung above Jesus' head, as well as the nails that had been hammered into his feet and wrists. But Helen had a problem. Which of the three crosses was the one on which Jesus died?

Macarius, the bishop of Jerusalem, came up with a solution. One of the local aristocrats was terribly ill, and all who knew of her condition believed the woman was near death. Macarius had the three found crosses brought to the woman's bedside (one can imagine the logistical nightmare of dragging three enormous crosses through the dusty streets of Palestine, but we'll overlook this unlikelihood), and touched each of the crosses to the dying woman. Two of them had no effect; one of the crosses restored the woman to perfect health.

The True Cross had been found.

St. Helen was ecstatic, and had full faith that she had identified this extraordinary relic. She saw to it that a church was built on the site where the cross had been found. She later traveled to Constantinople and presented a piece of the cross to her son Constantine, and she also provided a piece for a church in Rome. That piece is said to still exist as the Holy Cross of Jerusalem in a Rome cathedral.

Is it possible that a single piece of the True Cross actually exists somewhere on Earth? Is it possible that any of the True Cross relics believed to be authentic are, indeed, real?

The skeptic in me answers no to those questions. Until St. Helen purportedly unearthed the chamber where the three crosses lay undisturbed for almost four centuries, there wasn't even any mention of pieces of the cross in religious historical literature. The reasonable response to the story of St. Helen is that it is apocryphal, and probably nothing more than a fable conceived and written to instill piety and devotion to relics of all kind.

This rationalization, however, does not rule out the possibility that there is, indeed, a piece of the instrument of Christ's death somewhere in the world.

[1] Venantius Fortunatus (c. 530–c. 610), *Vexilla Regis*, "Analecta Hymnica, 50: No. 67.

[2] The "evidence" that does exist—the actual pieces of wood claimed to be from the True Cross—in no way can be proven to be authentic.

[3] Since we do not know for certain if any of the avowed pieces of the True Cross are real, we cannot know if they are actually responsible for miraculous healings and other paranormal, or spiritual miracles.

[4] *The Catholic Almanac* is published by *Our Sunday Visitor* Publishing and is not an official publication of the Catholic Church.

[5] *The Catholic Almanac* (1948), p. 250.

[6] *The Catholic Encyclopedia*, "Relics," online edition, www.newadvent.org.

73

Remote Viewing

HAIKU:

REMOTE VIEWING

Seeing from afar

Places in the mind's eye

Sight without the eyes

She gave us some latitude and longitude figures. We focused our satellite cameras on that point and the plane was there.

—Jimmy Carter[1]

DEFINITION: Remote viewing is a form of psychoenergetic perception; it is the ability to perceive people, objects, places, or events at a location removed from the "viewer" by space and/or time.

WHAT THE BELIEVERS SAY: Trained remote viewers can visualize distant locations in their mind, draw uncannily accurate images of what they see, and there is irrefutable evidence to prove it.

WHAT THE SKEPTICS SAY: The reality of actual remote viewing is highly unlikely, and the viewers' "hits" are probably more coincidence, imagination, or wishful thinking than anything else.

QUALITY OF EXISTING EVIDENCE: Excellent.

LIKELIHOOD PHENOMENON IS PARANORMAL: Very high.

Remote viewing is real. It is also indisputable evidence of psychic abilities in human beings.

Remote viewing, now considered a discipline requiring training, utilizes a viewer's unconscious mind, and has been so incredibly successful that military and intelligence organizations have used it (and may still be using it) in sensitive intelligence gathering operations. In 1995, the CIA acknowledged the existence of its Stargate program, which trained military intelligence personnel as psychic spies.

Remote viewing, far from being a paranormal or religious "power," seems to be a trainable scientific skill.

What, specifically, is remote viewing and how does it work?

A trained remote viewer sits with a paper and pencil and concentrates on a "target."

He or she then writes down their perception of the scene, sometimes doing sketchy line drawings of shapes that come to mind.

A session report from the Princeton Engineering Anomalies Research (PEAR) program[2] shows a target photo of a broken rock wall on a grassy bluff overlooking a bay. After concentrating, the remote viewer wrote, "I see rocks; with uneven holes . . . dark green in distance . . . ocean—dark, dark blue . . . tall structure . . . similar to a castle . . . ocean smells . . . old, unused feeling . . . moss or grass growing in walls."[3] This is extraordinarily accurate and achieved precision well beyond mere chance.

There is documented evidence that the U.S. military has used, and may still be using, remote viewers to identify the locations of foreign submarines all over the world. Interestingly, many remote viewers finding subs have also reported UFOs in the vicinity when they lock onto an underwater location.

As to how remote viewing works, its practitioners claim that there is a universal matrix (yes, like in the movie) in which everything in space and time exists. Remote viewing is the process of using our extrasensory abilities to "read" this matrix. Whether or not the actual mechanics of the process are as described, there is no question that it works, and that it might very well be a latent ability in us all. Remote viewing instructors emphasize that it is a skill—a *learnable* skill—and that even gifted viewers do not always get everything right. A 33 percent to 80 percent accuracy rate is considered successful. It is said that even beginners can achieve a 40 percent accuracy.

MY REMOTE VIEWING TEST

In an effort to serve you better, I delved deeply into the many remote viewing sites on the internet, and I took a test to evaluate the existence, or lack thereof, of my own remote viewing abilities.

The site I chose offered a very easy testing protocol, and provided detailed instructions for use ("make your mind an empty bowl . . .").

I was given a four-digit number and told to visualize a black window in my empty rice bowl, and then to repeat the number over and over in my mind until an image appeared in the window.

I concentrated as instructed, trying to shush away the million random thoughts and images that fly through our minds at any given moment. I did not want to visualize an image that was the product of my imagination, but rather one that supposedly resulted from the act of my subconscious tapping into the universal matrix.

After several minutes of staring into the black window, I actually began to see something. I had rejected many images that had popped up in this window, knowing that I was consciously imagining them, rather than allowing the target image to come to me. I had seen the Eiffel Tower, the Statue of Liberty, the Washington Monument, Stonehenge, and Cameron Diaz. (Like I said, I knew these images were coming from me.)

But then I began to see an expanse of golden sand, as though I was floating above an enormous desert. This sand was painted with undulating waves of curves as the sand formed dunes of wind-blown sand commonly seen in stretches of barren desert. In the distance was a thin strip of blue—the horizon. Somehow I knew that this was the image I was picking up by remote viewing. I committed the specifics of the scene to memory and then clicked on the four-digit number to see the actual photo.

A bottleneck dolphin leaping out of the water.

Alas, I was a failure as a remote viewer. Could there be anything more unlike a dolphin in water than dunes in a desert?

But since I am today the same intrepid researcher who once spent an entire day in Yale University's Sterling Memorial Library to dig up the date of a single Woody Allen short story, I did not give up.

I moved on to a new four-digit number and tried again. Perhaps my lack of success had robbed me of my concentration, or perhaps the matrix was busy, but all I could visualize for this second number was the same desert sand dunes from my first number.

I sighed in resignation, concluded that I was probably not the next Kreskin, and clicked on the number to see the photo.

Golden dunes of wind-blown desert sand with the blue horizon in the distance.

On second thought, maybe Kreskin might soon have some competition?

On third thought, maybe not.

[1] President Jimmy Carter, commenting on a 1978 remote viewing session convened to look for a lost U.S. military plane.

[2] http://www.princeton.edu/~pear/.

[3] http://www.princeton.edu/~pear/images/cstle3.gif.

74

Resurrection

HAIKU:

RESURRECTION

There can be no end
If Christ stepped out of his tomb.
Did Jesus conquer death?

The third day He arose again from the dead.

—The Apostles' Creed

What began in the simple story of Mark as a symbolic allusion to an ascended Christ soon to reveal himself in visions from heaven, in time led some Christians to believe that the resurrection was physical, and they heard or came up with increasingly elaborate stories proving themselves right.

—Richard Carrier[1]

DEFINITION: The belief that the dead can come back to life; most often used in the context of the Christian belief that Jesus Christ rose from the dead after he was executed by crucifixion in the first century.

WHAT THE BELIEVERS SAY: The dead can come back to life.

WHAT THE SKEPTICS SAY: Dead is dead.

QUALITY OF EXISTING EVIDENCE: Poor.[2]

LIKELIHOOD PHENOMENON IS PARANORMAL: Inconclusive.[3]

Victory over death. It is the driving impetus behind everything a doctor does in his practice; it is the goal of every human being who has done even *one thing* to improve their health; it is the promise of every religion on earth, each individual discipline providing the required steps to achieve immortality and eternal life.

As is often said, the big Clock of Life starts ticking backwards at the moment of birth, and when the clock reaches zero, we die.

But when is dead truly *dead?*

Modern medicine has perfected resuscitation of the clinically dead to such a level that terminally ill people now routinely make the decision *not* to be resuscitated if their heart stops. "Do Not Resuscitate" (DNR) orders are a common component of many patients' medical records. Medical technology today can keep hearts beating long after the body in which it is housed has degenerated beyond viability. Imagine telling people a thousand years ago that the day would come when people would choose whether or not to be brought back to life. Such a tale would undoubtedly convince the listener that the day was coming when man would rival God himself with his powers.

However, medical resuscitation is not what the faithful speak of when they refer to Christ's resurrection. Adherent Christians believe that Jesus was crucified on a cross, died, and was entombed for three days, after which he used God's divine power to come back to life and appear to more than five hundred people before ascending bodily into heaven. (Some also believe that the shroud in which he was wrapped retained the supernaturally imprinted image of Jesus following his return to life. See Chapter 79, "The Shroud of Turin.")

According to Christian dogma, Jesus's resurrection foreshadowed the resurrection of the dead that would occur at the Second Coming of Christ.

A comprehensive study of the Old and New Testaments shows that the Messiah's crucifixion was foretold (Psalm 22), as was his Resurrection.

But Jesus' return to life did not become part of the Christian corpus of doctrines until decades later and, all of the alleged deconstructionist evidence aside, it is possible that the *visionary* return of Christ may have metamorphosed into a *physical* return in later writings (the letters of Paul, and others).

Rising from the dead without medical assistance has been a hoary, horror movie device since the first silent movies. Such a supernatural act is always portrayed as something terrible and profane, and the reanimated dead are usually seen as shuffling, mindless ghouls, some of whom have come back to life with a taste for human flesh.

This is a far cry from the spiritually transcendent being Jesus Christ became upon his resurrection.

According to some Charismatic/Pentecostal Christians, resurrection is still going on around the world. One story that garnered a great deal of attention took place in 2001 in Nigeria. A pastor crashed his car into a tree, received life-threatening injuries, and was ultimately declared dead (although there are questions about the validity of the death certificate). The "dead" man's wife took the body home and, *three* days later (yes, *three*), attended a prayer meeting conducted by German evangelist Reinhard Bonnke. The grieving widow brought with her to the meeting her husband's corpse, which was now reportedly in advanced rigor mortis.

Bonnke recited a "prayer of resurrection" over the man, and soon the corpse started twitching and then began to breathe. Upon his full return to life, the man claimed to have visited Heaven and Hell and he said that an angel told him he was being sent back to save people's souls from Hell. A videotape of this miracle is available for purchase on the Reverend Bonnke's Web site.

People can come back to life after being thought dead. Drowning victims have been known to enter a state of suspended animation, with no heartbeat or breathing, and then be restored to life with no aftereffects.

This is not the same as being in the grave for three whole days, and then coming back to life.

Human death seems to be a process, rather than an event. If certain things are done before death becomes irreversible, sometimes life can be restored.

Resurrection with a capital "R," however, seems to belong solely to Jesus Christ, and that event has to be accepted solely on faith. Or not.

POSTSCRIPT

The Fall 2002 issue of *Skeptic* magazine featured an article titled "Science and the Resurrection" by Michael A. Persinger. In the article, Persinger attempts to explain the resurrection scientifically. He proceeds from four basic assumptions:

1. Jesus *did* exist.
2. Jesus *was* crucified and pronounced dead.
3. Jesus *was* seen alive three days after his death.
4. Jesus' resurrection was *not* a supernatural, divine miracle.

So how did Jesus "rise from the dead?"

1. He was a temporal lobe epileptic.
2. He was given large doses of the drug reserpine (found as a botanical extract in shrubs in the area at the time).
3. Tissue damage and being physically restrained caused a massive release of stress hormones into his bloodstream.

When these three factors were combined, Jesus entered a state of extreme hypothermia in which he appeared to be dead. It was during this time that he was removed from the cross and buried.

Forty-eight hours later, his body became euthermic (began to warm up) and he ultimately recovered from his coma on the third day.

However, by this time, he likely would have suffered extreme brain damage from his ordeal and could easily have not recognized his Apostles and walked right past them (as reported in the Gospels).

The author concludes:

If one assumes the reports concerning the events surrounding the crucifixion of Jesus were more or less accurate descriptions of his behavior, then his apparent death as inferred by immobility and protracted intense hypothermia and the subsequent sightings could be explained by a fundamental biochemical process rather than a highly improbably phenomena such as being raised from the dead by God.[4]

He describes Christ's resurrection as "the consequence of a relatively mundane synergism of physical and chemical processes, now replicable in the laboratory."[5]

If Persinger is correct, then one of the fundamental premises on which Christianity is based—Jesus Christ rose from the dead—is flawed.

[1]Richard Carrier, "Why I Don't Buy the Resurrection Story," a 2000 lecture at Yale University, available online at www.infidels.org/library/modern/ richard_carrier/resurrection/lecture.html.

[2]The "evidence" for Christ's resurrection comes solely from the New Testament, with its first mention appearing in *Mark*, the Gospel believed to have been written first. In the next two books written, *Matthew* and *Luke*, the resurrection story is embellished, and in *John*, the story achieves the richness of an epic. It is now known, however, that the original text of the book of Mark ended at Chapter 16, verse 8, with Mark talking about an empty tomb after Jesus' crucifixion. From 16:9, through the end of Mark, the specific details of Christ's appearances to people were added sometime in the second century, apparently as a tool to support the growth of Christianity, of which the guiding doctrine was Christ's resurrection. (See Carrier [fn.1].)

[3]Based on the gospel accounts of Jesus' resurrection, there is no concrete, *irrefutable* way of knowing whether or not Christ actually rose from the dead. Thus, our "inconclusive" rating.

[4]"Science and the Resurrection," *Skeptic*, Vol. 9. No. 4, p. 79.

[5]Ibid., p. 79.

75

Roswell

HAIKU:

ROSWELL

New Mexico crash
What was it fell from the sky?
Will the truth be told?

There can be no doubt that something dropped out of the skies near Roswell on July 4, 1947. The question is what. . . . Everyone agrees that no spaceship wreckage or alien bodies have been made public. Therefore, the truth seeker is left with only human testimony and official pronouncements. The basis for accepting the balloon version rests exclusively on government reports, which deny any unusual aspect to the Roswell case. A lengthy recitation of past official lies, disinformation, and deceit should not be necessary to establish that such pronouncements cannot be accepted at face value.

—Jim Marrs[1]

Air Force research did not locate or develop any information that the "Roswell Incident" was a UFO event. All available official materials, although they do not directly address Roswell per se, indicate that the most likely source

*of the wreckage recovered from the Brazel Ranch was from
one of the Project Mogul balloon trains. Although that
project was TOP SECRET at the time, there was also no
specific indication found to indicate an official pre-planned
cover story was in place to explain an event such as that
which ultimately happened.*[2]

DEFINITION: "Roswell" is the shorthand term used to describe an
event in the southeastern New Mexico desert where an alien spacecraft allegedly crashed in 1947.

WHAT THE BELIEVERS SAY: An alien spaceship crashed into the desert
outside Roswell, New Mexico on July 4, 1947, and the U.S. government recovered the ship and the bodies of aliens from the crash site.

WHAT THE SKEPTICS SAY: There was no alien spaceship—it was a top
secret weather balloon; there were no alien bodies—they were
anthropomorphic dummies; regarding the "eyewitness" testimony—
people were either mistaken, they deliberately lied, or they were delusional and began to believe their own prevarications.

QUALITY OF EXISTING EVIDENCE: Physical Evidence: Poor; Witness Testimony: Fair.

LIKELIHOOD PHENOMENON IS PARANORMAL: Nil, if you believe the official reports; Very high, if you don't.

I have a friend who has a friend . . .
That is usually how a firsthand Roswell story begins. Someone
knows someone who knows someone who was at or near Roswell in
July 1947, or saw the alien bodies being transported, or saw or held
the liquid foil that could not be made to hold a crease . . . etc.

In my case, the story happens to be true. I have a friend who has
a friend—he's former military—who *was* at Roswell in 1947 and who
claims to have witnessed alien bodies being loaded onto trucks and
transported away from the crash site.

My friend is credible; I must reluctantly assign similar credibility
to *his* friend. I say reluctantly because how can I be confident that
what he *said* he saw is what he actually saw? Did my friend's friend
truly see alien corpses—or were they anthropomorphic dummies
ejected from a top secret test balloon?

According to countless believers, in 1947, a flying saucer—an
actual extraterrestrial craft—crashed in the desert outside of Roswell,
New Mexico.

The legend continues: The wreckage of the saucer was recovered by the United States government, along with the actual bodies of extraterrestrials, the number of which varies, depending on the source. Most of these ETs were dead, but at least one was still alive; and they were all transported to Area 51, where our unfortunate visitors, along with the wreckage of their craft, remain to this day.

In 1994, the Air Force released its final statement on the Roswell incident. The Air Force has stated that what crashed at Corona was a Top Secret weather balloon that was part of a program called Project Mogul. It is an understatement to acknowledge that many UFOlogists do not believe the Air Force's "official" version of what happened in the New Mexico desert in 1947.

I have read the official report; I have also read much of the Roswell material out there, both pro-alien crash and skeptical; I have spoken with people who either saw something they did not understand, or know someone who reported such an experience; I even have a brochure from the Roswell UFO Museum.

When I first read the report, my initial thinking was to reject it as disinformation. It seemed suspicious that the U.S. government would feel the need to issue a lengthy, allegedly well-documented "final report" on something that happened in 1947, if what actually happened was as prosaic and inconsequential as a balloon crash. But the refutation to that is simple: an official request for anything and everything in the government files about what happened at Roswell was submitted by a U.S. Congressman, Steven Schiff (R., New Mexico), and the Air Force was legally obligated to fulfill his request.

The report, which is available many places online, seems to debunk every individual point about the Roswell crash.

It denied the existence of a cover-up; and it discredited point by point the alleged rumors about what actually happened.

What about the weird foil that flattened itself out like water after being crumpled into a ball? It has been suggested that it was nothing more than a type of aluminum foil that probably was a compound of aluminum and some kind of resin that gave it exceptional "memory," allowing it to flatten out without visible creases.

What about the alien bodies that many claim to have seen?

On June 24, 1997, the Air Force released its second report on the Roswell Incident. This is the press release from the Air Force News Service announcing the report:

WASHINGTON (AFNS)—The Air Force released its second report June 24 on what has become known as the "Roswell Incident." This report, "The Roswell Report: Case Closed," together with the one issued in September 1994, "The Roswell Report: Fact Versus Fiction in the New Mexico Desert," explains and demystifies events that occurred in New Mexico nearly fifty years ago.

During the 1940s and 1950s, the Air Force engaged in extensive high-altitude balloon experimentation. Some of the experiments involved using the balloons to carry and eject anthropomorphic dummies equipped with parachutes in order to learn how best to return pilots or astronauts to earth if they had to eject from high altitudes.

These experiments, as well as others described and explained in the report, including the 1947 crash of a balloon, correspond to many of the occurrences observed by local residents and later characterized as the "Roswell Incident."

This latest report is noteworthy for the extensive background it provides on the scope of the Air Force activities in the vicinity of Roswell, N.M., beginning in the mid-1940s and extending through the early 1960s.

"This is singularly the most exhaustive release of information on this subject," said Secretary of the Air Force Sheila Widnall. "In 1994, we made all records on this subject publicly available. This additional information will enlighten people about pioneer research and the challenging and often heroic work of Air Force personnel during those early years."

The Roswell incident is big business.

There are a wide array of books, videos, DVDs, and other materials about the crash. The aforementioned Roswell UFO Museum is a popular tourist attraction; the witnesses still living are regularly approached by researchers continuing to keep the legend alive.

The skeptics' conclusion is that a Project Mogul balloon crashed in the Roswell desert in July 1947. There were probably anthropomorphic dummies on the balloon that were mistaken for alien bodies. The "hieroglyphics" on the strips of metal found in the wreckage were probably nothing but some type of code or glyph-like symbols used in the experiment.

The believers' conclusion is that the Roswell crash was an extraterrestrial event, and that it is concrete evidence that we have been visited by aliens. The governments of the world know this, and there is a worldwide cover-up at the highest levels of all nations to keep this information from the public.

I believe Kenneth Arnold saw flying disks from his plane in 1947 before the Roswell crash.

I suspect we have been visited by other intelligences for millennia.

I am confident that consciousness survives death.

But I am not satisfied with either conclusion about what happened at Roswell.

The government's story is too pat and there are too many eyewitness accounts of exceedingly strange things that went on in Roswell to dismiss them all out of hand.

However, the believers' stories are often contradictory and the credibility of some can legitimately be questioned (and, in all fairness, should be).

What happened at Roswell?

We still do not know the answer to that question with certainty, other than the fact that something happened.

[1]*Alien Agenda*, p. 135.

[2]From the United States Air Force's 1994 official statement on the "Roswell Incident."

76

Runes

RUNES

Stick letters on stones
A tool for revelations?
Or merely dead words?

Thinking of his own Gods, a Greek
In pity and mournful awe might stand
Before some fallen Runic stone—
For both were faiths, and both are gone.

—Matthew Arnold[1]

DEFINITION: A script alphabet that originated in northern Europe as a means of communication and evolved into a divination tool. Today, runes are most commonly sold as sets of small imprinted stones that come with an instruction manual describing what each individual hieroglyphic-like symbol means.

WHAT THE BELIEVERS SAY: The ancient, mysterious roots of the symbolic language give runes their magical powers of divination. When they are read with humility, patience, and respect, they will reveal their secrets and provide much-needed answers to the questioner.

WHAT THE SKEPTICS SAY: Runes, like Tarot cards, can mean whatever the person reading them want them to mean. They hold no more precognitive powers than any other method of divination.

QUALITY OF EXISTING EVIDENCE: Poor.

LIKELIHOOD PHENOMENA ARE PARANORMAL: Low.

There are three basic surviving runic alphabets: The Anglo-Saxon alphabet of thirty-two letters; the Teutonic alphabet of twenty-four letters; and the Scandinavian alphabet of sixteen letters. It is believed that runes were used for both communication and divination for a thousand years, beginning sometime in northern Europe around the third century and dying out between the thirteenth and sixteenth century.

Yet as has been said, everything old is new again, and runes are an ancient pursuit popular today and sold everywhere from toy stores to New Age bookstores. British writer J.R.R. Tolkien designed alphabets inspired by runes for use by Hobbits, elves and other denizens of Middle Earth in his epic *Lord of the Rings* series.

"Rune" means mystery or secret, and the symbols and runic letters have a history that bears out their dark past.

Ancient Norse mythology tells the legend of the god Odin who hung suspended by a spear from a tree for nine days and nights as an occult ritual to gain control of the powers of the runes. On the ninth night, the runes materialized before him and he was able to seize them and claim dominion over them.

What was the first thing Odin did after gaining control of the runes? He cut runic symbols into stones and painted runes to bring back to life a corpse hanging from a gallows. According to the poem that tells of this, the spirits Odin summoned with the runes heard him and did, indeed, bring the dead man back to life on his behalf.

This is an ironic story about Odin. According to Norse mythology, Odin was not only the god of war, culture, art, wisdom, and the dead, he was also the supreme being that created the universe and all of humanity. It would seem that the "God of everything" would have been able to reanimate a corpse without having to rely upon the casting of runes to do so. But I suppose it is an exercise in futility to attempt to glean logic and consistent behavior from mythological contrivances.

Runes were (unfortunately) embraced and revived by the Nazis in the 1920s. German Nazi occultists used runic symbols in their military insignia, they used runes in their documents, and, perhaps most regrettable, they adopted two ancient Norse runic figures—the swastika and the sigil (the lightning "S")—as the symbols of the Nazi Party and Hitler's dreaded SS troops, respectively.

How is a rune reading cast?

The set of runes is mixed and then tossed out onto a flat surface. The symbols of the runes are then studied for their meaning as they relate to the questioner.

The individual hieroglyphic characters have names like Wyrd, Feoh, Thorna, Yra, Sigil, Ansur, Rad, Wynn, etc., and like Tarot cards, they are interpreted in both the upright and reverse positions.

Each symbol also has a planetary association. Ansur is associated with Mercury; Yra is associated with Jupiter, etc.

The meanings of the rune symbols are often general and vague. For instance, the Ansur stone indicates eloquence and intelligence. Reversed it means bad advice and the need for caution. Eolh means good luck; reversed, it means a susceptibility to be taken advantage of by others.

"Runeologists," like Tarot readers, can spend years studying the different meanings of the stones and interpreting them for a reading.

As a psychological tool, runes are often helpful in calling attention to a person's problem areas and stimulating self-evaluation and, hopefully, self-improvement.

As for whether or not there is genuine paranormal information communicated via the symbols, that, as with all methods of divination, is in the eye of the beholder.

[1]*The Grande Chartreuse*, lines 81–84.

77

Satanism[1]

HAIKU:

SATANISM

Praise to the carnal
Embracing glorious sins
Primacy of self

*Satanism is Satanism not due to our worship of any deity,
but for the philosophy that we stand for. We recognize
ourselves as gods, and we hold our own perspective on life
as holy and revere our own experiences as the only truth we
can ever know.*

—Vexen Crabtree[2]

DEFINITION: A Satanist is someone who either worships the Christian Devil, or who considers Satan a pre-Christian life *principle* (not an entity), and thus lives his or her life according to a number of quasi-religious traditions, mostly centering on personal indulgence and the primacy of the self.

WHAT THE BELIEVERS SAY: "Official" Satanism is the practice of embracing and exalting carnal and earthly human life. No redeemer ever lived, or will ever live; each person is his own redeemer. There is no Heaven or Hell; prayer is useless; indulgence instead of abstinence is true fulfillment; "equality for all" is insupportable.

WHAT THE SKEPTICS SAY: Worshiping Satan or simply indulging in Satanic life principles is an abominable betrayal of man's higher qualities and God-given soul. It is an excuse to wallow in sex, intoxicants, and violence without even a semblance of self-discipline. The fact that Satanists embrace and practice "with joy" what Christians call the "Seven Deadly Sins" (greed, pride, envy, anger, gluttony, lust, sloth) proves that Satanism is backwards, negative, and self-destructive, both for the individual and, if implemented as widely as they desire, for all of mankind.

QUALITY OF EXISTING EVIDENCE: Excellent.[3]

LIKELIHOOD PHENOMENON IS PARANORMAL: Low.[4]

The nine Satanic statements[5] of the Church of Satan, as developed by its founder Anton LaVey, are:

1. Satan represents indulgence instead of abstinence.
2. Satan represents vital existence instead of spiritual pipe dreams.
3. Satan represents undefiled wisdom instead of hypocritical self-deceit.
4. Satan represents kindness to those who deserve it instead of love wasted on ingrates.
5. Satan represents vengeance instead of turning the other cheek.
6. Satan represents responsibility to the responsible instead of concern for psychic vampires.
7. Satan represents man as just another animal—sometimes better, more often worse than those that walk on all-fours—who, because of his "divine spiritual and intellectual development," has become the most vicious animal of all.
8. Satan represents all of the so-called sins, as they all lead to physical, mental, or emotional gratification.

9. Satan has been the best friend the Church has ever had, as he has kept it in business all these years.

Paralleling these are the Church of Satan's nine Satanic sins:[6]

- Stupidity
- Pretentiousness
- Solipsism
- Self-Deceit
- Herd Conformity
- Lack of Perspective
- Forgetfulness of Past Orthodoxies
- Counterproductive Pride
- Lack of Aesthetics

THE BLACK MASS

The most important Satanic ritual is the Black Mass, a perversion of the traditional Roman Catholic mass.

In the past, the "altar" for a Black Mass was often the body of a naked woman with her head facing south, which signified that Satanism was a religion of the flesh. Today, a living altar is still used, but it is far less common. In fact, many Satanists rarely participate in Black Masses these days, unless the media requests one, or for a special occasion.

The male participants wear all black, the women often wear sexually suggestive clothing.

The participants also wear amulets of pentagrams or goat's heads; and several black candles are lit.

In addition to the Black Mass, there are many Satanic magical rituals performed by worshippers, including a destruction ritual, in which pins are stuck in a doll (similar to voodoo rituals), a happiness ritual, and a sex magic ritual, which includes masturbation, sometimes in public.

The language often used during Satanic rituals is known as "Enochian," which was supposedly revealed to Queen Elizabeth I's court astrologer's helper, Edward Kelley. Kelley reportedly received the language from the angels. Enochian sounds like a hodgepodge of Latin, Arabic, and Hebrew.

Satanists do not associate their concept of "Satan" with Christianity's image of a demonic entity of pure evil. To Satanists, Satan represents the base carnality of earthly human life.

In fact, some of their doctrinal statements sound blatantly "non-Satanic" (as Satanism is commonly perceived in today's culture:

> Satanism respects and exalts life. Children and animals are the purest expressions of that life force, and as such are held sacred and precious . . .[7]
>
> Satan . . . represents love, kindness and respect to those who deserve it.[8]

The essence of Satanism is worship of the self. A person's desires, motivations, fantasies, fetishes, urges, appetites, etc., should all be willfully and joyfully indulged.

True Satanists believe that Satan is not a being, but a life force.

Christian notions of compassion, selflessness, forgiveness, self-discipline, and asceticism are foolhardy, naïve, and a denial of man's innate instincts.

Not surprisingly, then, the most important "holiday" for a Satanist is their own birthday.

Satanists also espouse a political agenda, the gist of which seemingly goes against everything the United States holds sacrosanct.

They believe that equality for all is a myth and the efforts of governments striving for true equality for all people should be abandoned.

They want any and all religious beliefs, issues, doctrines, or statements in legislation removed.

They support total freedom for people to live within "a total environment of their choice."[9]

They also support the development and production of artificial human companions.[10]

Satanism is not Devil worship and they disassociate themselves from ritual "Satanic abuse" as is often read about in the media. True Satanists espouse their beliefs with pride and openness. They offer their belief system as the yin to Christianity's yang, yet the association many people have with "Satanism" will *always* prevent a calm, reasoned acceptance or rejection of its tenets.

"Satanism" is a buzzword with incredibly negative connotations and all of the Satanists' talk of the primal energies and powers of nature and sex will never disassociate the practice from being perceived as the worship of the Prince of Darkness.

---

[1]One of the main research sources for this chapter was the Web site www.religioustolerance.org. We recommend that readers interested in learning more about Satanism (and other religious traditions) visit that site where they will find much more material about the subject

than this space allows us to cover. Please note: This is not an endorsement of Satanism or any other religion by the author or the publisher; it is simply a referral to an extensive source of information.

[2]Quoted on www.religioustolerance.org.

[3]There are countless books and Web sites that explain and discuss Satanism. Also, Anton LaVey (1930–1997), the founder of the Church of Satan, wrote several books, all of which are in print and available.

[4]For all the trappings of "supernaturalism" attendant to Satanic rituals (the Black Mass, the incantations, the spells, the pentagrams, the upside-down crosses, etc.) there is little evidence that Satanism is anything more than a complex, fully developed belief system created by man and practiced by man.

[5]These are LaVey's original statements, which can also be found at their official Web site, www.churchofsatan.com.

[6]A.S. LaVey, "The Nine Satanic Sins," (1987), http://www.churchofsatan.com/Pages/Sins.html.

[7]www.churchofsatan.org.

[8]www.churchofsatan.org.

[9]A.S. LaVey, "Pentagonal Revisionism: A Five-Point Program," (1988) at: http://www.churchofsatan.com/Pages/PentRev.html.

[10]The Real Doll (www.realdoll.com) company creates life-like, life-sized, very expensive artificial "companions" for sex. Could this be what LaVey was suggesting?

78

Savant Syndrome[1]

SAVANTS

Islands of genius
In the minds of autistics
Who is the savant?

I am still learning.

—Michelangelo

DEFINITION: "An exceedingly rare condition in which persons with serious mental handicaps, either from developmental disability (mental retardation) or major mental illness (Early Infantile Autism or schizophrenia), have spectacular islands of ability or brilliance which stand in stark, markedly incongruous contrast to the handicap."[2]

WHAT THE BELIEVERS SAY: "Idiot" savants possess abilities that modern science cannot fully explain, and that is because these people may be blessed by God with a divine gift. It is quite possible (if not likely) that their talents are supernatural and beyond the understanding of man.

WHAT THE SKEPTICS SAY: Simply because science cannot fully explain how savants do what they do does not mean that their abilities are "from God" or are a supernatural power. It is likely that we will eventually identify the specific pathobiology that creates savantism. Genetics and reinforcement may play some role, but there is obviously some bizarre brain state that needs to be identified and studied and science will, ultimately, understand how the brains of savants "work."

QUALITY OF EXISTING EVIDENCE: Fair to Good.[3]

LIKELIHOOD PHENOMENON IS PARANORMAL: Nil to Low.[4]

Savant Syndrome, as it has come to be known, points up just how difficult it is to truly understand the functioning of the human brain.

Savants are usually male (six times more frequently than female), usually have extremely low IQs (some as low as in the 30s and 40s), and yet they possess "islands of ability" that are so extraordinary as to seem almost supernatural.

People who cannot see can draw like Old Masters; people who cannot speak can sing entire scores of Broadway musicals; people who appear almost catatonic in their daily lives can sit at a piano and flawlessly play complete classical concertos after hearing the piece only once.

Theories abound as to what role genetics and reinforcement play in these phenomenal abilities, but the truth is that much of what these people can do, and how they do it, is incredibly perplexing to the scientific and medical establishments.

One of the most recent cinematic portrayal of an autistic savant was in the 1988 movie *Rain Man*, which starred Tom Cruise and Dustin Hoffman. In that film, Hoffman played Raymond, a middle-aged autistic who manifested many of the abilities of the savant, including counting, memorization, and calculation. Filmgoers were astounded by what Raymond could do, and many challenged the veracity of the portrayal, but everything depicted in *Rain Man* was scientifically and medically accurate. In fact, as you'll see from the following discussion of savant abilities, *Rain Man* barely scratched the surface.

MUSICAL ABILITIES

Many savants manifest incredible musical talents. Sixteen-year-old Blind Tom, a blind and severely retarded slave who died in 1908, toured after the Civil War and played the piano at virtuoso level for audiences all over the United States. Tom had a musical repertoire of over five thousand pieces and, like many savants, could hear a piece of music once and then play it perfectly, no matter how difficult or complex the piece. Tom was also somehow capable of assimilating a particular composer's "style." On command, Tom could improvise a musical piece in the manner of any composer he had ever heard, including Beethoven, Bach, Chopin, Verdi, and many others. Tom once performed for President Buchanan.

Other documented musical savants:

- A twenty-three-year-old boy with an IQ of 47 who could play the piano by ear and could immediately sight-read sheet music.

- A girl named Harriet who had an IQ of 73 and who hummed perfectly the entire "Care Nome" aria from Verdi's opera *Rigoletto* at the age of seven months. (She was in her crib.) By the time she was four, she could play the piano, violin, trumpet, clarinet, and French horn, but she wasn't toilet trained until the age of nine. Harriet also manifested incredible memorization skills and could remember pages of the phone book and minute factual details about hundreds of symphonies. Like Blind Tom, she could also improvise in a composer's style and transpose between keys at will.

- A thirty-eight-year-old man with an IQ of 67 who had perfect pitch, could sight-read music, and had an enormous knowledge of facts about composers.

- A twenty-three-year-old girl with an IQ of 23 who could play on the piano any song or melody sung or hummed to her.

CALENDAR CALCULATING

Calendar calculating is the ability to tell what days dates fall on and when holidays will fall centuries into the future. Probably the most famous savant calendar calculators were twins named Charles and George. Charles's and George's IQs tested between 40 and 70. Some of their most amazing calendar abilities included the following:

- They could tell you on what day of the week any date fell in an eighty-thousand-year span. (They were proficient forty thousand years into the past and forty thousand years into the future.) The twins were able to account for changes in the ways calendars were designed over the centuries when calculating the dates.

- They could tell you in what years during the next two centuries that Easter would fall on March 23rd.

- They could remember and recite the exact weather of every single day of their adult lives.

Although Charles and George could not even do simple math, doctors were convinced that math and complex calculating abilities somehow played a role in the twins' date determinations. Memorization of date tables and calendars also played a part, but scientists are sure that somewhere in the twins' brains, an "island of ability" existed that could do high math.

MATHEMATICAL CALCULATING

The math skills exhibited by savants include incredibly rapid counting abilities (remember Raymond in *Rain Man* immediately being able to count the number of toothpicks that fell on the floor?), and the ability to do instantaneous complex mathematical calculations in their head. Some of the things savants have been known to count include the following:

- The hairs in a cow's tail
- The words spoken in a TV or radio broadcast
- The number of cars on a highway over a period of time

Some of the calculations savants have been known to make include the following:

- The number of seconds in a period of time
- The number of seconds in a person's life
- The multiplication of twenty-digit numbers
- Square root calculations involving huge numbers

Some of the calculations performed by savants have taken days, weeks, or even months to do. It seems as though some weird biological computer clicks on when the savant is given the problem and it doesn't turn off until the solution is arrived at. Many savants adept at calculating can usually add columns of numbers in seconds *without* paper and pencil (many can't even write for that matter), and they often exhibit the same level of problem-solving proficiency with division, multiplication, and subtraction problems as well.

INCREDIBLE MEMORIES

Decades ago, a physician named Dr. Witzman attempted to describe the incredible memory capabilities of some savants. He said that they are often capable of "reproducing at will masses of figures, like railway tables, budget statistics, and entries in bankbooks."[5] Eidetic (photographic) memories are one of the most amazing savant abilities. Anyone who has ever tried to memorize something knows just how incredible a photographic memory actually is. My wife told me that when she was studying for her speech pathology degree, everyone in her class grudgingly acknowledged that the only way to learn the necessary anatomical structures the course covered was by rote memorization. Med students have long turned to mnemonics to help them remember complex anatomical features of the human body. (Probably the most common mnemonic device we all used in school was "*All Good Boys Deserve Fun* [or *Fish*, depending on whether it was a Catholic school or not]," which is, of course, the lines of a musical stave.) Here is a look at some of the things individual savants have been reported as remembering:

- The exact configuration of the entire Milwaukee bus system
- The complete music and lyrics of thousands of songs
- The daily weather of a person's lifetime
- Thousands of meticulous details about wars and historical events
- Word-for-word recollections of complete short stories and, in some cases, entire novels
- The melodies, page numbers, and complete lyrics of every hymn in a specific hymnal
- Thousands of addresses, often "industry-specific." For instance, some savants will memorize only the addresses of car dealerships, but they will remember *every one* in an entire city
- Hundreds of foreign language phrases
- Detailed and comprehensive biographical details about hundreds of historical personages
- Decades of obituary records, including next of kin, addresses, and funeral homes
- The contents of entire newspapers, both forwards *and* backwards
- The exact number of bites of food taken during an entire month or longer
- The precise number of steps walked during a certain period of time
- The number of hotel rooms in every hotel in dozens of cities
- The distances between hundreds of cities
- The seating capacities of dozens of stadiums and arenas
- Every number seen on every railroad car over an entire lifetime (And in some cases, the savant has been known not only to recall the individual numbers on the trains, but to keep a running total of their sums as well.)

- Entire pages from phone directories
- The times of the comings and goings of hospital staff members over a fifty-seven year period
- Voluminous stock market statistical data
- The transcripts of entire radio and TV broadcasts

ARTISTIC ABILITIES

Savants with artistic abilities can produce impeccably artistic detailed renderings of something seen only once. Savants have been known to work with drawings and sculptures and they have created works depicting animals, insects, cats, and other forms of nature.

MECHANICAL ABILITIES

Savants occasionally are exceptionally good "with their hands." Some recorded mechanical abilities evidenced by savants include the following:

- One savant once took apart a clock and rebuilt it as a fully functioning windmill.
- Savants have been known to build detailed models of cars and boats after only seeing a picture of the vehicle.
- Some savants can draw accurately detailed blueprints.
- Some can instinctively repair appliances and other mechanical objects.
- Savants have been documented as being able to rebuild and *modify* multi-gear bicycles.

EXTRAORDINARY SENSORY PERCEPTION

Some savants have extraordinarily developed senses of sight, smell, hearing, taste, and touch.

- One blind savant was able to pick out his own clothes and shoes by smell alone.
- There is documentation of a savant whose sense of touch was so highly developed that he could split a sheet of newspaper into two thin leaves, resulting in two sheets of newsprint one-half the thickness of the original.

ESP

ESP, or *Extra*-Sensory Perception (which is different from *Extraordinary* Sensory Perception), appears to enter the realm of the almost impossible to explain. These abilities have often been considered paranormal and yet, there are savants who exhibit psychic and other "beyond nature" abilities. Some of the documented "powers" exhibited by savants include the following:

- Being able to hear (and repeat) conversations from outside his hearing range
- Being able to read another person's thoughts
- Being able to perform "distant viewing"; seeing accurately something happening rooms, or sometimes miles, away
- Being capable of precognition, i.e., being able to accurately predict the future

Evidence of these paranormal abilities further complicates our understanding of the *Savant Syndrome*. Or perhaps it clarifies it? Consider this: What if savants are using parts of their brains in bizarre ways that we still cannot understand and their manifestation of psychic abilities is something we might all be capable of, but savants are just tapping into them accidentally?

AN EXTRAORDINARY SENSE OF TIME

Some savants have an incredibly developed sense of the passage of time.

- One savant could tell to the minute the exact time at any time of the day or night, but could not read a clock.
- One savant knew exactly when commercials would begin and end, even when out of range of the TV.
- Savants can tell exactly how much time has passed during a specific period without looking at a watch or clock.

EXTRAORDINARY DIRECTIONAL PERCEPTION

Extraordinary directional perception is sometimes found in savants who have never been out of their house or have never traveled in their lives.

- Some savants can recall exact travel routes of individual trips taken, including every right and left turn made.
- Some savants can memorize maps and precisely reproduce them, to scale.
- Some savants can give detailed travel directions to a certain place even if they've never been there and often even if they're blind.

[1] Some of the material in this chapter appeared in a different form in the author's 1994 Plume book, *The Odd Index*.

[2] Dr. Darold Treffert. *Extraordinary People*.

[3] There is a great deal of data on specific savants and their abilities; the underlying explanation of how they became savants continues to elude medical science.

[4] Divine explanations notwithstanding, it seems likely that the final explanation for Savant Syndrome will look to the inner workings of the brain rather than the supernatural workings of God or some other paranormal force or source.

[5] *Extraordinary People*.

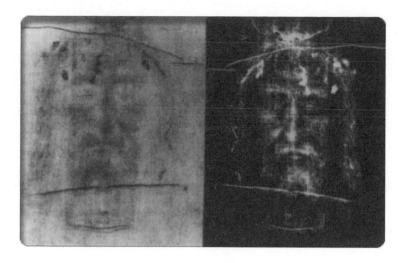

79

The Shroud of Turin

HAIKU:

THE SHROUD OF TURIN

Body wrapped in cloth
Image of crucified man
Can you be the Christ?

The church is not afraid of science.

—Archbishop Severino Poletto[1]

DEFINITION: The Shroud of Turin is a woven linen cloth fourteen feet, three inches long and three feet, seven inches wide, with front and rear images of a man on it that many believe is Jesus Christ.

WHAT THE BELIEVERS SAY: The Shroud is the actual burial cloth of Jesus Christ and His image was miraculously "burned" onto the cloth by an explosion of divine energy at the moment of His resurrection.

WHAT THE SKEPTICS SAY: The Shroud is a medieval painting, circa 1260–1390.

QUALITY OF EXISTING EVIDENCE: Fair.

LIKELIHOOD PHENOMENON IS PARANORMAL: Low.

The long linen cloth was stretched out and the body of the crucified man was laid on its bottom half.

The top half was then lifted and draped over the body, completely covering it, head to toe.

The man's body bore the signs of torture and death by crucifixion, and blood quickly stained the linen cloth. The shrouded body was then placed in a tomb, and the tomb was sealed with a large stone.

Three days later, the tomb was empty, and the shroud was all that remained in the cold sepulchre.

However, the cloth now displayed more than simple blood stains. The shroud now exhibited the complete image of the crucified man. His naked body was visible, albeit faintly, and it showed wounds from the crown of thorns used to torture him; blood dripping down his forehead; holes through the wrists where the nails had been mercilessly pounded; blood stains on his side where, according to Scripture, the biblical Christ had been pierced with a lance; and scourge marks on his back matching the dumbbell-shaped weights tied to the ends of whip lashes during Christ's time.

Although legend holds that the Shroud is two thousand years old, the first time it actually appears in the historical record is sometime around 1204, during the Crusades, when it was reported stolen during the sacking of Constantinople. The Shroud was later displayed in France in the 1350s, and ended up in the possession of the Archdiocese of Turin, where it has remained ever since. A fire in 1532 damaged the Shroud, and it was repaired by nuns with thirty pieces of cloth which were removed only recently during a major restoration of the cloth.

The most important event in the Shroud's history occurred in 1898, when its "negative" image was accidentally discovered. Since then, the Shroud has been hotly debated, with the faithful fully convinced of its authenticity, and most of the skeptics and those in the scientific community completely convinced that it is a medieval painting.

There is strong evidence that it is, indeed, a manmade artifact, most notably the carbon dating tests and the forensic reproduction of what Christ probably looked like (see below). The Church has never stated that it is the burial shroud of Jesus Christ, instead describing it as a "prayer aid." Nonetheless, they have never declared it to be a phony, and they protect it as though it were authentic.

ARGUMENTS FOR THE AUTHENTICITY OF THE SHROUD OF TURIN:

- The image on the Shroud is almost invisible, except as a photographic negative. How could a medieval forger have painted something that would only appear as a photographic negative, centuries before the invention of photography? How could he have "checked his work?": How could he have so meticulously created the details of the Shroud without being able to see what he was painting?

- The wounds and marks on the man on the Shroud's body correspond precisely with the description of Christ's crucifixion. Most compelling are the nail wounds on the wrist. Medieval paintings of the crucified Christ showed the nails through his hands. It was only centuries later that it was learned that the hands would not have been able to support the weight of a crucified body and that the Romans pounded the nails through the victim's wrists.

- Pollen grains removed from the Shroud were identified as a first century A.D. species of thistle indigenous to the Palestine area.

ARGUMENTS AGAINST THE AUTHENTICITY OF THE SHROUD OF TURIN:

- The "blood" on the Shroud was tested and proven to actually be red ocher and vermilion tempera paint.

- Carbon dating tests performed by three different laboratories (Arizona, Oxford, and Zurich) in 1988 confirmed that the linen of the Shroud dated from sometime between 1260 to 1390. (In 1994, German historian Holgar Kersten wrote a book called *The Jesus Conspiracy* in which he claimed that the samples tested in 1988 were *not* from the actual Shroud.)

- A mid-fourteenth century document exists in which a Bishop of the time recounts hearing the confession of the artist who created the Shroud. Also, in 1389, Pope Clement VII declared the Shroud to be a fraud.

- The physical characteristics of the Shroud (a single piece of linen fourteen feet long) contradict some of the Biblical accounts of Christ's burial, specifically, the book of John in the New Testament. In Matthew, Mark, and Luke, Christ's burial cloth is described, respectively, as "a clean linen cloth," "fine linen," and "linen."[2] But John is a different story completely:

John 19:40: "Then took they the body of Jesus, and wound it in linen clothes with the spices, as the manner of the Jews is to bury."

20:4-7: "So they ran both together, and the other disciple did outrun Peter, and came first to the sepulchre. And he stooping down, and looking in, saw the linen clothes lying, yet went he not in. Then cometh Simon Peter following him, and went into the sepulchre, and seeth the linen clothes lie, and the napkin that was about his head, not lying with the linen clothes, but wrapped together in a place by itself."

According to John, Christ was wrapped in linen *clothes*, and a separate piece of cloth ("the napkin that was about his head") was wrapped around his head. This completely contradicts the Shroud of Turin's one-piece nature, as well as its image of the crucified man's face.

- The Shroud image of a tall, long-haired, fair-complected Jesus is completely at odds with what men of Jesus' time and place looked like. Using skulls dated from the time of Jesus and sophisticated computer software, forensic anthropologists have recently concluded that Semite men of the first century were approximately five feet, one inch tall, with an average weight of 110 pounds, bearded, with short, curly hair. They were also dark-skinned, and had dark eyes. How do we know Jesus looked like the other men of his time? In the book of Matthew, we are told that Judas had to kiss Jesus in order to single him out for the Roman guards. If Jesus had been close to six feet tall, light-skinned, and had long, flowing hair, it is unlikely he would have needed to be identified.[3]

Who is the man on the Shroud? To this day, we still do not know, although a preponderance of evidence seems to preclude the possibility of it being Jesus Christ.

[1]Roman Catholic Archbishop Poletto made this widely cited statement during an August 2000 showing of the Shroud of Turin. The actions of the Catholic Church have, on occasion, contradicted this declaration.

[2]The passages:

- **Matthew 27:59:** "And when Joseph had taken the body, he wrapped it in a clean linen cloth."
- **Mark 15:44–46:** "And when he knew it of the centurion, he gave the body to Joseph. And he bought fine linen, and took him down, and wrapped him in the linen, and laid him in a sepulchre which was hewn out of a rock, and rolled a stone unto the door of the sepulchre."
- **Luke 23:52–53:** "This man went unto Pilate, and begged the body of Jesus. And he took it down, and wrapped it in linen, and laid it in a sepulchre that was hewn in stone, wherein never man before was laid."

[3]For a fascinating look at the "real face of Jesus," see the December 2002 issue of *Popular Mechanics*, which has a full-page color drawing of the forensic recreation of what Jesus probably looked like.

80

Spells

HAIKU:

SPELLS

Chant the magic words
Requesting intercession
Or simply a pox

*The priest shall write these curses in a book, and he
shall blot them out into the water of bitterness:
And he shall make the woman drink the water of
bitterness that causes the curse; and the water that causes
the curse shall enter into her and become bitter.*

—Numbers 5:23–24

DEFINITION: A spell is a word, phrase, formula, recipe, ritual, gesture,
or a curse that is believed to have magical powers and which can be
used for good or evil purposes.

WHAT THE BELIEVERS SAY: Spells work. When someone casts a magical spell or incantation, and they cast it with sincere intentions,

occult powers are accessed and the spirits will strive to help fulfill the person's desire. Good spells will summon good spirits; evil spells will summon evil spirits. Spells are cast for many reasons, including love, money, health, revenge, and power. Spells should not be cast frivolously.

WHAT THE SKEPTICS SAY: Spells and incantations most assuredly do *not* work. Any apparent results from a cast spell are due to coincidence, wishful thinking, faulty interpretation of a sequence of events, human interference, hoax, or error. The notion that reciting a scrap of doggerel (even *with* sincere intentions) can change the course of events in the real world is ridiculous.

QUALITY OF EXISTING EVIDENCE: Poor to Inconclusive.[1]

LIKELIHOOD PHENOMENA ARE PARANORMAL: Fair to Good.[2]

The adage "the pen is mightier than the sword" speaks to the power and the might of words. It affirms the damage that words can do, and it also points to the profound clout of the right words, when wielded in the right situation. "All men are created equal." "One small step for a man." "Ask not what you country can do for you." "Tear down this wall."

But words are only inanimate constructs developed to express ideas and the vagaries and complexities of reality, right?

Yes, but words are rocks, too.

Call an African-American the "n" word, say it with malice in your voice, and *see what happens*. Call a woman the "c" word with *anything* in your voice and *see what happens*.

Spells and incantations elevate to the supernatural level the notion of words having power. The belief in the efficacy of spells, then, actually endorses the notion that words *have* a power.

The West African spirit known as the Bori takes on human form, but has cloven feet. He is "allergic" to iron, so any "Bori repelling" spells should incorporate a piece of iron or, at the very least, should recite and repeat the word "iron" a few times. According to tradition, the Bori is a slave to his own name, which means that once a mortal learns the individual Bori's name, repeating it will enslave the demon to the "namer."[3]

Their pagan associations notwithstanding, spells are not only used for malefic purposes. Interestingly and ironically, benign "blessings" can be construed as spells "in reverse." Also, spells are a necessary part of the "demon casting out" rituals used in Christian exorcisms (see Chapter 27).

In the sixth century, St. Gregory named the Seven Deadly Sins, and his selection was later approved by St. Thomas Aquinas and included in his *Summa Theologica.*

The Seven Deadly Sins are greed, pride, envy, anger, gluttony, lust, and sloth. Christian theology states that the "opposing virtue" to any of the Seven Deadly Sins can be used as a spell to supplicate for forgiveness (if you happen to commit one—or more—of the Seven Deadly Sins); i.e., humility cancels out pride; fasting cancels out gluttony, chastity cancels out lust, patience cancels out anger; diligence cancels out sloth, etc.

In this case, a deed or action acts as a spell to negate sin.

Spells—if we use the exploded definition which includes prayers—are used in every religion of man.

Incantations and chants are akin to prayers and hymns.

Some of the connotations surrounding spells are, admittedly, blatantly negative. Our shared mythology regales us with stories of beak-nosed crones stirring a bubbling cauldron filled with bat's blood and eye of newt while chanting spells calling for the winning of a suitor's heart, or the destruction of someone's enemy.

Spells, when used as curses, can have profound effects. There are countless voodoo tales of someone dying after a curse is placed upon him—with no apparent cause other than fright. It is apparent that the power of suggestion can kill.

Spells are supersititous and range from the highly ritualized ceremonies involving props and substances, to a simple hand gesture thrown out a car window.

Do they work? People who have been prayed for and who have been granted health would likely say that all "exhortations for good."

Spells spoken for death or evil, if they succeed, do not leave witnesses to their effectiveness.

[1]If a person casts a malicious spell on an enemy and something bad happens to that person, they will claim victory in their spell-casting powers. This is not hard evidence that the spell actually worked. Thus, our mixed rating: the concrete evidence is poor; the results of spells are inconclusive.

[2]This rating stems from the understanding that prayer can be considered a spell—people chant words in hopes of a result. There are reports that praying for someone who is sick can result in improved health for the patient. (There are double-blind studies proving the connection.) We are not equating voodoo, witchcraft, or Satanic spells with praying; simply making the point that using words as a tool for a hoped-for effect does seem to have paranormal validation.

[3]*A Field Guide to Demons*, pp. 102–03.

81

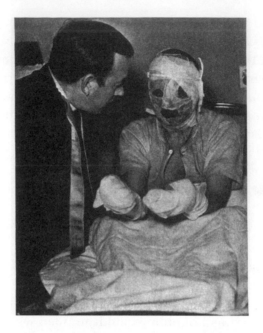

Spontaneous Human Combustion

HAIKU:

SPONTANEOUS HUMAN COMBUSTION

Engulfed in the flames
The helpless, moveless woman
Charred remains remain

*It is essential to find out whether a phenomenon does in fact
happen, even if we know not how it comes about or why it
occurs, regardless whether tradition or authority are opposed.*

—Dr. Lester S. King[1]

We are departing from our usual format in this chapter to turn the
podium over to the man many people consider to be the world's fore-
most authority on Spontaneous Human Combustion, Larry E.
Arnold. Larry is the author of the seminal book on the subject,
ABLAZE! The Mysterious Fires of Spontaneous Human Combustion,
and we are honored and pleased to present this fascinating and infor-
mative interview with Larry to our readers of *The Weird 100*.

1. What is Spontaneous Human Combustion?

Spontaneous Human Combustion (SHC) is the process whereby a person smokes, blisters or otherwise burns in the absence of a known, identifiable, external ignition source.

The historical depiction of SHC is what we now call *classic* SHC, in which a person is almost wholly transformed, skeleton included, to dry powder amid a fire scene exhibiting otherwise minimal heat or flame damage and without an accelerant. However, as research into this heatedly controversial subject has uncovered, the enigma of SHC presents many variations to this common depiction.

2. What are the most common theories regarding the cause of SHC?

The answer depends on how one evaluates evidence. Naysayers have but one theory (if one may term it that) for SHC: it doesn't happen. They assert that so-called SHC is 1) "fairy tale"; 2) "myth"; 3) "hoax"; 4) "superstition born of medieval ignorance"; or 5) proof of the "human wick effect" whereby a body, once *externally* ignited by a smoking mishap or an arson-murderer, will very slowly smolder in the fuel of its own body fat.

SHC proponents embrace these assertions too, *when* appropriate, including the theory that some people's physiology is preternaturally more flammable than the norm, hence will burn far more readily once lit (thus avoiding having to deal with authentic SHC). But believing the human body is a very complex bio-electrochemical cauldron not yet wholly understood, we consider other ideas when evidence belies such facile explain-aways.

Speculation posits many theories for spontaneous burning of humans, including these:

1. simultaneous discharge of electrical potential in millions (if not billions) of cells to produce an internal quasi-electrocution;
2. hormones, such as endogenous pyrogen, that over-stimulate the hypothalamus (body's thermostat) to trigger what one doctor terms "the body conflagration";
3. diphosphane and other radical chemistry in the body;
4. extreme cases of known toxic maladies, such as Strep-A necrotizing fasiatis, or a new form of etio-cholanone fever;
5. whole-body biophotolysis—dissociation of water via enzymes into hydrogen and oxygen and hydroxyl radicals (an electrically explosive mix);
6. auto-suggestion/hypnosis;

7. kundalini;[2]

8. ball lightning and fireballs;

9. a high-energy subatomic quantum photon impact;

10. unsuspected interplays between physiology and geomagnetism;

11. the science of New Chemistry, in which nanometer-scale collisions of atomic clusters yield temperatures as high as 7,000 degrees F.;

12. unknown telluric or atmospheric or cosmic energies that hyper-heat a person (or animal) who unfortunately is "in the right place at the wrong time."

3. Would you discuss your thoughts on whether or not you believe there is a paranormal (i.e., supernatural) component to SHC?

The Random House Dictionary (1966) gives two sets of definitions for supernatural. First, "above and beyond what is natural . . . abnormal." Second, "ghosts, goblins, or other unearthly beings; eerie; occult; direct influence or action of a god on earthly affairs." Paranormal is what which resides alongside *(para)* yet outside what is considered normal.

SHC is certainly eerie, no doubt. By the first definition, SHC is clearly *both* supernatural and paranormal; that is, it occurs in the normal world yet has explanation(s) alongside/outside what is currently understood scientifically about the human body, fire, and energy generally.

As science is presently practiced, it seems impossible to validate the supernatural as characterized by the second definition. Nonetheless, given a) the innumerable cross-cultural and metaphysical traditions referring to non-human consciousnesses (from fire-sprites to wrathful gods/God) and their interplay with humans that can result in combustion of the latter and b) our open-ended approach to theorizing, until we meet someone whose omniscience guarantees what can and cannot be, we will not rule out any aspect of the supernatural as a *possible* component to some quite eerie and enigmatic inflamings.

4. Would you summarize for us your theory regarding ley lines and SHC?

To preface our answer: the *best* fire investigators look for *patterns* at a fire scene to help them determine exactly how and where a fire began. Having been taught arson science by excellent fire instructors, we wondered if there might be a *larger* pattern to these odd, rare, and extraordinary fires that seemed spontaneous.

Consequently, in 1976 we plotted scores of such blazes in Great Britain on a map, a nation already renowned for alignments (leys) and odd energies associated with ancient megaliths. We chose Britain because a) it seems to host more cases of baffling blazes per capita than any other nation and b) spherical geometry was not a significant factor. To our astonishment and delight, fifty-one cases—84.3 percent of the total mapped—are linked by at least a three-point alignment. Many alignments link four (statistically significant) and more events. Along Britain's east coast, one astonishing 430-mile alignment unites perhaps as many as a dozen anomalous blazes befalling people and property.

For this discovery we coined the phrase *fire-leyne*. Two chapters in *ABLAZE!* detail this fascinating Cartography of Combustion.

Whether coincidental or meaningful, a mapping anomaly or the trackway to an invisible telluric energy that can kindle matter, the *fire-leyne* theory demands serious investigation. If a theory's proof is that it leads to findings predicted by the theory, then *fire-leynes* are well on their way to science fact . . . because their mapping fore-shadowed—even predicted—the locations of several future SHC-style fire fatalities.

5. What does modern forensic medicine have to say about the SHC phenomenon?

Consider this unequivocal declaration by Dr. Mark Benecke, who says he's investigated nearly two hundred alleged SHC cases in his international career as an esteemed forensic biologist, and which pretty much encapsulates the attitude of his colleagues toward SHC:

"In contrast to the first impression conveyed of gross destruction of the whole body, internal organs are frequently not essentially changed," he avows in *Skeptical Inquirer* (CSICOP, March/April 1998). "Even intestines, stomach, liver, heart, uterus, bladder, etc., are often well preserved . . . first-year medical students express surprise when shown burned corpses containing intact organs." This comment certainly applies to normal human fire fatalities, yes. But—

Dr. Benecke then attributes the absence of internal organs in some SHC-style fire photographs to misleading camera angles. "In forensic practice," he continues, "there are no known cases in which internal organs of a burned corpse were damaged more severely than the outer parts. This practical observation is further proof that combustion never starts from inside a human body."

Oh? We challenge Dr. Benecke to discover the camera angle that can conceal the skeleton and internal organs in what is arguably the world's most famous fire fatality photograph of an individual, Dr. John Bentley. Dr. Benecke will fail in all attempts.

Permit us to be blunt. Dr. Benecke is flat-out, brain-up-the-butt wrong. Since he errs on this point of photographic evidence, might he not also be wrong to declare impossible SHC itself?

6. You have been researching SHC for many years. Could you briefly summarize/discuss some of the most compelling cases you have investigated?

There are scores of compelling cases among the hundreds we have catalogued. Of these, a few have special significance to us.

1. *Mary Hardy Reeser:* Her death in 1951 as "The Cinder Woman" baffled local authorities in Florida, created an international sensation, and introduced us to the possibility of SHC. Her case is still "open," more than a half-century later.

2. *Dr. John Bentley:* His bizarre baffling burning in 1966 in our home state was the first of many cases we would investigate first-hand. Upon obtaining photographs of his death scene—the quintessential portrayal of classic SHC—we knew this was no ordinary fire fatality. His flaming fate became the first SHC-style death featured on American television, ABC-TV's "That's Incredible!" (1980).

3. *Helen Conway:* She was a known smoker and widow who burned up in a chair in southeastern Pennsylvania; the 1964 blaze was localized and intense and incredibly brief, if one accepts the testimony from Fire Chief Paul Haggarty, Assistant Fire Marshal Harry Lott and fire photographer (later Fire Marshal) Robert Meslin, who all agree the fire's duration was "not more than twenty-one minutes." Debunkers have no explanation, other than to allege the time factor—hence the fire officials themselves—must simply be wrong.

4. *George Mott:* He was a retired fireman in upstate New York; his 1986 localized cremation in a "tinderbox of a house" brought us together with Essex County's Tony Morette and Robert Purdy and other skilled, knowledgeable fire investigators. After 700-plus man-hours of investigation, SHC was declared the most reasonable cause-of-death to the exclusion of all other possibilities.

5. *Jack Angel:* This traveling salesman awoke in 1974 to find his right forearm "burned black, charred to a crisp." His pajamas, sheets on which he lay, and motor home in which he slept, were all unburned. Physicians diagnosed his multiple burn injuries as "internal in origin." The first survivor whom we had

the privilege to meet and interview, his 'unique' case challenged everything previously claimed about (and against) SHC.

6. *Peter Jones:* This Californian both witnessed and survived not one, but *two* bouts with self-combustion *in one day*. His wife, Barbara, witnessed one episode, to utter amazement and consternation. Their experiences and cooperation, honest frankness, and resulting friendship have been among the many blessings of our quest to document spon-com.

7. *Kay Fletcher:* This Ohio woman's diminutive body suddenly billowed smoke one Sunday morning in 1996. Her husband, who had worked at a crematorium, observed her predicament and rushed to her rescue. Together they observed the smoke originating from her body, not a garment or other external source. They, too, braved ridicule to tell their story about SHC—for which we are grateful.

7. What is the earliest mention of SHC in the historical literature?

The earliest SHC description we have located in the medical literature comes from Bartholini's obscure *Historiarum Anatomicarum Rariorum* (1654), which describes the death of a knight, Polonus, who "vomited flame and was thereupon totally consumed" sometime in the latter fifteenth century.

Earlier history, plus legends and myth, all suggest that SHC has plagued its victims and consternated its observers for millennia. The Ostrogoth king Theodoric the Great (ca. A.D. 454–526) is said to have emitted sparks from his body. Pliny the Elder (A.D. 23–79) wrote about two cases of "sudden fire" involving humans; and of "a flaming fire of some sort" that burned from the head of Lucius Marcius in 212 B.C. The Jewish Talmud alludes to an even earlier event, ca. 701 B.C., when soldiers of the Assyrian warrior-king Sennacherib were supernaturally "burnt, though their garments remained intact." *ABLAZE!* provides many more examples for the apparent antiquity of SHC.

8. How common is SHC? We know it has struck animals as well as humans. Is it more common in animals?

Given that we have identified approximately five hundred (and counting) examples that could be characterized as SHC during the past two thousand years, clearly SHC must be extraordinarily rare. Fortunately. However, we also believe that many episodes have been lost to history—unpublicized, misidentified, misrepresented, even willfully concealed. The true number will never be known, though being struck by lightning (odds of one-in-fifty thousand) is far more likely than by "internal fire."

Is spontaneous animal combustion more common? Probably not. Dogs and cats, some of them pets, plus sheep are among nonhuman species to have puzzlingly combusted.

9. What do the survivors of SHC say about the experience?

Ah, if only SHC survivors didn't exist—and wouldn't talk! But they do, to the endless consternation of SHC debunkers.

First, they say that they are surprised. Often times, they feel no discomfort; no pain. Kay Fletcher spoke of only mild warmth in her back before her shoulder erupted in smoke. Fear of a re-occurrence haunts, even terrifies, some survivors.

Often, the color of the "fire" is said to be electric-blue. Unlike the noxious odor normally associated with burning flesh, SHC survivors usually report either no smell or a sweet, redolent aroma. In one fatal case, the smell was characterized as "hickory incense."

Above all, survivors are mystified. They did not make contact with any ignition source, they affirm, consequently do not understand why their bodies would suddenly smoke, blister, or char. Nor do they get answers from their physicians.

10. Could you recommend some books and Web sites for readers interested in learning more about SHC?

Humbly, the standard reference book is Larry E. Arnold's *ABLAZE! The Mysterious Fires of Spontaneous Human Combustion* (1995); hardback, five-hundred plus pages with photographs, charts, maps. E-mail Larry at psinet@voicenet.com.

We also recommend John Heymer's *The Entrancing Flame* (1995); Jenny Randles and Peter Hough's *Spontaneous Human Combustion* (1992); Vincent Gaddis' *Mysterious Lights and Fires* (1967); Gerald N. Callahan's *Faith, Madness, and Spontaneous Human Combustion* (2002).

Some useful Web sites include:

- www.geocities.com/shashaeby/ablaze.html.
- www.diseaseworld.com/shc.htm.

---

[1] *The Growth of Medical Thought.*

[2] Energy that lies dormant at the base of the spine until it is activated, as by the practice of yoga, and channeled upward through the chakras in the process of spiritual perfection *(American Heritage Dictionary)*.

82

Stigmata

HAIKU:

STIGMATA

Bleeding wounds she wears
Hands and feet are bloody flags
Waving to her God

From now on, let no one cause me any trouble, for I bear the marks of the Lord Jesus branded on my body.

—St. Paul[1]

DEFINITION: Stigmata are bleeding marks, wounds, or sores corresponding to and resembling the crucifixion wounds, and sometimes the whip lashings, of Jesus Christ.

WHAT THE BELIEVERS SAY: Stigmata are divine wounds, sent as a sign from God.

WHAT THE SKEPTICS SAY: The bleeding and physical wounds of stigmata are self-induced by religious hysteria.

QUALITY OF SUPPORTING EVIDENCE: Excellent.

LIKELIHOOD PHENOMENON IS AUTHENTIC: Very high.

The August Catholic Encyclopedia begins its entry on "Mystical Stigmata" with the following proclamation: "Their existence is so well established historically that, as a general thing, they are no longer disputed by unbelievers . . ."2 Yet acceptance of their existence does not mean blanket acceptance of a divine source for these brutal, bloody wounds.

Stigmata are not painless; in fact, the Church states that suffering is a part of the miracle, asserting that "the wounds would be but an empty symbol, theatrical representation, conducing to pride. If the stigmata really come from God, it would be unworthy of His wisdom to participate in such futility, and to do so by a miracle."3

There is no record of stigmatics prior to the thirteenth century. It is generally accepted that the first stigmatic was St. Francis of Assisi, who manifested bloody wounds on his hands and feet. Remarkably, the wounds on Francis's hands and feet looked precisely like what such wounds would be expected to look like if they were made with thick, round-headed nails. The tops of his hands and feet showed rounded wounds; the bottoms, wounds appeared in which the skin was pierced and bent back, as if made by the point of a nail.

The Catholic Church does not accept stigmatization as an acceptable miracle for purposes of canonization. Yet, many officially canonized saints bore the marks of Christ's torture and crucifixion and the Church does consider stigmata as possible evidence of holiness on the part of the sufferer.

Stigmata is rarely seen in non-Catholics, yet recently, there have been reports of some Muslims displaying stigmata that correspond to the battle wounds of the Islamic prophet Mohammed. Also, Charles Fort wrote of a Protestant girl who bled for seventeen days before Easter in 1972, and of, of all things, a pigeon in the Philippines who developed stigmata matching wounds of another pigeon that had been stabbed.

Skeptics believe that all stigmata, without exception, are caused by autosuggestion. According to them, stigmata sufferers are usually so devout, and so obsessed with meditating on the agony Christ endured on the cross, that they cause their body to manifest bleeding wounds, always at the sites of Christ's suffering. It is written that St. Francis's stigmata first appeared after he fasted for a great length of time and meditated fiercely on Christ's crucifixion.

The literature is replete with similar stories of devout Catholics receiving Christ's wounds, and yet some stigmatics do not exhibit blatantly delusional, religio-obsessive behavior. The twentieth-century priest Padre Pio bore the stigmata every day of his life (sometimes producing as much as a water glass of blood in a single day), yet continued to fulfill his duties as a priest. He simply accepted the stigmata and went about his business, which is not the profile one might expect from a person so obsessed with piety that they could cause themselves to bleed. Many historical stigmatics, aside from being prayerful and obviously very devout, were also quite ordinary people and, in some cases, young children who likely had not had the time to develop extreme religious obsession.

Granted, there are stories of religious ecstatics who never slept, survived only on communion wafers (most notable, Therese Neumann), and essentially did nothing but pray, but for every one of these, there are countless stories of stigmatics who simply began bleeding one day, oftentimes after experiencing an unbidden vision of Christ. Usually, once a person became a stigmatic, the wounds were with them, at varying times and for varying durations, for the rest of their lives.

Medical science cannot explain three ubiquitous characteristics of stigmatic wounds:

- Physicians cannot cure or repair stigmata with conventional medical treatments.
- Stigmata wounds do not give off a foul, infected odor, a smell quite typical of most suppurating wounds.[4]
- Some stigmata wounds produce a wonderful, perfume-like smell.[5]

There are over four hundred documented cases of stigmata, beginning with St. Francis of Assisi, and with the majority being women. Also, the majority of the women stigmatics were members of a religious order.[6]

Supporters of the autosuggestion theory—physicians and scientists—have attempted to artificially "summon" stigmata on experimental subjects. These subjects have been hypnotized and told that they could make their hands and feet bleed. The results were not supportive of the autosuggestion hypothesis: none of the subjects actually caused themselves to erupt in wounds and bleed, although some were able to make red spots or rashes appear on their bodies.

* * *

The faithful will not accept scientific proof that stigmata are psychosomatic, if such proof were ever forthcoming and conclusive.

The religious accept stigmata as a miracle, and a mystery, and believe that those so afflicted are touched by God.

THIRTY-THREE FAMOUS STIGMATICS[7]

- St. Francis of Assisi (1186–1226)
- St. Lutgarde (1182–1246), Cistercian
- St. Margaret of Cortona (1247–97)
- St. Gertrude (1256–1302), Benedictine
- St. Clare of Montefalco (1268–1308), Augustinian
- Blessed Angela of Foligno (d. 1309), Franciscan tertiary
- St. Catherine of Siena (1347–80), Dominican tertiary
- St. Lidwine (1380–1433)
- St. Frances of Rome (1384–1440)
- St. Colette (1380–1447), Franciscan
- St. Rita of Cassia (1386–1456), Augustinian
- Blessed Osanna of Mantua (1499–1505), Dominican tertiary
- St. Catherine of Genoa (1447–1510), Franciscan tertiary
- Blessed Baptista Varani (1458–1524), Poor Clare
- Blessed Lucy of Narni (1476–1547), Dominican tertiary
- Blessed Catherine of Racconigi (1486–1547), Dominican
- St. John of God (1495–1550), founder of the Order of Charity
- St. Catherine de' Ricci (1522–89), Dominican
- St. Mary Magdalene de' Pazzi (1566–1607), Carmelite
- Blessed Marie de l'Incarnation (1566–1618), Carmelite
- Blessed Mary Anne of Jesus (1557–1620), Franciscan tertiary
- Blessed Carlo of Sezze (d. 1670), Franciscan
- Blessed Margaret Mary Alacoque (1647–90), Visitandine (crown of thorns only)
- St. Veronica Giuliani (1600–1727), Capuchiness
- St. Mary Frances of the Five Wounds (1715–91), Franciscan tertiary
- Catherine Emmerich (1774–1824), Augustinian
- Elizabeth Canori Mora (1774–1825), Trinitarian tertiary
- Anna Maria Taïgi (1769–1837)
- Maria Dominica Lazzari (1815–48)
- Marie de Moerl (1812–68) Franciscan tertiary

- Louise Lateau (1850–83), Franciscan tertiary
- Therese Neumann (1898–1962)
- Padre Pio (1887–1968), Franciscan

[1]Galatians 6:17. In the original Greek, the word "stigmata" was used for "marks." Some translations of the Bible have Paul writing that he bore the marks "in" his body and some have concluded that Paul was, thus, speaking metaphorically. This is a matter of interpretation.

[2]*The Catholic Encyclopedia*, www.newadvent.org.

[3]Ibid.

[4]The only known exception to this rule was the forehead "crown of thorns" wound of St. Rita of Cascia (1381–1457, canonized 1900). Rita, a devout Augustinian nun, began bleeding from her forehead after listening to a sermon about Jesus' crown of thorns, and the wound gave forth a putrid odor, although there was never any sign of infection.

[5]Blessed Lucy of Narnia and St. John of the Cross are two stigmatics whose wounds reportedly emitted a sweet, floral smell.

[6]Ted Harrison, *Stigmata*.

[7]Adapted and expanded from *The Catholic Encyclopedia*.

83

Stonehenge

HAIKU:

STONEHENGE

Silent standing stones
Astronomical wisdom
A circle of stars

Stonehenge stands as lonely in history as it does on the great plain.

—Henry James

DEFINITION: Stonehenge is a group of enormous standing stones on Salisbury Plain in central southern England that are believed to have been constructed in three phases between 2950 and 1600 B.C.

WHAT THE BELIEVERS SAY: We do not know why Stonehenge was built, but there had to have been some kind of extraterrestrial or paranormal participation or influence. Perhaps aliens built the site, as some suspect they built the Easter Island *moai* (see Chapter 31) and the pyramids at Giza. Solving the mystery of Stonehenge may provide the key to confirmed extraterrestrial contact.

WHAT THE SKEPTICS SAY: The arrangement of the stones suggests that Stonehenge was used as a religious center and also as an astronomical observatory, but it is assuredly manmade and there is no evidence that aliens were involved in its construction. Some archaeologists believe Stonehenge may have been an ancient sacred burial site.

QUALITY OF EXISTING EVIDENCE: Excellent.[1]

LIKELIHOOD PHENOMENON IS PARANORMAL: Low to Fair.[2]

A PREHISTORIC MEETING

It is dawn.

A great crowd is gathered on the plain, for it is a special occasion—the day of decision.

The sky brightens in the east . . .

There has been laughing, earlier, and jostling to keep warm. The English night can be cool, even at midsummer. But now the people grow silent. They stand looking toward the horizon, toward the two lone trees on the skyline. Above those trees, radiating from them as a focus, the brightening sky is spreading its color out in a fan.

The priest speaks.

"People, look carefully. If God appears at the sacred place, it is good. The prophecy is fulfilled. All omens are favorable. We will build the temple here, and God will be pleased. He will protect you in life, and he will guard your spirits in death."

The chieftain, tall and strong, with the high forehead typical of his race, speaks.

"We are honored that our land has been chosen, by God himself, for his holy temple. It will be well."

The people murmur assent.

(And "Yes," thinks the priest, "by this temple I will know when to call the people to this place on this one day, to see God enter his sanctuary, and by this temple I will know other things, many things." And "Yes," thinks the chieftain, "this temple will be our alliance with God, a mighty fortress and monument to our power. Already we have pleased God so that he will tell the priest the good times for planting and for hunting—with this temple we will please him more—we will be great." And "Yes," think the people, "a lot of work—but worth it . . .")

The sky brightens.

The priest spreads out his arms.

Beside him, the chief stands as in prayer.

There is a moment of intolerable brilliance—an instant from eternity, the high magic moment of birth—a flash—and, exactly between those distant trees, red-gold, immense—God appears . . .

. . . And the next day, the enormous sanctified work began . . .[3]

* * *

Is this imagined scene a true account of how the ancient builders of Stonehenge decided to begin work?

Did they interpret the sunrise as a sign from God?

And if this was the moment when they were convinced that the land on which they prayed was the divinely mandated location for the monument, were they all standing inside a crop circle that would ultimately be mirrored by the design of the standing stones?

There are hundreds of stone circles scattered throughout England, yet few of them are true circles (most are ellipses), and none of them is anywhere near as well-known as Stonehenge.

Some of the Stonehenge stones weigh upwards of sixty tons, and scientists believe that many of the largest pieces were transported from a quarry over two hundred miles away in Wales. The logistics of such a task are daunting *today*; imagine moving the Stonehenge standing stones using nothing but logs, rope, stone axes, and tools made from deer antlers.

Regardless of the wild theories about extraterrestrial involvement in the construction of Stonehenge, it has been confirmed with relative certainty that the site is a giant astronomical calculator. Dr. Gerald Hawkins, the author of the excerpt reprinted at the beginning of this chapter, determined that the placement of the stones was directly linked to a fifty-six-year cycle of eclipses. Later research confirmed that sticks of varying heights, when placed in the fifty-six Aubrey holes at the site on specific days of the year perfectly aligned with the positions of stars and planets.

How was Stonehenge built?

Dr. Hawkins meticulously calculated the expenditures of time and materials required, and arrived at the staggering figure of 1,497,680 man-days of physical labor. One of his calculations boggles the modern mind:

> Transporting 80 sarsens, average weight thirty tons, twenty miles by land at seven hundred men per stone, one mile per day: 1,120,000 man-days of labor[4]

Seven hundred men per stone.

Such a commitment is impressive, and, at the same time, bewildering.

Why would a people devote generations to such grueling work? As Hawkins tells us, "For generations the work on Salisbury Plain must have absorbed most of the energies—physical, mental, spiritual—and most of the material resources of a whole people."[5]

Again, we ask *why?*

The reasons for such an enormous channeling of resources into the construction of Stonehenge will never be fully known, although we can hazard a guess.

Stonehenge was built as an astronomical computer that its builders seem to have believed would provide them with insights and information that would serve and protect them, and also connect them to God and the universe in ways mere prayer and obedience to Scripture could not.

The religious significance and underlying motivation cannot be dismissed. As has often been the case with momentous expressions of the human spirit like Stonehenge, the Great Pyramids, the Easter Island monuments, etc., the hope of the builders has clearly been to understand, honor, and unite with God and all of eternity.

Perhaps that, in the end, is the true key to understanding *why*.

---

[1] Stonehenge has been measured, studied, x-rayed, and analyzed for centuries.

[2] There really isn't very much concrete evidence that there is a paranormal component to the Stonehenge site. There are theories, and those are acknowledged by the "Fair" ranking, but in all likelihood, Stonehenge was built by man, for his own purposes.

[3] Gerald Hawkins, *Stonehenge Decoded*, pp. 61–2.

[4] Ibid., p. 73.

[5] Ibid., p. 73

84

Subliminal Messages

HAIKU:

SUBLIMINAL MESSAGES

Hidden images
Secret messages are there
Or is it a hoax?

*Lulled in the countless chambers of the brain, our thoughts
are linked by many a hidden chain; awake but one, and in,
what myriads rise!*[1]

DEFINITION: Subliminal messages are hidden pictures, words, or sounds in photographic ads, or sound recordings. The theory behind them is that the subconscious mind can see and hear (and remember) these messages even if they are unrecognizable and inaccessible to the conscious mind. Some theorists also claim subliminal "pro-something" or "anti-something" messages can be embedded metaphorically in the lyrics and sound (the production) of songs. (See the discussion of "Bridge Over Troubled Water" on next page.)[2]

WHAT THE BELIEVERS SAY: Advertisers regularly embed hidden messages in ads. They are there, and they are real. The subconscious mind is like a computer and it remembers everything, so putting the image of a naked woman in ice cubes in a liquor ad will register with the reader, associate sex with the brand, and spur him to buy that brand the next time he is buying alcohol.

WHAT THE SKEPTICS SAY: There is no empirical evidence that subliminal messaging works, and the advertising agencies deny ever deliberately hiding images or words in ads. Anything people see in ads—unless it is deliberately placed there as a goof, as in the Chivas ad on the back of the 2003 *Sports Illustrated* swimsuit issue[3]—is completely in the imagination of the person spending way too much time trying to find things in ads.

QUALITY OF EXISTING EVIDENCE: Fair to Good.[4]

LIKELIHOOD PHENOMENA ARE PARANORMAL: Inconclusive.

Do you like the Simon & Garfunkel song "Bridge Over Troubled Water"? Almost everyone does. Did you know, however, that the subliminal story being told in the song's lyrics is of a drug dealer comforting his customer, a heroin addict, while providing him or her with the fix they so desperately need? So says Wilson Bryan Key, the guru of subliminal communication. If you listen to the song as though a drug dealer is the one singing, Key tells us in his 1976 book *Media Sexploitation*, the meaning in the lyrics is blatant.

Paul Simon begs to differ, however.

In an interview with Paul Zollow for *SongTalk* magazine, Simon says, "There was a whole period of time where 'Bridge Over Troubled Water' was supposed to be about heroin." Zollow replies, "Yeah, 'silvergirl' was supposed to be a syringe," to which Simon responds, "That's a tough one. It's a tough one to prove 'cause, of course, it's absolutely not so, so how are you going to do it?"

This epitomizes the problem with the theory that subliminal messages are embedded in advertising, movies, TV shows, and songs. If you listen to the song with Key's interpretation in mind, it absolutely works. And yet we have the songwriter himself telling us this reading of the song is solely in the mind (ear) of the beholder (listener). However, Key provides concrete evidence in his book that advertisers do, indeed, embed words and images in their ads, none of which are evident on first perusal of the ad.

He shows photographs[5] of Ritz Crackers with the word "sex" imprinted on them in their nooks and crannies.[6] He shows ads with erect penises and naked women in them. He points out the vaginal symbols in ice cubes and the phallic symbols in mail-order catalog ads. Can any of this be true? In an article in the March 31, 2003 issue of *Advertising Age*,[7] advertising execs and art directors dismiss the practice as an urban legend. Jeff Goodby, co-creative director of Goodby, Silverstein & Partners in San Francisco, said, "In my twentysomething years of doing this, I have never been asked to airbrush a single breast into an ad." In the same article, a representative for the American Association of Advertising Agencies states emphatically, "It does not exist, it's not real, and agencies don't do it."

Then what are all those breasts and deathhead masks and phalluses doing hidden in the ads? Once they are pointed out, they are impossible to "not see." Are they purely imaginary, like seeing cities in the clouds? Perhaps, yet some of the pointed-out images are quite vivid in their detail and specificity and seem too well-defined to manifest solely by chance.

Subliminal messaging was "born," so to speak, in 1957 when James M. Vicary conducted a little experiment in a movie theater. Using a new strobe-light projection machine from Eastman-Kodak called the Tachistoscope, Vicary projected on the screen, at 1/30,000th of a second, the messages "Drink Coke" and "Eat Popcorn." Reportedly, popcorn sales in the theater went up 57 percent, while Coke sales increased 18 percent. This experiment caused a furious uproar and lawmakers responded to the public outcry by actually passing laws against something that advertisers said they weren't doing anyway. Vicary's experiment was later dismissed as a hoax, since his results could not be duplicated under controlled circumstances.

All of the ad folks' denials aside, are there subliminal embeds in ads being run today?

I perused the May 2003 issue of *Playboy* (just doing what I can to serve you better), specifically looking at ads carefully and trying to find the hidden images.

I did not study ads with a magnifying glass; I simply looked at them for a longer period than I normally would have while flipping through the pages to get to the . . . articles.

My findings were . . . let's say "interesting":

- **Pg. 12: A Columbia Sportswear ad for stonewashed canvas men's shorts.** The outline of an erect penis is clearly visible in the folds of the top leg of the shorts.
- **Pg. 42: An ad for Jack Daniels whiskey.** The bottom half of a woman clad in a bikini bottom can clearly be seen in the striations of the glass window on the left side of a distilling chamber.

- **Pg. 56: An ad for the Toyota Matrix.** Two clearly discernible alien, cat, or demon faces can be seen as reflections in the windows of the building in front of which sits the Matrix.

- **Pgs. 62–3: A two-page ad for Winston cigarettes.** When the magazine is turned upside down, an alien face (it looks exactly like the gray-type extraterrestrial shown on the cover of Whitley Strieber's book *Communion*) can be seen in the foam of the waves. (This one gave me chills when I first recognized it.)

- **Inside back cover: An ad for Miller Lite.** This ad is blatantly sexual, and the subliminal message is charged and very direct. A woman is telling the story of the time she saw a dog stick its snout under a woman's skirt at a party. The party scene itself is depicted in a large photo filling the top two-thirds of the page. The dog looks like a beagle, he has his nose under the skirt, lifting it, and the woman's thong-clad buttocks are exposed. The dog is thrusting himself out of the lap of a smiling woman looking away, not noticing what Fido is doing. The suggestion of bestiality is obvious and somewhat unsettling. The woman telling the story is part of a group of six, two male/female couples, and two men. Interestingly, one of the men in the two men couple seems to have been cut and pasted into the picture. It looks like a man's laughing face has been placed over another face. His hair doesn't match and looks like it is in two sections. The sexual connotations in this ad are numerous and had to have been placed deliberately.

Also worth noting from this issue is an ad on page fifteen for Molson's Beer, which blatantly (and satirically) acknowledges the power of subliminal advertising, and suggests it can influence women.

The ad talks about Molson Twin Advertising Technology (which it wryly states is a trademarked technology). The ad tells the reader (a single man, of course) that as he is reading this ad, women are reading a different ad currently running in *Cosmopolitan* magazine. This other ad shows a handsome man holding two adorable puppies— and a bottle of Molson. "Hundreds of thousands of women. Pre-programmed for your convenience," the headline shouts. The ad in *Cosmo*, we learn, is "a perfectly tuned combination of words and images designed by trained professionals. Women who are exposed to it experience a very positive feeling." These woman can be triggered to transfer this feeling to you, the reader, the ad goes on to say, by simply (wait for it) *ordering a Molson beer!* Cute.

* * *

In conclusion, it would seem that subliminal messages are being used in expensive ads. (It costs too much to do them in small, limited market ads.) Today, with the amazing array of digital imaging software available to advertising art directors, it's a wonder it is not used more often.

Then again, maybe it is?

[1] Alexander Pope.

[2] Also see Chapter 14, "Backwards Messages and Reverse Speech."

[3] Playing on the urban legend of naked women in ice cubes, the Chivas ad said, "Some see a naked woman in the ice cubes. Others simply see the need for more Chivas." The naked woman is at the top of the lower right cube.

[4] There are undoubtedly hidden images in some ads. I myself have seen them and many of them were obviously planted. Some are subjective, like seeing vaginal images in the shape formed by a woman's thumb and index finger, but some are detailed and obvious.

[5] *Media Sexploitation*, Figure 4, photo insert.

[6] The words are definitely there, but one cannot help but wonder how this was done. Do the Ritz people at Nabisco have special presses which have the word sex on them and they use these to stamp the word into the dough? Key claims the holes in the crackers are arranged in specific ways so that they spell out the word "sex" repeatedly. Sounds ridiculous, doesn't it? And yet Key finds "sex" all over the crackers and points them out to us in his book. Coincidence?

[7] "Sex, Crackers and Subliminal Ads" by Eleftheria Parpis.

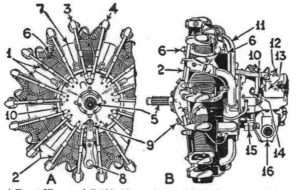

85

A Front View, and *B* Side View, of a Radial Engine. 1 Cylinders; 2, 2 Housings for rods actuating valves; 3 Housing for intake valve rocker; 4 Housing for exhaust valve rocker; 5 End of crankshaft on which propeller is mounted; 6, 6 Spark Plugs (two for each cylinder); 7 Wind Deflector; 8 Sump; 9 Controllable Pitch Mechanism; 10 Ignition Manifold; 11 Intake Manifold; 12 Electric Starter; 13 Magneto; 14 Tachometer Drive; 15 Fuel Pump; 16 Oil Temperature Regulator. the crankshaft the engine is called a ***rotary engine.*** When the cylinders are stationary and the crankshaft revolves it is called a ***fixed radial engine,*** or simply, a radial engine.
radial feeder. *Elec.* See FEEDER, 6.

Suppressed Inventions

HAIKU:

SUPPRESSED INVENTIONS

A cure for cancer

A car that runs on water

Can these really be?

Americans have come to depend largely upon synthetic compounds designed to mimic natural plant compounds. Because these drugs—unlike herbs—are patented, the exclusive rights to sell them are held by drug companies, and there is correspondingly less commercial incentive to invest money in collecting and preparing herbs or testing and promoting the compounds extracted from them. Thus, as little as 1 percent of all plant species on Earth today—estimates range between 250,000 to a half-million species—has been extensively studied for medicinal applications.

—Dr. William F. Williams[1]

DEFINITION: Suppressed inventions are those inventions, technological developments, medical breakthroughs, and incredible archaeological and astronomical discoveries that have been deliberately withheld from the public at large for alleged security, financial, or public safety reasons.

WHAT THE BELIEVERS SAY: Incredible medical cures, limitless sources of non-polluting energy, and the truth about UFOs and extraterrestrials exists and is known at the highest levels of governments around the world, but have been deliberately covered up and withheld from the citizenry of the world.

WHAT THE SKEPTICS SAY: Rumors of suppression stem from unfounded conspiracy theories. All medical and energy breakthroughs, as well as government knowledge regarding UFOs, is freely available to all.

QUALITY OF EXISTING EVIDENCE: Excellent.

LIKELIHOOD PHENOMENA ARE AUTHENTIC: Very high.

> Cures for cancer and AIDS?
> A car that runs on water?
> Fully functional anti-gravity devices?
> Wireless transmission of electricity?
> Can it be possible that these things exist?
> Seems so.

Comedian Chris Rock did a bit in his HBO stand-up concert *Bigger and Blacker* that not only got laughs, but applause and knowing nods. He started out by telling the audience that he doesn't think there will ever be cures for cancer or AIDS because there's "no money" in a cure. "The money's in the medicine!" he proclaims. His point is that medical science probably already has cures for mankind's deadliest diseases, but they deliberately suppress them because of the staggering loss of income doctors and pharmaceutical companies would undoubtedly experience if the cures were released. Rock then went on to attack the car companies, making the following cogent point: If technology is capable of creating materials for the heat shields of the space shuttle that can withstand incredible temperatures and stresses, why can't car manufacturers make a car "that the bumper don't fall off?" Because then cars would last a long time and no one would need to buy them very often.

It's all about the money. It's *always* all about the money.

* * *

Two of the most compelling cases of institutional suppression of important breakthroughs are the stories of Dr. Harry Hoxsey (his degree was in naturopathy) and New Zealand inventor Archie Blue.

Dr. Hoxsey had what seemed to be a cure for cancer, but the American Medical Association threatened him with prison if he did not sign over all his rights and research to them.

Hoxsey's cure consisted of an internal herbal tonic and an external herbal paste. He discovered the power of certain herbs when he saw one of his horses that was suffering from cancer repeatedly eating weeds from a certain spot in the pasture. The horse got better, and the Hoxsey family created a cancer cure from almost completely natural substances.[2]

In 1947, Hoxsey's remedies seemed to cure a man with cancer who had days to live. The man's "medical" doctors watched with astonishment, and shortly thereafter, Hoxsey was offered a contract which outlined a ten-year clinical study of his treatments and then a 10 percent cut of all net profits once the remedy was marketed. The doctors at the hospital where Hoxsey cured the man would receive the other 90 percent. Hoxsey refused to sign and at that moment made himself an enemy of the AMA.[3] Today, various companies offer combinations of the Hoxsey formula, and his treatment protocols are used in some alternative therapy clinics, but it is not widespread and still has not been accepted by the mainstream medical community.

Archie Blue figured out a way to run a vehicle on water.

Archie Blue invented a device that would allow any car with a gasoline engine to run solely on the hydrogen in ordinary water. One test car using Blue's device got one hundred miles to the gallon. He was awarded a patent, garnered the support of investors, publicly demonstrated his invention in 1979, and shortly thereafter, everything stopped. Blue stopped talking about his device, and all testing of it ceased. After Blue's death in 1991, his daughter disposed of much of what was in his laboratory and workshop.

Engines that run on water still exist and are known to the automotive industry all over the world. Many inventors have come up with prototypes that burn water as fuel and emit nothing but water vapor in the process. But you won't find a car powered by such an engine on the showroom floor of your local car dealership.

Herbal "cures" for cancer and other diseases are also known to the medical establishment, but are dismissed and derogatorily lumped into that weird half-cousin of medicine, "alternative therapies." There are countless stories of people who were cured by many of these treatments after the standard therapies failed them. They're just not in the usual medical journals.

The burning of fossil fuels is polluting the Earth and threatening future generations. The scourge of cancer in all its Hydra-headed incarnations is a public health issue that consumes untold billions of health care dollars that could be put to use fighting hunger and poverty all over the world.

Is it really possible that solutions to the world's worst problems exist, but are being suppressed in the name of monolithic corporate greed?

Could this be?

[1] *Encyclopedia of PseudoScience*, p. 144.

[2] The ingredients of Dr. Hoxsey's internal tonic are potassium iodide, red clover, buckthorn bark, burdock root, stillingia root, berberis root, pokeberries and root, licorice root, Cascara amarga, and prickly ash bark. The external paste is made from zinc chloride, antimony trisulfide, and bloodroot.

[3] Hoxsey's story, in his own words, can be found in the article "The AMA's Successful Attempt to Suppress My Cure for Cancer," in *Suppressed Inventions and Other Discoveries* by Jonathan Eisen, pp. 117–124.

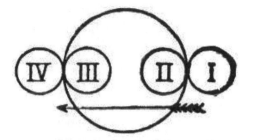

86

Synchronicity

HAIKU:

SYNCHRONICITY

A coincidence?
How can chance be meaningful?
Synchronicity?

A star fall, a phone call, it joins all, synchronicity . . .[1]

DEFINITION: The coincidence of events that seem to be meaningfully related, conceived in the theory of Carl Jung as an explanatory principle on the same order as causality.[2] The key to synchronicity is that the events seem related *outside the normal laws of cause and effect*; i.e., beyond random occurrence.

WHAT THE BELIEVERS SAY: All events have a deeper meaning in a mindful, purposeful universe. All events are inextricably connected in many ways, and there is a spiritual, "enlightened consciousness" underpinning to seemingly unrelated occurrences.

WHAT THE SKEPTICS SAY: The complexities of life and its infinite number of variables make unrelated events that seem related inevitable. There is no fabric of causality in which every thread leads to another thread, connecting everything that happens in some way or another. Coincidence is coincidence, although some events do seem more coincidental than others.

QUALITY OF EXISTING EVIDENCE: Excellent.[3]

LIKELIHOOD PHENOMENON IS PARANORMAL: Good to High.[4]

Carl Jung developed the concept of synchronicity to explain coincidences that quite simply could not be accepted by mortal men as mere coincidences. These seemingly random events were so *meaningful* in their totality, there had to be an underlying principle of causality to explain them, so the theory suggests.

For instance, ponder this true story: One day, a man riding a moped was killed in Bermuda when he was struck by a taxi carrying one passenger. Exactly one year later, the man's brother was also killed in Bermuda by a taxi. The brother was riding the *same moped* as his brother had been when he was killed, he was struck by the *same taxi*, which was being driven by the *same driver*. Also, the taxi was carrying the *same passenger* as the year before, and the incident happened on the *same street*.[5]

Or how about this one? In 1911, three men were hanged for the murder of Sir Edmund Berry at Greenberry Hill. The murderers' names were Green, Berry, and Hill.[6]

And this: In 1883, Henry Ziegland of Honey Grove, Texas, callously dumped his girlfriend, upsetting her to the point that she committed suicide. (Henry must have been quite a catch, eh?) The girl's brother blamed Henry for his sister's death and decided to avenge her death and kill Henry. He went to Henry's farm, where he took a shot at him, but the bullet only grazed Henry's face and lodged in a tree on the property. The brother mistakenly thought he had successfully killed Henry, however, and then he took *his* own life, joining his sister in that great Texan pasture in the sky. Henry, however, recovered and went on to live a full life on his farm. Thirty years after being shot at, Henry decided to take down the tree in which the bullet had lodged. The tree was enormous, so Henry used dynamite to blow it up. The explosion sent his ex-girlfriend's brother's thirty-year-old bullet flying through the air. It struck Henry Ziegland in the head and instantly killed him.[7]

And this: In the sixties, in Lake Charles, Louisiana, a man named Eddie Bordelon was involved in a minor traffic accident. The driver of the other car was named Eddie Bordelon. The accident occurred in a small community of Lake Charles called Bordelonville. The accident was investigated by a cop named Eddy Bordelon. None of the Bordelons were related nor knew each other.[8]

Is it possible that some force, some guiding hand played a role in the sequence and culmination of these events? Is that force synchronicity? This leads to the question, is there any scientific evidence whatsoever for the existence of synchronicity?

We understand chance. We understand the odds of certain things happening. Probability can be understood mathematically.

Realizing this, Carl Jung used probability to illustrate the principles of synchronicity with the following example:

You take matchboxes, put one thousand black ants in the first, ten thousand black ants in the second and fifty in the third, together with one white ant in each, shut the boxes and bore a hole in each of them, small enough to allow only one ant to crawl through at a time. The first ant to come out of the boxes is always the white one.[9]

Can the principle of random chance be responsible for the white ant exiting the boxes first, out of ten thousand, one thousand, and fifty black ants? Synchronicity says no, and states that there is some causal connection that may or may not ultimately be understood.

Jung believed that synchronicity permeates and orders the essence, function, and structure of the universe and all that occurs in reality in a manner similar to the way archetypes permeate and order the essence, function, and structure of the human subconscious. A network of relationships exists, and our goal should be to fully understand the connections between all that happens, all that may happen, and all that cannot happen.

It seems, though, that science may not be the only path to this ultimate understanding.

POSTSCRIPT

The winning three-digit New York lottery number on September 11, 2002 was 9-1-1.

The September Standard & Poor's 500 Futures and Options Contract closed Tuesday, September 10, 2002 at 911.00.

Officials for the New York Lottery and Standard & Poor's issued statements that both results were due to pure chance.

[1] "Synchronicity I," The Police (Words and music by Sting).

[2] *American Heritage Dictionary.*

[3] Accounts of astonishing coincidences are voluminous and easily accessible. (The Ripley's people have created an entire "Believe It or Not!" subculture based, in large part, on amazing coincidences.)

[4] It seems likely that some esoteric force or principle will one day be discovered or developed that explains seemingly impossible coincidental randomness.

[5] *The Liverpool Echo*, July 21, 1975.

[6] *The New York Herald*, November 26, 1911.

[7] *Ripley's Believe It or Not!*, p. 133.

[8] *Fate*, May, 1967, p. 98.

[9] Carl Jung, *Collected Works.*

87

The Sun

Tarot

HAIKU:

TAROT

The Wheel of Fortune
Major, minor arcana
Fate is in the cards?

*It may be that the deepest occult wisdom of the Tarot
cannot be put into words at all . . . in the end, the seeker is
told only what he cannot find for himself.*

—E. Gray[1]

DEFINITION: A Tarot deck is a set of seventy-eight playing cards separated into two parts, the Major Arcana and the Minor Arcana. The Major arcana consists of twenty-two key, or "trump" cards; the Minor Arcana consists of the remaining fifty-six cards, divided by suit into fourteen cards each.

WHAT THE BELIEVERS SAY: Tarot readings are a form of occult divination that can reveal hidden truths and offer guidance to the one seeking knowledge.

WHAT THE SKEPTICS SAY: The Tarot deck is nothing but a stack of picture cards and any interpretations gleaned from a reading are from self-evaluation that could have been arrived at through nothing but deliberate, contemplative thought.

QUALITY OF EXISTING EVIDENCE: LOW.

LIKELIHOOD PHENOMENA ARE PARANORMAL: LOW.

The number of Tarot trump cards—twenty-two—is symbolically important. The number twenty-two in the Cabala is the number of all things, including the twenty-two letters of the Hebrew alphabet, and the Twenty-Two Paths, the lines drawn on the Tree of Life; the lines of truth and power representing the design of the universe and the path to God.

Is a paranormal power summoned or "tapped" when a Tarot reader throws a spread and reads the cards for a questioner?

Your answer to that question depends solely on whether or not you accept the assignation of mystical significance to numbers and, by extension, cards. Many do.

Many also believe that the Tarot is a tool; nothing but a means for exploring a person's subconscious. The iconography of the cards, combined with their traditional interpretations, trigger an evaluation process by the person being read. Symbols transmute into messages relevant to the subject; an evaluation process takes place by which a person discerns possible meaning in what they have been told as it applies to his or her life.

For instance, if during a Tarot reading a person is told the cards are saying be cautious and avoid danger, and this person has just begun, oh, say, bungee jumping for fun, the reading could easily spur the funster into taking up a less hazardous hobby. Did the Tarot deck know that the person had begun participating in a dangerous sport? Maybe? Maybe not? It must be acknowledged that the meanings of the cards are general and oftentimes vague and, thus, great import can easily be applied (in a willing subject) to an individual's specific situation.

Is this a paranormal occurrence?

Is it synchronicity?

Is it meaningless coincidence?

Anecdotal accounts of Tarot readings that, in a sense, saved lives (or money, or relationships, or property) are commonplace. Believers are certain that some type of extrasensory abilities on the part of the reader, possibly connecting with the person being read via the cards, are tapped upon embarking on the Tarot ritual.

The Tarot's roots are ancient. A card game developed in Italy during the fourteenth century called "Taroks" used the tarot cards as trumps, suggesting Tarot had been around prior to Taroks. Some scholars date the deck to ancient Egypt.

THE MAJOR ARCANA

These are the main cards of a Tarot reading, and the interpretation of each card depends on whether it is cast in the upright or reversed (upside down) position.

- The Fool
- The Magician (aka The Juggler)
- The High Priestess (aka The Female Pope)
- The Empress
- The Emperor
- The Hierophant (aka The Pope)
- The Lovers
- The Chariot
- Strength
- The Hermit
- The Wheel of Fortune
- Justice
- The Hanged Man
- Death
- Temperance
- The Devil
- The Tower (aka The Falling Tower)
- The Star
- The Moon
- The Sun
- Judgment (aka The Day of Judgment)
- The World

THE MINOR ARCANA

Each suit is comprised of ten number cards from ace through ten, plus four "Court" cards, consisting of the King, Queen, Knight, and Page.

- Pentacles (corresponds to Diamonds)
- Wands (Clubs)
- Cups (Hearts)
- Swords (Spades)

The Tarot, unlike the Ouija, is not used to summon spirits. It is a tool for divination. How much supernatural foreknowledge is assigned to an individual reading is, in the end, up to the individual.

[1] *The Tarot Revealed.*

88

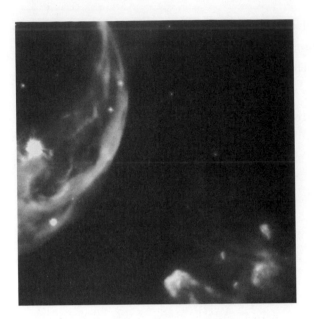

Teleportation

HAIKU:

TELEPORTATION

Atoms sparkling
You are light sent across space
Briefly part of all

Energize.[1]

DEFINITION: Dematerializing an object or a person, sending his, her, or its atomic configuration through space to another location, and then reconstructing said transportee perfectly.

WHAT THE BELIEVERS SAY: Teleportation is theoretically possible, has been successfully achieved in the laboratory and will someday be commonplace.

WHAT THE SKEPTICS SAY: Scientists may be able to teleport subatomic particles in a laboratory, but the days of someone beaming across town at will are nothing but science fiction and will never be a reality.

QUALITY OF EXISTING EVIDENCE: Very good.[2]

LIKELIHOOD PHENOMENON IS PARANORMAL: Nil.[3]

TOMORROW

The aide knocked on the door, waited two seconds, and entered the room.

"Good morning, Mr. President."

"Good morning, Major. Am I late?"

The aide suppressed a smile. "Slightly. But not enough to affect the fate of the free world, sir."

The President looked up from the papers he was reading, a pensive and bemused look on his face. "Have I ever been on time for anything since I was elected, Don?"

"Since you were elected? Yes, sir. I believe you were punctual for your inauguration."

The President nodded. "It's the Jumper, you know. Ever since that thing replaced Air Force One."

Major Donald Andrews nodded and remained standing at ease in front of the President's desk.

"Simply because I can be anywhere I need to be in . . . what is it?"

"Three-millionths of a second, sir."

"Three-millionths of a second. I think that all the other stuff I have to do before I travel that three-millionths of a second doesn't count."

"It's a common misjudgment, sir. Teleportation technology does not eliminate the human element."

The President laughed. "The human element. Right." He closed his folder and stood. "Where am I going?"

The Major flipped open a small black PDA and began to read.

"Moscow. Eleven A.M. Thirty minutes with the President. London. Eleven thirty-five. Ten minutes with the Prime Minister. Tokyo. Eleven fifty. Five minute photo op with the emperor. Back to the White House by noon."

"Okay. Let's go."

The President led the way out of the Oval Office, down a hallway to a flight of stairs. He bounded down the stairs to a circular vestibule. He stopped and turned to the Major who was right behind him.

"The big one?"

"Door Four, sir. It has a capacity of twelve."

The President looked at the ten people who would accompany him all over the world this morning. He remembered back to the days when the three-stop trip he was taking in an hour this morning would have required months of preparation, dozens of support staff, Air Force One, escort planes, weather experts, and days in the air.

The Jumper changed all that.

The President walked to Door Four, which a military aide opened for him. He stepped inside, and was immediately followed by six men and three women.

Each of them stepped onto a slightly raised circular platform. The President waited until everyone was in place and then stepped onto the blue platform in the middle of the room.

"We're ready."

Three levels under the White House, in a room that could withstand a direct hit from a nuclear missile, a team of twenty-one men and women sat in front of computer consoles, screens, and keyboards.

Cameras showed the faces of everyone in Room Four, and a picture of the entire room could also be seen. Next to the screen showing the President and his party was a screen showing an empty Jumper Room in Moscow.

"Moscow, this is Blue Team."

"Blue Team, go ahead."

"Rover plus nine ready to jump."

"Roger that. Rover plus nine. Green to go, JAW. I repeat, green to go. Jump at will."

"Roger. Jumping now."

The Jump Commander hit a blue button and on his screen he saw "Nine jumpers confirmed."

He then hit a round red button embossed with the image of an American flag, its stripes and fifty-three stars glowing in the room's dim light.

Instantly, Jump Room Four was empty and in less time than it took the Jump Commander to blink, the nine Americans were standing in the Jump Room in Moscow.

He heard the Moscow JC say, "Jump Joy, Jump Joy, Jump Joy."

The Commander hit the reset button, said, "Jump Joy confirmed. Thanks, Ivan."

"My pleasure, Tom. My best to Brenda."

Tom smiled and leaned back in his chair. Sure beats flying through a lightning storm, he thought.

In Moscow, the President and his team left the Jump Room and headed for his meeting with the President of Russia.

Science fiction? A mini-short story inspired by *Star Trek?*
Or a glimpse at our possible future?
It depends on who you talk to.
Scientists have successfully transported a photon and a laser

beam across a distance. The original photon was destroyed and its identical duplicate was created one meter away.

Does this mean that human teleportation will require the transporting human to be destroyed and an exact duplicate be created at the destination?

That is apparently what happens on *Star Trek*. The transporter locks onto every one of the trillions upon trillions of atoms in Captain Kirk's body, reads each one's molecular information, and then sends all of these atoms through space and creates the exact duplicate of the person, down to the molecule. According to Kevin Bosnor, writing on the *howstuffworks.com* Web site,[4] a true transporter will not actually transport anything—it will act as a really powerful fax machine, creating a duplicate of the original at the receiving end of the system. (This analogy doesn't really work, though, since a fax machine does not destroy the original, whereas this type of transporter would.)

Do the principles of quantum physics render the concept of teleportation impossible?

Not necessarily (as evidenced by the aforementioned experiments). But the practicality of implementing theoretical principles—*Star Trek*'s apparent success notwithstanding—seem far beyond the reach of man and computer for the foreseeable future.

The problem lies in the amount of information needed to be read, stored, and transmitted in order to teleport a human being over a distance. The number of binary digits comprising such a digital profile of a human is almost beyond imagination. It takes well over a million binary digits for a computer to perform a relatively straightforward mathematical calculation. The digital data stream for a person could feasibly take years or even longer for a computer to process—unless future computers are able to process data at speeds inordinately greater than even today's fastest computers. And the amount of energy required for such a feat is well beyond our capabilities now, and perhaps forever.

All that said, though, matter transmission is an enduring fantasy of science. If it ever becomes a reality, it would essentially eliminate the transportation industry overnight.

In fact, the changes routine teleportation would bring to the human condition are almost beyond imagination. Everything would change, and for the better.

And perhaps that is why, odds aside, scientists continue to transport photons and laser beams, in the hope that someday, a heart needed for transplant in Dubuque could be there in, say, three-millionths of a second, from New Zealand.

Farfetched? Perhaps. But most miracles usually are.

[1] Any *Star Trek* character who was transported anytime during the series.

[2] We understand the science underlying the principle of teleportation. Accomplishing it is another story altogether.

[3] If teleportation ever becomes a reality (which is unlikely) it will not be a paranormal or supernatural occurrence, but rather a scientific achievement.

[4] http://www.howstuffworks.com.

89

Theosophy

HAIKU:

THEOSOPHY

Oh, bodhisattva
Won't you take me by the hand?
Help me rise above?

*The interior world has not been hidden from all by
impenetrable darkness. By that higher intuition acquired by
Theosophia—or God-knowledge, which carried the mind
from the world of form into that of formless spirit, man has
been sometimes enabled in every age and every country to
perceive things in the interior or invisible world.*

—Madame Helena Petrovna Blavatsky

DEFINITION: "A supposed intercourse with God and superior spirits,
and consequent attainment of superhuman knowledge, by physical
processes, as by the theurgic operations of some ancient Platonists,
or by the chemical processes of the German fire-philosophers."[1]

WHAT THE BELIEVERS SAY: Theosophy is the only path to fully understanding that the physical body is an impediment to true spiritual
unfoldement and enlightenment. Spiritual progress is unceasingly
hindered by physical matter and it is the goal of humans to tap into
their innately divine source to truly know God.

WHAT THE SKEPTICS SAY: Theosophy is a hodgepodge of Egyptian mythology, Hindu philosophy, Brahmanism, neo-Platonism, pre-Christian Gnosticism, pantheism, and ancient legends like Atlantis, taught by the charlatan Madame Blavatsky, a prototypical Ron Hubbard of sorts, who shamelessly invented her own religion.

QUALITY OF EXISTING EVIDENCE: Inconclusive.[2]

LIKELIHOOD PHENOMENON IS PARANORMAL: Inconclusive.[3]

Theosophy posits three basic principles of belief.

The first principle is that there is an eternal, omnipresent "force" or spirit permeating all existence. (George Lucas may have been influenced by Theosophical principles when he introduced *Star Wars* fans to the notion of a "force" running through all of reality.) This absolute, unchangeable agency is beyond our understanding, and any and all attempts at divining the nature of God are really our attempts at understanding this infinite principle.

The second principle is the universal law of the cyclical nature of all existence, which manifests at every level of reality. The cycle of days (morning, day, night) is paralleled by the cycle of birth, life, and death. In Theosophy, this principle is extrapolated to "prove" the existence of reincarnation. As morning follows night, so does new life follow death. In order to prevent an infinite cycle of deaths and rebirths, Theosophy brings the concept of karma into the mix, asserting that our good deeds during life determine the elevation—or demotion—of our eternal soul after death.

The third Theosophical principle states that all souls are part of the Oversoul, the aforementioned unknowable spiritual force permeating all existence. The Oversoul transcends individual consciousness, and all humans (actually, our invisible souls) are on a pilgrimage from birth, with the final goal being to become one with the Oversoul. At birth, the human soul is a blank sheet. Good works and living a life of kindness and love adds "points," so to speak. Each reincarnation *should* be a climb to a higher rung on the ladder of eternal existence.

Again, spiritual evolution mirrors and parallels physical evolution. According to the Theosophists, there have been only a handful of elevated, fully evolved souls during the period of man's existence on Earth. Jesus and Buddha were two of these "perfected" beings and their purpose on Earth was to teach the rest of us how to achieve oneness with God.

For many of the spiritually minded among us, all this makes a lot of sense and simply restates what many religions have been teaching for centuries: God is everywhere and eternal; we must live a loving life ("all you need is love"); and our ultimate goal is to become one with God at the moment of our death. Some theologies accept reincarnation as part of this paradigm; many believe an individual's soul never again exists in our corporeal reality after we die. Nonetheless, the underlying principles are the same.

Then why have there been attacks against Blavatsky and her teachings, and why is there a great deal of skepticism regarding Theosophy? Blavatsky's goals were ostensibly noble: according to the 1875 mission statement of her Theosophical Society, she hoped to form a universal brotherhood of man; to study the ancient religions; and to investigate the laws of nature with the goal of developing man's spiritual essence.

The problems lie with Madame Blavatsky herself, not her teachings. She claimed that she had direct contact with astral mahatmas and that she was given secret teachings. This is not in and of itself culpable, but she apparently also used deception and trickery to convince followers that she had paranormal powers. She faked the materialization of a tea cup and saucer, and she also claimed that writings she possessed were from the astral realm, even though it was obvious that she had written them herself. There were also many other occasions where her alleged supernatural "miracles" were revealed to be nothing but clever parlor tricks; common deceptions that had been used by mediums and magicians for centuries.

So, as is often the case with spiritual leaders, Madame Blavatsky's personal life and her actions were sometimes in contrast with her teachings.

Is the fact that she tricked some of her believers into thinking she had "powers" relevant to the philosophies she championed? Yes, but only if a person misguidedly transfers their respect for the teachings onto the teacher—always a mistake—and which always devalues the spiritual message of the religion or philosophy.

At the time of Blavatsky's death, she had over 100,000 adherents, and today Theosophy is an accepted spiritual path toward enlightenment. It is safe to say that Theosophy practitioners of today do not factor Madame Blavatsky's personal shortcomings into their pursuit of the ultimate goals espoused in her teachings.

---

[1] *Webster's Dictionary.*

[2] How can the principles of Theosophy or any other religion or philosophical doctrine be concretely *proven?* That's why it's called *faith.*

[3] Again, we simply do not know with certainty if religious dogma is truly paranormal or simply created by man out of whole (holy) cloth.

90

Time Travel

HAIKU:

TIME TRAVEL

Time is but a book
With pages forward and back
Can we read ahead?

*The laws of physics do not rule out time travel,
but building a time machine would probably pose
insurmountable difficulties.*

—Gary T. Horowitz[1]

*That which hath been is now, and that which is
to be hath already been . . .*

—Ecclesiastes 3:15

DEFINITION: The ability to physically travel into the past and the future.

WHAT THE BELIEVERS SAY: Time travel is theoretically possible. It is simply a matter of time until we achieve the level of technological advancement required to resolve the problems with time travel, especially the energy requirements and the necessity of traveling close to the speed of light.

WHAT THE SKEPTICS SAY: Time travel is a science-fiction device; incredible quantum physics theories aside, time travel will never be something mankind will ever be able to achieve. Ever.

QUALITY OF EXISTING EVIDENCE: Excellent.

LIKELIHOOD PHENOMENON IS PARANORMAL: Nil.[2]

What is time? Dictionaries tell us time is "a nonspatial continuum in which events occur in apparently irreversible succession from the past through the present to the future;"[3] and "a limited stretch or space of continued existence, as the interval between two successive events."[4]

Many are familiar with at least one variation of this classic time travel conundrum: Let's say you are able to time travel. You go back in time and kill your grandfather before your own father is born, thereby preventing your own birth. How, then, could you even exist, since you have made it impossible for you to be born? And if you were never born, how could you kill your grandfather? But then if you did not kill your grandfather, then you *would* be born, and then you could go back in time and kill your grandfather, preventing your birth . . . and so on and so on . . . ad infinitum. Carl Sagan summed it up for *Nova*: "The heart of the paradox is the apparent existence of you, the murderer of your own grandfather, when the very act of you murdering your own grandfather eliminates the possibility of you ever coming into existence."[5]

Is time a river that flows? And if so, can the flow be stopped, or reversed; or can we visit different locales along the banks of this river, some behind us, some ahead of us?

And what about "time slips?" The late scientist and naturalist Ivan Sanderson, along with his wife, once saw fifteenth century Paris while walking along a path in Haiti. He and his wife both saw the same thing, at the same time, and they were very precise about the vivid details of the past reality they simultaneously witnessed.

Let's imagine that every person's life is a collection of individual frames of existence, single moments lasting, perhaps, a thousandth (a millionth?) of a second, and the sum total of all of these slices of reality comprise a single being's life. Picture a long trough with all of these images lined up, one after the other, from the moment of birth until the moment of death. Trillions upon trillions of individual slivers of a person's reality. Now imagine that one single slice from this long collection falls out of order, or somehow gets entangled with someone else's reality. Perhaps a life frame from a fifteenth-century Frenchman somehow gets mixed in with Ivan Sanderson's twentieth-century collection of life frames. Sanderson, for only a moment, sees this "foreign" frame within his own reality, until the river of time rights itself, moves on, and he returns to his own trough of realities.

A time slip (and they are reported regularly, often by highly credible people) is compelling evidence of the fluidity of time, and provides some validity to the notion that the construct of time comprises an infinite number of these slices of reality. Science-fiction writer Alfred Bester, in his novel, *The Men Who Murdered Mohammed*, described these time lines as "like millions of strands of spaghetti." Every living thing would have its own trough of frames—its own strand of spaghetti—and perhaps these instances of reality are accessible across space and time—accidentally, in the case of time slips; intentionally, after science progresses to the point at which we know how to circumvent the "normal" passage of time.

This leads to the question of whether or not a functional time machine can be built.

The answer is yes—theoretically. Ronald L. Mallet, a professor of physics at the University of Connecticut, in the fall of 2002, embarked on constructing an operative time machine that would send a single neutron into the past by means of a circulating laser that would bend light and slow it down. The theory is that if it works for a subatomic particle, it could someday work for people.

But that someday is a long way off, considering that just the problems with creating the massive amounts of energy required seem almost insurmountable.

Travel into the future has already been proven possible. The Russian Cosmonaut Sergei Avdeyev lived in the MIR space station for 748 days, traveling in Earth's orbit at seventeen thousand miles per hour. (Light travels at 186,000 miles per second.) It was calculated that during his two years in space, Avdeyev traveled into the future by approximately 1/50th of a second.

The *Back to the Future* movies made time travel seem like a trip across town, with the energy required no more than is contained in a bolt of lightning.

But reality is not the movies.

We can see the past when we look into deep space. What we see is the light sent out from other planets and stars hundreds of millions of years ago. We actually watch the past happen. If we can already *see* the past, is it only a matter of time before we figure out how to *visit* it?

[1] *The New Haven Register*, May 21, 2002, p. B10. Horowitz is a physicist at the University of California in Santa Barbara.

[2] Remember, we are using the dictionary definition of "paranormal" for this evaluation: "Beyond the range of normal experience or *scientific explanation*" (*American Heritage Dictionary*, emphasis added). It is widely accepted that time travel—*within* the realm of scientific explanation—is possible.

[3] *American Heritage Dictionary.*

[4] *The Oxford English Dictionary.*

[5] www.novaonline.com.

91

Transubstantiation

HAIKU:

TRANSUBSTANTIATION

Bread becomes true flesh
Wine is the blood of Jesus
Miracles of faith

Jesus therefore said to them, "Most assuredly I tell you, unless you eat the flesh of the Son of Man and drink his blood, you don't have life in yourselves. He who eats my flesh and drinks my blood has eternal life, and I will raise him up at the last day. For my flesh is food indeed, and my blood is drink indeed."

—Gospel of John[1]

DEFINITION: Transubstantiation is the doctrine holding that the bread and wine of the Eucharist are transformed into the *actual* body and blood of Jesus, although their appearances remain the same.[2]

WHAT THE BELIEVERS SAY: The consecrated host and wine are the *real* flesh and blood of Jesus Christ and remain so until they are digested and no longer resemble the host or wine.

WHAT THE SKEPTICS SAY: The consecrated host and sacramental wine are nothing but unleavened white flour and ordinary table wine.

QUALITY OF EXISTING EVIDENCE: Negligible.[3]

LIKELIHOOD PHENOMENON IS PARANORMAL: Inconclusive.

According to the Roman Catholic doctrine of the *real presence*, at the moment of consecration during the celebration of the Mass, the priest transforms the host and wine into the actual flesh and blood of Jesus Christ. This is called transubstantiation and it is an integral part of the liturgy of the Eucharist. The *Catechism of the Catholic Church* tells us that, "The Eucharistic presence of Christ begins at the moment of consecration and endures as long as the Eucharistic species exists."[4] According to the Church, when the faithful receive Communion, they are literally consuming real flesh and, if they take the cup, drinking real blood.

Protestants do not accept the doctrine of transubstantiation. Non-Christians not only do not accept the concept, many of them are repulsed by the entire notion of "holy cannibalism" and many reject even the symbolism of consuming flesh and blood.

As the epigraph introducing this chapter illustrates, the concept of transubstantiation stems from the words of Jesus at the Last Supper, which the church tells us was the first mass. (Although skeptics and historians do not hesitate to remind the Catholic faithful that pagans believed in transubstantiation long before the time of Jesus, and many suggest that Catholicism "borrowed" heathen dogma.) Also, the Church did not decree that the Eucharist contained the "real presence" of Christ until the thirteenth century Council of Trent (although it had been written about as early as the ninth century). For twelve centuries, the act of consecration was believed to be symbolic, rather than literal.

"My flesh is food indeed," Jesus told his disciples. This apparently did not go over very well with some of his followers: "Therefore many of his disciples, when they heard this, said, "This is a hard saying! Who can hear it?"[5] Jesus understood their doubts and asked them if they wished him to ascend into heaven before their eyes to prove that he was the Son of God. Perhaps then they would accept his words? Interestingly, Jesus then offered an explanation that seemed to contradict the literal interpretation of his words. "It is the *spirit* who gives life. The flesh profits nothing. *The words that I speak to you are spirit*, and are life."[6] [emphasis added]

This sounds like Jesus is telling them that he had previously been speaking symbolically, using the metaphor of food to herald the spiritual "nourishment" that would inure to them through their faith.

Can such a thing as transubstantiation ever be scientifically proven? The only "scientific" evidence for the actual transformation of the Eucharist into human flesh seems to be a series of 1970 tests of a transubstantiated Lanciano, Italy host. A priest experiencing a crisis of faith witnessed the host that he had consecrated transform into human flesh. The host was tested thirteen hundred years later and the tests revealed that the "wafer" was actual human flesh, specifically myocardium (heart) tissue. It also contained proteins found in human flesh, and the blood in it tested AB (which, believers tell us, was the same blood type found on the Shroud of Turin (see Chapter 79).

However, we do *not* have proof that what was tested is the host from the 700 A.D. Lanciano Mass in which it transformed into actual flesh before the eyes of the priest and the parishioners. We also do not have proof that the wine and host ensconced in a monstrance in Lanciano is the actual "miraculous" substances.

The belief that the Eucharist and wine transforms into the flesh and blood of Jesus Christ is an issue of faith. Even though the substances appear to remain bread and wine, the faithful tell us they have changed at a level our "normal" senses cannot perceive, and that faith is the filter which allows our *soul* to recognize that it has, indeed, transubstantiated. This *cannot* be proven or disproved, thus, our "Inconclusive" rating as to whether or not transubstantiation is a paranormal event.

There are rules regarding the Catholic faithful's taking of Communion. One cannot accept Communion if he or she has an unrepented mortal sin on their soul. One must fast out of respect for taking the body of Christ into the body of the faithful. Initially, fasting was required from midnight the night before taking Communion. It has since been revised to fifteen minutes. The church now also allows the faithful to accept the Host into their hand and place it into their own mouth.

Transubstantiation, like resurrection and the Virgin Birth, are blatantly supernatural occurrences that many non-Catholics simply cannot accept as being possible.

The Catholic faithful believe otherwise.

[1]John 6:53–55.

[2]*American Heritage Dictionary.*

[3]See the Lanciano story for details as to why we consider existence of hard evidence to be negligible.

[4]*Catechism of the Catholic Church*, p. 385.

[5]John 6:60.

[6]John 6:62.

92

The Tunguska Explosion

HAIKU:

TUNGUSKA

The morning silence
Shattered by the voice of God
Thunder from above

On an average of every few hundred thousand years or so, asteroids larger than a kilometer could cause global disasters. In this case, the impact debris would spread throughout the Earth's atmosphere so that plant life would suffer from acid rain, partial blocking of sunlight, and from the firestorms resulting from heated impact debris raining back down upon the Earth's surface. Since their orbital paths often cross that of the Earth, collisions with near-Earth objects have occurred in the past and we should remain alert to the possibility of future close Earth approaches.[1]

DEFINITION: The Tunguska event was a fifty-megaton[2] explosion in the wilderness of Siberia at 7:17 A.M. on June 30, 1908.

WHAT THE BELIEVERS SAY: The Tunguska explosion was the Earth colliding with a black hole, or the explosion of an extraterrestrial spacecraft's engine, or a piece of antimatter, or a Russian nuclear bomb explosion gone bad.

WHAT THE SKEPTICS SAY: The Tunguska explosion was most likely an asteroid or a meteorite that exploded above the Earth. A new theory suggests it could have been a fluid jet shooting up from the Earth's depths. Whatever it was, it seems not to have been a paranormal occurrence.

QUALITY OF EXISTING EVIDENCE: Good.

LIKELIHOOD PHENOMENON IS PARANORMAL: Low.

The fabulation-minded would so like to believe that the Tunguska "event" was the type of spectacular occurrence seen on the covers of science fiction magazines and novels:

- *Black Hole Collides with Earth!*
- *Alien Spacecraft Explodes in Earth's Atmosphere!*
- *Time Warp Blows Hole in Earth!*
- *Antimatter Meteor from Another Dimension Decimates Siberia!*
- *Doomsday in Russia! The Rapture Has Begun!*
- *Russia Explodes Nuke! Shockwaves Felt in U.S.!*

The seductive appeal of a conspiracy theory or a bizarre explanation for a seemingly unexplainable event is powerful. The Tunguska event has generated this type of mania. Books have been written discussing nothing but speculation about the explosion; elaborate Web sites exist to discuss the possibilities of what *might* have happened; experts on one theory or another are seemingly everywhere.

It is understandable why such wild-eyed conjecturing and guessing regarding the Tunguska event took hold of both the mainstream and scientific communities. The explosion occurred in 1908, and yet the site of the catastrophe was not visited until 1930, when an expedition of Soviet geologists traveled to the desolate northern reaches of Siberia to investigate the then twenty-two-year-old scene of the cataclysm.

What they found astounded them. There was no impact crater. Trees at ground zero were stripped of their bark, but still standing. Trees in a three- to ten-mile radius were knocked over, their tops pointing away from the blast area. Testing of soil, wood, and water samples from the blast zone did not provide any answers as to what actually happened in 1908.

For decades, the Tunguska enigma endured, the theories propagated, and the research continued.

But in 2001, a group of Italian scientists announced that they had finally solved the mystery.

The Tunguska event was the explosion in the Earth's atmosphere of a low-density asteroid comprised of space rubble, and containing a high volume of water. The scientists, led by Dr. Luigi Foschini, studied seismic records from several Siberian monitoring stations, and analyzed the fall direction and wood of sixty thousand trees in the area of the explosion.

Their conclusions are grounded in science. The asteroid came from the southeast traveling at seven miles a second. Its high water content caused it to explode in the atmosphere rather than surviving long enough to strike the ground. The shock wave of the explosion did hit the ground, however, resulting in the destruction noted by scientists.

The people of Earth were lucky. The Tunguska asteroid exploded in a barren, almost unpopulated area of Siberia. Reindeer died, as did many other animals, but the human toll was essentially zero.

If the Tunguska asteroid had approached the Earth on a trajectory a few degrees in either direction, and exploded over, say, London, or Paris, or Berlin, the death toll would have been in the hundreds of thousands and the destruction would have been thousands of times worse than what we saw in Hiroshima after the bomb was dropped.

Regarding NEOs (Near Earth Objects capable of colliding with our planet), NASA tells us, "It seems prudent to mount efforts to discover and study these objects, to characterize their sizes, compositions and structures and to keep an eye upon their future trajectories."

The people of Earth were lucky in 1908. It remains to be seen if our luck will persist as our blue planet spins through a galaxy of silent, yet biding hazards.

---

[1] NASA.

[2] The Tunguska explosion was equivalent to fifteen million tons of TNT, or 2,000 Hiroshima A-bomb explosions.

UFOs
(Unidentified Flying Objects)

HAIKU:

UFOs

Visions in the sky
Visitors from other worlds?
Or fanciful dreams?

Of course the flying saucers are real—and they are interplanetary . . . the cumulative evidence for the existence of UFOs is quite overwhelming and I accept the fact of their existence.[1]

Flying saucers are real. Too many good men have seen them, that don't have hallucinations.[2]

DEFINITION: UFOs are unidentifiable aerial phenomena that includes visible crafts, circular objects, and balls and beams of light, many of which manifest bizarre flight behaviors not currently possible by any known flying vehicles.

WHAT THE BELIEVERS SAY: Some UFO sightings are definitely explainable as *non*-extraterrestrial, but many are actual craft from other planets or dimensions, and the governments of the world not only know the truth, but have concealed this information from the public for decades.

WHAT THE SKEPTICS SAY: All UFOs are explainable as natural phenomena, hallucinations, birds, terrestrial aircraft, or secret government aircraft. None—and we emphasize the finality of that word—*none* are from other planets or dimensions.

QUALITY OF SUPPORTING EVIDENCE: Excellent.

LIKELIHOOD PHENOMENA ARE EXTRATERRESTRIAL: Very high.

Those who say there is no visual photographic evidence of UFOs have not been paying attention.

On June 24, 1947, pilot Kenneth Arnold saw nine objects flying in formation at speeds between 1,300 and 1,700 m.p.h. Arnold reported that their formation was approximately five miles long and that each object was approximately two-thirds the size of a DC-4. He described them as looking like saucers and the term "flying saucers" was born.[3] A couple of weeks later, the Roswell crash happened. Was the craft that allegedly crashed in the New Mexico desert one of Arnold's UFOs?

Arnold's sighting marked the beginning of the modern age of UFO sightings, although unidentified aerial phenomena, including things that looked like, yes, saucers, have been reported for centuries. A few years back, an Italian art scholar published a monograph that examined all the UFOs visible in medieval paintings.

There is photographic evidence of UFOs. Some UFOlogists, if asked, can produce any number of scrapbooks filled to bursting with UFO photos.[4]

Granted, the overwhelming majority of these pictures are, without a doubt, certainly *not* images of extraterrestrial crafts. But after all the mundane explanations for the pictures have been factored in—after all the birds, balloons, satellites, lenticular clouds, planets, hoaxes, and terrestrial aircraft have been ruled out—there still remains a solid core of truly baffling photos, most of which, to this day, have not been satisfactorily explained.

Reasonableness is key when looking at and attempting to understand the UFO experience.

The pendulum swings widely in the arena of UFO debate. On one side we have the True Believers. These are the people who would flip through the aforementioned scrapbooks and accept every picture as a genuine photo of an extraterrestrial craft. *Every picture.*

On the other side are the True Skeptics. These are the folks who dismiss even the possibility that any of the photos are real. UFOs simply do not exist to these people and, no matter how compelling is some of the evidence and how convincing are some of the personal sighting accounts, their position is, "UFOs are not extraterrestrial, and an extraterrestrial craft has never visited our planet's airspace." *Never.*

Both of these doctrines are unreasonable.

Why would an Air Force pilot—someone meticulously trained to make sober, reasoned judgments and decisions—make up a report in which he tells of a craft spiraling around his plane and then flying off at speeds impossible for known aircraft?

Most reasonable people would respond, "He wouldn't."

But there are dozens of such reports in the U.S. Government's abandoned UFO project, *Project Blue Book*. Remember: these reports come from people to whom we would accede credibility in almost any other matter. Yet, when it comes to a UFO sighting, they suddenly become unbelievable? Why?

Project Blue Book looked at over twelve thousand UFO sightings during its period of operation, and it ruled out all but seven hundred or so sightings as explainable. As part of my research for my earlier book, *The UFO Book of Lists*, I culled through those seven hundred unexplainable sightings and extracted only the sightings reported by trained military personnel and members of law enforcement, including pilots, air traffic controllers, radar operators, highway patrolmen, state troopers, and sheriffs. Personnel who are trained to be observant, and to make sober and reasoned judgments on a daily basis. There were over two hundred of these sightings and the complete list with details of what they saw are in my book.

These more than two hundred sightings are the most credible reports to date.

For the *UFO Book of Lists*, I also reviewed the most credible *photos* of UFOs to date.

In July 1998, *Popular Mechanics* magazine published a feature story on what they determined to be the six most baffling UFO sightings and photographs. They occurred in Oregon, Brazil, Michigan, Ohio, Iran, and England, from 1950 through 1980. Personally, I think the Iran sighting was of a top-secret stealth jet. Here is a look at the remaining five, all of which are still unexplained:

- On Thursday May 11, 1950, farmer Paul Trent took two black-and-white photographs of a UFO hovering above his farm. The UFO Trent saw and photographed was a flat-bottomed disk with a pointed top. Later, Trent described the craft as being about the size of a "good-sized parachute canopy without the strings." He described its color as "silvery-bright mixed with bronze." The two Trent photos were subjected to all manner of analysis. Conclusion? Fabrication, hoax, hallucination, military traffic, and natural explanation have mostly been ruled out. So far, the McMinnville sighting can only be explained as an authentic sighting of an extraterrestrial craft, although there are still some debunkers who claim the Trents faked the shots, the logistical improbability of this notwithstanding.

- On January 16, 1958, forty-seven members of a Brazilian oceanographic and meteorological research team saw a Saturn-shaped UFO and it was photographed by a civilian photographer. Many of the eyewitnesses were professional oceanographers and meteorologists. The UFO was estimated to be traveling at approximately six hundred miles per hour. An airplane and hoax were ruled out later when the photos were analyzed. NICAP later issued a report that included this astonishing statement: "Weighing all the facts, we conclude that the pictures appear to be authentic. They definitely are one of the potentially most significant series of UFO photographs on record." Ground Saucer Watch declared the pictures as authentic; i.e., not faked.

- On the evening of March 21, 1966, an estimated 140 students at Hillsdale college in Hillsdale, Michigan, reported seeing a glowing object maneuvering above a swamp near the school. None other than J. Allen Hynek himself was dispatched by the Air Force to investigate the sighting. Initially, swamp gas, students with flares, and the planet Venus were all suggested as explanations for the sighting. Ultimately, all of these were dismissed as not possible and to date, there has not been a credible explanation for the Hillsdale sighting.

- On Sunday, November 13, 1966, Ralph Ditter, a barber and amateur astronomer, snapped two photographs of a hat-shaped UFO hovering above his house in broad daylight. The pictures are crisp and detailed and they show UFOs that match the description of UFOs reported by law enforcement personnel in the area in the prior months. The Ditter photos have not yet been satisfactorily explained, although the Condon Committee[5] declared them to have been faked.

- On August 13, 1956, RAF radar at the Bentwaters, England picked up objects traveling at upwards of nine thousand miles per hour and under apparent intelligent control. Fourteen years later, a triangular-shaped craft was seen hovering above

Rendlesham Forest in the same area. Also, circular depressions in the forest floor were found the following day, looking precisely like the indentations landing gear would make in the soft earth. These two sightings have never been adequately explained.

Carl Jung believed that UFOs were a projection of mankind's collective unconscious, that subconscious place we all share and can tap into; the place where the archetypes live. Jung was obviously reaching for a explanation for UFOs that did not involve the word "extraterrestrial." He came up with what he believed was a rational theory and many psychologists and even some parapsychologists signed on to this explanation, gladly attributing millennia of sightings as nothing but collective hallucinations.

The notion of UFOs being a projection of a Jungian archetype simply does not make sense when the eyewitness accounts of military pilots and other credible people are factored in.

Conclusion?

Something is going on in the skies. And it is quite likely that the day is nearing when we will confirm once and for all that it is certainly not our imagination.

---

[1]From an August 1954 statement by Royal Air Force Commanding Officer Air Chief Marshall Lord Hugh Dowding.

[2]From a statement by World War I flying ace Captain Eddie Rickenbacker.

[3]Well, sort of. Arnold is rightfully credited with popularizing the term, but the word "saucer" had been used to describe a daylight UFO sighting in January 1878 by a farmer named John Martin in Denison, Texas. The account of his UFO sighting appeared in the January 25, 1878 issue of the *Denison Daily* and Martin described what he saw as a "large saucer."

[4]For an amazing gallery of UFO photos, see http://www.ufopicture.info/pictures/galleryindex.htm.

[5]The government-sponsored investigation into alleged UFO phenomena.

94

The Ultimate Lincoln/Kennedy Coincidences List

HAIKU:

LINCOLN & KENNEDY

Commonalities
Similiarities galore
A coincidence?

Coincidences are spiritual puns.

— G.K. Chesterton

DEFINITION: There are many seemingly amazing coincidences between the lives and assassinations of Presidents Abraham Lincoln and John F. Kennedy.

WHAT THE BELIEVERS SAY: There are too many coincidences to be merely coincidences. There must be some kind of paranormal connection between John F. Kennedy and Abraham Lincoln. Subsequently, there must also be some type of profound meaning for the United States (and possibly the world) in their lives and how they were killed.

WHAT THE SKEPTICS SAY: The coincidences between Kennedy and Lincoln are just that: coincidences. All of the seemingly bizarre similarities in their histories can be attributed to nothing but chance. Anyone attempting to find a meaning in these weird occurrences is on a futile mission. There simply is no connection between the two men and their assassinations other than the fact that they were both Presidents of the United States. That, we will concede.

QUALITY OF EXISTING EVIDENCE: Excellent.[1]

LIKELIHOOD PHENOMENON IS PARANORMAL: Nil to Low.

You've heard many of these before. There is a core group of Lincoln/ Kennedy coincidences that has been circulating for years. Lately, more research has been done and even more commonalities in the lives and deaths of the two Presidents has been uncovered.[2]

This chapter looks at seventy of these eerie similarities, including some of the newer ones. Some are not the least bit surprising; some are undeniably stunning in their synchronous connections.

Are all these coincidences simply due to mere chance? (See Chapter 86, "Synchronicity.")[3] Here is a list of the many coincidences:

- Both Presidents liked rocking chairs.
- The name of Lincoln's assassin, "John Wilkes Booth," contains fifteen letters. The name of Kennedy's assassin, "Lee Harvey Oswald," contains fifteen letters.
- The name of Lincoln's successor, "Andrew Johnson," contains thirteen letters. The name of Kennedy's successor, "Lyndon Johnson," contains thirteen letters.
- "Lincoln" and "Kennedy" each consist of seven letters.
- Both presidents were named after their grandfathers.
- Both Presidents were second children.
- Both Presidents experienced the death of a sister before they became President.
- Both Presidents did not marry until they were in their thirties: Lincoln was thirty-three; Kennedy was thirty-six.
- Both Presidents married socially prominent, twenty-four-year-old brunettes who were fluent in French, known for their fashion sense, and had been previously engaged.

- Both First Ladies oversaw major renovations of the White House.
- Each President experienced the death of a son while president.
- The Lincoln and Kennedy children rode ponies on the White House lawn.
- Lincoln's son Tad's funeral was held on July 16, 1871. John F. Kennedy Jr. died on July 16, 1999. Mary Todd Lincoln died on July 16, 1882.
- Two of Lincoln's sons were named Robert and Edward; two of Kennedy's brothers were named Robert and Edward.
- Both Presidents were related to United States Senators.
- After Lincoln was assassinated, his family moved into a house at 3014 N Street, N.W, in Georgetown. After Kennedy was assassinated, his family moved into a house at 3017 N Street, N.W, in Georgetown.
- Both Presidents were related to Democratic United States Attorney Generals who were graduates of Harvard University.
- Both Presidents were related to ambassadors to the Court of St. James in Great Britain.
- Both Presidents were friends with an Adlai E. Stevenson. Lincoln's friend would become Grover Cleveland's second Vice President. Kennedy's friend would twice be the Democratic Presidential nominee.
- Both Presidents knew a Dr. Charles Taft. Lincoln was treated by Dr. Charles Sabin Taft; Kennedy knew Dr. Charles Phelps Taft (the son of President Taft).
- Both Presidents were advised by a Billy Graham: Lincoln's friend was a New Salem, Illinois schoolteacher; Kennedy's was the Reverend Billy Graham.
- Kennedy had a secretary named Evelyn Lincoln. Her husband's nickname was Abe.
- Lincoln was first elected to the U.S. House of Representatives in 1846; Kennedy was first elected to the U.S. House of Representatives in 1946.
- Lincoln was runner-up for his party's Vice Presidential nomination in 1856; Kennedy was runner-up for his party's Vice Presidential nomination in 1956.
- Lincoln was elected President in 1860; Kennedy was elected President in 1960.
- Both Presidents were involved in seminal political debates: Lincoln participated in the Lincoln-Douglas debates in 1858; Kennedy participated in the Kennedy-Nixon debates in 1960.

- Both Presidents were concerned about African-Americans. Lincoln wrote the Emancipation Proclamation; Kennedy submitted a report on civil rights to Congress.
- Both Presidents were writers and were well-read; both Presidents were versed in Shakespeare and the Bible.
- Both had genetic diseases: Kennedy had Addison's disease; Lincoln (it is suspected) had Marfan Syndrome.
- Both Presidents were in the military.
- Both Presidents had been skippers of a boat: Lincoln had been captain of the *Talisman*; Kennedy had captained the *PT 109*.
- Both Presidents did not worry about their personal safety, much to the consternation of their Secret Service protection.
- In the year of his death, Abraham Lincoln received eighty death threats in the mail. In the year of his death, John F. Kennedy received eight hundred death threats in the mail.
- Both Presidents were shot in the back of the head.
- Both Presidents were shot on a Friday before a holiday: Lincoln, Easter; Kennedy, Thanksgiving.
- Both Presidents were sitting next to their wives when they were shot.
- Neither of the First Ladies was injured in the shootings.
- Both Presidents were with another couple when they were shot: Kennedy was with Governor and Mrs. John Connally; Lincoln was with Major and Mrs. Henry Rathbone.
- Both of the men with the Presidents, Major Rathbone and Governor Connally, were injured but not killed.
- Lincoln was shot at Ford's Theater; Kennedy was shot in a Ford motor vehicle (a Lincoln).
- Lincoln was shot in Box 7 at the theater; Kennedy was shot in car 7 of his motorcade.
- Both Presidents received closed chest massage after the shooting; in both cases, it was ineffective.
- Both Presidents died in a place with the initials "P.H.": Lincoln died in the Peterson House; Kennedy died in Parkland Hospital.
- Both Presidents were buried in mahogany caskets.
- The coffins of both Lincoln and JFK were displayed in the Capitol Rotunda and the same black-draped catafalque was used for both men.
- Both assassins were known by three names: John Wilkes Booth and Lee Harvey Oswald.

- Both assassins were in their mid-twenties when they shot the President.
- Both assassins had brothers with successful careers that they envied: Booth's brothers were acclaimed actors; Oswald's brothers had successful military careers.
- Both assassins never went past the rank of private in the military.
- Both assassins were born in the South.
- Both assassins ideologically supported enemies of the United States: Booth supported the Confederacy; Oswald endorsed Marxism.
- Both assassins kept a journal or diary.
- Booth shot Lincoln in a theater (Ford's Theater) and was cornered in a warehouse; Oswald shot Kennedy from a warehouse and was cornered in a theater (the Texas Theater).
- The concession stand operator at Ford's Theater was named Burroughs. The concession stand operator at the Texas Theater was named Burroughs.
- Booth was aided in his escape by a man named Paine. Oswald got his job at the School Book Depository with the help of a woman named Paine.
- Booth was trapped on Garrett's farm by an officer named Baker. Oswald was questioned on the second floor of the School Book Depository by a cop named Baker.
- Both assassins were killed by a single shot from a Colt revolver.
- Both assassins were murdered before they could be questioned about their crimes.
- Oswald and Booth were both shot by religious zealots: Booth by Boston Corbett; Oswald by Jack Ruby.
- Both Presidents were succeeded in office by Southern Democrats named Johnson: Lincoln, by Andrew Johnson; Kennedy by Lyndon Johnson.
- Both Vice President Johnsons became President in their fifties: Andrew Johnson was fifty-six; Lyndon Johnson was fifty-five.
- Andrew Johnson's father once worked as a janitor; Lyndon Johnson's father once worked as a janitor.
- Andrew Johnson was born in 1808; Lyndon Johnson was born in 1908.
- "Andrew" and "Lyndon" both have six letters.

- Both President Johnsons had two daughters.
- Both President Johnsons served in the military.
- Both President Johnsons had previously been Senators from a southern state.
- Both President Johnsons suffered from kidney stones. They were the only two Presidents ever to experience this malady.
- The re-election opponents of both President Johnsons were men whose name began with G: Andrew Johnson against Ulysses S. Grant; Lyndon Johnson against Barry Goldwater.
- Andrew Johnson chose not to run for re-election in 1868. Lyndon Johnson chose not to run for re-election in 1968.

[1] The historical record on both Presidents is extensive and complete.

[2] Also, one glaring error in the earlier list has been corrected. One of the coincidences that regularly made the rounds was: "Lincoln's secretary was named Kennedy; Kennedy's secretary was named Lincoln." Not so. Apparently, Lincoln never had a secretary named Kennedy.

[3] Special acknowledgment must go to Lu Ann Paletta and Fred L. Worth's *World Almanac of Presidential Facts*, a valuable resource in the compiling of this list.

95

Unicorns

HAIKU:

UNICORNS

The spiraling horn
Silently leads through the woods
Creature of a dream

Hunters can catch the unicorn only by placing a young virgin in his haunts. No sooner does he see the damsel than he runs towards her, and lies down at her feet, and so suffers himself to be captured by the hunters.

—Clerc de Normandie[1]

Now I will believe that there are unicorns . . .

—William Shakespeare[2]

DEFINITION: A unicorn is (depending on who you talk to) either a mythical or real creature, most often represented as a horse with a single straight spiraled horn projecting from its forehead.

WHAT THE BELIEVERS SAY: Unicorns were real and are now extinct; or, unicorns are real and still exist somewhere in the world, although they are elusive creatures, akin to Bigfoot or the Loch Ness Monster.

WHAT THE SKEPTICS SAY: Unicorns are imaginary creatures.

QUALITY OF SUPPORTING EVIDENCE: Good.

LIKELIHOOD PHENOMENA ARE AUTHENTIC: Good.[3]

There are seven references to unicorns in the Old Testament, yet rather than confirming the reality of this now perhaps-extinct creature, these mentions illustrate the problem not only with text translation of ancient documents, but also with literal interpretation of the Bible. Unicorns are mentioned specifically in *only* the King James version of the Bible. In many other translations, the term "wild ox" replaces "unicorn" in the text.

So the answer to the question, "Does the Bible establish as true the existence of the unicorn?" is "Not really."

Were—or are—unicorns real?

There are many historical accounts of unicorn sightings. Are they credible? It depends on your belief system, I suppose.

Genghis Khan reportedly did not invade India because a unicorn knelt down before him. Khan interpreted this as a sign from God and a warning not to invade. Julius Caesar claimed to have seen a unicorn in the forests of Germany, and Alexander the Great is said to have ridden a unicorn into battle. Herodotus wrote of a "horned ass" in the third century B.C.; Aristotle believed that the unicorn was probably real, and in the first century A.D., Pliny the Elder described the unicorn in his thirty-seven-volume encyclopedia, *Historia Naturalis*. In the late 1200s, Italian traveler Marco Polo wrote of seeing a unicorn during his journeys through China, although many historians today believe what he had actually seen was a rhinoceros.

During the Middle Ages, there was a profound belief not only in the existence of unicorns, but in the magical and healing powers of its horn. There were tests to determine whether or not a horn was really from a unicorn, since it was quite common for hoaxsters to sell goat horn, dog bones, or other animal horns as unicorn horns.[4] Known as alicorn, a unicorn's horn could allegedly cure epilepsy, the gout, rabies, and could lower fevers. Royalty had their eating utensils made from what they believed was unicorn horn to assure their protection from poisoning. Other parts of the unicorn also possessed great power. Its liver could cure leprosy, and wearing its hide guaranteed overall good health.

In all the mythologies and accounts of unicorns, the animal is always associated with purity and great virtue. As the first epigraph above describes, the only way to capture a unicorn alive was to tempt it with a virgin. Apparently, unicorns could not resist virgins and, upon encountering one, would walk up to her and lay its head in her lap. He could then be captured. In religious symbology, the unicorn represented Christ, and its horn represented the unity of Christ with God the Father. It was also believed that the reason a virgin was the only human who could subjugate a unicorn was because the Virgin Mary herself had originally been the one to tame the noble beast.

Over the years, there have been attempts to "manufacture" a living unicorn. A white Angora goat named Lancelot the Living Unicorn was a popular attraction with the Ringling Brothers-Barnum & Bailey Circus for years. The horn buds of a baby goat were manipulated and shaped so that they grew into a single horn. A living unicorn? Hardly. Yet Lancelot did look like what a small unicorn would look like, and many visitors to the circus headed home feeling like they had seen something magical.

Today, there are occasional unicorn sightings, yet, like the sightings of the legendary Bigfoot, Nessie, angels, elves, and dragons, they still reside more in the realm of mystery than anywhere else.

[1]*Le Bestiaire Divin de Guillame* (c. thirteenth century).

[2]*The Tempest* (1612).

[3]In this case, an authenticity likelihood rating of "Good" refers to the possibility that the phenomena (the unicorn) *was* real at one time.

[4]One particularly nasty test was to feed a quantity of arsenic to several pigeons, followed by a dose of what was believed to be ground-up alicorn. If the pigeons lived, it was real unicorn horn. This test often resulted in a large number of dead pigeons.

Vampires

HAIKU:

VAMPIRES

Creature of the night
Empty coffin, lid open
Blood hunger rages

There was nobody about, and I made a search over every inch of the ground, so as not to lose a chance. I went down even into the vaults, where the dim light struggled, although to do so was a dread to my very soul. Into two of these I went, but saw nothing except fragments of old coffins and piles of dust. In the third, however, I made a discovery.

There, in one of the great boxes, of which there were fifty in all, on a pile of newly dug earth, lay the Count! He was either dead or asleep. I could not say which, for eyes were open and stony, but without the glassiness of death, and the cheeks had the warmth of life through all their pallor. The lips were as red as ever. But there was no sign of movement, no pulse, no breath, no beating of the heart.[1]

DEFINITION: A vampire is traditionally defined as a reanimated corpse that rises from the grave at night to suck the blood of living people. He is often disguised as a bat during his nocturnal wanderings. People who fall victim to a vampire's bite become vampires when they die; sometimes (depending on the source of the legend), they transform into vampires immediately.

WHAT THE BELIEVERS SAY: Vampires are real supernatural creatures that feed on blood, are vulnerable to sunlight, crosses, and garlic, and sleep in coffins during the daytime.

WHAT THE SKEPTICS SAY: There are no such creatures as real vampires. Throughout history, there have been people who suffered from a rare genetic disease called porphyria, which made them sensitive to light and gave them chronic and grave anemia, which many may have tried to treat by drinking blood. These people were mythologized over the centuries into the modern-day icon of the bloodsucking vampire of movies and fiction. The descriptions of disinterred corpses believed to be vampires (blood on the mouth, bloating, longer hair and nails, etc.) are all explainable by the normal process of decomposition. Corpses who exhibited signs of trying to escape the coffin were more than likely poor souls who were buried a little too early—like when they were still alive.

QUALITY OF EXISTING EVIDENCE: Poor.

LIKELIHOOD PHENOMENA ARE PARANORMAL: Low.

In the sixteenth century, Countess Elizabeth Bathory bathed in and drank human blood. She believed that the blood of virgins had restorative powers and for years she had her lackeys round up chaste young girls from the surrounding towns for her to use as she desired. She would often torture these hapless victims before exsanguinating them, and she delighted in inflicting unimaginable pain on the poor young ladies imprisoned in her castle dungeons.

A century earlier, Vlad the Impaler—Count Dracul—committed similarly unspeakable acts and was likewise known to drink blood. During one abominable event, Vlad had thousands of people dismembered and impaled as he feasted, pausing now and then to dip his bread in the blood of the dying.

The legend of Vlad the Impaler was the main source for Bram Stoker during his writing of his classic novel *Dracula*, and it is believed Stoker also studied the legend of Elizabeth Bathory for further inspiration.

In modern times, novelists Stephen King and Anne Rice (both of whom owe an enormous debt to Bram Stoker) have each made major contributions to the modern perception of the vampire. In *Salem's Lot*, King created the vile and repulsive Kurt Barlow, the ageless vampire who set up shop in Jerusalem's Lot, Maine; and in *The Vampire LeStat*, Rice gave us the charming and seductive LeStat, who likewise was eternal and changed personas depending on the period in which he "lived."

Were Bathory and Vlad supernatural, demonic creatures? In addition to unspeakable cruelty, did they also possess the powers attributed to the vampire?

It seems that these two lunatics were simply psychopaths with power; individuals with sadistic, bestial urges they were permitted to indulge at will, thanks to their power and wealth.

Their stories inspired Stoker, yet there are countless surviving legends from many eastern European cultures that certainly sound like stories of vampires.

Today, the Internet has spawned a global community of vampire scholars, vampire fans, vampire wannabes and, yes, real vampires. One highly trafficked site (which I'll not promote here) is the work of a young woman who states with certainty that she is, indeed, a real vampire. She admits to drinking a shot glass or two of human blood each week and she reveals that most modern vampires enlist the help of "donors," friends who are fully aware of the vampire's true nature and needs and willingly provide him or her with some of their own blood on a regular basis.

According to these people, vampirism is not porphyria, nor is it demonic. It is an elevated state of being which manifests sometime in late adolescence and which is inherent to the individual, much the way blond hair or a tendency towards alcoholism is genetically predisposed.

In addition to modern-day blood vampires, there also exists a subset of vampires known as psi-vampires. These are humans who believe they can absorb (drain) energy from others and in many cases, are convinced they need to do so for both increased well-being and sometimes survival.

The legend of the vampire—in all its horror and science fiction incarnations—is one of the most beloved and enduring myths in the history of man's myth-making. The metamorphosis of the stories of people like Bathory and Vlad into tales of supernatural powers and passions speaks to the need for myth in the human experience.

---

[1]Bram Stoker, *Dracula*, ch. 4.

97

Voodoo and Zombies

HAIKU:

ZOMBIES

Death is a mirror
Some can look behind the glass
The shambling raggedy man

"They're dead. They're all messed up."[1]

DEFINITION: Voodoo is a religion practiced chiefly in Caribbean countries, especially Haiti, syncretized from Roman Catholic ritual elements and the animism and magic of Dahomean slaves, in which a supreme God rules a large pantheon of local and tutelary deities, deified ancestors, and saints, who communicate with believers in dreams, trances, and ritual possessions.[2] A zombie is a corpse revived by voodoo practices, although the "corpse" is a drugged and paralyzed living person, rather than actually being dead.

WHAT THE BELIEVERS SAY: Zombies are bodies without souls and they are reanimated by the dark power of the voodoo rituals.

WHAT THE SKEPTICS SAY: Zombies are living people who are given paralyzing, hallucinogenic, mind-altering drugs after which they are enslaved.

QUALITY OF EXISTING EVIDENCE: Low.[3]

LIKELIHOOD PHENOMENA ARE PARANORMAL: Poor.

The sorcerer tapped the side of the clay bowl and the brown dust inside the bowl settled. The dust was a combination of ground puffer fish, porcupine fish, and a certain deadly toad, and he slowly poured it into a leather satchel, being careful not to get even a grain of the powder on his skin.

The sorcerer placed the satchel in the side pocket of his coat and immediately left his house. It was a fifteen minute walk to the home of the man he had elected to transform into a zombie and he wanted to arrive there before the man left for his job in the fields.

The sun was not up when the sorcerer arrived at Claude Jean's house. He looked around and assured himself no one was watching. He then withdrew the leather satchel, crouched, and carefully sprinkled the powder on the path leading to Claude Jean's house. He then hid behind a line of bushes across the lane from the house and waited and watched.

Mere minutes later, Claude Jean emerged from his small ramshackle house and walked down the path leading to the road. His bare feet stepped in the sorcerer's powder at least four times.

The paralyzing powder did its job and Claude Jean fell to the ground. The sorcerer quickly ran to the prone man, picked him up, swung him over his shoulder, and hurried away, the rising sun barely beginning to illuminate the houses.

The sorcerer kept Claude Jean locked in a closet in his house until night fell. He then carried him into the deep woods where a grave lay open, awaiting its sleeper. He placed Claude Jean in a wooden coffin, and hammered the top into place. One of the nails pierced the wood and struck Claude Jean in the cheek. He felt it, and it drew blood, but he could not cry out. The sorcerer then slid the coffin into the grave and covered it up with dirt.

Claude Jean would lay paralyzed and conscious for four days and nights before the sorcerer dug him up. As soon as he ripped off the cover of the coffin, the sorcerer would pick Claude Jean up by the throat and throw him out of the grave. He would then beat him with his fists and a whip for almost an hour, after which he would force him to consume a piece of a plant with powerful hallucinogenic and psychoactive properties.

Within minutes of the plant taking effect, Claude Jean would be a zombie, renamed by the sorcerer, and completely under the magician's control.

In the classic 1968 black-and-white movie, *The Night of the Living Dead*, the dead are brought back to life after the Earth passes through the tale of a comet. After being reanimated, they are mindless, violent cannibals. This was a horror movie fantasy about how reanimated zombies would act. Apparently, being brought back to life made them hungry for human flesh.

This was an effective plot for a movie, but it was pure fantasy. As illustrated in the above vignette, there are beings—*people*—that are considered zombies, but the truth is that they have been "zombified" by the process of being given paralytic, mind-altering drugs; by the trauma of being buried alive; and due to the submission that follows severe and violent physical abuse. Ongoing administration of psychoactive drugs keeps these poor saps in this terrible state and these shambling raggedy men are the source of the zombie legend.

The power of belief is strong. The people of undeveloped, Third World cultures that place great store in superstitions are highly susceptible to mind control—i.e., if a witch doctor known to practice voodoo creates a zombie, the people will believe a supernatural transformation has occurred.

The legend of zombies is another instance where the pervasive and enduring myth emerged from all-too-real horrible events and practices, and merged with the realm of the paranormal.

[1]*The Night of the Living Dead*, George Romero, 1968.

[2]*American Heritage Dictionary.*

[3]The quality of evidence that "zombies" exist is good, but the quality of evidence proving the existence of *real* zombies, i.e., the reanimated dead, is poor.

98

Werewolves

HAIKU:

WEREWOLVES

Hairy face and hands
A supernatural beast?
Or a fantasy?

I saw a werewolf with a Chinese menu in his hand
Walking through the streets of Soho in the rain . . .

—Warren Zevon[1]

DEFINITION: Werewolves are human beings who are magically transformed into wolves. Tales about werewolves appear in many countries and in many literary works. Werewolves, according to the stories, prowl at night, devour babies and dig up corpses, and cannot be killed with ordinary weapons or ammunition. They are particularly associated with the full moon.[2]

WHAT THE BELIEVERS SAY: Werewolves are real, supernatural creatures. Do not confuse the true werewolf with the human lycanthrope, the mentally ill person who believes he or she transforms into a wolf (or some other animal, often a tiger or a bear) under a full moon. Werewolves exist, and they walk the Earth hungering for prey.

WHAT THE SKEPTICS SAY: All supposed "werewolves" are lycanthropes; there are no human beings who can actually transform into wolves. Also, there are known medical conditions such as hypertrichosis (excessive hair growth on the face and upper body), and porphyria (skin lesions and extreme sensitivity to light) that could have, in less enlightened times, caused people to believe that their sufferers were werewolves.

QUALITY OF EXISTING EVIDENCE: Poor.

LIKELIHOOD PHENOMENA ARE PARANORMAL: Low.

According to legend, when a pack of werewolves refused to listen to St. Patrick preach about Christianity, he prayed to God that they be punished and God quickly obliged. The Lord reportedly sentenced their race and all their descendants to periodically live as wolves, while retaining human thought and will, so that they might fully understand the consequences of their choosing the soulless, primitive being of the wolf over the spiritual, human form given to them by God.

Folklore has been filled with tales of werewolves for centuries. All over the world, dozens of cultures have their own name for the human that transforms into a beast and then goes on a bloody rampage, slaughtering and eating whomever is ill-fated enough to cross their path.

Many of these tales are classic *Twilight Zone*-type tales. A person is attacked by a werewolf and manages to cut off its hand, or pokes out its eye, or shoot or stab it, and then the almost-victim escapes. The following day, the werewolf's prey comes upon a person he or she knows—but now that person is missing a hand, or an eye, or is wearing a bandage from a gunshot or knife wound. Werewolf identified. Let the torture begin!

Horror writer Stephen King paid homage to this classic conceit in his 1983 novella, *Cycle of the Werewolf*, in which a marauding werewolf is shot in the eye with a firecracker rocket—and the following day, the town's minister shows up with a patch over his eye.

One of the earliest mentions of a man that turned into a wolf was in the Roman Petronius Arbiter's first century comic novel, *Satyricon*. St. Augustine also wrote of a werewolf four centuries later in his classic, *City of God*. However the most detailed accounts of werewolves and their deeds are from the Middle Ages. In many works, the transformation ritual is described, as well as instructions on how to identify a werewolf. The trials of people accused of committing crimes while changed into a werewolf are also recounted in detail.

Over the centuries, the myth has evolved to a point where we now know of the three ways a person can become a werewolf:

The first way is unwittingly. A person is inherently a werewolf and first discovers the truth during the period of a full moon when he or she transforms. Often the victim will "awaken" (become human again) surrounded by the bloody remains of their victims.

The second way is willingly. A person strips naked and slathers himself with a grease made from several herbs, some of which are hallucinogenic. Sometimes he wears the skin of a wolf, or of another animal. He then dances around, essentially summoning the transformation into a werewolf. Mayhem ensues.

The third way is as a victim of a werewolf bite. As with the legend of the vampire (see Chapter 96), if a person is bitten by a werewolf, he or she will become a werewolf. (This scenario was convincingly depicted in the 1981 John Landis movie, *An American Werewolf in London*.)

It has been suggested that the legend of the werewolf was conceived as a way of explaining seemingly inhuman crimes; assaults that were so vicious and grotesque, it was impossible to believe that a human being could have committed them. Cannibalism, dismemberment, torture-murders, rape-murders, incest, and other horrific crimes were, in earlier times, believed to have been supernatural in origin. Today, the literature of contemporary serial murder is replete with stories of just-plain-humans committing such incredibly heinous atrocities, including the horrors cited, as well as even more bizarre barbarities made possible by technology. Jeffrey Dahmer drugged, sodomized, killed, and then cut up and ate young black boys. Albert Fish cooked and ate a stew made from the genitals of children. And there are many more similar stories. It is easy to see how such unimaginable evils could have been attributed to a non-human beast. Today, we know better.

[1] "Werewolves of London" © Warren Zevon. All rights reserved.
[2] *Dictionary of Cultural Literacy.*

99

Who Is the Antichrist?

HAIKU:

WHO IS THE ANTICHRIST?

No one knows his name

Jesus is his enemy

Mankind must beware

A survey of Russian peasants in the mid–1920s suggested that 55 percent of them remained active Christian worshippers. The Red worker and the Communist intellectual were city phenomena . . . [Rural villagers] mocked Bolshevik agitators . . . "Your nails are very long," one young militant was greeted in a village. "You're not the Antichrist, are you?" With that he was attacked to see "if he didn't have a tail or whether he was covered in hair."[1]

DEFINITION: The Antichrist is the great enemy of Jesus Christ; he is the entity who was predicted by the early Church and Scripture to set himself up against Christ in the last days before Christ's Second Coming.

WHAT THE BELIEVERS SAY: The Antichrist is a real being whose coming is foretold in the Bible. Once his identity is known, the time is short before Christ returns to vanquish evil and govern the world. Those who survive will be the ones who renounce the Antichrist and align themselves with Jesus in this monumental final battle between good and evil.

WHAT THE SKEPTICS SAY: The Antichrist is just one more doctrinal, archetypal element of the mythology of the Christian religions; his persona symbolizes the pervasive spread of evil throughout the world. Almost any religious text can be interpreted within a context that seems relevant to the times in which it is being read.

QUALITY OF EXISTING EVIDENCE: Inconclusive.[2]

LIKELIHOOD PHENOMENON IS PARANORMAL: Inconclusive.[3]

Nostradamus scholars (see Chapter 59) believe that the legendary French psychic told us that the world is destined to know three Antichrists, and that Napoleon and Hitler were the first two. Some speculate that Saddam Hussein is the third, but that theory has not yet been widely accepted. The degenerate emperor Nero has also been named as a possible candidate, as was Joseph Stalin. (Nostradamus also predicted that the Antichrist would appear when the two great leaders will be friends.[4] Many interpret this to describe the recent alliance of the United States and Russia.)

Some religious scholars make the distinction between Antichrists, of which they say there are many, and the Antichrist himself, who most agree, has not yet come to Earth.

Satan is not the Antichrist, although some do believe that the Antichrist will be the *Son* of Satan, thereby mocking the very nature of Christ's incarnation as the Son of God. The majority of theological scholars, as well as many card-carrying Satanists, are in agreement that the Antichrist will be a human being. The *Catholic Encyclopedia* also weighs in on his identity:

> The individual person of Antichrist will not be a demon, as some of the ancient writers believed; nor will he be the person of the devil incarnated in the human nature of Antichrist. He will be a human person . . .[5]

There are very few references to the Antichrist in the Bible, and they all appear in the Epistles of John. In 1 John 2:18 it is written, "Little children, these are the end times, and as you heard that the Antichrist is coming, even now many Antichrists have arisen. By this we know that it is the end times." In 1 John 2:22, we are told that the Antichrist denies that Jesus is the Christ, and in 2 John 1:7, we learn that "many deceivers" are in the world and that they "confess not that Jesus Christ is come in the flesh." These are *all* Antichrists, further confusing the issue. Will there be a single Antichrist? Or should the world prepare for an army of evildoers, all of whom deny Jesus Christ, and all of whom are harbingers of the end times?

Many religious analysts are conflicted about the true nature, as well as the true identity, of the Antichrist. Some tracts speak of the Antichrist as a demonic force rather than a single being; a cadre of evil manifested in many people throughout the world, all working to vanquish the powers of good and God and prevent the return of Christ. Alternatively, some, including the Catholic Church, speak of a single person.

From *The Catechism of the Catholic Church*:

> Before Christ's second coming the church must pass through a final trial that will shake the faith of many believers. . . . The supreme religious deception is that of the Antichrist, a pseudo-messianism by which man glorifies himself in place of God and of his Messiah come in the flesh.
>
> The Antichrist's deception already begins to take shape in the world every time the claim is made to realize within history that messianic hope which can only be realized beyond history through the eschatological judgment.[6]

Who have the primary contenders for the title of Antichrist been?

On August 18, 1520, Martin Luther concluded that the Pope himself was the Antichrist, describing the papacy as "the seat of the true and real Antichrist."[7] (Protestants later took that back.)

As we have seen, Adolf Hitler, Joseph Stalin, Saddam Hussein, Napoleon, Nero, Frederick II, and Caligula have all been named as possible Antichrists. Following the events of September 11, 2001, Osama bin Laden came to be spoken of as the Antichrist.

Is the Antichrist walking the Earth today? Does the Bible tell us what to watch out for before the end times?

Earthquakes, floods, droughts, famines, plagues, unrest, violence, unprecedented storms, epidemics, religious strife—all of these terrible things are cited as evidence of the collapse of civilization, the turning away from God, and the presence of the Antichrist.

But, playing Devils' advocate (not literally, of course, and no pun intended) all of these tribulations have been present on Earth since the earliest days of human civilization. Even during periods of relative peace (i.e., a time when there were only many small wars being waged rather than one elephantine global conflict), one could find countless examples of great storms, great hunger, religious conflict, plagues and illnesses, and many other of the supposed "signs of the end."

The interpretation of the religious texts of one's choosing can easily provide validation and verification of many end-time prophecies.

The ultimate question, then, is how will man be able to identify the Antichrist when he arrives on Earth? The answer to that is depressing: There are so many evil people at any given moment in the history of mankind that we can, in essence, take our pick.

[1] Brian Moynahan, *The Faith: A History of Christianity*, p. 671.

[2] What can reasonably be considered evidence? Religious texts? Not really. Eye of the beholder, as it were.

[3] Again, an individual's faith will be the final determinant as to whether or not the Antichrist is real and, if so, paranormal.

[4] *The Prophecies of Nostradamus*, translated by Erika Cheetham, Century II, Quatrain 89.

[5] *The Catholic Encyclopedia*, "Antichrist," online at http://www.newadvent.org.

[6] *The Catechism of the Catholic Church*, Part 1, passage 657, p. 194.

[7] LeRoy Froom, *The Prophetic Faith of Our Fathers*, Vol. 2, p. 121.

Witches and Witchcraft

HAIKU:

THE WITCH

Gruesome hag of old
Does she have evil powers?
And should she be burned?

Thou shalt not suffer a witch to live.
—Exodus 22:18

I am no witch. I am innocent. I know nothing of it.
—Bridget Bishop[1]

DEFINITION: Witchcraft is the "magical manipulation of supernormal forces through the casting of spells and the conjuring or invoking of spirits."[2] Witchcraft can be used for good or evil purposes. Malevolent use (black magic) involves entering into compacts with the Devil and other demonic spirits, often to do evil to others; use for good (white magic, practiced by Wiccans[3]) involves casting spells for health and healings, good harvests, and other beneficent purposes.

WHAT THE BELIEVERS SAY: Witches can summon supernatural forces and use them for both good and evil.

WHAT THE SKEPTICS SAY: Witchcraft is impossible and all belief in it is nothing but pure, unadulterated delusional thinking.

QUALITY OF EXISTING EVIDENCE: Fair.

LIKELIHOOD PHENOMENA ARE PARANORMAL: Low.

The torture chamber reeked with the smell of burnt hair. Elizabeth, the accused witch, lay naked on a wooden table, her arms and legs spread and tied to iron rings. The torturer had poured a bucket of pure alcohol on Elizabeth's head and then set fire to it. He had watched carefully as flames engulfed her face and hair, as he did not want to kill her here. Her screams were loud enough to make his ears ring. When most of her hair had burned off and her skin was beginning to turn black, he dumped a pail of cold water on the flames, extinguishing them. Elizabeth's face was a charred wound; what was left of her hair was black and smoldering; her eyes and mouth were swollen and burned almost shut.

"Confess," the torturer said softly.

Elizabeth was panting in agony, but somehow managed to squeak out the words, "I am not a witch."

"Very well."

The torturer reached for the *turcas* and moved to the bottom of the table. He picked up Elizabeth's bare left foot, and positioned the turcas over her big toe.

"Confess in the name of God."

Elizabeth said nothing, but shook her head from side to side.

The torturer then applied the instrument to her toe and yanked the nail out in one swift move. Elizabeth's entire body tensed and she let out a blood-curdling scream.

"Nineteen to go, woman. Perhaps one will spur you to confess."

The torturer continued to remove her toe nails, one at a time, as Elizabeth entered a realm of pain so intense, she felt as though her entire body was one raw, exposed nerve.

Elizabeth eventually did confess to being a witch, after which her eyes were gouged out with a hot iron and she was flogged until the skin fell from her back in strips. As she was marched naked to her burning stake, her mangled fingers were individually hacked off and collected in a basket for nailing to the burning platform. The executioner was given a bonus for the additional amputation work.

* * *

Three of every ten Americans believe in the existence of witches—beings with evil, supernatural powers who may be in cahoots with the Devil himself. Contrarily, "good" witches, those who practice the Wiccan religion, are seen as "New Age chanter-types" who dance in circles in fields and pray to the gods of nature—earth, sea, fire, and sky.

The traditional portrayal of the "evil" witch is of a crone with a hook nose, dressed in all black, wearing a black pointed hat, having a black cat as a familiar, and often getting around on a flying broom. There are adults who still get the shivers when they watch the *Wizard of Oz* ("I'll get you, my pretty!").

The belief in witchcraft has been a powerful, influential, and pervasive force throughout history, beginning sometime around the fourth or fifth century.

The Catholic Church's fourteenth- and fifteenth-century Inquisition, for instance, while targeting all infidels and heretics in general, over time increasingly focused on women believed to be witches, often burning and hanging village-fuls of females. There are records of some European villages being so decimated by the Church's misogynous tirade that they ended up with one sole surviving female by the time the slaughters of the Inquisition were abolished.[4] Granted, witch's covens did exist and accounts of crazed orgies and bacchanalia do permeate the historical record. Many students of witchcraft now believe, however, that witches used an ointment on their bodies which contained hallucinogenic drugs, which would definitely explain the stories of flying, and apparitions, and other supernatural occurrences.

Witchcraft and the persecution of witches both made the journey across the Atlantic to the New World. The most notorious episode of anti-witch hysteria in America was the period from January through November 1692, the time of the Salem Witch Trials, when 141 people were arrested and twenty were executed for being witches. American writer Nathaniel Hawthorne was so ashamed of his ancestor John Hathorne's contemptible actions as a magistrate during the Salem Witch Trials that he added the "w" to his name to sever the familial association.

Witchcraft is still practiced today, both as a black art and as white magic. There are countless books to instruct proselytes on casting spells, mixing potions, and summoning demons.

Advocates of both schools of witchcraft claim paranormal validity.

Skeptics dismiss it all as make-believe.

[1] Bridget Bishop was the first woman executed for being a witch during the Salem Witch Trials. She was hanged on June 10, 1692.

[2] Rosemary Ellen Guiley, *The Encyclopedia of Witches and Witchcraft*, Second Edition, p. 366.

[3] Wicca is a pagan nature religion which had its roots in pre-Christian western Europe. Since the 1940s, Wicca has been undergoing a twentieth-century revival, especially in the United States and Great Britain.

[4] Interestingly, four centuries before the Inquisition there is an admirable record of at least a semblance of sanity in the Catholic Church regarding sorcery and witches. In 900 A.D. the Church issued the *Canon Episcopi*, an ecclesiastical document which essentially proclaimed that there was no such thing as witchcraft and that anyone who believed was not only "stupid and foolish," but also an infidel. Four hundred years later, no less a thinker than Thomas Aquinas, however, denounced the *Canon Episcopi* and asserted that witches could fly, copulate with the Devil, raise storms, and change their appearance at will. A "pervasive force," indeed.

Select Bibliography

Adams, Cecil. *The Straight Dope*. New York: Ballantine Books, 1984.

Baum, Richard, and William Sheehan. *In Search of Planet Vulcan: The Ghost in Newton's Clockwork Universe*. New York: Plenum Press, 1997.

Benham, William G. *The Laws of Scientific Hand Reading: A Practical Treatise on the Art Commonly Called Palmistry*. New York: Hawthorne Press, 1974.

Berliner, Don, and Stanton T. Friedman. *Crash at Corona*. New York: Marlowe & Company, 1997.

Berra, Tim M. *Evolution and the Myth of Creationism: A Basic Guide to the Facts in the Evolution Debate*. Stanford, Calif.: Stanford University Press, 1990.

Best, Robert M. *Noah's Ark and the Ziusudra Epic: Sumerian Origins of the Myth*. Winona Lake, Ind.: Eisenbrauns, 1999.

Bord, Janet, and Colin Bord. *Unexplained Mysteries of the 20th Century*. Chicago, Ill.: Contemporary Books, 1989.

Calkins, Carroll C., editor. *Mysteries of the Unexplained*. Pleasantville, N.Y.: Reader's Digest Association, 1982.

Catholic Encyclopedia, The. http://www.newadvent.org.

Cavendish, Richard, editor. *Encyclopedia of the Unexplained: Magic, Occultism and Parapsychology*. London: Arkana, 1989.

Cheetham, Erika, translator. *The Prophecies of Nostradamus*. New York: Berkley, 1973.

Childress, David Hatcher. *Extraterrestrial Archaeology*. Stelle, Ill.: Adventures Unlimited Press, 1994.

Clark, Jerome. *The UFO Book: Encyclopedia of the Extraterrestrial*. Detroit, Mich.: Visible Ink Press, 1998.

Clark, Jerome. *Unexplained!: 347 Strange Sightings, Incredible Occurrences, and Puzzling Physical Phenomena*. Detroit, Mich.: Visible Ink Press, 1993.

Condon, Edward U. *Scientific Study of Unidentified Flying Objects*. New York: Bantam, 1969.

Corliss, William R. *Ancient Man: A Handbook of Puzzling Artifacts*. Glen Arm, Md.: The Sourcebook Project, 1978.

———. *Incredible Life: A Handbook of Biological Mysteries*. Glen Arm, Md.: The Sourcebook Project, 1981.

———. *Mysterious Universe: A Handbook of Astronomical Anomalies*. Glen Arm, Md.: The Sourcebook Project, 1979.

———. *Unknown Earth: A Handbook of Geological Enigmas*. Glen Arm, Md.: The Sourcebook Project, 1989.

Corso, Philip J. *The Day After Roswell*. New York: Pocket Books, 1997.

Cousineau, Phil. *UFOs: A Manual for the Millenium.* New York: Harper-Collins, 1995.

Drosnin, Michael. *The Bible Code.* New York: Touchstone, 1997.

———. *Bible Code II: The Countdown.* New York: Viking, 2002.

Eisen, Jonathan. *Suppressed Inventions and Other Discoveries: Revealing the World's Greatest Secrets of Science and Medicine.* Garden City Park, N.Y.: Avery Publishing Group, 1999.

Fodor, Nandor. *Encyclopœdia of Psychic Science.* New Hyde Park, N.Y.: University Books, 1966.

George, Leonard. *Alternative Realities: The Paranormal, the Mystic and the Transcendent in Human Experience.* New York: Facts on File, 1995.

Gittelson, Bernard, and Laura Torbett. *Intangible Evidence.* New York: Simon & Schuster Fireside, 1987.

Gray, E. *The Tarot Revealed.* New York: Inspiration House, 1960.

Guiley, Rosemary Ellen. *The Encyclopedia of Witches and Witchcraft, Second Edition.* New York: Facts on File, 1999.

Harrison, Ted. *Stigmata: A Medieval Mystery in a Modern Age.* New York: Penguin Putnam, 1996.

Heintz, Peter. *A Guide to Apparitions of Our Blessed Virgin Mary.* Sacramento, Calif.: Gabriel Press, 1993.

Hesemann, Michael. *The Fatima Secret.* New York: Dell, 2000.

Hoagland, Richard C. *The Monuments of Mars: A City on the Edge of Forever.* Berkeley, Calif.: North Atlantic Books, 1992.

Jung, Carl. *Collected Works.* Routledge, London: Princeton University Press, 1953–1963.

Key, Wilson Bryan. *Media Sexploitation.* New York: Signet, 1976.

Landsburg, Alan, and Sally Landsburg. *The Outer Space Connection.* New York: Bantam, 1975.

Mack, Carol K., and Dinah Mack. *A Field Guide to Demons, Fairies, Fallen Angels, and Other Subversive Spirits.* New York: Henry Holt and Company, 1998.

Marrs, Jim. *Alien Agenda: Investigating the Extraterrestrial Presence Among Us.* New York: HarperCollins, 1997.

Mitchell, John, and Robert J.M. Rickard. *Phenomena: A Book of Wonders.* New York: Pantheon Books, 1977.

Moss, Dr. Thelma. *The Probability of the Impossible.* New York: Plume, 1974.

Moynahan, Brian. *The Faith: A History of Christianity.* New York: Doubleday, 2002.

Nichols, Peter. *The Science in Science Fiction.* New York: Alfred A. Knopf, 1983.

Nickell, Joe. *Looking for a Miracle: Weeping Icons, Relics, Stigmata, Visions & Healing Cures.* Amherst, N.Y.: Prometheus Books, 1998.

Paletta, Lu Ann, and Fred L. Worth. *World Almanac of Presidential Facts*, rev. ed. New York: World Almanac, 1988.

Randi, James. *An Encyclopedia of Claims, Frauds, and Hoaxes of the Occult and Supernatural.* New York: St. Martin's Press, 1995.

Randle, Kevin D. *A History of UFO Crashes.* New York: Avon, 1995.

Rawcliffe, D.H. *Illusions and Delusions of the Supernatural and the Occult.* New York: Dover Publications, 1959.

Rich, Jason. *The Everything Ghost Book.* Avon, Mass.: Adams Media, 2001.

Ripley's Believe It or Not! New York: Warner Books, 1976.

Sagan, Carl. *The Cosmic Connection: An Extraterrestrial Perspective.* New York: Dell, 1973.

Selzer, Richard, M.D. *Mortal Lessons: Notes on the Art of Surgery.* New York: Simon & Schuster, 1974.

Singer, Barry, and George O. Abell, editors. *Science and the Paranormal.* New York: Charles Scribner's Sons, 1981.

Smaart, Ninian, and Richard D. Hecht, editors. *Sacred Texts of the World: A Universal Anthology.* New York: Crossroads Publishing, 1982.

Southwell, David, and Sean Twist. *Conspiracy Files.* London: Carlton Books, 1999.

Spence, Lewis. *An Encyclopaedia of Occultism: A Compendium of Information on the Occult Sciences, Occult Personalities, Psychic Science, Magic Demonology, Spiritism, Mysticism and Metaphysics.* New Hyde Park, N.Y.: University Books, 1960.

Spignesi, Stephen J. *In the Crosshairs: 75 Assassinations and Attempts, from Julius Caesar to John Lennon.* Franklin Lakes, New Jersey: New Page Books, 2002.

———. *The Odd Index.* New York: Plume, 1994.

———. *The UFO Book of Lists.* New York: Kensington Publishing, 2001.

Thurston, Herbert. *Beauraing and Other Apparitions.* London: Burns Oates & Washbourne Ltd., 1934.

Von Däniken, Erich. *Chariots of the Gods?* New York: Putnam, 1970.

Welfare, Simon, and John Fairly. *Arthur C. Clarke's Mysterious World.* New York: A & W Publishers, 1980.

White, John. *Pole Shift: Predictions and Prophecies of the Ultimate Disaster.* New York: Doubleday, 1980.

Williams, William F. *Encyclopedia of Pseudoscience.* New York: Facts on File, 2000.

Wilson, Colin, and Damon Wilson. *The Mammoth Encyclopedia of the Unsolved.* New York: Carrol & Graf Publishers, 2000.

Wilson, Ian. *The Blood on the Shroud: New Evidence That the World's Most Sacred Relic is Real.* New York: Touchstone, 1998.

Woodward, Kenneth L. *Making Saints: How the Catholic Church Determines Who Becomes a Saint, Who Doesn't, and Why.* New York: Simon & Schuster, 1990.

INDEX

Abominable Snowman, 60
Albee, Arden, 141
Alexander the Great, 393
alien abductions, xiv, 1–4, 195–97, 217–19
"alien autopsy" film, 5–7
aliens, 1–11, 22–25, 29–32, 53, 59–64, 73–76, 97–100, 122–25, 198–201, 206–8, 220–22, 302–6, 342–45, 381–85
Allende, Carlos Miguel, 264–65
Almost Famous (film), 46n
American Werewolf in London, An (film), 403
"ancient astronaut" theory, 8–11
Andrews, Colin, 97–100
Angel, Jack, 334
angel hair, 12–14, 207
angels, 4, 15–18, 27, 31
animal psi, 19–21
anti-gravity technology, 187
Antichrist, 404–7
Antikythera Mechanism, 10
apparitions, 155–58
Area 51, 22–25, 304
Argosy magazine, 52
Aristotle, 42, 393
Ark of the Covenant, 26–28
Armstrong, Neil, 49
Arnold, Kenneth, 207, 306, 382
Arnold, Larry E., 330–36
artistic abilities, 320
asteroids, 378–80
astral body, planes, and projection, 33–35, 157, 226
astrology, 36–39
Atkov, Oleg, 16
Atlantis, 40–43, 162, 165
atmospheric phenomena, 12–14, 82, 100, 143–46, 207

Augustine, Saint, 402
auras and halos, 33–35, 44–46, 180–83, 283
automatic writing, 77–80, 190
Avdeyev, Sergei, 372

Back to the Future (film series), 372
backwards messages, 47–50
Baghdad Battery, 10
Balducci Levitation, 185
Bathory, Countess Elizabeth, 396–97
Beatles, the, 47–50, 249–59
Bender, Albert, 207
Benecke, Dr. Mark, 333
Benham, William, 245
Bentley, Dr. John, 333–34
Berlitz, Charles, 52
Bermuda Triangle, 43n, 51–54
Bernadette, Saint, 169–71
Bernard, Dr. Raymond, 159–63
Berra, Dr. Tim, 90–96
Best, Robert M., 230
Bester, Alfred, 372
Betz, Hans-Dieter, 115
Bible, 17–18, 26–32, 55–58, 89–96, 104–5, 129, 153, 186, 202, 228–31, 286–87, 325–27, 337, 374–76, 393, 404–7
Bible Code, the, 55–58
Bigfoot, 59–64
bin Laden, Osama, 56, 58, 406
bio-physical phenomena, 33–35, 44–46, 65–68, 147–50, 168–71, 172–75, 184–87, 245–48, 315–22, 330–36, 362–66, 398–400
biorhythms, 65–68
Bird, Roland T., 94

Bishop, Bridget, 408
Blackmore, Susan, 224
Blaine, David, 86
Blavatsky, Madame Helena, 35n, 367–69
bleeding/weeping religious icons, xiv, 69–72, 213
Blind Tom, 316–17
Blue, Archie, 353
Bonnke, Reinhard, 299
Bosnor, Kevin, 365
Braun, Wernher von, 90
Briggs, Benjamin, 216–19
Brown, Rosemary, 79–80
Browne, Dr. Charles Albert, 116
Bush, George W., 177, 179
Byrd, Rear Admiral Richard E., 161–62

Caesar, Julius, 393
calendar calculating, 317–18
Carlotto, Mark, 140–41
Carmichael, Alexander, 210
Carrier, Richard, 297
Carroll, Marion, 203
Carroll, Robert Todd, 2, 50, 115–16, 166
Carter, Jimmy, 293
catastrophism, 165–67
Catholic Almanac, The, 290–92
Catholic Church, 39, 71–72, 105–7, 169–71, 203–5, 213–14, 338–41, 375–77, 406, 410
Catholic Encyclopedia, 17, 135, 405–7
cattle mutilations, 73–76
Cavett, Dick, 179
Cayce, Edgar, 43n, 126–29
channeling, 77–80, 190, 242–44, 287
Cheetham, Erika, 234
chiropractic, xiv
Chorvinsky, Mark, 119
Clinton, Hillary Rodham, 176–77
cold reading, 86–88
Columba, Saint, 192–93
Columbus, Christopher, 53
communication with the dead, 85–88, 97–100, 287

communications, 47–50, 55–58, 77–80, 249–59, 307–9, 327–29, 346–50
Conny, Dr. Robert, 143
Conway, Helen, 334
Cook, Nick, 22
Crabtree, Vexen, 310
creationism, 89–96
creatures and beings, 15–18, 59–64, 104–7, 118–21, 130–32, 191–94, 209–11, 392–403, 408–11. *See also* aliens
crop circles, 60, 97–100, 138
crosses of light, 101–3
Crowe, Cameron, 46n
CSICOP, 38
Curran, Pearl, 78–79
Cuvier, Georges, 165
Cyril, Saint, 103

Dahl, Harold, 207
Dahmer, Jeffrey, 403
Däniken, Erich von, 8–11, 124, 220–22
Dante Alighieri, 156–57
Dare, Virginia, 196
Darwin, Charles, 13
Davis, Gladys, 128
dead, the, 77–80, 85–88, 155–58, 168–71, 188–90, 223–27, 285–88, 297–301, 398–400
demons, 104–7, 158, 242, 328
Devil's Sea, 54n
DiPietro, Vincent, 141
directional perception, 321
disappearances, unexplained, 51–54, 195–97, 216–19
Discover magazine, 160
Ditter, Ralph, 384
divination and prophecy, 36–39, 55–58, 108–13, 226–27, 232–48, 274–78, 307–9, 358–61
Dowding, Lord Hugh, 385n
dowsing, 114–17
dragons, 4, 118–21
Drosnin, Michael, 56–58
dwarves, 130–32

Easter Island, 9–10, 122–25, 342
Edward, John, 87

Einstein, Albert, 189, 264, 269–70
Einstein, Alfred, 268
elves, 4, 130–32
Ephron, Nora, 179
ESP, 3, 133–36, 320–21. *See also*
    psychic phenomena
eugenics, 179
evolution, 89–96
exorcism, 104–7, 242, 328
Exorcist, The (film), 242

fairies, 4, 130–32
falling objects, 143–46
Fate magazine, 119
Fatima, 204–5
fire immunity and firewalking,
    147–50, 283
Fish, Albert, 403
flat earth, 151–54
Fleiss, Dr. Wilhelm, 67
Fletcher, Kay, 335–36
Fort, Charles, 12, 81–84, 114, 116,
    146, 338
Fortean phenomena, 81–84
Foschini, Dr. Luigi, 380
Frakes, Jonathan, 5
Francis of Assisi, Saint, 186,
    338–39
Fuld, William, 243

Gaddis, Vincent, 52
Gaia Theory, 100
Gauquelin, Michel and Françoise,
    38
Genghis Khan, 393
geo-physical phenomena, 40–43,
    51–54, 97–100, 114–17,
    151–54, 159–63
Ghost (film), 79
ghosts, 155–58, 190, 287
Gibb, Russ, 250
Gittelson, Bernard, 237
Goodby, Jeff, 348
Gray, E., 358
Griswold, Chuck, 226
Grossinger, Richard, 137

haunted places, 155–58
Hawkins, Dr. Gerald, 222, 344
Hawthorne, Nathaniel, 410

healing powers, 126–29, 212–15,
    393
Helena, Saint, 291
Hendrix, Jimi, 71
Herodotus, 393
Heyerdahl, Thor, 123–24
Hill, Betty and Barney, 3
Hill, Thomas, 210
Hitler, Adolf, 234, 405
Hoagland, Richard, 140–42
hoaxes, 5–7, 60, 70–71, 86–88,
    93–94, 98–100, 150, 174,
    186–87, 191–94, 198–202, 207,
    249–59, 289–92, 348, 393
hollow earth, 159–63
holy water, powers of, 205, 271–73
Home, Daniel, 186
Hooton, E.A., 179
Horowitz, Gary T., 370
Houdini, Harry, 147
Hoxsey, Dr. Harry, 353
Hudson, Henry, 210
Hussein, Saddam, 405
Hynek, J. Allen, 384

incorrupt corpses, 168–71
Indian rope trick, 186–87
inventions, suppressed, 260–62,
    351–54
invisibility, 172–75, 263–66
Ivy League nude posture photos,
    176–79

James, William, 214–15
Jessup, Morris K., 264–65
Jesus, 29–32, 186, 286–87, 289–92,
    297–301, 323–26, 337–41,
    374–77, 404–7
Jesus Tortilla, 102, 204
John of the Cross, Saint, 341n
Johnson, Charles K., 151–53
Jones, Peter, 334–35
Joseph of Cupertino, Saint, 186
Jung, Carl, 355–57, 385

karma, 286–87, 368–69
Kelley, Edward, 312
Kennard, Charles, 243
Kennedy, John F., 49, 234, 386–91
Kersten, Holgar, 325

Key, Wilson Bryan, 347–48
King, Dr. Lester S., 330
King, Stephen, 37, 144, 158, 283, 396–97, 402
Kirlian photography, 180–83
König, Wilhelm, 10

LaBour, Fred, 250–51
Lamont, Peter, 187n
Landis, John, 403
Lapseritis, Jack Kewaunee, 59–64
Larry King Live (TV show), 87
LaVey, Anton, 311, 314n
Lawson, John, 197
Lazar, Robert, 24
Le Verrier, Urbain, 268–69
leprechauns, 131–32
Lescarbault, Dr. Edmond Modeste, 267–70
levitation, 184–87, 208
Lewisohn, Mark, 254, 257
life after death, 188–90
Lincoln, Abraham, 386–91
Loch Ness Monster, 63, 191–94
Lord of the Rings, The, 131–32, 308
Lourdes, 169–70, 204–5, 272–73
Lucius Marcius, 335
Lucy of Narnia, Blessed, 341n
lunar anomalies, 198–201, 401–3
Luther, Martin, 406

Mack, Dr. John, 3
MacLaine, Shirley, 78
magnetism, xiv, 100, 115–16, 184, 187, 263–66
Mahesh Yogi, Maharishi, 186
Mallet, Ronald L., 372
Marian apparitions, 102, 169, 190, 202–5
Marrs, Jim, 302
Mars, face on, 137–42
Martin, John, 385n
Mary Celeste mystery, 216–19
mathematical calculating, 318
McCartney, Paul, 249–59
mechanical abilities, 320
Medici, Catherine de, 38
memories, incredible, 318–20

Men in Black, 206–8
mermaids, 119, 209–11
miracles, 69–72, 168–71, 202–5, 212–15, 271–73, 289–92, 337–41
Mohammed (prophet), 17, 338
Molenaar, Gregory, 141
monuments, 8–11, 122–25, 137–42, 198–201, 220–22, 342–45
Moody, Raymond, 224, 226–27
Moray, Henry, 262
Morehouse, Benjamin, 218
Mott, George, 334
Muetzenberg, Martin, 68n

Napoleon, 405
NASA, 17, 138–42, 153, 161
Nazca lines, 9–10, 138, 220–22
Nazis, 199, 309
near-death experiences, 190, 223–27
Nickell, Joe, 71, 182
Night of the Living Dead, The (film), 400
Noah's Ark, 228–31
Nostradamus, 38, 232–35, 405
numerology, 236–40, 359

Oates, David, 49–50
Ouija board, 241–44
out-of-body experience, 33, 226
outer space, 16–17, 137–42, 164–67, 198–201, 267–70. *See also* aliens; UFOs
Owen, Tobias, 139

palmistry, 245–48
Paracelsus, 46
Parade magazine, 16
past-life regression, 285–88
Patterson, Roger, 60
"Paul is Dead" mystery, 249–59
Penn & Teller, xiv–xv
perpetual motion, 260–62
Persinger, Michael A., 299–300
Petronius Arbiter, Gaius, 402
Philadelphia Experiment, 175, 263–66
Pillinger, Dr. Colin, 140
Pink Floyd, 48

Pio, Padre, 339
Plato, 40–43
Pliny the Elder, 119, 145, 211, 335, 393
Poletto, Severino, 323
Polo, Marco, 393
poltergeists, xiv, 155–58, 287
Popular Mechanics magazine, 383
possession, 104–7, 158
Poundstone, William, 48–49
Project Blue Book, 383
prophecy. *See* divination and prophecy
pseudosciences, 36–39, 65–68, 89–96, 236–40, 280
psychic phenomena, 19–21, 34–35, 62–63, 77–80, 85–88, 108–13, 126–29, 133–36, 155–58, 232–35, 279–84, 293–96. *See also* divination and prophecy
psychokinesis, 279–84
pyramids, 185, 190, 342
pyrokinesis, 282–84
Pythagoras, 236

Queen, 48–49

Rabin, Yitzhak, 56
Raiders of the Lost Ark (film), 28
Rain Man (film), 316, 318
Rajneesh, Osho, 44, 180, 184
Ramsey, Patsy, 49
Raynor, Robert, 210
Reagan, Nancy, 39
Reeser, Mary Hardy, 334
Reeve, Andru, 257
reflexology, xv
Reiche, Maria, 222
reincarnation, 285–88, 368–69
relics, 289–92, 323–26
religious phenomena, 15–18, 26–35, 55–58, 69–72, 101–7, 147–50, 168–71, 184–90, 202–5, 212–15, 223–31, 271–73, 285–92, 297–301, 310–14, 323–29, 337–45, 367–69, 374–77, 398–400, 404–11

remote viewing, 190, 226, 280, 293–96, 321
resurrection, xx, 297–301
reverse speech, 47–50
Rhine, J.B., 135, 279
Rice, Anne, 396–97
Rickenbacker, Eddie, 385n
Riker, Joe, 272–73
Rips, Eliyahu, 57
Rita of Cascia, Saint, 341n
Roanoke, lost colony of, 195–97, 217
Robertson, Morgan, 274–78
Rommel, Kenneth, 74–75
Roswell incident, 5–7, 58, 207, 302–6, 382
Rubio Maria, 204
runes, 307–9
Russian Journal of Scientific and Applied Photography, 181
Ryerson, Kevin, 78

Sagan, Carl, 133, 225, 371
saints, 169–71
Sanderson, Dr. Ivan T., 62, 371–72
Santilli, Ray, 6–7
Sasquatch, 59–64
Satanism, 310–14
Satanists, 405
Savant Syndrome, 79, 315–22
Sawyer, Diane, 177, 179
Schiff, Steven, 304
Scot, Reginald, 115
Selzer, Dr. Richard, 272–73
Sennacherib, Assyrian king, 335
sensory perception, 320
September 11 attacks, 56, 58, 105, 406
Sheldon, W.H., 179
Shipton, Mother, 108
shrines, 101–3, 169–70, 204–5, 272–73
Shroud of Turin, 298, 323–26
Simon & Garfunkel, 347
Simpson, O. J., 49
Six Feet Under (TV series), 86
Sixth Sense, The (film), 79
60 Minutes (TV show), 24
Smart, Elizabeth, 213

Smithsonian Institution, 178
Soffen, Gary, 139
Sopranos, The (TV series), 242
spells, 327–29
Spielberg, Steven, 28
Splash (film), 209
spontaneous generation, 145
spontaneous human combustion, 283, 330–36
Stannard, Neville, 254
Star Trek (TV series), 63, 267–70, 364–65
Star Wars (film series), 368
Statistical Science, 57
stigmata, 213, 337–41
Stoker, Bram, 395–97
Stonehenge, 9, 342–45
Streep, Meryl, 179
subliminal messages, 346–50
suppressed inventions, 260–62, 351–54
Suzek, Barbara, 249
Swoboda, Dr. Hermann, 67
synchronicity, 244, 355–57, 386–91

Tachi, Susumu, 172
tarot, xx, 358–61
Tartikoff, Brandon, 179
Taylor, Lt. Charles, 52
telekinesis, 279–84
teleportation, 362–66
Teresa, Mother, 106, 214
Teresa of Avila, Saint, 186
Tesla, Nikola, 262
Thayer, Tiffany, 83
Theodoric the Great, Ostrogoth king, 335
Theosophy, 35n, 367–69
Thomas Aquinas, Saint, 411n
time sense, 321
time travel, 370–73
time warps and wormholes, 53, 60, 63–64, 217–19
Titanic, predicted sinking of, 274–78
Tlacote, 273
Todeschi, Kevin J., 129
Tolkein, J.R.R., 131–32, 308

transubstantiation, 374–77
Trent, Paul, 383–84
True Cross, relics of, 289–92
Tunguska explosion, 378–80

UFOs, 2–3, 5–7, 12–14, 22–25, 29–32, 61, 64, 73–76, 97–100, 143–46, 160–63, 187, 198–201, 206–8, 294, 302–6, 378–85
unicorns, 4, 392–94
U.S. government, 5–7, 22–25, 116, 153, 162, 187, 207–8, 263–66, 280, 293–96, 302–6, 383

vampires, 395–97, 403
Van Flanders, Dr. Tom, 141–42
Velikovsky, Immanuel, 164–67
Verne, Jules, 163
Vicary, James M., 348
visual phenomena, 101–3, 105, 137–42, 155–58, 180–83, 202–5, 346–50
Vlad the Impaler, 396–97
voodoo, 398–400
Voorman, Klaus, 252
Vulcan, planet, 267–70

Walton, Travis, 3
Wasserstein, Wendy, 179
Wells, H.G., 175
werewolves, 119–20, 401–3
White, John, 1, 149, 196–97, 225
Wiccans, 408, 410
Williams, Dr. William F., 351
Wilson, Robert, 194n
Witchboard (films), 242
witches and witchcraft, 113n, 115, 408–11
Woodward, Bob, 179
Wyatt, Ron, 28n

Yeti, 59–62
yoga, 184, 186

Zener Cards, 135
Zero-Point Energy, 261–62
Zollow, Paul, 347
zombies, 398–400

About the Author

Stephen J. Spignesi is a full-time writer who specializes in popular culture subjects, including historical biography, television, film, American and world history, and contemporary fiction.

Spignesi—christened "the world's leading authority on Stephen King" by *Entertainment Weekly* magazine—has written many authorized entertainment books and has worked with Stephen King, Turner Entertainment, the Margaret Mitchell Estate, Andy Griffith, Viacom, and other entertainment industry personalities and entities on a wide range of projects. Mr. Spignesi has also contributed essays, chapters, articles, and introductions to a wide range of books.

Mr. Spignesi's more than thirty books have been translated into several languages and he has also written for *Harper's*, *Cinefantastique*, *Saturday Review*, *TV Guide*, *Mystery Scene*, *Gauntlet*, and *Midnight Graffiti* magazines; as well as the *New York Times*, the *New York Daily News*, the *New York Post*, the *New Haven Register*, the French literary journal *Ténèbres* and the Italian online literary journal, *Horror.It*. Mr. Spignesi has also appeared on CNN, MSNBC, Fox News Channel, and other TV and radio outlets; and also appeared in the 1998 E! documentary, *The Kennedys: Power, Seduction, and Hollywood*, as a Kennedy family authority; and in the A & E *Biography* of Stephen King that aired in January 2000. Mr. Spignesi's 1997 book *JFK Jr.* was a *New York Times* best-seller. Mr. Spignesi's *Complete Stephen King Encyclopedia* was a 1991 Bram Stoker Award nominee.

In addition to writing, Mr. Spignesi also lectures on a variety of popular culture and historical subjects and teaches writing in the Connecticut area. He is the founder and Editor-in-Chief of the small press publishing company, The **StephenJohn Press**, which recently published Mr. Spignesi's first novel, *The Husbands of Coventry*.

Mr. Spignesi is a graduate of the University of New Haven, and lives in New Haven, CT, with his wife, Pam, and their cat, Carter, named for their favorite character on *ER*.

BOOKS BY STEPHEN J. SPIGNESI

- *Mayberry, My Hometown* (1987, Popular Culture, Ink.)
- *The Complete Stephen King Encyclopedia* (1990, Contemporary Books)
- *The Stephen King Quiz Book* (1990, Signet)
- *The Second Stephen King Quiz Book* (1992, Signet)
- *The Woody Allen Companion* (1992, Andrews and McMeel)
- *The Official "Gone With the Wind" Companion* (1993, Plume)
- *The V. C. Andrews Trivia and Quiz Book* (1994, Signet)
- *The Odd Index: The Ultimate Compendium of Bizarre and Unusual Facts* (1994, Plume)
- *What's Your* Mad About You *IQ?* (1995, Citadel Press)
- *The Gore Galore Video Quiz Book* (1995, Signet)
- *What's Your* Friends *IQ?* (1996, Citadel Press)
- *The Celebrity Baby Name Book* (1996, Plume)
- *The* ER *Companion* (1996, Citadel Press)
- *J.F.K. Jr.* (1997, Citadel Press; originally titled *The J.F.K. Jr. Scrapbook*)—*New York Times* best-seller
- *The Robin Williams Scrapbook* (1997, Citadel Press)
- *The Italian 100: A Ranking of the Most Influential Cultural, Scientific, and Political Figures, Past and Present* (1997, Citadel Press)
- *The Beatles Book of Lists* (1998, Citadel Press)
- *Young Kennedys: The New Generation* (1998, Avon; written as "Jay David Andrews")
- *The Lost Work of Stephen King: A Guide to Unpublished Manuscripts, Story Fragments, Alternative Versions, & Oddities* (1998, Citadel Press)
- *The Complete Titanic: From the Ship's Earliest Blueprints to the Epic Film* (1998, Citadel Press)
- *How To Be An Instant Expert* (2000, Career Press)
- *She Came In Through the Kitchen Window: Recipes Inspired by The Beatles & Their Music* (2000, Kensington Publishing)
- *The USA Book of Lists* (2000, Career Press)
- *The UFO Book of Lists* (2001, Kensington Publishing)
- *The Essential Stephen King: The Greatest Novels, Short Stories, Movies, and Other Creations of the World's Most Popular Writer* (2001, New Page Books)
- *The Cat Book of Lists* (2001, New Page Books)

- *The Hollywood Book of Lists* (2001, Kensington Publishing)
- *The Essential Stephen King: The Complete & Uncut Edition* (2001, GB Books)
- *Gems, Jewels, & Treasures: The Complete Jewelry Book* (2002, QVC Publishing)
- *100 Greatest Disasters of All Time* (2002, Kensington Publishing)
- *In the Crosshairs: The 75 Most Famous Assassinations and Assassination Attempts, from Julius Caesar to John Lennon* (2002, New Page Books)
- *Crop Circles: Signs of Contact* (with Colin Andrews) (2003, New Page Books)
- *American Firsts* (2004, New Page Books)
- *The 100 Best Beatles Songs* (with Michael Lewis) (2004, Black Dog & Leventhal)
- *What's Your Red, White & Blue IQ?* (2004, Kensington Publishing)
- *The Husbands of Coventry* (2004, The StephenJohn Press)